Why do societies vary in their tolerance for deficits and public debt? This groundbreaking book shows the power of deep historical expertise to illuminate a central issue of our times.

Isaac Martin, *UC San Diego, US*

Deficits and Debt in Industrial Democracies provides a sweeping yet detailed exploration of the politics of debt in the postwar period. In some countries, supportive governmental institutions help political actors win taxpayer consent and resolve conflicting social interests; whereas in others, the struggle for fiscal consolidation seems futile. Gene Park, Eisaku Ide and their collaborators enlighten us about these national, long-term patterns of fiscal performance with their insightful comparative case studies of seven advanced economies. This impressive work is highly relevant to anyone concerned about the future of advanced industrial democracies in a debt-ridden world.

Cathie Jo Martin, *Boston University, US*

Deficits and Debt in Industrialized Democracies

Since the global financial crisis, government debt has soared globally by 40 percent and now exceeds an astonishing $100 trillion. Not all countries, though, have fared the same. Indeed, even prior to the financial crisis, the fiscal fates of countries have been diverging, despite predictions that pressures from economic globalization push countries toward more convergent fiscally conservative policies.

Featuring the work of an international interdisciplinary team of scholars, this volume explains patterns of fiscal performance (persistent patterns of budget deficits and government debt) from the 1970s to the present across seven countries—France, Italy, Germany, Japan, South Korea, Sweden, and the United States. Employing a comparative case study approach, seldom employed in studies of fiscal performance, contributions illuminate the complex causal factors often overlooked by quantitative studies and advances our theoretical understanding of fiscal performance. Among other things, the cases highlight the role of taxpayer consent, tax structure, the welfare state, organization of interests, and labor and financial markets in shaping fiscal outcomes.

A necessary resource to understand a broader array of factors that shape fiscal outcomes in specific national contexts, this book will reinvigorate the study of fiscal performance.

Eisaku Ide is Professor in the Department of Economics at Keio University. He is also affiliated with the Center for Risk Management and Safety Sciences at Yokohama National University. Dr. Ide is an expert on Japanese fiscal and financial policy.

Gene Park is Associate Professor in the Department of Political Science at Loyola Marymount University. Dr. Park has researched and written extensively on the politics of public finance in Japan.

Routledge research in comparative politics

1 **Democracy and Post-communism**
Political change in the post-communist world
Graeme Gill

2 **Sub-State Nationalism**
A comparative analysis of institutional design
Edited by Helena Catt and Michael Murphy

3 **Reward for High Public Office**
Asian and Pacific Rim States
Edited by Christopher Hood and B. Guy Peters

4 **Social Democracy and Labour Market Policy**
Developments in Britain and Germany
Knut Roder

5 **Democratic Revolutions**
Asia and Eastern Europe
Mark R. Thompson

6 **Democratization**
A comparative analysis of 170 countries
Tatu Vanhanen

7 **Determinants of the Death Penalty**
A comparative study of the world
Carsten Anckar

8 **How Political Parties Respond to Voters**
Interest aggregation revisited
Edited by Kay Lawson and Thomas Poguntke

9 **Women, Quotas and Politics**
Edited by Drude Dahlerup

10 **Citizenship and Ethnic Conflict**
Challenging the nation-state
Haldun Gülalp

11 **The Politics of Women's Interests**
New comparative and international perspectives
Edited by Louise Chappell and Lisa Hill

12 **Political Disaffection in Contemporary Democracies**
Social capital, institutions and politics
Edited by Mariano Torcal and José Ramón Montero

13 **Representing Women in Parliament**
A comparative study
Edited by Marian Sawer, Manon Tremblay and Linda Trimble

14 **Democracy and Political Culture in Eastern Europe**
Edited by Hans-Dieter Klingemann, Dieter Fuchs and Jan Zielonka

15 **Social Capital and Associations in European Democracies**
A comparative analysis
Edited by William A. Maloney and Sigrid Roßteutscher

16 **Citizenship and Involvement in European Democracies**
A comparative analysis
Edited by Jan van Deth, José Ramón Montero and Anders Westholm

17 **The Politics of Foundations**
A comparative analysis
Edited by Helmut K. Anheier and Siobhan Daly

18 **Party Policy in Modern Democracies**
Kenneth Benoit and Michael Laver

19 **Semi-Presidentialism Outside Europe**
A comparative study
Edited by Robert Elgie and Sophia Moestrup

20 **Comparative Politics**
The principal–agent perspective
Jan-Erik Lane

21 **The Political Power of Business**
Structure and information in public policymaking
Patrick Bernhagen

22 **Women's Movements**
Flourishing or in abeyance?
Edited by Marian Sawer and Sandra Grey

23 **Consociational Theory**
McGarry and O'Leary and the Northern Ireland conflict
Edited by Rupert Taylor

24 **The International Politics of Democratization**
Comparative perspectives
Edited by Nuno Severiano Teixeira

25 **Post-communist Regime Change**
A comparative study
Jørgen Møller

26 **Social Democracy in Power**
The capacity to reform
Wolfgang Merkel, Alexander Petring, Christian Henkes and Christoph Egle

27 **The Rise of Regionalism**
Causes of regional mobilization in Western Europe
Rune Dahl Fitjar

28 **Party Politics in the Western Balkans**
Edited by Věra Stojarová and Peter Emerson

29 **Democratization and Market Reform in Developing and Transitional Countries**
Think tanks as catalysts
James G. McGann

30 **Political Leadership, Parties and Citizens**
The personalisation of leadership
Edited by Jean Blondel and Jean-Louis Thiebault

31 **Civil Society and Activism in Europe**
Contextualizing engagement and political orientation
Edited by William A. Maloney and Jan W. van Deth

32 Gender Equality, Citizenship and Human Rights
Controversies and challenges in China and the Nordic countries
Edited by Pauline Stoltz, Marina Svensson, Zhongxin Sun and Qi Wang

33 Democratization and the European Union
Comparing Central and Eastern European post-Communist countries
Edited by Leonardo Morlino and Wojciech Sadurski

34 The Origin of Electoral Systems in the Postwar Era
A worldwide approach
Krister Lundell

35 The Globalization of Motherhood
Deconstruction and reconstructions of biology and care
Edited by Wendy Chavkin and JaneMaree Maher

36 Parties, Elections, and Policy Reforms in Western Europe
Voting for social pacts
Kerstin Hamann and John Kelly

37 Democracy and Famine
Olivier Rubin

38 Women in Executive Power
A global overview
Edited by Gretchen Bauer and Manon Tremblay

39 Women and Representation in Local Government
International case studies
Edited by Barbara Pini and Paula McDonald

40 The Politics of Charity
Kerry O'Halloran

41 Climate Policy Changes in Germany and Japan
A path to paradigmatic policy change
Rie Watanabe

42 African Parliamentary Reform
Edited by Rick Stapenhurst, Rasheed Draman and Andrew Imlach with Alexander Hamilton and Cindy Kroon

43 The Politics of International Law and Compliance
Serbia, Croatia and The Hague Tribunal
Edited by Nikolas M. Rajkovic

44 The Funding of Political Parties
Edited by Keith Ewing, Joo-Cheong Tham and Jacob Rowbottom

45 Parliamentary Oversight Tools
A comparative analysis
Riccardo Pelizzo and Frederick Stapenhurst

46 Inclusion and Exclusion in the Liberal Competition State
The cult of the individual
Richard Münch

47 New Challenger Parties in Western Europe
A comparative analysis
Airo Hino

48 Metropolitan Governance and Policy
Jen Nelles

49 **Rewards for High Public Office in Europe and North America**
Edited by B. Guy Peters and Marleen Brans

50 **International Security, Conflict and Gender**
'HIV/AIDS is another war'
Hakan Seckinelgin

51 **Young People and Politics**
Comparing Anglo-American democracies
Aaron J. Martin

52 **Immigration and Public Opinion in Liberal Democracies**
Gary P. Freeman, Randall Hansen, and David L. Leal

53 **Russia's Regions and Comparative Subnational Politics**
Comparing Anglo-American democracies
Edited by William M. Reisinger

54 **Protecting Immigrant Rights in Mexico**
Understanding the state–civil society nexus
Laura Valeria González-Murphy

55 **The Public Sector Performance**
Pockets of effectiveness
Edited by Michael Roll

56 **The Organization of Political Interest Groups**
Designing advocacy
Edited by Darren R. Halpin

57 **Electoral Systems and Governance**
Diversity and policy-making
Salomon Orellana

58 **Government Accountability and Legislative Oversight**
Riccardo Pelizzo and Frederick Stapenhurst

59 **Corruption and Legislatures**
Riccardo Pelizzo and Frederick Stapenhurst

60 **Global Perspectives on the Politics of Multiculturalism in the 21st Century**
A case study analysis
Edited by Fethi Mansouri and Boulou Ebanda de B'béri

61 **Party Organization and Electoral Volatility in Central and Eastern Europe**
Enhancing voter loyalty
Sergiu Gherghina

62 **Politics of Religion and Nationalism**
Federalism, consociationalism and seccession
Edited by Ferran Requejo and Klaus-Jürgen Nagel

63 **Deficits and Debt in Industrialized Democracies**
Edited by Eisaku Ide and Gene Park

Deficits and Debt in Industrialized Democracies

Edited by Eisaku Ide and Gene Park

Routledge
Taylor & Francis Group
LONDON AND NEW YORK

First published 2015 by Routledge

2 Park Square, Milton Park, Abingdon, Oxon OX14 4RN
711 Third Avenue, New York, NY 10017, USA

Routledge is an imprint of the Taylor & Francis Group, an informa business

First issued in paperback 2017

Library of Congress Cataloging in Publication Data
Deficits and debt in industrialized democracies/edited by Gene Park and Eisaku Ide.
pages cm. – (Routledge research in comparative politics; 63)
1. Finance, Public–Developed countries. 2. Debts, Public–Developed countries. 3. Budget deficits–Developed countries. 4. Fiscal policy–Developed countries. I. Park, Gene, II. Ide, Eisaku.
HJ235.D44 2015
336.3'4–dc23 2014040033

ISBN: 978-1-138-82132-3 (hbk)
ISBN: 978-1-138-06659-5 (pbk)

Typeset in Times New Roman
by Wearset Ltd, Boldon, Tyne and Wear

Contents

Figures

Tables

Contributors

Editors

Eisaku Ide is Associate Professor in the Department of Economics at Keio University. He is also affiliated with the Center for Risk Management and Safety Sciences at Yokohama National University. Dr. Ide is an expert on Japanese fiscal and financial policy. He has published numerous books on Japan's budgetary and monetary policy, including *A Study on Takahashi Economic Policy* (Yuhikaku, 2006) and *Fiscal Sociology of the Central Bank* (Chisen Shokan, 2006).

Gene Park is Associate Professor in the Department of Political Science at Loyola Marymount University. Dr. Park has researched and written on the politics of public finance in Japan including a book entitled *Spending without Taxation: FILP and the Politics of Public Finance in Japan* (Stanford University Press, 2011).

Contributors

W. Elliot Brownlee is Professor Emeritus of History at the University of California, Santa Barbara. He earned his PhD in History from the University of Wisconsin. He is the author or editor of nine books and numerous articles on the fiscal, economic, and general history of the United States. His most recent books are *The Political Economy of Transnational Tax Reform: The Shoup Mission to Japan in Historical Context* (Cambridge University Press, 2013), co-edited with Eisaku Ide and Yasunori Fukagai; *Federal Taxation in America: A Short History*, second edition (Cambridge University Press, 2004); and *The Reagan Presidency: Pragmatic Conservatism and its Legacies* (University Press of Kansas, 2003), co-edited with Hugh Davis Graham.

Jonas Edlund is Professor of Sociology at Umeå University, Sweden. His main areas of interest are comparative political sociology and social stratification.

Edward A. Fogarty is Associate Professor of Political Science at Colgate University, US. His work focuses on global governance, international economic institutions, and the European Union, and has appeared in the *Journal of*

European Integration, *International Studies Review*, and *Journal of Civil Society*, among others. His book, *States, Nonstate Actors, and Global Governance: Projecting Polities*, was published by Routledge in 2013.

Morinao Iju is Associate Professor in the Department of Economics at Yokohama National University. Professor Iju is an expert on public finance and intergovernmental fiscal relations. He has published articles on Swedish tax policy and intergovernmental fiscal transfer during the 1990s.

Myung-koo Kang is Assistant Professor in the Department of Political Science at Baruch College, City University of New York. Dr. Kang is an expert in Korean and Japanese fiscal and financial policy. He has conducted research on financial crises and government responses, focusing on both cross-national and Asia-specific context.

Achim Kemmerling is Associate Professor of Political Economy in the Department of Public Policy, Central European University Budapest. He has published in academic journals of various disciplines (*Public Choice*, *JEPP*, *EUP*, and *JCMS*) on issues of tax policy, social and labor market policies, and fiscal federalism. His monograph *Taxing the Working Poor* (Edward Elgar, 2009) deals with the political and economic tradeoffs between redistribution and job incentives for poor workers.

Anna Konishi is a PhD candidate in the Department of History, Panthéon-Sorbonne University, France. She began her research on taxation in France at the University of Tokyo in 2007, receiving a Master's degree in Economics in 2009 with a thesis entitled *The Creation of Modern Income Taxation in France* in 1959. Since 2010 she has been a PhD student at Pantheon-Sorbonne University and is currently writing her dissertation on the history of tax harmonization in Europe after the Treaty of Rome.

Benedicta Marzinotto is Lecturer in Political Economy at the University of Udine and Visiting Professor at the College of Europe (Natolin Campus).

Takaharu Shimada is Lecturer in the Faculty of Economics at Shimonoseki City University, Japan. He is a specialist in the field of public finance, fiscal policy, and monetary policy. His research has focused on the relationship between fiscal and monetary policy in West Germany, especially in the 1970s. He now studies childcare and taxation issues in Germany. His works have been published in various journals including *Keio Economic Studies* and *Local Fiscal Administration* (Chihou Zaimu).

Masayuki Takahashi is Associate Professor in the Graduate School of Humanities and Social Sciences at Saitama University, Japan. Dr. Takahashi is a specialist in the field of public finance, public administration, and fiscal policy. His works have been published in various journals including *Local Public Finance* (Chihou Zaisei) and *Annual Bulletin of Japan Association of Local Public Finance* (Chihou Zaisei Gakkai Nenpou). He has also co-authored several books on fiscal and monetary issues in Japan.

Joseph J. Thorndike is Director of the Tax History Project at Tax Analysts. Dr. Thorndike is also a Visiting Scholar in History at the University of Virginia and an adjunct faculty at Northwestern University Law School. He is the author (with Steven A. Bank and Kirk J. Stark) of *War and Taxes* and the editor (with Dennis J. Ventry, Jr.) of *Tax Justice: The Ongoing Debate*. His new book, *Their Fair Share: Why Americans Tax the Rich*, was published by the Urban Institute Press in 2013. He is a regular columnist for *Tax Notes* magazine.

Frédéric Tristram is Associate Professor in the Department of History at Panthéon-Sorbonne University, France. He is also a Lecturer at Sciences Po. He is the author of *Une fiscalité pour la croissance : La direction générale des Impôts et la politique fiscale en France de 1948 à la fin des années 1960* (CHEFF, 2005).

Zbigniew Truchlewski is a PhD candidate in Political Economy at the Central European University, Budapest. There, he started researching the comparative politics of austerity in the UK and France after having worked at the European Central Bank in Frankfurt. He has been a visiting researcher at Cornell University, the London School of Economics, and the European University Institute in Florence. He has published in the *Journal of Common Market Studies* and the *Journal of European Public Policy* and contributed to reports on public finance by the European Commission.

Preface

The genesis for this project dates back to the fall of 2011. Elliot Brownlee and Eisaku Ide hosted a conference at Keio University—"Two Political Economies in Crisis: Historical and Comparative Perspectives on the Fiscal Dilemmas Facing Japan and the United States"—that focused on the consequences of the global financial crisis in the US and Japan and how each government was responding. The conference brought together a group of experts on Japan and the US to compare the experiences of both countries.[1]

Both of the editors of this book had until then focused largely on Japanese fiscal issues, and both were increasingly drawn to understanding the origins of Japan's debt problem, which even at that time was over 200 percent of GDP. After the successful conference in Tokyo, we decided that the best way to approach this question was through a more systematic comparative study of the determinants of fiscal performance.

As we began planning for our project, we were struck by the lack of research based on in-depth comparative case studies. The large majority of the research is based on large-*n* statistical analysis operating at a relatively high level of abstraction that did not delve into the thicket of budget institutions and their complex social and political contexts. There are certainly case studies and in some cases edited volumes that included case studies, such as Poterba and Von Hagen's outstanding and influential *Fiscal Institutions and Fiscal Performance*. Few studies, though, have relied on comparative case studies. In retrospect, this should not have been surprising. Undertaking such a project has very high start-up costs. Budgets themselves are immensely complex and those of us that have largely focused on one country have spent countless hours trying to understand them. A comparative project would require deep cross-country expertise and language skills.

This project is an attempt to fill this lacuna. Thanks to generous funding from the Japan Foundation Center for Global Partnership, we were able to assemble a team of international scholars with expertise and knowledge of all of our seven country cases—France, Germany, Italy, Japan, South Korea, Sweden, and the US. We met twice to present our papers, to engage in discussion, and to draw out comparisons across our cases. The first conference was held January 6–7, 2013 at Keio University in Tokyo, and the second conference took place on August 11–12, 2013 at Loyola Marymount University in Los Angeles. The result is this volume.

The authors would like to thank the Center for Global Partnership. This project would not have been possible without their support. The staff in the Los Angeles, New York, and Tokyo offices were exceedingly helpful, and their flexibility in adjusting to changes as they arose greatly facilitated completing the project. Special thanks to Lisa Wong and Carolyn Fleischer in the New York office. We would also be remiss not to acknowledge our home institutions—Loyola Marymount University and Keio University—that also provided valuable support. Chris Eaton, Rechard Francois, and Michael George provided research assistance, while Michelle Larson helped keep the administration of the project running smoothly.

Note

1 Participants included: Morinao Iju, W. Elliot Brownlee, Takehiko Ikegami, Eisaku Ide, Gene Park, Takaharu Shimada, Masaru Kaneko, Yukiko Yamazaki, Shigeru Sato, Ajay K. Mehrotra, Joseph J. Thorndike, Satoshi Sekiguchi, Andrea Louise Campbell, Cathie Jo Martin, Mari Osawa, Masayuki Takahashi, Masaya Ueda, Isaac William Martin, Gareth Davies.

1 Introduction

Gene Park and Eisaku Ide

Fiscal issues are one of the defining political challenges for many nations. We have witnessed this through recent events. A series of global crises has left many governments straining under growing public debt and high budget deficits. The global financial crisis (GFC) from 2008 was the first blow, causing revenues to decline and social expenditures, such as unemployment benefits, to rise. In the eurozone, the GFC morphed into a sovereign debt crisis starting with Greece and then threatening contagion in Italy, Portugal, and Spain. The sovereign debt crisis has led to historic changes in the nature of fiscal governance within the European Union with the signing of a new fiscal compact. At the global level as well, high deficits and mounting public obligations have led to serious discussions about how to restore fiscal sustainability within the IMF, G-7, and G-20.

These events have understandably grabbed headlines, but there are also other fundamental shifts that will continue to strain the public finance systems of the advanced industrialized democracies even after the global economy fully recovers from the aftermath of the GFC. Populations are aging, in some cases rapidly, and other demographic trends such as lower fertility mean that the share of the working age population will continue to decline. As the population ages, welfare programs, especially health insurance and public pensions, will come under growing financial stress, a problem exacerbated by the shrinking tax base resulting from low fertility rates. This problem is particularly advanced in the industrial democracies in Western Europe and Japan, however other countries will also face similar pressures. Other Northeast Asian countries have very low fertility rates and will in the not-too-distant future face a fiscal squeeze, in some cases even more acutely. How governments handle these pressures will continue to shape the political agenda for years to come. Moreover, how they do so may have profound impacts. The fiscal sustainability of the state will determine the nature of tradeoffs that governments face in providing basic functions, particularly the level of social services, the largest (and growing) area of expenditure. Government fiscal choices also impact the distribution of the debt burden across generations.[1] If governments leave large debts to be serviced by future generations, this can raise ethical concerns about intergenerational equity (Shaviro 1995). And while often overblown by the media,[2] high deficits and debt can have negative economic effects, crowding out private investment and possibly leading to higher interest rates and slower growth rates.[3] This volume seeks to shed light on what determines how governments manage their public finances.

The Focus of the Study

This volume focuses on explaining fiscal performance through the lens of long-term variations in the successes and failures of the government to restore fiscal balance, i.e., fiscal consolidation. As Dellepiane-Avellaneda and Hardiman (2009) have noted, many studies view fiscal consolidation relatively as discrete, short-term episodes (such as a multi-year improvement in budget balance). Short-term changes, however, are often driven by the rate of economic growth or exogenous shocks rather than policy choices, which are the focus of this book. Furthermore, in any given business cycle, economists and policy makers can have legitimate debates over whether governments should purse fiscal stimulus or fiscal consolidation. Indeed, this debate is unfolding across nearly every country and within international forums such as the G-20 and international organizations like the International Monetary Fund (IMF).

Our study avoids these debates and instead shifts the focus to understanding longer patterns in how governments respond to fiscal challenges. We can see these longer-term periods relatively clearly. Japan, for instance, has been unable to staunch chronic deficits and rapidly accumulating debt for decades, despite repeated efforts since the 1990s. Italy faced a similar situation to Japan until the start of the 1990s. Then, through reforms spanning over a decade, the government restored fiscal balance that stabilized but did not substantially reduce debt. After the bursting of a financial bubble and large deficits, the Swedish government lowered deficits and debt through a sustained, multi-year fiscal adjustment across several administrations. We can see the wide degree of variation in the willingness and ability of governments to engage in fiscal adjustments reflected in fiscal outcomes (Figure 1.1 and Table 1.1).

This volume uses comparative case studies of seven countries—France, Germany, Italy, Japan, South Korea, Sweden, and the US—to explore these questions. The advantage of case studies is that it allows us to explore both

Table 1.1 Budget balance, cyclically adjusted primary balance as share of GDP

	1980–89	*1990–99*	*2000–09*	*2010–11*
France	–0.6	–1.0	–1.5	–2.6
Germany	0.4	–0.8	0.5	–0.1
Italy	–3.3	2.6	1.1	2.0
Japan	–0.1	–3.0	–4.5	–7.3
South Korea*	–	3.1	3.4	0.8
Sweden	–0.7	–0.7	1.9	0.8
USA	–1.1	0.7	–2.4	–7.3

Source: OECD Economic Outlook Database.

Note

* For South Korea, the data starts from 1996.

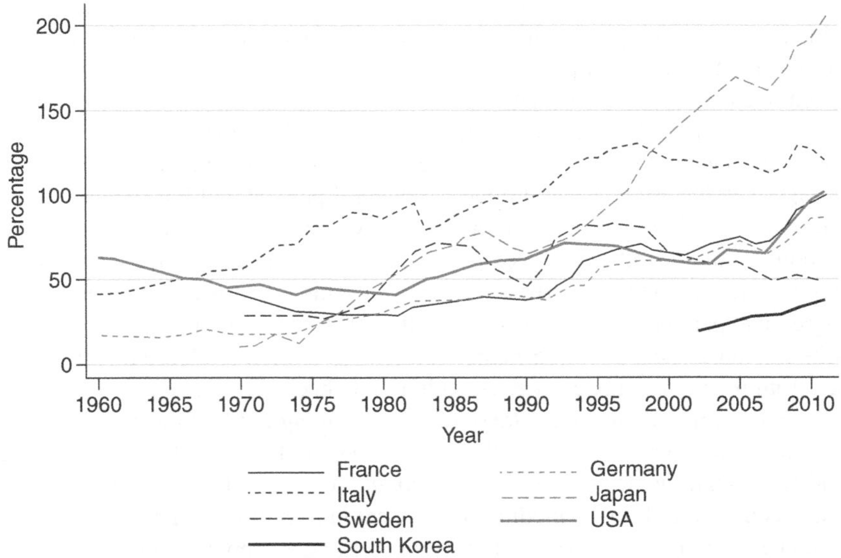

Figure 1.1 Gross government debt as share of GDP (source: OECD Economic Outlook Database).

(1) cross-country variation and (2) within-country temporal variation. Indeed, much of what is driving cross-country variation has been changes within countries over time. We selected our countries to include a diversity of industrialized democracies. We also wanted to control for level of socioeconomic development by focusing on the advanced industrial democracies. Expanding our study beyond the OECD is something that should be considered for the future. We also did not want to include in our study—given limited resources—too many cases whose fiscal outcomes have been heavily shaped by large exogenous shocks. For this reason, we did not include Ireland, which has had a very costly bail-out of its financial sector and Spain, which experienced the collapse of a housing bubble.

Common Trends and Divergent Paths

Since the end of World War II, there has been a growing trend toward increasing public debt across the industrialized democracies. These changes have not, however, been uniform. Indeed, the variation across countries in fiscal performance in terms of budget deficits and public debt has increased over time, particularly since the 1980s. For the first decades after the war, during the "30 glorious years," a confluence of factors led to a large expansion of the public sector with relatively mild deficits and moderate growth in government sector debt. Governments across the industrialized world increased public spending, particularly in the area of social welfare, and to pay for this spending the government increased tax revenues. Governments, to varying degrees, also relied on Keynesian fiscal stimulus to manage aggregate demand in order to smooth out the business cycle and maintain high employment. In retrospect, the increase in spending and taxation and relatively sound public finances seem like a remarkable achievement. Several factors supported this period of 30 glorious years of fiscal management.

First, the period through the 1960s was one of rapid global economic growth. During the 1960s, the global economy grew 5.5 percent annually. By contrast, during the 1970s, growth rate dropped to under 4 percent and fell steadily to 2.6 percent for the first decade of the new century.[4] Rapid economic growth eased the politics of the otherwise vexing challenge of raising revenue. Economic growth generated natural increases in revenue. This effect was amplified by the progressive personal income tax. Growth combined with moderate inflation pushed incomes naturally into higher income tax brackets. Consequently revenues from the income tax grew even without rate hikes.

Second, demographics were favorable to managing public finances. After the war, populations grew rapidly with the baby boom. The fertility rate increased steadily through the mid-1960s, and the population was relatively young. These trends reduced the short- to medium-term fiscal impact of the expansion in social insurance programs. The large and growing working age population paid into the tax system and the relatively low number of elderly made modest demands on social security systems.

Third, the Bretton Woods monetary regime supported some degree of fiscal discipline. With a pegged (but adjustable) exchange rate, governments faced an external constraint to running current account deficits. In the event of a current account deficit, governments had to respond through domestic adjustment, including reining in budget deficits, to maintain their exchange rates. In contrast to the classical gold standard, however, the postwar monetary system did not place the entire onus for adjustment on the domestic economy. In some cases, governments could devalue their currency, as France, Italy, and others did. Capital controls and the relatively low extent of trade also shielded domestic economies partly from international pressures.

The situation began to change starting in the 1970s as governments began to face growing fiscal pressures. The two oil shocks in 1974 and 1979 brought two spikes in inflation, and unlike in earlier decades, high inflation coincided with high unemployment, i.e., stagflation. To cope with high unemployment, many governments resorted to fiscal stimulus. Although there were varying degrees of success in reviving economic growth, overall fiscal stimulus appeared to be less effective and the relationship between inflation and employment deviated from the Phillips curve.[5]

The Bretton Woods system (BWS) also came under strain and then collapsed during the 1970s, which had significant implications for fiscal management. Under President Johnson, the government expanded domestic programs. In the realm of foreign policy, the US involvement in Vietnam grew increasingly costly, and the government chose to finance these expenditures largely through borrowing. Rather than pursue domestic adjustment, the Nixon administration chose to devalue and then the government moved to a floating exchange rate, effectively bringing an end to the BWS. With the collapse of the BWS, the US freed itself of the external constraint of its own making, paving the way for the huge increases in debt during the 1980s under Ronald Reagan.

The European Community (EC) responded to the collapse by pushing for exchange rate coordination with measures to limit exchange rate fluctuation—first with the so-called "snake in the tunnel" and later with the European Monetary System (EMS)—that reimposed some degree of external constraint. The move toward economic and monetary union (EMU) in the 1990s led to more explicit fiscal rules. The Maastrict Treaty of 1992 required governments to limit budget deficits to 3 percent of GDP and government debt to 60 percent of GDP and also forbade governments to finance government debt. The Stability and Growth Pact, which came into force in the late 1990s, created a framework for preventing excessive deficits and debt—the "preventative arm"—and also a procedure for reducing fiscal imbalances when the targets were exceeded—the "corrective" arm.

Other changes created downward pressure on government revenues. During the 1980s, a wave of countries experimented with tax reform, starting with the US and UK. Both governments lowered the capital gains and corporate tax; they also lowered progressive personal income tax rates and reduced the number of tax brackets. These reforms reflected the growing influence of supply-side economics and growing skepticism of Keynesianism. They also triggered international tax competition. During the late 1970s and 1980s, industrialized countries liberalized their capital accounts. With increased capital mobility, governments grew increasingly sensitive to tax policy changes in other countries, and many countries followed suit by lowering taxes on the wealthy, corporations, and capital gains. Since this first wave of the tax reforms, many countries have continued to lower corporate taxes and taxes on capital. Cuts in statutory rates, though, have not always led to lower revenue; in some cases closing loopholes and economic gains led to growing corporate tax revenues. Some governments also offset these tax cuts by hiking VAT rates and social insurance contributions.

Pressures for increased expenditures also grew. Governments continued to enhance welfare policies over the 1960s and 1970s. Furthermore, demographic changes gradually shifted. Fertility rates declined and to varying degrees, populations grew older. Japan is the most extreme case: its fertility rate has hovered around 1.3; its working age population has been declining since 1995; and its total population has been shrinking since 2007. Japan, however, is not an exception. From 1950 to 2011, the dependence ratio (the ratio of those over 65 to those between 20 and 64) for 23 advanced industrial democracies increased from 15.7 to 27.5 percent.[6] These changes have increased demands for welfare spending, particularly pensions and healthcare. In the case of pensions, the fiscal effects of the demographic squeeze have been amplified by the use of pay-as-you-go (PAYG) pensions systems, in which pension benefits are paid out of current revenues rather than being funded in advance.

These secular trends have created broad fiscal pressures. As Figures 1.2 and 1.3 show, however, cross-country variation has been increasing over time, even

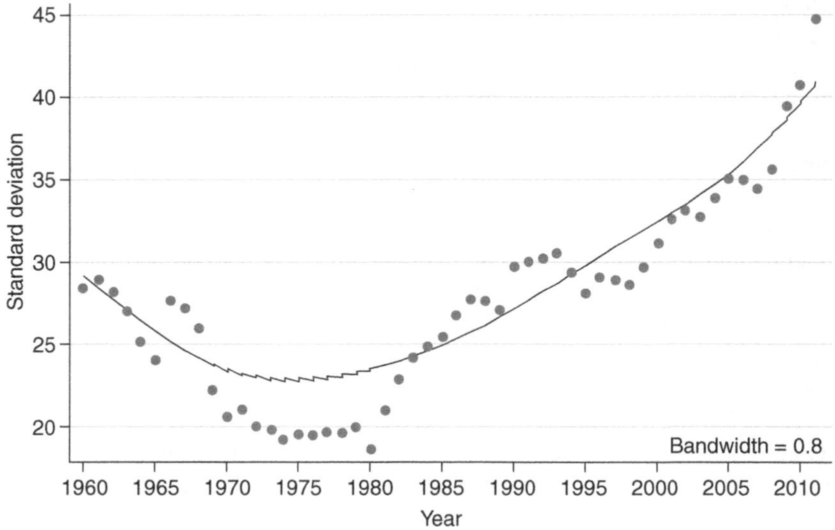

Figure 1.2 Standard deviation of gross government debt as share of GDP of 23 OECD countries, with Lowess smoothing line (source: OECD and author calculations).

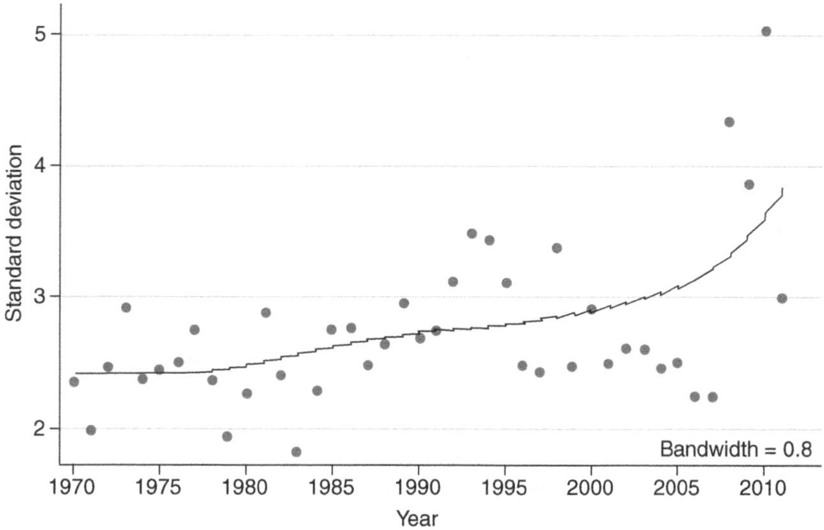

Figure 1.3 Standard deviation of cyclically adjusted annual deficit as share of GDP of 23 OECD countries, with Lowess smoothing line (source: OECD and author calculations).

prior to the start of the GFC. This is in spite of the prediction by some that economic globalization would heighten the costs of fiscal indiscipline giving governments greater incentives to converge in their fiscal policies.

The rate and timing of economic growth partly accounts for this variation. In some countries, fiscal pressures were alleviated or obscured temporarily by spurts of economic growth. In Japan and Sweden asset bubbles stemming from the process of financial deregulation and monetary decisions led to temporary increases in revenue, but then required public bailouts. In the US, the dot-com bubble at the turn of the century also inflated government revenues. More recently, the asset bubbles in the US, UK, and Spain had a similar effect. After the bubbles burst, there was an immediate impact on government finances, through slower economic growth and in cases when there were financial crises through the need to recapitalize banks.

Government choices have also contributed to different fiscal outcomes. Some countries have done a remarkable of job of restoring fiscal discipline, such as Sweden, despite very high levels of social expenditures. Others, though, have had steady deficits and mounting public debt like Japan, whereas countries such as Italy and Belgium have stabilized their finances though failed to significantly lower their accumulated public debt.

Existing Approaches

What factors influence when a government is likely to confront deficits and growing debt and what determines the likelihood of its success in doing so? A broad literature has looked at the factors that shape these questions. This research is reviewed below.[7] The subsequent section then discusses the approach of this book and how it can complement the existing work by opening up new avenues of inquiry.

Ideology and Partisan Politics

The effect of partisan politics on fiscal policy has been one of the major avenues of research on fiscal policy. According to this theory, parties enact policies that reflect the economic interests of their support base (Hibbs 1977). Left parties, supported by lower income groups, prefer low unemployment and high inflation, while right parties prioritize low inflation over employment. Thus, right parties should be more likely to implement fiscal consolidation (and budget cuts) than left parties (Mulas-Granados 2003, 2006; Perotti and Kontopoulos 2002; Tavares 2004). However, there are important exceptions. Kitschelt (2001) shows that sometimes even left parties engage with retrenchment and fiscal consolidation. He argues that partisan competition can force these parties to act. Sometimes it takes a Nixon to go to China (Ross 2000); left parties are also office seeking and hence feel forced to consolidate the budget for their own political survival.

Some have argued that economic globalization has rendered Keynesian demand management less feasible over the long term (Boix 2000). Garrett

(1998), however, finds that globalization has not forced governments to converge on a set of fiscal policies. In fact, he finds directly counter to the globalization argument that partisanship has become even more salient with increased capital mobility and trade dependence. Specifically, left governments tend to run higher deficits under higher levels of globalization. Oatley (1999) also finds that capital mobility has not eroded partisan distinctions in fiscal policy. In an analysis that considers the role of exchange rate regimes and central bank independence, however, Clark and Hallerberg (2000) find that partisanship does not have any statistically significant effect.

Other research has studied the effect of the ideology of ruling party in explaining the composition of fiscal adjustments, specifically the ratio of expenditure cuts and revenue increases (Castles 2007; Mulas-Granados 2003, 2006). This research shows that the ideology of party in power predicts the composition of fiscal consolidation strategies. Right governments focus on cutting spending to lower taxation, while left governments seek to preserve spending and pursue revenue-based approaches. Some scholars argue that this choice of strategy affects the outcome of consolidation. The more fiscal consolidation relies on expenditure cuts rather than revenue increases, the more successful it tends to be (Alesina and Perotti 1997a; Cournede and Gonand 2006; McDermott and Wescott 1996).

Fiscal Institutions and Fiscal Rules

Fiscal institutions have also been found to impact fiscal management. The central challenge from this perspective stems from the common pool resource (CPR) problem. Taxes are a resource shared by all. Spending, however, can be concentrated or targeted toward specific constituencies. Since the cost of such spending is spread out across all taxpayers, the beneficiaries of such spending do not bear the full cost of spending. Thus, there is an incentive to overspend.

Institutions that centralize control over fiscal policy make it more likely that governments will internalize the costs of their spending. Thus, strong fiscal institutions should facilitate fiscal consolidation in the event that deficits arise. Empirical work has found that fiscal institutions that limit special interests, curtail the ability of the legislature to amend bills, and increase transparency all are associated with greater fiscal discipline (Alesina et al. 1999; Fabrizio and Mody 2006; von Hagen 1992; Wehner 2007). Conversely, the fragmentation of power—veto players, complex checks and balance and fiscal federalism, etc.—can make fiscal consolidations more difficult (Ganghof 2006; Obinger et al. 2005; Rodden and Wibbels 2002; Tsebelis and Chang 2004).

A related vein of research has analyzed the role of the budget process and how it unfolds sequentially. Von Hagen (1992) finds that voting on aggregate fiscal targets, such as spending and deficits beforehand, produces greater fiscal discipline. In later work, however, Hallerberg and von Hagen (1997) contend that the centralization of budget-making authority rather than sequencing of legislative votes matters. Alesina et al. (1999) find that there is greater fiscal discipline when deficit levels are decided first.

Fiscal rules that impose budget restrictions—such as limits on deficits (Eichengreen and Bayoumi 1994; Feld and Kirchgässner 2001) and balanced budget requirements (Bohn and Inman 1996)—have been found to increase fiscal discipline and increase the likelihood that fiscal consolidations achieve budget balance (Guichard et al. 2007).

Government Fragmentation, Electoral Systems, and Elections

In addition to fiscal institutions, the degree of government fragmentation can influence the severity of the CPR problem. Roubini and Sachs (1989) find that coalition government generates higher deficits, and Alt and Lowry (1994) looking at US states find that divided government has a similar effect. Subsequent empirical analyses provide further support for this view (Fabrizio and Mody 2006; Perotti and Kontopoulos 2002). Other work has found that electoral systems impact fiscal discipline (Persson and Tabellini 2003, 2004a). Proportional representation (PR) tends to create a more fragmented party system than majoritarian systems. The greater number of parties in government leads to electoral competition in the coalition inducing greater spending Persson et al. (2007).

The timing of elections influences whether or not a government is likely to initiate fiscal consolidation. A government is more likely to embark on fiscal consolidation soon after an election when electoral pressures are lower (Buti and van Den Noord 2004; Mulas-Granados 2006).

The Approach of this Volume

The literature discussed above has enhanced our understanding of fiscal performance, but this volume is motivated by the belief that there is a room for an approach that takes into fuller account the role of institutions, history, and social context. The mainstream approach has relied on quantitative analysis that relies on simplifications of fiscal institutions, fiscal rules, electoral systems, partisanship, etc., in some cases with inadequate attention to the larger context. For instance, the work on fiscal institutions, discussed above, relies on the use of numerical indices. In reality, budgets and budget institutions are highly complex, and such indices do not come close to capturing their full complexity. Poterba and von Hagen (1999: 4) who have used such indices in their analyses, caution that researchers must be sensitive to the limitations of these approaches: "institutional environments of national fiscal policy are complex and therefore, difficult to model and to characterize empirically." Moreover, quantitative analyses can only test for variables for which there are quantitative measures; this makes it harder to explore a wider range of factors and also creates the possibility that the findings might be skewed by omitted variables.

In an attempt to address some of these limitations, this volume relies on comparative cases studies written by an interdisciplinary team of scholars. The work is historical institutional in its approach, which we believe can help bring a range of new factors into consideration. While historical institutionalism has been widely applied in comparative political economy, and even to fiscal issues, especially taxation,[8] it has rarely been applied to understanding deficits and fiscal adjustment, with the notable exception of Dellepiane-Avellaneda and Hardiman (2009). We draw from historical institutionalism three key starting points. First, actor preferences are situational. Preferences cannot be assumed, but rather they are mediated by a large number of factors. Research has shown, for instance, that the organizational structure of interest groups can shape preferences (Vogel 1999). As work in fiscal sociology has shown, voter preferences toward taxes are also shaped by policy. Wilensky (2002) has attributed tax resistance to the structure of taxes; visible taxes such as property and income taxes engender the greatest resistance while invisible taxes such as taxation of consumption are less prone to backlash. Martin and Gabay (2012) argue that tax protests stem from the fit between tax policy and social spending commitments. Similarly, the welfare state can shape spending preferences; welfare policies that are widely distributed can create lock-in effects if programs are popular (Pierson 1994, 2001). While the CPR problem arises when expenditures are targeted, in many countries, social spending, such as on health or pensions, is largely universal. In thinking about fiscal politics, the formation of preferences should clearly matter, yet it has seldom figured in the studies on deficits, debt, and fiscal consolidation.

Second, ideas and non-material factors influence elite and societal views. Beyond economic interests, ideas create cognitive frameworks that shape perceptions about cause and effect or what is normatively desirable. Research in comparative political economy has shown how ideas have, among other things, contributed to the spread of Keynesianism (Hall 1989), the diffusion of central bank independence (McNamara 2002), and mode of economic regulation (Vogel 1996; Blythe 2001). In addition to ideas, non-material factors, such as diffuse forms of support, can impact politics and policy. Scholars working on taxation have drawn attention to the role of "tax consent," the acceptance by individuals to pay taxes as part of a diffuse social contract (Levi 1988; Martin et al. 2009). As a result of this research, we know that patriotism (Felman and Slemrod 2009) as well as trust and confidence (Ide and Steinmo 2009; Park and Ide 2014) enhance tax consent. Considering that fiscal adjustments can require hard choices on both the revenue and expenditure side, one would expect levels of diffuse support and trust to come into play.

Third, causal complexity and timing matter. Events and causality unfold in time and how they do so can be highly consequential. Sequencing, path dependence, exogenous shocks, and feedback mechanisms can all shape causal pathways (Pierson 2004; Martin et al. 2009; Thelen 2004). Starting with this assumption determines both the nature of the questions posed and the kind of explanations that are considered. When thinking about fiscal performance, one of the challenges is to explain both how some patterns are locked-in and how they change over time (Pierson 2004; Thelen 2004). Indeed, it is these longer-term patterns that are the object of this study. There is strong path dependency to fiscal performance. Yet there also have been remarkable changes in fiscal performance over time within countries. This is clear in our case countries, from Japan's rapid transition from remarkable fiscal discipline to chronic deficits to

Italy's stabilization of its public debt. For this project, our authors have taken their own approach in defining what specific pattern and time period to focus on. This broadening of the notion of fiscal performance also helps bring into focus the fact that commonly accepted measures of fiscal performance (such as IMF or OECD statistics) are not necessarily straightforward. Recent work has highlighted that fiscal systems often rely on mechanisms outside of the formal budget, and thus standardized statistics on deficit and debt can in fact be misleading (Park 2011). The chapter on South Korea in this volume further develops this point.

Attention to causal complexity and timing also influences the kind of explanation we seek. In this volume, we try to identify underlying structural causes. Many studies analyze fiscal performance using cross-sectional time-series data. Statistical models often attempt to strip out the effects of country and time, making it difficult to analyze underlying effects that may shape longer-term patterns of fiscal performance. This volume by contrast leverages within-country variation to identify and unravel these country specific and time effects by delving into the historical evolution of institutions and preferences.

The work on budget institutions illustrates the need for greater sensitivity to these issues. Fiscal institutions—as well as other institutions such as electoral systems or federalism—do not change frequently. Since they are often time invariant, budget institutions in many cases cannot explain temporal change within a country. There are, however, times when governments do change budget institutions, but we need a better understanding of what drives such change. Furthermore, closer attention is needed to parse the effects of budget institutions from the factors that gave rise to these budget institutions in the first place; it may be that these underlying factors in fact explain changes in fiscal performance rather than the budget institutions themselves (Poterba and von Hagen 1999). We believe that a greater sensitivity to these issues can help illuminate our understanding of fiscal performance.

Roadmap for the Volume

This volume is a collective effort to advance a new approach to studying fiscal performance. The aim was to leverage the collective knowledge and expertise of our contributors to carry out in-depth comparative research. The next eight chapters focus on individual countries and are followed by a penultimate chapter that covers fiscal governance in the eurozone. The chapters are summarized below.

In Chapter 2, Konishi and Tristam explain why France has had problems pursuing fiscal consolidation, leading to accumulating government debt. Their analysis focuses on the French government's challenges on the expenditures side; France has one of the highest levels of expenditure in the OECD. Several factors make it harder for the government to slow expenditure growth: strong social consensus around high social expenditures, an inefficient organization of the state, and the ease with which the French state has been able to finance its deficits. With a tradition of statism in France, both the right and the left have been committed to a vision of large government, and there is a pervasive distrust of neo-liberalism. Although the government is centralized, France has a complex system of local government with many jurisdictions and overlapping responsibilities that contributes to public sector inefficiency and creates fragmented responsibility for controlling expenditures. The government also has faced little restraint to growing spending in part because it has been able to finance its deficits relatively easily, something that European monetary union actually enhanced by eliminating exchange rate risk.

In Chapter 3 Kemmerling and Truchlewski use Germany as a critical case to explore the conditions that facilitate fiscal consolidation. Germany is a country with moderate debt, even despite costly reunification, and relatively high fiscal discipline. The authors argue that traditional explanations such as partisan politics and fiscal institutions cannot explain Germany's fiscal performance. Even a constitutional "debt brake" introduced in 1969 did little to restrain deficits. Instead, Kemmerling and Truchlewski find that electoral competition is the key variable. Fiscal consolidation is only successful when a government can avoid the blame for unpopular measures. When electoral pressure was high and governments could not easily blame others, consolidation efforts remained limited or led to severe adverse political consequences for the government. Their findings suggest that an overemphasis on debt rules may be misguided, particularly if they create a political liability for incumbent politicians. Instead, governments might be better off in finding mechanisms that mitigate the political consequences of consolidation by, for instance, facilitating fiscal pacts.

Marzinotto uses an historical institutional analysis to explain in Chapter 4 how Italy was able to rein in rapid growth in public debt. In contrast to the conventional narrative that budget reforms and external EMU constraints are responsible for the stabilization of Italy's debt in the 1990s, Marzinotto highlights how incremental changes produced shifting socioeconomic preferences that paved the way for fiscal adjustment. The chapter locates the path to a new fiscal regime in Italy's shift to central bank independence in 1981 and later monetary union. Both changes led business and labor to become more sensitive to inflation, allowing them to build consensus around fiscal consolidation. While the budget reform in 1988 also facilitated consolidation by helping the government overcome political instability during the 1990s, this reform itself was a consequence of changing socioeconomic preferences. The chapter concludes by showing how these preferences have continued to shape the politics of fiscal adjustment up to and beyond the sovereign debt crisis.

In contrast to Italy, Japan experienced a sharp rise in public debt during the 1990s and beyond. In Chapter 6, Takahashi and Shimada lay out the reasons for this development. Conventional explanations that emphasize party politics, electoral reform, and changes in budget institutions cannot fully explain the Japanese case. Instead, Takahashi and Shimada show that Japan's problem is rooted in two historical institutional features of Japan's political economy. First, the government relied over the postwar period on a model of social protection that relied on tax cutting and highly targeted welfare spending. This form of "discriminatory" welfare provision and habituation to tax cuts weakened the link between taxation and benefits, which in turn has fed tax resistance. Second, specific institutional features have allowed the government to circumvent this resistance through debt financing. The government's direct control of financial resources, macroeconomic and financial conditions that produced a large pool of domestic savings, and bond absorption by the central bank all provided the government access to low cost financing.

To understand the South Korean case, Kang shows in Chapter 6 that the analysis needs to go beyond the formal budget. On the one hand, South Korea has relatively low public debt and a history of fiscal discipline, partly a legacy of the government's adherence to a balanced budget policy during the period of authoritarian rule in the 1980s and a high degree of centralization of budget-making authority in the executive. Democratization unleashed greater political pressure for spending and the legislature began to play a larger role in the budgeting process. Still, by comparative standards the executive remains strong and, during the first part of the new century, the government passed reforms to enhance budget transparency. Kang points out though that while South Korea's level of public debt appears comparatively low the government has increasingly relied on off-budget borrowing through public corporations and special funds to circumvent the legislature. This debt now exceeds the level of budget debt and may pose serious financial liabilities in the future.

In Chapter 7 Edlund and Iju explain why Sweden was first able to restore fiscal discipline successfully after experiencing a financial and economic crisis in the early 1990s and then maintain a high degree of fiscal discipline subsequently. To restore the fiscal balance, the government relied on revenue enhancements and sizeable cuts to spending and also implemented a far-reaching budget reform, which the authors conclude helped the government maintain future fiscal balance. Edlund and Iju then turn to the conditions that made the fiscal adjustment and budget reform possible. Their chapter highlights the role of the economic crisis, which created a broad perception that action was necessary, and cross-party cooperation around a broad package of reforms that voters and social partners accepted.

Chapters 8 and 9 cover different aspects of US fiscal performance. Elliot Brownlee in Chapter 8 analyzes every long-run period of fiscal consolidation since the formation of the first government under the US constitution in 1789. This broad historical perspective presents the US's current fiscal challenges in a novel light. As Brownlee shows, the US has a long history of "fiscal virtue" and the government has succeeded in fiscal consolidations in the face of tremendous challenges. From this perspective, it is even questionable if there really is a fiscal crisis currently. Brownlee finds several common threads behind the successful consolidations. The government succeeded in part because fiscal consolidations have not engendered much political backlash, a surprising and somewhat counterintuitive finding. This is in part due to their timing—largely during periods of buoyant economic growth—and to serendipitous circumstances, particularly large peace dividends after wars. Brownlee also finds, though, that consolidations succeeded in part for two important reasons: (1) the government avoided retrenchment of domestic programs and (2) fiscal consolidations relied on revenue enhancements. Brownlee shows that voter perceptions of fairness were a critical precondition to making tax hikes politically palatable. Also important for pushing fiscal consolidation agenda forward has been the nation's financial leadership both inside and outside the government. While the long-view of history offers a more sanguine view of the current US situation, especially since interest rates remain very low, Brownlee does not discount the fact that the economic and political conditions have become more unfavorable to fiscal consolidation, particularly since 2001.

Joseph Thorndike focuses on these more recent trends in Chapter 9. His chapter looks at developments in the US since 1970 assessing the impact of various attempts to tinker with budget institutions and the budget process. The US political context is not particularly conducive for limiting deficits. Although reforms early in the twentieth century enhanced the role of the executive in budgeting, the legislature has jealously guarded its budget authority. Large budget deficits tend to spark a push for fiscal consolidation, but legislators have had to contend with partisan differences, narrow interests and gridlock. In an attempt to overcome these problems, the congress has devised rules to enforce budget discipline, such as pay-as-you-go (PAYGO) rules that require deviations from budget targets to be offset with revenue or corresponding cuts and sequestration, automatic spending cuts. While congress is prone to change or dispense with these rules when they conflict with their larger goals, Thorndike finds that these devices have played a constructive political role in brokering compromises. He adds a note of caution, though, suggesting that we may be in a new era, in which there is growing legislative polarization; thus, even the threat or reality of painful measures from sequestration cuts may not be adequate to force parties to the bargaining table.

Chapter 10 shifts to the supranational level—the European Union. In this chapter, Edward Fogarty analyzes the origins and effects of the fiscal rules in the eurozone. He finds that the fiscal regime from the early 1999s suffered from design flaws that undermined their credibility. Thus, the fiscal rules have had only weak effects on national fiscal policy. With the sovereign debt crisis, the EU created a stronger fiscal regime—the new fiscal compact—but Fogarty argues that the new regime fails to deal with the basic flaws in the fiscal regime, namely the structural imbalances between northern and southern Europe. Thus, he concludes on a pessimistic note about the new supranational fiscal regime.

Finally, a brief conclusion discusses the larger implications of the findings from this project. The concluding chapter draws together cross-case generalizations and suggests directions for future research.

Notes

1 The intergenerational effect depends on the nature of the spending; investments in human capital or infrastructure, for instance, will yield benefits for future generations as well.

2 The concern over deficits and debt has partly been driven by the sovereign debt crisis, but this comparison has been exaggerated, since the crisis stems in part from the design and management of the eurozone—see Chapter 10 in this volume by Fogarty. The public debate has also been animated by a controversy over work by Reinhart and

Rogoff (2009, 2010), which suggested that there is debt threshold above which growth slows. Subsequent work found mistakes with the data (Herndon et al. 2014).

3 When governments run deficits they must finance themselves through borrowing. The increased demand from the government may drive up interest rates. In some cases, the effect of deficits may depend on the debt level. A high level of debt makes interest rates more sensitive to deficits (Aisen and Hauner 2007; Ardagna 2007). Despite the controversy over the work of Reinhart and Rogoff, others have found support for the claim that debt can slow growth (Checherita and Rother 2010), or that while there may be a negative effect there is no clear threshold and that the effect of debt depends on whether it is growing or not (Chudik et al. 2013).

4 Based on author calculations from World Development Indicators from World Bank. (http://data.worldbank.org/indicator/NY.GDP.MKTP.KD.ZG).

5 For instance, the German government was able to use fiscal stimulus more effectively by cooperating with labor unions to keep wages low.

6 OECD.Stat at http://stats.oecd.org (accessed December 20, 2013).

7 The literature is extensive and this is only a partial review.

8 There is a long line of historical institutionalist work on taxes, including, but not limited to Levi 1988; Martin 1989; Steinmo 1993; Wilensky 2002. The new fiscal sociology (see the edited volume by Martin, Mehotra, and Prasad 2009) builds on this existing work, but again largely focuses on taxation.

References

Abbas, S.M. Ali, Olivier Basdevant, Stephanie Eble, Greetje Everaert, Jan Gottschalk, Fuad Hasanov, Junhyung Park, Cemile Sancak, Ricardo Velloso, and Mauricio Villafuerte. 2010. *Strategies for Fiscal Consolidation in the Post-Crisis World*. International Monetary Fund.

Aisen, Ari and David Hauner. 2007. *Budget Deficits and Interest Rates: A Fresh Perspective*. International Monetary Fund.

Alesina, Alberto and Roberto Perotti. 1995a. "The Political-Economy of Budget Deficits." *International Monetary Fund Staff Papers* 42(1): 1–31.

Alesina, Alberto and Roberto Perotti. 1995b. *Fiscal Expansions and Fiscal Adjustments in OECD Countries*. National Bureau of Economic Research Working Paper 5214.

Alesina, Alberto and Roberto Perotti. 1999. "Budget Deficits and Budget Institutions." In *Fiscal Institutions and Fiscal Performance*, edited by James M. Poterba and Jürgen von Hagen, 13–36. Chicago: University of Chicago Press.

Alesina, Alberto, Nouriel Roubini, and Gerald D. Cohen. 1997. *Political Cycles and the Macroeconomy*. Cambridge, MA: MIT Press.

Alesina, Alberto, Ricardo Hausmann, Rudolf Hommes, and Ernesto Stein. 1999. "Budget Institutions and Fiscal Performance in Latin America." *Journal of Development Economics* 59: 253–273.

Alt, James E. and R.C. Lowry. 1994. "Divided Government, Fiscal Institutions, and Budget Deficits: Evidence from the States." *American Political Science Review* 88(4): 811–828. doi:10.2307/2082709.

Alt, James E. and David Dreyer Lassen. 2005. "Fiscal Transparency, Political Parties, and Debt in OECD Countries." *European Economic Review* 50: 1403–1439.

Amable, Bruno, Donatella Gatti, and Jan Schumacher. 2006. "Welfare-State Retrenchment: The Partisan Effect Revisited." *Oxford Review of Economic Policy* 22(3): 426–444.

Ardagna, Silvia, Francesco Caselli, and Timothy Lane. 2007. "Fiscal Discipline and the Cost of Public Debt Service: Some Estimates for OECD Countries." *The B.E. Journal of Macroeconomics* 7(1).

Benito, Bernardino and Francisco Bastida. 2009. "Budget Transparency, Fiscal Performance, and Political Turnout: An International Approach." *Public Administration Review* 69(3): 403–417.

Blythe, Mark. "The Transformation of the Swedish Model: Economic Ideas, Distributional Conflict, and Institutional Change." *World Politics* 54(1): 1–26.

Bohn, H. and R.P. Inman. 1996. "Balanched-Budget Rules and Public Deficits: Evidence from the U.S. States." *Carnegie-Rochester Conference Series on Public Policy* no. 45: 13–76.

Boix, Carles. 2000. "Partisan Governments, the International Economy, and Macroeconomic Policies in Advanced Nations, 1960–93." *World Politics* 53(1): 38–73.

Buti, M. and P. Van den Noord. 2004. "Fiscal Discretion and Elections in the Early Years of EMU." *Journal of Common Market Studies* 42(4): 737–756. doi:10.1111/J.0021–9886.2004.00527.X.

Cambpell, Andrea. (forthcoming). *How Americans Think about Taxes: Public Opinion and the American Fiscal State.*

Castles, Francis G. 2007. "Introduction." In *The Disappearing State? Retrenchment Realities in an Age of Globalisation*, edited by Francis G. Castles, 1–18. Cheltenham, UK; Northampton, MA: Edward Elgar.

Checherita, Cristina and Philipp Rother. 2010. *The Impact of High and Growing Government Debt on Economic Growth: An Empirical Investigation for the Euro Area*. European Central Bank: Working Papers Series no. August (1237).

Chudik, Alexander, Kamiar Mohaddes, M. Hashem Pesaran, and Mehdi Raissi. 2013. *Debt, Inflation and Growth: Robust Estimation of Long-Run Effects in Dynamic Panel Data Models*. CESifo Working Paper, No. 4508.

Clark, William Roberts and Mark Hallerberg. 2000. "Mobile capital, domestic institutions, and electorally induced monetary and fiscal policy." *American Political Science Review* 94(2): 323–346.

Cournede, B. and F. Gonand. 2006. *Restoring Fiscal Sustainability in the Euro Area: Raise Taxes or Curb Spending?* OECD Economics Department Working Papers 520.

Dellepiane-Avellaneda, Sebastiá and Niamh Hardiman. 2009. *Explaining Variations in Patterns of Fiscal Consolidation*. UCD Geary Institute Discussion Paper Series.

Eichengreen, B. and T. Bayoumi. 1994. "The Political-Economy of Fiscal Restrictions: Implications for Europe from the United-States." *European Economic Review* 38(3–4): 783–791. doi:10.1016/0014–2921(94)90114–7.

Fabrizio, Stefania and Ashoka Mody. 2006. *Can Budget Institutions Counteract Political Indiscipline?* IMF Working Paper no. 6 (123): 1–49.

Feld, L.P. and G. Kirchgassner. 2001. "The Political Economy of Direct Legislation: The Role of Direct Democracy in Local and Regional Decision-Making." *Economic Policy* 16(33): 329–367.

Feldman, Naomi and Joel Slemrod. 2009. "War and Taxation: When does Patriotism Overcome the Free-Rider Impulse." In *The New Fiscal Sociology: Taxation in Comparative Perspective*, edited by Isaac William Martin, Ajay K. Mehotra and Monica Prasad, 138–154. New York: Cambridge University Press.

Ganghof, Steffen. 2006. *The Politics of Income Taxation: A Comparative Analysis*, ECPR monographs. Colchester: ECPR Press.

Garrett, Geoffrey. 1998. *Partisan Politics in the Global Economy*. New York: Cambridge University Press.

Guichard, Stephanie, Mike Kennedy, Eckhard Wurzel and Christophe Andre. 2007. *What Promotes Fiscal Consolidation: OECD Country Experiences*. OECD Economics Department Working Papers (553): 5–31.

Hagen, Jürgen von. 1992. *Budgeting Procedures and Fiscal Performance in the European Communities*. European Commission Economic Paper 96.

Hagen, Jürgen von and Ian J. Harden. 1995. "Budget Processes and Commitment to Fiscal Discipline." *European Economic Review* 39: 771–779.

Hahm, S.D., M.S. Kamlet, and D.C. Mowrey. 1996. "The Political Economy of Deficit Spending in Nine Industrialized Parliamentary Democracies: The Role of Fiscal Institutions." *Comparative Political Studies* 29(1): 52–77.

Hall, Peter A. 1989 *The Political Power of Economic Ideas: Keynesianism across Nations*. Princeton, NJ: Princeton University Press.

Hallerberg, Mark and Jürgen von Hagen. 1997. *Sequencing and the Size of the Budget: A Reconsideration*. Centre for Economic Policy Research Discussion Paper No. 1589.

Herndon, Thomas, Michael Ash, and Robert Pollin. 2014. "Does High Public Debt Consistently Stifle Economic Growth? A Critique of Reinhart and Rogoff." *Cambridge Journal of Economics* 38(2): 257–279.

Hibbs, Douglas A. 1977. "Political Parties and Macroeconomic Policy." *The American Political Science Review* 71(4): 1467–1487.

Ide, Eisaku and Sven Steinmo. 2009. "The End of the Strong State? On the Evolution of Japanese Tax Policy." In *The New Fiscal Sociology: Taxation in Comparative Perspective*, edited by Isaac William Martin, Ajay K. Mehotra and Monica Prasad, 119–137. New York: Cambridge University Press.

Kirchgässner, Gebhard. 2001. *The Effects of Fiscal Institutions on Public Finance: A Survey of the Empirical Evidence*. CESifo Working Paper Series (617): 1–30.

Kitschelt, Herbert. 2001. "Partisan Competition and Welfare State Retrenchment: When do Politicians Choose Unpopular Policies?" In *The New Politics of the Welfare State*, edited by Paul Pierson, 265–302. Oxford: Oxford University Press.

Levi, Margaret. 1988. *Of Rule and Revenue*. Berkeley, CA: University of California Press.

Manasse, Paolo and Nouriel Roubini. 2008. "'Rules of Thumb' for Sovereign Debt Crises." *JEL* no. F35.

Martin, Cathie Jo. 1989. "Business Influence and State Power: The Case of U.S. Corporate Tax Policy." *Politics and Society* 17: 189–223.

Martin, Isaac William and Nadav Gabay. 2012. "Fiscal Protest in Thirteen Welfare States." *Socioeconomic Review* 11(1): 107–130.

Martin, Isaac William, Ajay K. Mehrotra, and Monica Prasad. 2009. *The New Fiscal Sociology: Taxation in Comparative and Historical Perspective*. New York: Cambridge University Press.

McDermott, C. John and Robert F. Wescott. 1996. "An Empirical Analysis of Fiscal Adjustments." *IMF Staff Papers* 725–753.

McNamara, Kathleen. 2002. "Rational Fictions: Central Bank Independence and the Social Logic of Delegation." *West European Politics* 25(1): 47–76.

Mulas-Granados, Carlos. 2003. "The Political and Economic Determinants of Budgetary Consolidations in Europe." *European Political Economy Review* 1(1): 25–49.

Mulas-Granados, Carlos. 2006. *Economics, Politics and Budgets: The Political Economy of Fiscal Consolidations in Europe*. Basingstoke; New York: Palgrave Macmillan.

Oatley, Thomas. 1999. "How Constraining is Mobile Capital? The Partisan Hypothesis in an Open Economy," *American Journal of Political Science* 43(4): 1003–1027.

Obinger, H., S. Leibfried, and F.G. Castles. 2005. *Federalism and the Welfare State: New World and European Experiences*. Cambridge: Cambridge University Press.

Park, Gene. 2011. *Spending without Taxation: FILP and the Politics of Public Finance in Japan*. Palo Alto, CA: Stanford University Press.

Park, Gene and Eisaku Ide. 2014. "The Tax–Welfare Mix: Explaining Japan's Weak Extractive Capacity." *The Pacific Review* 27(5): 675–702.

Perotti, R. and Y. Kontopoulos. 2002. "Fragmented Fiscal Policy." *Journal of Public Economics* no. 86 (2): 191–222. doi:10.1016/S0047–2727(01)00146–3.

Persson, Torsten and Guido Enrico Tabellini. 2000. *Political Economics: Explaining Economic Policy*, Zeuthen lecture book series. Cambridge, MA: MIT Press.

Persson, T. and G. Tabellini. 2003. *The Economic Effects of Constitutions*, Munich lectures in economics. Cambridge, MA: MIT Press.

Persson, T. and G. Tabellini. 2004a. "Constitutional Rules and Fiscal Policy Outcomes." *American Economic Review* 94(1): 25–45. doi:10.1257/000282804322970689.

Persson, T. and G. Tabellini. 2004b. "Constitutions and Economics Policy." *Journal of Economic Perspectives* 18(1): 75–98.

Persson, T., G. Roland, and G. Tabellini. 2007. "Electoral Rules and Government Spending in Parliamentary Democracies." *Quarterly Journal of Political Science* no. 2 (2): 155–188. doi:10.1561/100.00006019.

Pierson, Paul. 1994. *Dismantling the Welfare State? Reagan, Thatcher, and the Politics of Retrenchment*. Cambridge: Cambridge University Press.

Pierson, Paul. 2001. *The New Politics of the Welfare State*. Oxford, UK; New York: Oxford University Press.

Pierson, Paul. 2004. *Politics in Time: History, Institutions, and Social Analysis*. Princeton: Princeton University Press.

Poterba, James M. and Jürgen von Hagen. 1999. "Introduction." In *Fiscal Institutions and Fiscal Performance*, edited by James M. Poterba and Jurgen von Hagen, 1–12. Chicago: University of Chicago Press.

Reinhart, Carmen M. and Kenneth S. Rogoff. 2009. *This Time is Different: Eight Centuries of Financial Folly*. Princeton: Princeton University Press.

Reinhart, Carmen M. and Kenneth S. Rogoff. 2010. "Growth in a Time of Debt." *American Economic Review* 100 (May 2010): 573–578.

Rodden, J. and E. Wibbels. 2002. "Beyond the Fiction of Federalism: Macroeconomic Management in Multitiered Systems." *World Politics* 54(4): 494–531.

Ross, Fiona. 2000. "'Beyond Left and Right': The New Partisian Politics of Welfare." *Governance* 13(2): 155–183.

Roubini, Nouriel and Jeffrey Sachs. 1989. "Political and Economic Determinants of Budget Deficits in the Industrial Democracies." *European Economic Review* 33(5): 903–933.

Ruggie, John. 1982. "International Regimes, Transactions, and Change: Embedded Liberalism in the Postwar Economic Order." *International Organization* 36(2): 379–415.

Sears, David O. and Jack Citrin. 1985. *Tax Revolt: Something for Nothing in California*. Enlarged edn, Cambridge, MA; London, England: Harvard University Press.

Shaviro, Daniel. 1995. *Budget Deficits and the Intergenerational Distribution of Lifetime Consumption*. John M. Olin Law and Economics Working Paper no. 29 no. 2D Series: 1–44.

Steinmo, Sven. 1996. *Taxation and Democracy: Swedish, British, and American Approaches to Financing the Modern State*. New Haven, CT: Yale University Press.

Strauch, Rolf R. and Jürgen von Hagen. 2000. "Introduction." In *Institutions, Politics and Fiscal Policy*, edited by Rolf R. Strauch and Jurgen von Hagen. Norwell, MA: Kluwer Academic Publishers.

Tavares, Jose. 2004. "Does Right or Left Matter? Cabinets, Credibility and Fiscal Adjustments." *Journal of Public Economics* 88(12): 2447–2468.

Taylor, Lance, Laura de Carvalho Proaño, and Nelson Barbosa. 2012. "Fiscal Deficits, Economic Growth and Government Debt in the USA." *Cambridge Journal of Economics* 36: 189–204.

Thelen, Kathleen Ann. 2004. *How Institutions Evolve: The Political Economy of Skills in Germany, Britain, the United States, and Japan*, Cambridge Studies in Comparative Politics. Cambridge; New York: Cambridge University Press.

Tromborg, Mathias Wessel. 2014. "Bringing the Median Voter back in: The Relationship between Government Debt, Median Voter Preferences, and Welfare State Spending." *Journal of European Social Policy* 24(107): 107–121.

Tsebelis, G. and E.C.C. Chang. 2004. "Veto Players and the Structure of Budgets in Advanced Industrialized Countries." *European Journal of Political Research* 43: 449–476.

Vogel, Steven Kent. 1996. *Freer Markets, More Rules: Regulatory Reform in Advanced Industrial Countries*, Cornell Studies in Political Economy. Ithaca, NY: Cornell University Press.

Vogel, Steven Kent. 1999. "When Interests are Not Preferences: The Cautionary Tale of Japanese Consumers." *Comparative Politics* 31(2): 187–297.

Wehner, J. 2007. "Budget Reform and Legislative Control in Sweden." *Journal of European Public Policy* 14(2): 313–332. doi:10.1080/13501760601122704.

Wilensky, Harold L. 2002. *Rich Democracies: Political Economy, Public Policy, and Performance*. Berkeley: University of California Press.

2 The Difficulty of Fiscal Consolidation in France

Anna Konishi and Frédéric Tristram
Translated by Zbigniew Truchlewski, CEU

Introduction

In the past few years, the subject of public debt has been center-stage. This is particularly the case in France, where the issue of debt has both political and economic dimensions. This chapter will focus on the specificities of French debt and deficits, and will seek to explain why France accumulated deficits during the last three decades and why such deficits make debt stabilization so difficult today.

The chapter proceeds as follows: First, we describe the situation in France by exploring the dependent variables. Second, we will focus on the causal mechanisms that explain the current situation in French public finances.

A Worrisome Budgetary Situation

Five characteristics define the French situation currently: First, French public debt grew continuously but irregularly over the last 30 years. Measured according to the Maastricht criteria, public indebtedness rose from just over 20 percent of GDP in 1980, to 92.7 percent of GDP in the last quarter of 2013, which amounts to €1,900.8 billion. Figure 2.1 shows that four time periods can be identified.

Between 1980 and 1991, public indebtedness grew slowly from 20 to 35 percent of GDP. Then it skyrocketed between 1991 and 1997, reaching almost 60 percent of GDP.[1] From 1998 to 2007, debt stabilized at a high level, between 60 and 65 percent of GDP. This result stems from a lack of fiscal consolidation despite good economic conditions. The fourth and last period comes in the aftermath of the Great Recession, common to all developed countries. Public debt increased by 30 percent due to the financial crisis in less than five years.

Clearly, economic activity is the determining factor behind these successive increases, especially the two major economic crises in the last 30 years in France, the one of 1992–93 and 2008–12.

Second, the high level of public expenditures, significantly higher than in other countries, characterizes French budgeting (see Figure 2.2). In 2012, it was second to Denmark only, with public expenditure at 56.1 percent of GDP vs. 59.3 percent in Denmark. French public expenditures are thus 7 percent higher

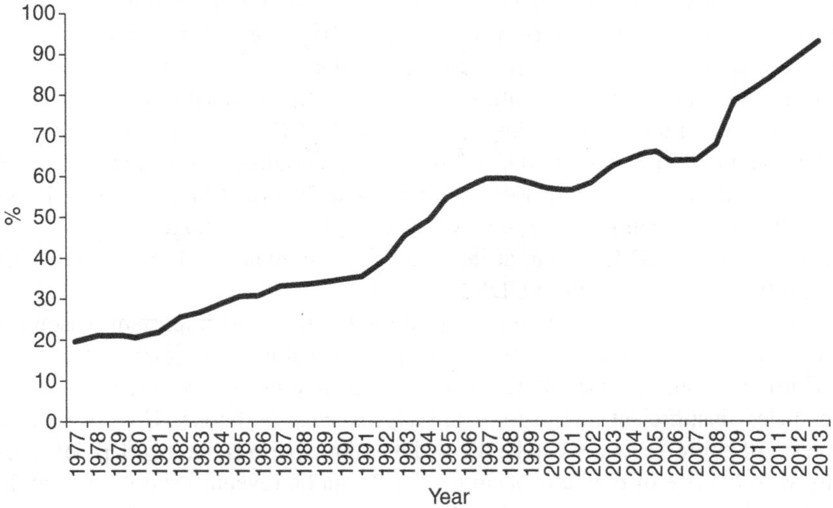

Figure 2.1 Growth of French public debt since end of 1970s (source: INSEE, percentage of GDP).

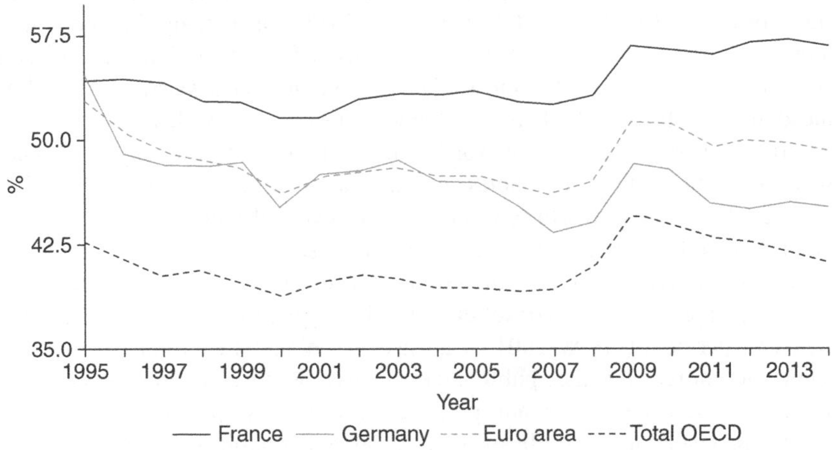

Figure 2.2 Public expenditures as percentage of GDP, 1995–2013.

than the eurozone average (49.2 percent) and 10 percent higher than in Germany (45.7 percent).[2]

This is not news: since the middle of the twentieth century, France has had a significantly higher level of public expenditures than her main partners. At the beginning of the 1960s, public expenditures reached 35 percent of GDP in France, which was approximately 10 percent above the OECD average.[3] However, this gap has continued to grow in recent years due to the fact that other

European countries—above all those who posted high levels of public expenditures like France—implemented reforms entailing expenditure control. Sweden's public expenditure, for instance, was more than 10 percent higher than France in 1995, but almost 7 percent lower in 2012 according to the OECD.

The growth of public expenditures in France stems primarily from the growth of social expenditures.[4] According to the latest OECD data, social expenditures will amount to 33 percent of GDP in 2013, i.e., the highest among the developed countries, ahead of Denmark (30.8 percent) and Sweden (28.6 percent). These expenditures will continue to grow apace, around 2.8 percentage points of GDP between 2008 and 2013, while at the same time Germany will reduce its social expenditures by 5.8 percent of GDP.[5]

This lack of control over public expenditures is the most important reason for high deficits. This chapter investigates the reasons behind this situation.

Third, high public expenditure levels have led to a heavy tax burden, which is nonetheless insufficient to close the gap and balance the books. This increase in the level of public revenues can be divided into three periods that overlap only partially with the rise of public debt. In the 1970s public revenues shoot up from 34 percent of GDP to 42.8 percent in 1984. A second acceleration, though more modest, can be noticed between 1992 and 1995, when France had to qualify for membership in the eurozone, and when revenue peaked at 45.1 percent of GDP in 1999.[6] Lastly, revenues increased again after the Great Recession, reaching 45.1 percent of GDP in 2012.[7] Forecasts suggest that public revenues could amount to 46 percent of GDP in 2013 and 47 percent in 2017.[8] Once again, France is in a unique situation among Western countries. Only a few of the Nordic countries have higher taxation levels but most of them have, in recent years, stabilized or reduced their taxation levels. This is particularly the case in Sweden.

Fourth, and perhaps the most worrisome, is the poor smoothing of cyclical policies over time. French policies are indeed asymmetric in general, being counter-cyclical when growth is weak, and pro-cyclical when growth is robust (Champsaur and Cotis 2010). This distortion raises three kinds of problems. First, it is partly responsible for the build-up of outstanding debt. France is not able to implement efficient consolidation policies once cyclical problems fade away. The period of 1998–2001 is a case in point, when robust growth (3 percent) did not really reduce public indebtedness, because governments refused to reduce public expenditures and preferred to use the surplus to reduce taxes. Now, it is precisely during spells of robust growth that public debt can be significantly reduced, as the American example in the late 1990s suggests.[9]

This asymmetry of policies hinders the implementation of counter-cyclical policies. Countries which can post surpluses during economic expansions are also those which can smooth out the business cycle more effectively thanks to dynamic budgetary policies (Poterba and von Hagen 2000). Finally, this asymmetry can, under certain circumstances, force governments to conduct pro-cyclical policies during recessions, thus jeopardizing the efficiency of those policies and increasing their cost. The rare examples of fiscal consolidations implemented in France happened in the context of slow growth and were only modest successes obtained at a high price in terms of economic activity and employment. This was the case in 1987, in 1995–97, and in 2004–07. It is, most importantly, also the case today. Indeed, since 2011, strong increases in taxation may have reduced the structural deficit, as shown in Table 2.1, but they have hardly reduced net lending.

Thus, France finds it difficult to fulfill its European commitments and to stick to its own forecasts to balance its budget. The objective of limiting the public deficit to 3 percent of GDP in 2013 has not been reached, even though it was specified in all budgetary documents published before the end of 2012.[10] This objective had to be postponed by two years after the European Council agreed to it in June 2013. The final deficit (4.1 percent) is even higher than what was planned in the Stability Program sent to the European Commission in April 2013 (3.7 percent). This poor performance is due to lower than expected public revenues stemming from sluggish growth and an important decrease of the elasticity of public revenues to the GDP (Cour des Comptes 2014).

Fifth, and finally, the consensus on the priority given to balancing the books is fragile. The public debate seized on this topic only very late in the 2000s, after the publication of the "Pébereau Report" in the fall of 2005 which was a crucial step (Pébereau 2006).[11]

After the crisis of 2008–09, the center-right government of Nicolas Sarkozy was slow to tackle exceptionally high fiscal deficits. Despite the joint pressure of higher interest rates on the public debt and the sovereign debt crisis in the eurozone, it was not before August and November 2011 that two successive plans of increasing taxation were presented.[12]

This policy of fiscal consolidation has been broadly continued with the new socialist government elected in May and June 2012.[13] This policy is nonetheless subject to a double opposition, which subsumes fiscal and budgetary policies under a larger contestation including national economic and social policy as well as EU integration and the single currency.

This contestation of fiscal consolidation has, first, a political nature, which stems from French partisan cleavages and their recent evolution. On the left, a neo-communist and anti-capitalist movement (the Left Front or varied declinations of the Trotskyist movement) carries out this contestation. On the right side of the political spectrum, it is carried out by a populist and nationalist stream, the National Front (FN), which had some real successes in elections. Looking more closely at the first round of the presidential elections in 2012, almost a third of

Table 2.1 Net lending/borrowing of public administrations, as percentage of GDP

	2007	*2008*	*2009*	*2010*	*2011*	*2012*	*2103 (provisional)*
Net lending	–2.7	–3.3	–7.5	–7.1	–5.3	–4.8	–4.1
Cyclical element	0.7	0	–2.0	–1.6	–0.3	–0.8	–1.4
Structural element	–3.5	–3.3	–4.5	–4.8	–5.1	–4.0	–2.6
Temporary operations	0.1	0	–1.0	–0.7	0.1	0	–0.1

Source: Cour des Comptes 2012, 2013, 2014.

the electorate contested the policy of fiscal consolidation. But this contestation can also gain mainstream governmental parties (PS (Parti socialiste) and UMP (Union pour un mouvement populaire)), especially the socialist party currently in office and where minority currents hostile to governmental and austerity policies undermine the current effort to consolidate public finances.[14]

Numerous social groups echo the left-wing contestation. Several trade unions like CGT (Confédération générale du travail), FO (Force ouvrière), or SUD (Solidaires Unitaires Démocratiques) are hostile to the consolidation of public expenditures, and are all the more powerful hindrances by virtue of being well entrenched in the public and para-public sectors. Some associations like ATTAC (Association for the Taxation of financial Transactions and Aid to Citizens) also joined the chorus of contestation and some voices are heard among academics, especially sociologists, political scientists, and a few "heterodox" economists.[15] For these intellectuals, the debt crisis is a construction stemming from national and international choices made over 30 years: using financial markets to refinance public debt, forbidding monetary financing, dismantling the "circuit" as a means to finance deficits, the primacy of fighting inflation, conceptualized as an antinomy of economic growth.[16] Rather, even if these people contend that solutions are to be found on the national level, they still argue that EU member states should benefit from being allowed to maneuver on the EU level, for instance by changing the mandate of the European Central Bank (ECB) and allowing it to finance national deficits. This would mean that the economy of indebtedness should be reconstructed on the European level.

These five characteristics suggest a very specific budgetary situation that makes France stand apart from other Western capitalist democracies. The next section will now turn to the determinants of this situation.

The French Budgetary Exception: Loose Expenditure Control and Relaxation of Financial Constraints

In France, persistent debt and deficits can be explained by three factors: the difficult control of public expenditures, weak financial constraints, and the belated implementation of institutional mechanisms to control the budget.

Difficult Control of Public Expenditures

Two types of expenditures played a key role in the increase and preservation of a high level of public outlays. On the one hand, these are—as seen above—social expenditures and, in particular, healthcare and old-age insurance policies. On the other hand, these are expenses stemming from the territorial organization of the country.

1 A High Level of Social Expenditures

The high level of social expenditures answers a collective preference that is clearly expressed. There is strong consensus in France on maintaining a high level of social protection and on a collective insurance mechanism to cater for healthcare, old age, and family policies. But there is a weaker consensus on social expenditures earmarked for peculiar situations of distress, as witnessed during the recent polemics on the dependence on social welfare. Those polemics entail a paradox in the French debate. On the one hand, it appears clear that in order to control public expenditures and to increase the fairness of the French welfare state—which carries out little redistribution—social policies have to be reformed thoroughly, and switch from a Bismarckian paradigm of insurance to a Beveridgian logic of assistance. On the other hand, consensus on assistance is much weaker: the French strongly favor the more expensive logic of social insurance.

A few factors underpin this strong consensus: The first, which is worth recalling, is that the social security system dramatically improved sanitary norms and living conditions. Pension policies have, for instance, largely contributed to the eradication of poverty among old people, which existed until the 1960s. France has the best results among the developed nations for social indicators, especially as far as life expectancy is concerned (83.5 years on average for women, and 78.2 years for men in 2010). These good results can explain why this social system benefiting everyone is strongly supported in a consumer-oriented logic.

Furthermore, the "Sécu"—the social security program within France—benefits from the historical conditions of its creation. The choice made in 1945 to implement an extensive system of social protection through the creation of, in particular, the Social Security, is strongly linked to the experience of the Liberation and to the inheritance of the Résistance movement. On a political level, this system is underpinned by a broad consensus—including all left-wing parties and, on the right, the Gaullists families and the Christian Democrats—whose political identity it partly structures. Thus, the French right, influenced for a long time by social Gaullism, is hardly neo-liberal. In France, there was only a short episode during which the right adopted the neo-liberal and conservative policies of its Anglo-Saxon peers, in 1986–88, when the right regained office for a brief time. Explicit references were made to the contemporary experiences of Ronald Reagan in the US and Margaret Thatcher in the UK (Tristram 2008).[17] Conversely, the hallowed experience of the Liberation is used regularly in the French political debate. In recent years, explicit references to the Program of National Council of the Résistance (a fundamental text of the policies implemented after 1945) have reappeared in the debates on the current evolution and reforms of the social security system (Andrieu 2006).

Other, debatable, explanations may shed light on the reasons behind the high level of public expenditures.

First, the system of social insurance lacks unity. Despite the unifying ambition of 1945, particular regimes of healthcare, unemployment, and pension insurance have survived in the French system. These regimes include civil servants, independent workers, farmers, and the so-called special regimes of the workers of public firms like SNCF (National Railway Service) or EDF (National Electricity Service). The multiplication of these regimes entails some serious problems of transparency and governance. Besides, those special regimes are more generous than the general regime and are thus one of the main sources of deficits. The pension system of the civil servants has structural deficits that are compensated by budgetary resources. In the same vein, the National Court of Accounts regularly criticizes the unemployment regime of casual entertainment workers due to its yearly structural deficit estimated at €1 billion (Cour des Comptes 2013, 2012).

The increase in social expenditures is finally also the result of some untimely decisions in certain public policies. The choice to remove the older generations from the labor market is perhaps the best example. This was decided at the end of the 1970s in order to fight rising unemployment. A series of decisions have contributed to this state of affairs: a relatively low legal retiring age—60 years after 1981, sometimes earlier in the special regimes of the public or para-public sector—and, above all, policies of early retirements, like pre-retirement schemes. There is a large consensus on the perverse effects of these policies on the balance of French social accounts, and on the competitiveness of the French economy (Hairault 2012). But despite reforms, especially concerning the pension system, retirement age in France is on average lower than in other OECD countries, particularly in the civil service.[18]

2 Weaknesses in the Organization of the State

A large literature has dealt with the weaknesses and reforms of the organization of the French state for several years (Picq 1992). The topic is way beyond the narrow focus of this chapter. We will thus focus only on two major issues, on which there is a strong consensus, and which have tremendous financial consequences.

The first issue is the poor organization of the country. While it has traditionally been a unitary and centralized state, France has been engaged in a process of decentralization since the outset of the 1980s that confers new competences to local governments and loosens the grip of the central state. But if the principle of decentralization is not questioned, its modalities are targeted by numerous critiques. Those focus first on the excessive number of levels of local and regional governments: this hardly manageable "millefeuille" (a cake made of alternate layers of cream and pastry) is composed by the municipalities, the departments, the regions, to which one can add an increasing number of inter-municipalities enabled by the law of December 16, 2010. Second, the poor distribution of competencies between these structures, which has been incremental rather than implemented with a clean slate, is very much criticized. On the other hand, a very debatable "clause of general competence" enables local governments to intervene outside their jurisdictions if they can prove that it is in their interest to do so.[19] Finally, the very existence of mixed sources of financing (several municipalities can manage the same project) blurs the inner workings of the system and the respective responsibilities of the actors. This triple dysfunction entailed an increase in responsibilities that is well beyond the transferred competences. Thus, local government expenditures rose from 8 percent of GDP in 1980 to more than 11 percent in 2007, which represents an average yearly increase of 3.4 percent (Cour des Comptes 2009: 18). In the meantime, the tax burden of local governments increased from 3 percent of GDP at the end of the 1970s, to around 6 percent of GDP from the beginning of the 2000s (it was 5.9 percent in 2011 and 6.1 percent in 2012; see MINEFI 2013c: 61).

The second factor of this drift is the increased current expenditures and, more precisely, the rise of staff costs. Between 1982 and 2003, the total number of civil servants (in the central and local government as well as in hospitals) increased from 4,025 million to 4,980 million, that is, an increase of 23.7 percent (Pébereau 2006: 73). This phenomenon is particularly clear at the level of the central government: the budget tends to be allocated more and more to expenditures related to staff or to the interest paid on the public debt, at the expense of public investment. This situation suggests a state that can be described as "employer-debtor" (Siné 2006: 35ff.). This bias strengthens the incremental nature of French budgets and makes it more difficult to use the budget as an instrument for economic policies.

3 Piecemeal and Unbalanced Reforms

Government response to these pressures for increased expenditures has been muted: Indeed, France did not implement any structural reforms that would have reduced public expenditures significantly, as did other countries with high public expenditures (e.g., Sweden in the 1990s). What comes closest to examples set by other countries is the attempted paradigmatic reform of the social security system by Alain Juppé in 1995. The Prime Minister's plan, announced on November 15, was to increase the power of the state over the finances of social security, and to limit the costs of the welfare state. Juppé was nonetheless on a collision course with social movements. Strikes—the most important ones since 1968—forced the government to withdraw its consolidation project in December 1995. This failure weakened the main reformist trade union, the CFDT (Confédération française démocratique du travail), which backed the government's consolidation. This failure also bridled policy makers. But it strengthened the political and intellectual opposition to reform of the protesting left parties. They consider any reform of social security as a process calling into question the very principle of social security.

The failure of 1995 thus sheds a particularly raw light on the major hindrances to the control of public expenditures, i.e., the lack of a culture of social compromise in France. Countries that managed to retake control over public expenditures had unified trade unions that were heeded and very representative. This is particularly the case of Sweden, where social dialogue led to an agreement on the adopted solutions. France is in a different situation: trade unions are fragmented, civil servants are over-represented, and the culture is impregnated with conflict and radicalism. The same applies to the employers' association, the MEDEF (Mouvement des entreprises de France), despite its reform in 1998 (Woll 2006).

In these conditions, only partial and progressive reforms were implemented. This is especially the case with pensions. For 20 years, the strategy of the government has been to maintain the PAYGO system by increasing the years of contributions and, to a lesser extent, the retirement age.[20] Systemic reforms, like the transition to a defined contribution regime as advocated by the CFDT, have been brushed aside. The results of these incremental reforms have been mediocre and did not solve the fundamental problems of the pension system, e.g., the recurrent structural deficits, the inequality between general and special regimes, and the insufficient employment rate of workers who are more than 50 years old. Regarding healthcare, the definition of a spending cap was very difficult to put into place and yielded very poor results (Pierru 2011).

Finally, those reforms had a different impact on different public actors—central government, local governments, or Social Security—as Figure 2.3 suggests.

The control of expenditures has essentially put the burden of adjustment on the central government. Its expenditures peaked at 29 percent of GDP in 1985, but have since been reduced to less than 25 percent, bringing it back to the level of the 1970s. This relative stabilization—in nominal terms the expenditures of the central government increased—stands in stark contrast with the significant increases of public expenditures in other sectors. Thus, expenditures of local governments soared from 8 percent of GDP at the end of the 1970s to 12 percent

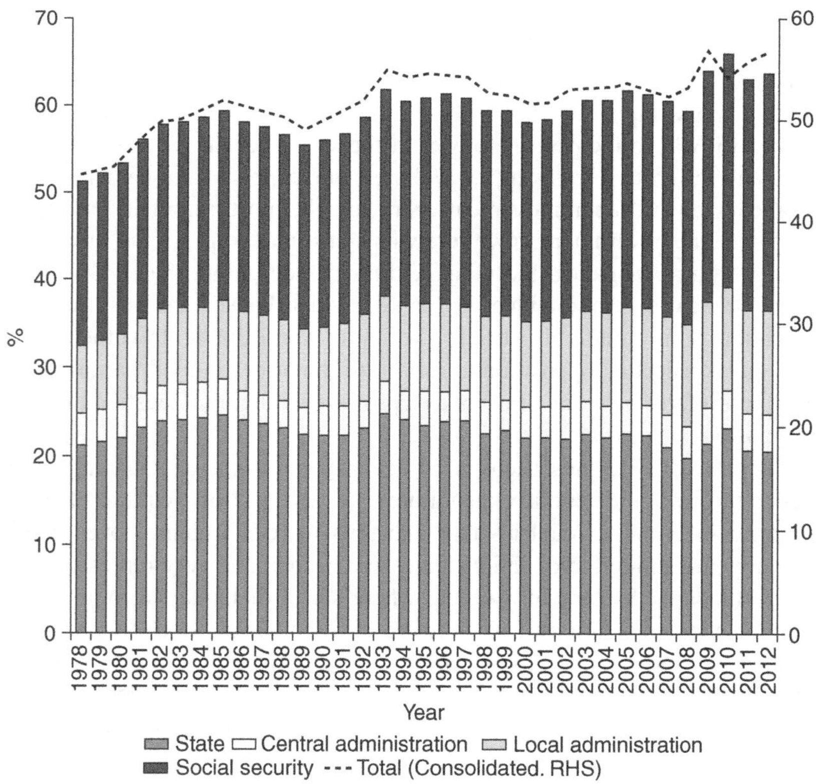

Figure 2.3 Allocation of public expenditures in France, 1978–2012 (source: INSEE, percentage of GDP).

of GDP today. Social security expenditures skyrocketed from 19 to 27 percent of GDP over the same period. These results are not a coincidence. They mirror trends of decentralization and the increasing burden of social expenditures, as well as the fact that the control of expenditures has been taken into account unequally.

The central government has thus shouldered the bulk of the efforts by implementing control mechanisms to a larger extent than other entities. The state first strengthened budgetary procedures. In 2001 a new organic law on public finances (LOLF, *Loi organique sur les finances publiques*) was voted to replace the old organic ordinance from 1959. The main innovation was the new budgetary nomenclature that underlined the concept of "mission" and thus introduced a logic of new public management focused on results and subject to regular evaluations. The administrations have thus more room for maneuver, and can redeploy their budgets according to their priorities. In return, the Parliament has access to more information on the state's actions thanks to reports provided by the government during budgetary debates. The LOLF was strongly inspired by new public management and the search for greater efficiency in the administration of the state. Importantly, the LOLF also stemmed from the will of the Members of Parliament to relax the constraining ordinance of 1959, which limited the influence of the Parliament over the budget. Thus the LOLF was started at the initiative of socialist MP Didier Migaud—who is also the current president of the National Audit Office, the Cour des Comptes. Drawing inspiration from New Public Management, the LOLF is a rare example of bi-partisan consensus on the need for reform (Arkwright et al. 2007). Yet, to this day, the LOLF has yielded no significant results regarding the control of public expenditures, perhaps due to great fluctuation of the boundaries of public policies or more fundamentally due to cyclical reasons. The LOLF was introduced in 2006 and was thus rapidly followed by the Great Recession of 2008. On another level, the state made an effort to control growth forecasts that form the basis of budgetary laws, though it was a requirement of the TSCG (Treaty on Stability, Coordination and Governance, signed by eurozone members). Therefore, the High Council of Finances was created in December 2012 to give its opinion on macro-economic forecasts.

Meanwhile, the implementation of the General Review of Public Policies (RGPP) was the most significant policy initiative to control public expenditures (on the link between the LOLF and the RGPP, see Kott 2010). Started in 2007, and ending in 2012, the RGPP was supposed to review all the missions of the state and included policies to reduce public expenditures, among which the most important was not to replace half of the retiring civil servants. The financial effects of the RGPP are debatable. If the RGPP did not help to stabilize public expenditures by itself, including expenditures on staff, it did allow a reduction of the rate of increase in expenditures (Cour des Comptes 2010).[21] The RGPP has nonetheless proven to be a real watershed in the management of the state, not only because of its global approach, but also due to its mobilization of resources and processes taken from the private sector (Bezès 2010).

The constraints on the other sectors of public expenditures are far less important. Concerning social security, reforms have been modest and very progressive. Still, the state implemented a potentially efficient instrument: the parliamentary vote on a cap for the social security budget. This is an important step towards budgetary centralization, which is an essential condition to control public expenditures.

There is no such mechanism for local governments and it would certainly face theoretical and institutional obstacles strengthened by the process of decentralization. There are, to be sure, a few rules guiding local finances, but they remain insufficient. Local governments are, for instance, required to vote balanced operating budgets. This does not apply to investment, which can spur considerable indebtedness.

Above all, the financing modes of local governments are themselves an incentive to spend and are a clear example of a common pool resource problem (Poterba and von Hagen 2000). Local governments face only a part of the political consequences of an increase in taxation, even though the revenues of local governments stem from their own resources (among which are highly territorialized taxes—50 percent of total revenues), while state subsidies represent only 28 percent of their revenues (Laignel and Guené 2014: 58).[22] But these data are misleading because the central government compensates a large share of tax deductions for local taxpayers (especially for the more modest households and firms) which in fact increases state subsidies to local government. The central government has thus become the "first local tax payer."[23]

More broadly, the whole financing system of local governments would need to be reconsidered, in particular the poorly aging taxation system and the financial relations between the central and local governments. Such a reform is hindered by strong opposition, of which the difficult reform of local taxation of firms has offered a foretaste.[24]

The difficulty of imposing financial norms conducive to expenditure control on local governments can be explained by political and institutional reasons, in particular the old tradition of cumulating local and national mandates by the same representatives. This difficulty can be analyzed through the lens of the common pool resource problem, applied by some authors to the question of public finance (Poterba and von Hagen 2000). The common pool resource problem refers to the fact that some policy makers use a common resource (the state budget) towards particular ends (in the interest of local or regional governments and their constituency) at the expense of the national collectivity, with no rules limiting this bias, such as forbidding the accumulation of local and national mandates. Other common pool problems, very frequent in France, could be identified.

France, thus, largely failed to control its expenditures for technical and, more fundamentally, political and historical reasons that make any compromise more difficult. A weak financial constraint, to which we now turn, did not help either.

Weak Financial Constraints

Until now, weak financial constraints meant that there were no strong incentives for the state to reform itself. Indeed, until recently, the French state benefited from the concurrence of three favorable factors: an electorate highly tolerant to taxes, historically low interest rates, and lax European fiscal surveillance. The real question is how to know whether this situation is structural or whether it is due to peculiar cyclical reasons, i.e., the end of a weak financial constraint. The latter may define a peculiar moment in French fiscal history, which progressively disappears and calls for adjustments that are more severe because they were long postponed.

1 High Tolerance for Taxation among French Voters

The steep increase of public expenditure was enabled by an exceptional acquiescence to taxation, which may seem paradoxical. French society had been very reticent about paying taxes until the middle of the twentieth century, a fact often underlined by historians. But French society entered, after World War II, a period of "fiscal appeasement" (Delalande and Spire 2010). Some contestation movements against the increase in the tax burden erupted, such as "poujadisme" between 1953 and 1958, or the CID-UNATI (Comité interprofessionnel de défense-Union nationale des travailleurs indépendants) at the end of the 1960s. But these movements remained sporadic, limited to certain social categories (independent small shopkeepers and craftsmen), and they never significantly influenced the effectiveness of the tax system (Tristram 2012).

From this, France achieved a very high level of taxation without provoking real opposition, at least until recently. The reasons for this tax tolerance are diverse. It comes partially from the above-mentioned collective choices, but also from the taxation structure and the improvement of fiscal techniques. The increase of the tax burden has been focused on two taxes, the CSG (Contribution Sociale Généralisée) and VAT, which have several common attributes. First, these taxes are relatively "painless": in contrast to personal income tax (PIT), the CSG is a withholding tax. The VAT is collected using the technique of segmented payments: this means that through repercussion mechanisms, it is not always guaranteed that the taxpayer will pay all the tax. The other common attribute of these two taxes is that they are not progressive, or only to a small extent for the CSG. Thus the French welfare state developed thanks to proportional, or even regressive taxes, like other industrialized countries (Katō 2003). On the other hand, increases in income tax have been used only rarely, and it is only after the recent financial crisis that its marginal rate has been increased. This voluntary abstention, coupled with a policy of reducing rates between 1999 and 2005 led to a decrease of the weight on income revenue in total taxation.[25]

This exceptional tolerance for taxes explains revenue-based fiscal consolidations in France. A good example of this bias can be found between 1995 and 1997 during the important fiscal consolidation required for qualification to the Economic and Monetary Union (EMU) in 1998. Under the government of Alain Juppé, the tax burden increased by 1.5 percent of GDP. The choice was clearly to use taxation, for instance by increasing the normal rate of VAT by 2 percent, from 18.65 to 20.6 percent (Law of July 28, 1995). Nonetheless, the share of public expenditures in GDP only decreased in 1997, but rather due to the mechanical effect of increased economic growth. The only real exception to this use of taxation was the short period between July 2011 and May 2012. Then reduced expenditures represented half of the fiscal consolidation. But since the election of François Hollande, only taxation has been used to consolidate public finances, creating a "fiscal shock" of more than €40 billion and increasing the tax burden to 46 percent of GDP at the end of 2013.

In the meantime, it is not certain that the ability to increase taxation is sufficient to define a good fiscal performance for two reasons: First, the tolerance of French voters for taxation is probably reaching its limits. Contestation movements that were long forgotten have started to reappear. This resurgence affected first small entrepreneurs of the IT sector who created the "Pigeons" movement in the Fall of 2012 (in French argot the term "pigeons" refers to people who are swindled). They managed to prevent the government from increasing capital gains taxes. Of another importance is the recent movement of the Breton "red caps" that mobilized in the Fall of 2013 against the creation of a tax on heavy vehicles. For the first time since the 1970s, vandalism—repeated attacks on roadside posts set up to administer the "ecotax"—and street violence have accompanied fiscal contestation. The magnitude of these manifestations may be explained by the exceptional burden of taxation in France, above its previous peak of 1999. But the source of this contestation can also be found in the types of taxes that are used to reduce the deficit. Indeed, since 2011, governments have refused to increase the main taxes on income and consumption that would weigh on all taxpayers and have instead opted for inefficient and targeted taxes that focus on a particular social category: savers, business leaders, or landlords. The result is a general effect of accumulation and an increased sensitivity for those who are particularly affected. These two phenomena have doubtlessly favored rejection movements.

A second caveat should be added to the performance of the French fiscal system, which stems from its opaqueness and the poor distribution of the taxation burden. In the last few years, recurrent critiques have developed in academia and in public debates focusing on the small share of income tax in the total tax burden, as well as its extreme complexity and its lack of progressivity. A widely read book concentrates most of these critiques, spurring a real debate on the eve of the 2012 presidential election around the main policy proposal: the creation of a great progressive tax that would merge income tax and the CSG (Landais et al. 2011).[26] François Hollande adopted this idea during the electoral campaign without giving more technical details. It seemed that this idea was abandoned after the election, however the former Prime Minister Jean-Marc Ayrault put it back on the table again in November 2013 by announcing a comprehensive fiscal reform. Whatever the future of this tax proposal, the French fiscal system is heavily burdened by numerous deficiencies that make it unlikely to afford an increase in the taxation burden. There are thus clear technical and political limits to the increase of fiscal pressure.

2 Using the Debt Market to Relax the Financial Constraint

The French state not only benefited from an exceptional tax tolerance for a relatively long time, it was also able to reform and build a reliable and efficient financing system that considerably weakened financial constraints and thus enabled high deficits and public debt. The reforms of the financial system were motivated by the necessity to finance budgetary deficits. On the other hand, European monetary integration and the movement towards the euro decreased interest rates thanks to the removal of the exchange rate risk.

A massive use of debt markets has developed since the mid-1980s. Since World War II, the French state favored non-negotiable monetary resources (bank credits offered by the central bank to the state and not subject to being traded on any market), which covered 75 percent of the deficits at the end of the 1970s. By then, the French state was using all the advantages of an economy of indebtedness, in particular the mechanism of the "circuit" (Quennouëlle-Corre 2000). In less than a decade, the public financing modes changed radically: in 1993, the former proportion was totally reversed and the public debt was financed at 93 percent on the debt market (Percebois 1991).

This brutal policy U-turn has several explanations: The first is economic, and relates to the modes of financing of public and private actors. The former economy of indebtedness led to a questionable allocation of savings. But it mostly had inflationary effects that were hardly compatible with international economic openness. The increasing use of financial markets is thus to be seen in a wider context of the diffusion of neo-liberal ideas and the fight against inflation that was the hallmark of the beginning of the 1980s.

But other domestic reasons related to the financing of the state have to be taken into account. The former system, despite the reforms of the 1960s, was not compatible with frequent high deficits, except if high inflation could be tolerated. This system was suitable for France from the 1960s until the mid-1970s, when the budget was balanced and financing needs were relatively small. It was also compatible with the situation of the years 1976–81, during which Prime Minister Raymond Barre contained all the major deficits. But the entrenchment of high deficits after the second oil shock made a reform of these modes of financing inevitable.

From this point of view, the French financing difficulties between 1981 and 1983 clearly signaled the need for reform. In its first months in office, the newly elected socialist government implemented a Keynesian reflationary policy. But despite the limited scope of this policy and the low level of public indebtedness, the French treasury had great difficulty to refinancing itself (Feiertag 2001). This was a traumatic episode for French policy makers, politicians, and top civil servants who were often close to the Socialist government. They remember the humiliating request for help addressed to the Central Bank of Saudi Arabia in 1982, and the risk of going cap-in-hand to the IMF. In these conditions, socialist leaders deemed a financing reform essential for conducting a dynamic budgetary policy, or at least to avoid brutal expenditure cuts that were hard to conceive ideologically or from an electoral point of view. All in all, this reform helped tremendously to refinance deficits.

From 1983 onwards, the finance minister—and future president of the European Commission—Jacques Delors initiated a large movement of liberalization that focused on the issuance of bonds. This had the double advantage of giving an abundant and regular resource to the state, and enlivening a quickly modernizing financial market that would become the primary source of financing for the economy. Thus the transformation of the modes of financing of the state is the other side of the coin of the larger and simultaneous reform of the financing of the economy. But it is also seen, at least implicitly, as an alternative to the control of public finances. Since then, policies have increasingly sought to improve the efficiency of the bond debt: creating a brand for banks specialized in government securities, establishing a precise management of the timetable of bond issuance, increasing debt maturity, and creating the Agence France Trésor in 2001, an administrative structure dedicated to the good management of public debt.

What are the results of this change in the mode of financing? They are globally positive, as Figure 2.4 suggests. Indeed, the burden of the interest rate did not follow the accumulation of outstanding debt. To be sure, the interest rate on debt increased faster than the outstanding debt until the beginning of the 1990s, and thus the new system of financing could appear more expensive than the previous one. But this trend changed quickly and since the mid-1990s, the burden of servicing the debt stabilized in terms of GDP share and even started to decrease. In other words, France has found a way to pile up public debt without paying the full price for this policy.

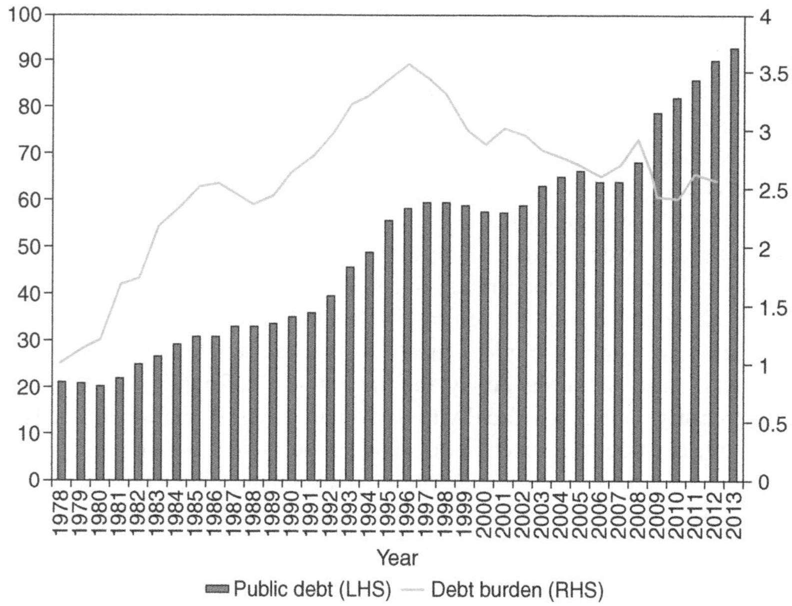

Figure 2.4 Evolution of outstanding French debt and interest burden, 1978–2012, as a percentage of GDP (source: INSEE).

This very favorable result in terms of interest rates stems doubtlessly from the improvement of the techniques related to the issuance of public bonds. But this is mostly the consequence of the creation of the single currency, which allowed, after 1997, French spreads to close on German bonds, which are traditionally the safest haven in Europe. Figure 2.5 clearly shows this movement. Between 1997 and 2009, the spread between German bunds and French Treasury bonds was almost zero because the inception of the Euro by definition eliminated exchange rate risks on the French franc. It is only with the eruption of the sovereign debt crisis since 2009 that financial markets started taking into account a new risk of solvency and that a spread reappeared on the sovereign debt of some countries, among which was France. After the peaks of 2009 and, most importantly, 2011, this spread came down nonetheless by a few dozens basis points. The degradation of France's sovereign rating by international rating agencies did not stop these spreads from decreasing.

The creation of the euro was a real breath of fresh air because it decreased the cost of debt by maintaining low interest rates. This situation is not risk-free nonetheless: France could see its interest rates rise and, given the stock of French debt, this would have a tremendous impact on its budgetary balance making it very difficult to achieve the objective of reducing deficits.

It is indeed uncertain that historically low interest rates mirror financial markets' trust in the health of the French economy and its capacity to generate long-term growth. Those rates are rather the result of three cyclical factors that can change swiftly.

The first is the accommodating monetary policy, especially of the FED (Federal Reserve System), which aims at injecting liquidities into the economy and at maintaining low interest rates. This policy has helped to limit the fallout of the great recession. But the progressive healing of the American economy—seen through lower unemployment rates in the US—could lead to a progressive tightening of monetary policy and to an increase in interest rates.

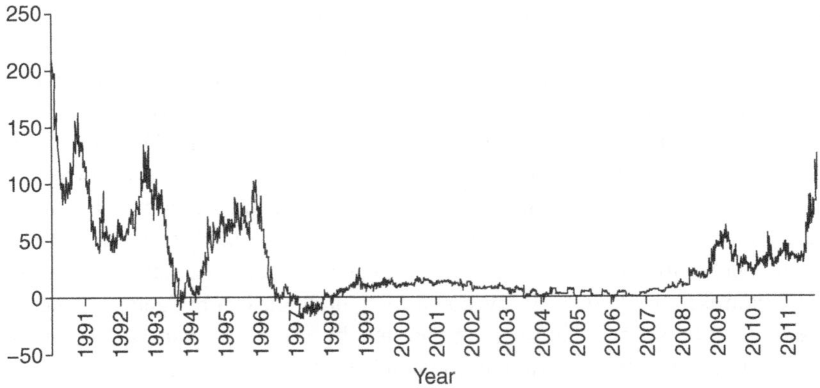

Figure 2.5 Spread between French and German sovereign bond yields (source: Agence France Trésor).

The second factor is the difference in credibility between France and the southern countries of the eurozone. Until now, it has been mostly positive because France seemed to have, for good or bad reasons, higher potential growth and more stable governments, and was thus more able to conduct policies leading to balanced budgets. It is uncertain whether this difference in credibility will persist, given the considerable reforms enacted by Spain and Italy.

The last and most important factor is the peculiar position of France in the eurozone, which makes it a vital partner for the survival of the eurozone. France enjoys a paradoxical advantage because a crisis in France would lead to a systemic financial crisis in the eurozone. It is uncertain however that France can continue hiding behind this comfortable, but dangerous, position that allows her to postpone essential reforms. Such an attitude, if it were to last, would certainly lead to a deterioration of the Franco-German relationship, and to a crisis of confidence between the two states. This very peculiar context explains certainly the more and more uncompromising stance of the European institutions towards France.

Weak European Fiscal Surveillance

This was not always the case. European authorities have long been indulgent towards France, which has not helped the government to balance its books.

The single currency entails that member states keep a lid on their budgets. This obligation is inherent to the existence of the common good that is the euro for reasons both theoretical and practical. Indeed, in a unified monetary zone, excessively expansionary fiscal policies of one member state could have negative consequences on its partners. Having no alternative adjustment mechanisms—such as central bank finance or devaluation—this member state would rapidly be confronted with a series of non-cooperative choices: either default, which has the immediate effect of weakening the common currency; or asking the European Central Bank to refinance it, which is, in theory, forbidden by the Treaties because it would create inflation for the whole eurozone; or, lastly, to ask to be bailed out by its main partners either through loans or transfers.

To avoid the free riding problems, strict rules have been established. Since 1992, the Maastricht Treaty established two budgetary conditions to participate in the single currency: public debt should not exceed 60 percent of GDP and the deficit of public administrations should not exceed 3 percent of GDP. These conditions have been extended with the inception of the Stability and Growth Pact (SGP) signed in Amsterdam in 1997. The SGP also entails a common surveillance by member states in order to incentivize them to stick to their commitments in a preventive manner. Each year, they have to submit a stability program to the Commission where they lay down their medium-run budgetary forecasts (in general, four years). Those are examined by the Economic and Financial Affairs Council (ECOFIN) formation, which leads to recommendations proposed by the Commission. Concerning the punitive side of the SGP, a deficit procedure can be initiated by the Commission, which can lead to sanctions amounting to 0.5 percent of GDP if voted by the Council.

One should notice that France has not respected her obligations since the creation of the euro. Although in the first years (1999 to 2001) the 3 percent threshold was not exceeded, this was mainly due to the good economic conditions. But from 2002 to 2004, France again posted excessive deficits. The slight improvement of 2005–07 did not resist the eruption of the financial crisis of 2008 that provoked soaring deficits. In reality, it appears that France relaxed its budgetary discipline and renounced improving her structural deficits once it qualified for the euro after all the efforts it made to achieve this objective. This attitude can be all the more criticized since France fully benefited from reduced interest rates enabled by the eurozone since the end of the 1990s.

If one considers not the obtained results but the commitments made by France towards the other member states, France does not fare better. As Figure 2.6 suggests, since 1999 France has broken all the promises to balance its budget laid out in the stability programs.

These repeated breaches of procedure did not provoke any firm response from the European institutions and the sanctions planned in the SGP have remained a dead letter.

This lack of firm surveillance at the European level can first be explained by technical reasons. The procedures established in the pact in 1997 immediately appeared imperfect. Their length and their complexity delayed any potential sanctions, which could have been counter-cyclical in a context where deficits varied a lot (at least before 2008). Above all, the budgetary obligations of the member states were not modulated according to the economic cycle and did not specify objectives of structural deficits. In these conditions, the 3 percent threshold appeared less like a limit not to be crossed than a target around which states could tailor their budgetary policies and which could easily be breached in case of an economic slowdown. Lastly, the SGP did not give any incentives to implement counter-cyclical fiscal policies in times of high economic growth (for

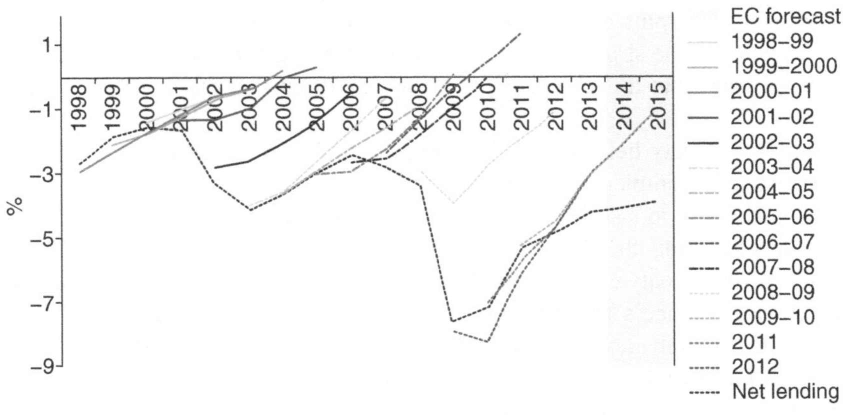

Figure 2.6 Budgetary commitments in stability pacts, 1999–2014, as a percentage of GDP (source: Compiled by Zbigniew Truchlewski based on Stability Programs of the French Government submitted to the European Commission).

instance between 1997 and 2001) if the objectives of 3 percent and 60 percent were not formally breached (Cimadomo 2005).[27] To be sure, a reform of the SGP by the European Council of March 22–23 in 2005 enabled to take into account the economic cycle.[28] This reform has been nonetheless limited, due to the lack of precise definition of an objective for structural deficits, and it appeared, rather, to be used as a means to relax budgetary constraints on member states, making sanctions even more uncertain.

But another reason, perhaps more determinant than the technical elements of the SGP, explains the European inertia. It stems from the political nature of the decisions regarding excessive deficits. Indeed, the final decision is for the Council to make, and the Council can be influenced by opportunistic arguments, or by political considerations exceeding budgetary matters. A good example is when, in 2003, France and Germany—the two main economies of the eurozone—posted deficits above the 3 percent threshold. On November 25, the excessive deficit procedure launched by the Commission was refused by the Council, which is the only institution empowered to decide on sanctions. The conditions of the vote with a qualified majority have been contested: indeed, 40.6 percent of the votes were concentrated among the big states—France, Germany, the UK, and Italy, which all had at that time deficits above 3 percent—against the "small" virtuous countries.[29] Retrospectively, the episode of 2003 has been analyzed by numerous European policy makers as one of the clearest signs of the loss of credibility of mechanisms of collective discipline. Ultimately, a de facto suspension of European obligations happened after the 2008 financial collapse, when almost all the countries of the eurozone increased their debt and deficits.

The sovereign debt crisis represents, nonetheless, a turning point in European budgetary policies. It ended the tolerant attitude that prevailed until then, and led to the adoption of stricter and improved surveillance rules. Those rules were formalized in the Treaty on Stability, Coordination, and Governance (TSCG) signed on March 2, 2012. The TSCG states the principle of public budgets close to balance or in surplus (article 3). It replaces the old 3 percent threshold with a norm related to the structural deficit.[30] Lastly, it strengthens the sanctions against member states that do not respect their objectives and makes them more easily applied.[31]

The new Treaty helped to redirect fiscal policies of deficit countries, France in particular. Its implementation consecrated the policy turn operated in August 2011, enabling it to last. François Hollande, once elected to the Elysée, refrained from renegotiating the Treaty as he promised during his electoral campaign. Above all, the Treaty enables to tighten the budget constraint and to increase the influence of France's European partners on its adjustment policies. The European Commission may have accepted on May 29, 2013, to postpone by two years (from 2013 to 2015) the objective of reducing the deficit beneath the 3 percent limit, but it has nonetheless imposed a strict and tight schedule with strings attached in the form of neo-liberal structural reforms. These were focused on three points for the Commission: the simplification of the fiscal system, reducing labor costs, and simplification in the service sector. This new conditionality can explain a certain number of policy decisions taken by François Hollande, either the pension reform of Fall 2013 and which was not included in his initial program, or the acceleration of supply side reforms undertaken since January 1, 2014 with the "Responsibility Pact". The European Commission decided to enhance this conditionality by putting France under intensified surveillance on March 5, 2013.

To conclude, whatever the level of analysis, French financial constraints seem to tighten up. This new conjuncture has, without doubt, contributed much to the current reorientation of budgetary policies in France.

Conclusion

France should thus implement a robust policy of fiscal stabilization as soon as possible. This indispensable reorientation, lest the choice of European integration and international openness decided in 1958 be challenged, calls for three types of remarks.

First, this reorientation has been badly timed: it happens precisely at a moment when a convalescent economy with sluggish growth has to bear the burden of increased taxes and lower expenditures, which can have a recessionary effect in the short run. The root of this problem can be found in the decades-old poor management of policies supposed to smooth the business cycle, in debatable political choices, especially in times of strong growth, and in deficient control mechanisms. The topic of consolidation has appeared in the public debate only since the mid-2000s, and it imposed itself very late in 2011 due to the threat of a systemic crisis in the eurozone. Consolidation in France is far from being underpinned by a large consensus in French society that is still not aware of the consequences of the choices made in 1992, and of the adaptions required by the creation of the single currency.

The second remark is that the problem and the solutions are well known in France. They were the topic of a myriad of notes and reports, often drafted by high civil servants, less by private think tanks, and which were regularly published for 20 years. Some of these problems and solutions have been cited in this chapter—territorial reform of the administrative *millefeuille*, unification and reform of the pension system, reform of the financing modes of the local governments, or the improvement of the university system with their increased autonomy. Some institutions like the Cour des Comptes (National Court of Accounts) have even progressively reoriented their activity to specialize on this audit mission, with some results very well publicized in public opinion.

The challenge in France is thus not to know what is to be done, but how to do it. This leads to questions about the political and institutional model of the country. Major obstacles to deficit reduction seem to be an over-centralization of power, the difficulty to establish social dialogue, and the low representativeness of interest groups and intermediary bodies. This is true also of the Constitution of 1958, which was adopted—paradoxically—in the name of stability and efficiency in decision-making. The concentration of power in the hands of the President of the Republic, the narrowness of Parliamentary debates, the extreme polarization of the public sphere hinder the necessary maturation of policy decisions and their acceptance by stakeholders. It is thus the difficult revision of a whole political system and mode of social regulation that is entailed by the reordering of French public finances.

Notes

1 Public debt peaked in 1998 at 59.6 percent of GDP, but the bulk of the increase happened in 1992–95, with public indebtedness soaring from 36.0 percent in 1991 to 55.5 percent of GDP in 1995 (source: INSEE (Institut national de la statistique et des études économiques, French national statistics office)).
2 See OECD 2013, Statistical Annex, table 25. Expenditure forecasts suggest that French public expenditures will peak at 57.1 percent of GDP in 2013 before reducing to 56.6 percent of GDP in 2014.
3 See MINEFI 2013a: 12ff. Until the outset of the 1970s, public expenditure represented rather more than 35 percent of GDP. Between 1974 and 1991, it increased from 37 to 50 percent. Afterwards, public expenditure continued to grow but more slowly, at a rate of 2 percent per year.
4 See MINEFI 2013a: 17. Between 1978 and 2011, social expenditure increased by 7.8 percent of GDP, while public expenditure increased by 11.3 percent of GDP. Expenditures on human resources increased by 0.7 percentage points and the debt burden increased by 1.6 percentage points. On the other hand, investment expenditures decreased by 0.1 percentage points.
5 See www.oecd.org/els/social/depenses.
6 OECD.
7 These are data from INSEE. OECD data are slightly higher.
8 Data from MINEFI 2013b.
9 See Chapters 8 and 9 in this volume. Brownlee (Chapter 8) shows for instance that the first balanced budget in the US since 1968 was voted in 1998.
10 See the 2012 Stability Program (published in April 2012), the initial Loi de Finances for 2013 and the Loi de Programmation for 2012–17 of December 31, 2012.
11 Michel Pébereau, former general inspector of finances, took the helm of the first French private bank, BNP Paribas, after a career in the civil service. The task force responsible for drafting the report was composed of high-ranking public officials from the Finance Ministry, often from the directorate of the Finance Inspection (Inspection des finances), on duty or on leave. They include Michel Camdessus and Jacques de Larosière, former governors of the French central bank (Banque de France) and former managing directors of the IMF, Pascal Lamy (former Director General of the WTO), Budget Director, Pierre-Matthieu Duhamel, the General Director of the INSEE, Jean-Pierre Charpin, and Jean-Philippe Cotis, chief economist of the OECD. A few public intellectuals joined them, such as Jacques Julliard or Philippe Herzog, and a business leader, Edouard Michelin.
12 The consolidation plan of August 24, 2011 foresees €11 billion of new revenues in a full fiscal year, and the consolidation plan of November 7, 2011 €8 billion.
13 A rectified budget was passed on August 16, 2012, increasing public revenues by €7.2 billion (€4.4 billion in 2013) and the budget law for 2013 foresees €15.8 billion of additional tax revenues.
14 This contestation could be seen through the hostile vote of 20 socialist deputies and 12 deputies from the Green party during the ratification at the National Assembly of the Treaty on Stability, Coordination and Governance in the Economic and Monetary Union, through recurrent criticisms of the 3 percent threshold of public deficits, and through the lack of government solidarity by some ministers.
15 One could cite several groups like the *Economistes atterrés* ("Appalled Economists"), created after a manifesto published in 2010, or "Roosevelt 2012," which advocates a

New Deal. Interesting research could be undertaken on these groups and their respective positions as well as their connections. ATTAC wants to come back to an economy of indebtedness where the central bank would finance deficits and banks, as was the case before the liberalization of capital movements. But unless ATTAC is ready to accept higher inflation, this position is a contradiction in terms: indeed, reverting to the old system would tighten the financial constraint and would thus force policymakers to adopt the very austerity that is contested by ATTAC.

16 See Lemoine (2011) for an elaboration on these topics and especially the idea of a progressive construction of the problem of public debt.

17 The right's failure, symbolized by the defeat of Jacques Chirac in the presidential elections of 1988, provoked a lasting rejection of liberal policies in the French right. This rejection was only partially questioned by Nicolas Sarkozy at the outset of his government.

18 For the private sector, retirement age is 61.9, while it is 57.1 in the civil service (COR 2013).

19 This clause of general competence stems from the great communal law of 1884, which conceptualizes the local public interest very broadly. This clause was extended to the other regional and local governments in the decentralization law of 1982 and is more and more contested. It has thus been reformed in the law of December 16, 2010, which maintains it for municipalities but limits it at the regional and the departmental levels. Starting from 2015, those can only intervene in the domains of their competencies or "for every issue of departmental (or regional) interest for which public law has not attributed any competency to any other public person." This limitation has nonetheless sparked strong antagonism from local representatives. The law on the "modernization of territorial public policies and the affirmation of the cities," voted on December 19, 2013 (under review in the Constitutional Court) re-established the clause of general competence.

20 Five major reforms were passed in 1993, 2003, 2008, 2010, and 2013. The contribution period increased from 37.5 to 41.5 years (and will be increased to 43 years in 2035 according to the law of December 2013), while the legal age of retirement is 62 years (67 years without any discount). But there are many exceptions to these rules.

21 The RGPP helped to reduce the number of civil servants by 3,000 a year; however, it did not stabilize state expenditures on human resources which continue to increase by 1 percent a year due to the promotion of civil servants, and also due to the fact that the benefits of not replacing half of retiring civil servants were repaid to the remaining civil servants in the form of increased salaries.

22 Respectively €113.6 billion and €67 billion of a total of €227 billion in 2012. The rest comes from non-tax revenues and indebtedness.

23 In order to compensate for the inequalities generated by local taxation, the government has implemented fiscal shields limiting local taxes to a fraction of taxable income. The difference is then paid by the state to local governments.

24 The old professional tax created in 1975 had a certain number of shortcomings, especially concerning its distribution and its economic effects (it inhibited investment). In 2009, the government reformed this tax to base local taxation on the added value of firms.

25 The marginal rate of the income revenue increased from 40 to 45 percent between 2010 and 2013.

26 The authors show that the French fiscal system is not only regressive as a whole once a certain threshold of high incomes has been reached, but also that the supposedly progressive income tax is also regressive on a small number of tax payers. The authors propose a radical reform which would entail the merger of the general social contribution (CSG) and the progressive income tax (IR) into a new tax with a large base with a high degree of progressivity and which would not take into account household taxes.

27 Cimadomo asks whether the SGP has increased the pro-cyclicality of fiscal policies but answers negatively to this question.

28 Breaching the 3 percent threshold can be allowed in case of recessions. The Commission takes into account all the "relevant factors" when it launches an excessive deficit procedure, for instance the implementation of structural reforms, R&D policies, unemployment and public investment policies.

29 From a strictly legal perspective, the ECJ condemned the attitude of the Council in the ruling of July 13, 2004.

30 The structural deficit is limited to 0.5 percent of GDP and is defined as a "medium term objective" (1 percent for states having public debts above 60 percent of GDP).

31 When a case is brought before the court by a member state, the ECJ can fine an errant/lawbreaking state up to 0.1 percent of its GDP.

References

Andrieu, Claire. 2006. "Le Conseil National de la Résistance." In *Dictionnaire Historique de La Résistance*, edited by François Marcot. Paris: Robert Laffont.

Arkwright, Andrew, Christian de Boissieu, Jean-Hervé Lorenzi, and Julien Samson. 2007. "Economie politique de la LOLF." 65. Paris: Conseil d'Analyse Economique, la Documentation Française.

Bezès, Philippe. 2010. "Morphologie de la RGPP. Une Mise en Perspective historique et comparative." *Revue Française D'administration Publique* 136(4): 775–802.

Champsaur, Paul and Jean-Philippe Cotis. 2010. *Rapport sur la Situation des Finances Publiques*. La Documentation Française, Paris. www.ladocumentationfrancaise.fr/rapports-publics/104000234.

Cimadomo, Jacopo. 2005. "Le Pacte de Stabilité a-t-il renforcé la pro-Cyclicité de la Politique budgétaire?" *Lettre du CEPII*, 247.

COR. 2013. "Retraites: Un État des Lieux du Système français." Paris: Conseil d'Orientation des Retraites.

Cour des Comptes. 2009. "La Conduite par l'Etat de la Décentralisation." Rapport thématique. Paris.

Cour des Comptes. 2010. "Les Conditions d'une Stabilisation en Valeur de la Masse salariale de l'Etat." Paris.

Cour des Comptes. 2012. "Le Régime des Intermittents du Spectacle, la Persistance d'une Dérive Massive." Rapport Public annuel T. 2. Paris: La Documentation française.

Cour des Comptes. 2013. "Le Régime d'Indemnisation Chômage à l'Issue des Emplois précaires." Référé du premier Président de la Cour daté du 19 Septembre.

Cour des Comptes. 2014. "La Situation et les Perpectives des Finances Publiques". Paris.

Delalande, Nicolas and Alexis Spire. 2010. *Histoire sociale de l'Impôt*. Paris: La Découverte.

Feiertag, Olivier. 2001. "Finances publiques, 'Mur d'Argent' et Genèse de la Libération financière en France de 1981 à 1984." In *François Mitterrand. Les Années du Changement, 1981–1984*, edited by Serge Berstein, Pierre Milza, and Jean-Louis Bianco, 431–455. Paris: Perrin.

Hairault, Jean-Olivier. 2012. *Pour l'emploi des Seniors, Assurance Chômage et Licenciement*. Collection du CEPREMAP. Paris: ENS Ulm.

Katō, Junko. 2003. *Regressive Taxation and the Welfare State: Path Dependence and Policy Diffusion*. Cambridge: Cambridge University Press.

Kott, Frédéric. 2010. "La RGPP et la LOLF: Consonances et Dissonances." *Revue française d'Administration publique* 136(4): 881–893.

Laignel, André and Charles Guené, eds. 2014. *Les Finances des Collectivités Locales en 2013*. Paris: Observatoire des Finances Locales.

Landais, Camille, Thomas Piketty, and Emmanuel Saez. 2011. *Pour une Révolution fiscale. Un Impôt pour le XXIe Siècle*. Paris: Le Seuil.

Lemoine, Benjamin. 2011. "Les Valeurs de la Dette. L'Etat à l'Épreuve de la Dette publique." Thèse de doctorat sous la direction de Michel Callon, Paris: École nationale supérieure des mines de Paris.

MINEFI. 2013a. "Rapport sur la Dépense publique et son Évolution." Annexé au PLF 2013. Paris: Ministère de l'Economie, des Finances et du Commerce Extérieur.

MINEFI. 2013b. "Rapport sur les Prélèvement obligatoires et leur Évolution." Annexé au PLF 2013. Paris: Ministère de l'Economie, des Finances et du Commerce Extérieur.

MINEFI. 2013c. "Rapport économique, social et financier." Annexé au PLF 2014, tome 2. Paris: Ministère de l'Economie, des Finances et du Commerce Extérieur.

OECD. 2013. *Perspectives économiques de l'OCDE*. Paris: Organisation for Economic Co-operation and Development.

Pébereau, Michel. 2006. "Rompre avec la Facilité de la Dette publique. Pour des Finances publiques au Service de notre Croissance économique et de notre Cohésion sociale." Paris: La Documentation française.

Percebois, Jacques. 1991. *Économie des Finances publiques*. Paris: Armand Colin.

Picq, Jean. 1992. "L'Etat en France, servir une Nation ouverte sur le Monde." Ministère de la Fonction publique.

Pierru, Frédéric. 2011. "Budgétiser l'Assurance Maladie. Heurs et Malheurs d'un Instrument de Maîtrise des Dépenses publiques: L'Enveloppe globale (1976–2010)." In *Gouverner (par) les Finances publiques*, edited by Philippe Bezès and Alexandre Siné, 395–449. Paris: Presses de Sciences Po.

Poterba, James M. and Jürgen von Hagen. 2000. "Introduction." In *Institutions, Politics and Fiscal Policy*, edited by Rolf R. Strauch and Jürgen von Hagen. Alphen aan den Rijn, Netherlands: Kluwer Academic Publisher.

Quennouëlle-Corre, Laure. 2000. *L'Etat-Banquier et La Croissance, La Direction du Trésor 1947–1967*. Paris: CHEFF.

Siné, Alexandre. 2006. *L'Ordre budgétaire: L'Économie politique des Dépenses de l'État*. Economica.

Tristram, Fréderic. 2008. "Libéralisme." In *La France de la Ve République*, edited by Jean Garrigues, 535–540. Paris: Armand Colin.

Tristram, Fréderic. 2012. "Combat d'Arrière-garde ou Mouvement social précurseur? Le Poujadisme à la Croisée des Analyses." In *Histoire des Mouvements sociaux en France*, edited by Michel Pigenet and Danielle Tartakowsky, 446–455. Paris: La Découverte.

Woll, Cornelia. 2006. "La Réforme du MEDEF, Chronique des Difficultés de l'Action collective patronale." *Revue Française de Sciences Politiques* 2: 255–279.

3 Fiscal Performance in Germany

The Role of Electoral Competition

Achim Kemmerling and Zbigniew Truchlewski

Introduction: Fiscal Performance, Political Survival and Electoral Competition

In this study we will argue that German fiscal performance depends on the political survival of governments. If the electoral risks of fiscal consolidation are high, governments will be very reluctant to introduce harsh measures. Active fiscal consolidation is therefore bound to the political context and the electoral fate of governments in particular.

Hypothesizing the link between political survival and fiscal consolidation idea is not trivial. Germany is well known for its relatively conservative and moderate economic policies in general, and its fiscal conservatism in particular. In this sense, Germany is a least likely case for the problem of political survival. Moreover, reunification has increased the fiscal pressure on governments enormously and could make electoral pressures secondary. Finally, we will see that in some instances, governments managed to avoid the blame of consolidation relatively well. Yet, we will also see that fiscal consolidation put governments under substantive electoral pressure and political survival risk.

How is fiscal consolidation possible, and under which circumstances? We find that in Germany, reforms entailing fiscal consolidations are mainly observed under highly restrictive circumstances, namely huge external pressures (as qualifying for the euro or restoring competitiveness) that can serve as mechanisms of blame avoidance. If these circumstances are absent, projects of fiscal consolidation either have disastrous electoral consequences, such as the second Schröder government, or they will not happen. Hence, the German case is an important, and somewhat counterintuitive, illustration of the nexus between political survival and fiscal consolidation.

We start our overview briefly narrating the evolution of German fiscal performance over the last 30 years. We link this discussion to the major episodes of fiscal consolidation and the socioeconomic background factors that delimit governments' room to maneuver. In section three we identify six major episodes of fiscal consolidation in the last three decades. In sections four to six, we go through these episodes highlighting the role of electoral competition in the size and occurrence of fiscal consolidation. Section seven develops further implications of the German case.

Long-Term Evolution and Structural Context of Fiscal Performance

The overall fiscal performance of Germany shows two somewhat contradictory features. On the one hand, the overall level of debt has continuously risen across the last decades and put governments under increasing pressure. There are two factors that are important to explain this rising trend: socioeconomic changes and a large welfare state. On the other hand, German public finance shows remarkable resilience and the capacity for significant corrections. This is due to a combination of fortunate economic factors as well as the government's attempts to keep public debt at bay.

Let us begin with the rise in debt. Figure 3.1 shows that the overall trend of cumulative debt in Germany increased over the last 30 years. This rising trend reveals enormous **socioeconomic pressure**. Germany is one of the OECD countries in which population aging takes place the fastest and population growth has been negative for the last 40 years except for several waves of immigration. This has had a tremendous impact on the level of explicit government debt. Its impact is even stronger on the implicit debt of the PAYGO pension system, where estimates go up to 200 percent of GDP.[1] Economic growth has been moderate since the end of the golden era of the 1950s and 1960s, and the international

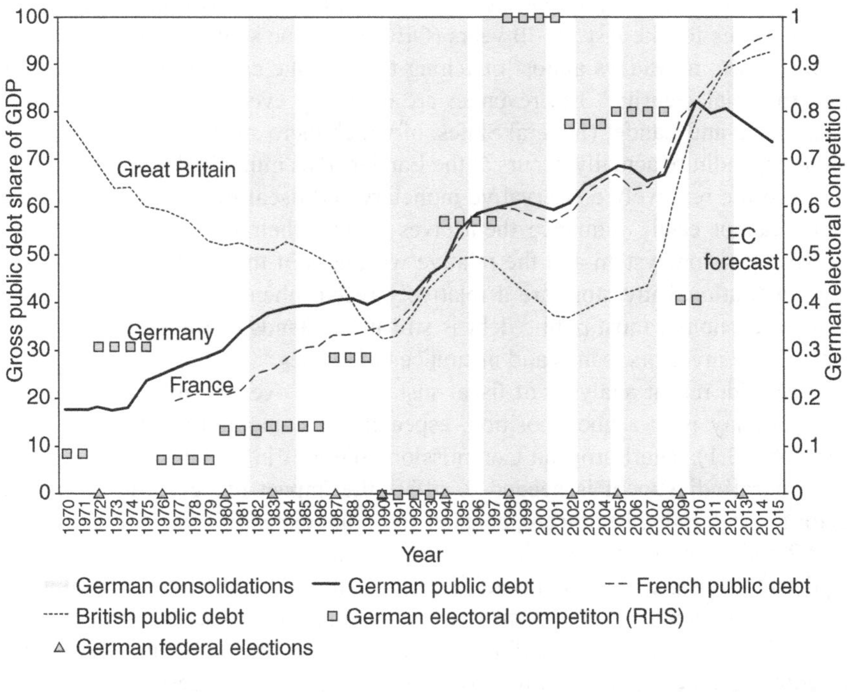

Figure 3.1 Comparing public debt in Germany, France and Great Britain (source: Authors' compilation from the AMECO, Devries et al. (2011) and Politbarometer, cumulative file (Leibniz Institute for the Social Sciences (GESIS)) databases).

exposure of the country, otherwise a hugely beneficial factor for the economy,[2] puts more mobile forms of tax revenues under strain.[3]

Part of this increase in public debt is related to the German welfare state, which is large in international comparison.[4] To be fair, a huge part of increasing public deficits was due to German reunification, which led to some 5 percent of Western German GDP being redistributed to the Eastern parts per year. Yet how the government reacted to the crises exacerbated the situation,[5] as most of the automatic adjustment fell on employees. Indeed, since the 1990s, competitiveness had become a big issue in Germany since it had entered the euro with an overvalued exchange rate. Because of the Reunification, the current account plunged from 4 percent of GDP (its average level since the mid-1980s) to a –2 percent of GDP in 1999. The Schröder reforms were partly a reaction to this lost competitiveness and Merkel's effort to reduce debt and deficits can be seen as a continuation of this policy. If anything, this suggests that fiscal rules are endogenous: fiscal performance and fiscal rules are driven to a great extent by the political dynamics in Germany.

These fundamentals have left their mark also on the German **budget structure**. On the expenditure side, the welfare state and the debt burden dominate every other category. The share of federal budget spent on subsidies to social security and on debt service reached 50 percent in 2006 (Streeck 2007: 25). The tax mix is strongly tilted towards payroll taxation (including social security contributions). Income from corporate and personal taxation has been stagnating in relative terms for the last 25–30 years (OECD revenue statistics), whereas VAT is on the rise, nowadays almost matching the revenue capacity of the contributions to social security.[6] Tax revenues are relatively evenly distributed between the national and Länder (Federal States, of which there are 16) level, while most of the expenditure actually occurs at the Länder (plus municipality) level.

Given the relatively conservative monetary and fiscal rules, German governments cannot easily refinance themselves or buy their own debt. Due to the PAYGO pension system and the relative weakness of the stock market,[7] "new" large institutional investors are a relatively recent phenomenon. In Germany's political economy, most public debt is still in the hands of traditional domestic institutional investors, banks and insurance companies.[8]

That said, recent analyses of fiscal sustainability over the long term suggest that Germany is in a good position, especially if compared to other countries (see Table 3.1). The European Commission compiles information showing how much fiscal adjustment is needed to offset the impact of aging on the public sector through rising healthcare, pension and other expenditures. More precisely, the S2 indicator below (which indicates the short- and long-term adjustment required to satisfy an inter-temporal budget constraint in which the cost of aging is included) shows that Germany has public finances as sound—if not more so—as France, and finds itself in a much stronger position than the United Kingdom and the EU in general. Furthermore, Figure 3.1 suggests that the Great Recession seems to have proved to be a structural break in fiscal politics in Germany: while the German debt to GDP ratio was highly correlated with the French one (R squared is 0.98 for the period 1977–2010, see Figure 3.1), after

Table 3.1 Long-term sustainability of public finances in Germany

S2 Indicator	*2006*	*2009*	*2012*
Germany	4.4	4.2	1.4
France	4.0	5.6	1.6
United Kingdom	4.9	12.4	5.2
EU average	3.4	6.5	2.6

Source: European Commission 2006, 2009, 2012.

2010 the German debt path seems to have bifurcated towards a lower trend, while the French and the British ones are still rising.

Some authors argue that this sustainability is perhaps the consequence of **fiscal institutions**. Indeed, fiscal governance is fairly tough in Germany. Regarding fiscal rules, a standardized measure comparing 27 EU member states over the time span of 1990–2011[9] shows that Germany was always above average (value of 0.72 and increasing to 1.19 in 2011). The same was true of the index on Medium Term Budgetary Frameworks (MTBF),[10] indices of fiscal delegation (power of the finance minister to manage the public purse) and of the fiscal contract (ability for a government to set binding guidelines that limit deficits).[11]

And yet, fiscal rules and institutions did not prevent German governments from running high deficits and piling on debt. A good example of this is the German "debt brake." It was introduced as Article 115 of the German *Grundgesetz* (Basic Law or Constitution) in 1969 to limit the increase in federal debt. At that time the ratio of federal public debt to GDP was 20 percent.[12] Despite the debt brake this ratio increased to around 80 percent over the next 40 years and some observers even went as far as to claim that Germany was in a state of "fiscal crisis."[13] Because of the failure of the "old" debt brake, Germany replaced it with a new legal provision in 2009. The new debt brake aims at reducing the structural deficit of the Bund (Federation) and the Länder to 0.35 percent of GDP by 2016 and 2020 respectively. These reforms have also to be seen against the backdrop of the reform of federalism in Germany.[14]

International fiscal rules, so much promoted by the German government and international institutions like the European Commission, the European Central Bank or the International Monetary Fund, are sometimes even blander. The clearest example of this is the Stability and Growth Pact (SGP, introduced under German pressure in 1997), which stipulates that deficits of member countries should not go beyond 3 percent of GDP and their debt should not go beyond 60 percent of GDP. The compliance rate with the SGP over the first ten years among eurozone members was as low as 42.8 percent (the compliance rate was higher in non-eurozone members: 46.2 percent in Central and Eastern European countries and 81.6 percent for the UK, Sweden and Denmark) with Germany posting a dismal 30 percent rate of compliance on the preventive arm of the SGP[15] and slightly better 60 percent compliance rate with the corrective arm of the SGP. Both of these results were lower than EU averages.[16] Five years after its inception, the SGP went through a major crisis due to the fact that Germany, France and other members of the eurozone refused to abide by the rules (their deficits were above 3 percent), and decided to hold the SGP in abeyance. All in all, the case for an independent effect of fiscal institutions on the budget balance is not as strong as it seems at first sight.

Other institutions such as the federalist structure or the corporatist insertion of industrial partners did not stem the tide of rising debt, either. Similar considerations apply to social pacts that were rarely successful in post-war Germany. A good case in point is the Alliance for Jobs, initiated by the Schröder government in 1998, which soon proved a failure. No significant reform was enacted and soon Schröder changed towards a unilateral strategy, bypassing the trade unions in the the Agenda 2010 and the so-called Hartz reforms.[17]

Instead, **economic fundamentals** played a more fortunate role for the fiscal performance of Germany. First, domestic savings are traditionally among the highest in the world.[18] Second, the sheer size of Germany's industrial base has given the German economy a pivotal role in European financial markets. Third, and perhaps most importantly, Germany has been a relatively safe haven for capital inflows in times of financial crises after World War II. Due to the conservative stance of the German Bundesbank, German governments face relatively low interest rates, with a very low risk premium compared to other countries.[19] This has become particularly evident again in recent times, when the government refinanced its debt at negative real interest rates. Finally, fourth, German governments occasionally managed to reduce, successfully, part of the implicit and explicit debt. It is to these instances of fiscal consolidation that we now turn.

Six Episodes of Success and Failure in Fiscal Consolidation

Between 1970 and 2012, the German CAPB (Cyclically Adjusted Primary Balance) has been in balance or close to balance only five times: in 1970, 1971, 1973, 1989, 2012–13 (AMECO database). This data also reveals that Germany only consolidated in 17 years after World War II (AMECO database). A word of caution is necessary: First, CAPB data can be erroneous in periods of booms and bust due to high volatility of economic activity and asset prices.[20] Second, the CAPB does not inform us about the intentions of policy makers. For instance, those may decide to tighten policy to cool down an overheating economy rather than to set debt on a sustainable path (cf. Finland or Ireland in the 2000s). Third, CAPB does not reflect more structural problems of long-term, contingent liabilities such as pension debt.

Hence, CAPB data only reveals the fiscal performance, but not the role government policy plays in fiscal performance. To find out about actual efforts of fiscal consolidation, one needs to triangulate CAPB data with two other sources of information. First, episodes of fiscal consolidations are recognized by using governmental plans.[21] Second, those episodes are cross-checked with qualitative case studies.[22] The qualitative evidence can help to check whether the Devries' dataset is complete. One of the major problems of the Devries data is that it does not yield information about efforts of fiscal consolidation, unless they were officially listed.

But in fact, many implicit measures might have an enormous effect on public finance and fiscal performance in the long run: changing the formula for social benefits, increasing the retirement age, increasing sanctions on benefit recipients etc. For each episode we will check whether the explicit measures were supported or counteracted by implicit measures.

This procedure leads to six major episodes of consolidation out of German fiscal history from 1980 to 2012 (Figures 3.1 and 3.2, Table 3.2). Those six episodes followed in the wake of four conjectural shocks (the recession of the 1970s, the early 1990s, 2000s and 2010s) and one historical shock (German reunification in 1990). The first episode took place in 1982–84, with the inception of the Kohl administration in the shadow of the oil crisis. The Kohl government did consolidate the budget somewhat in the first years, but later on, the government's attention moved away from consolidation. Consolidation returned to the fore after reunification. The later Kohl governments struggled with the simultaneous challenges of applying the Maastricht criteria for EMU access and financing the reunification of the country. Despite these efforts, the 1990s saw a period of unprecedented new debt. The next consolidation already happened under a new Red–Green government. Initial consolidation efforts were backed by a benevolent economic environment, but were soon abandoned. The Schröder government returned to consolidation after the dot-com crisis and launched a series of structural reforms that eventually led to its demise in 2005. The incoming grand coalition of Christian (CDU/CSU) and Social Democrats (SPD) had to consolidate the budget again until the international financial crisis led to a complete reversal towards deficit spending. In the sixth and last consolidation, the second Merkel government reversed

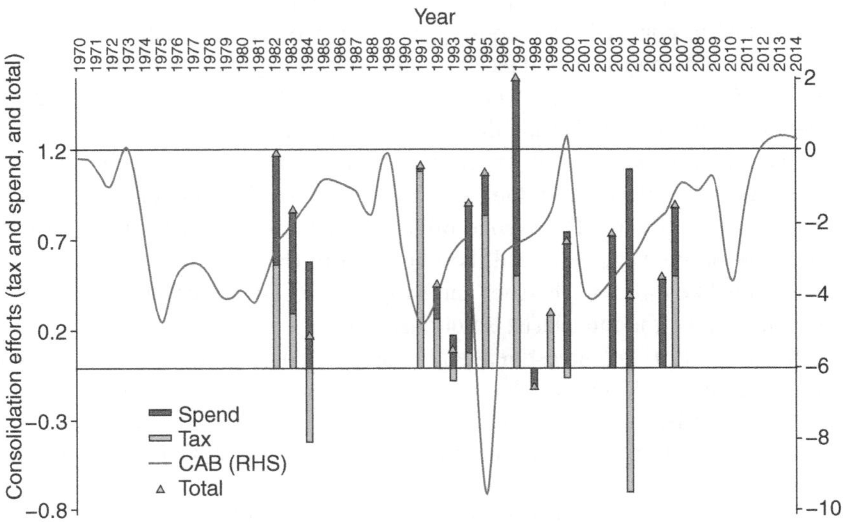

Figure 3.2 German cyclically adjusted balance (CAPB) and episodes of consolidations (source: CAPB is from the AMECO database and episodes of consolidation are from Devries et al. (2011)).

Table 3.2 Tax/expenditure mix in German consolidation episodes

	Total	*Tax*	*Spend*	*% Tax*	*% Expenditure*	*Δ Debt*[a]
Kohl I	2.23	0.45	1.78	20.18	79.82	2.46
Kohl II (EMU)	5.27	2.7	2.57	51.23	48.77	17.30
Schröder I	0.9	0.25	0.65	27.78	72.22	–0.31
Schröder II	1.14	0.04	1.1	3.51	96.49	1.82
Grand Coalition	1.4	0.5	0.9	35.71	64.29	–2.89
Merkel 2010–13	4.1	0.9	3.2	22	78	–3.8

Source: Devries et al. (2011) and AMECO (European Commission's Directorate General for Economic and Financial Affairs, Annual Macro-Economic Database).

Note

a In percentage points of GDP.

course again, but the consolidation only partially offset the additional debt due to the global financial crisis.[23]

All in all, we see that fiscal performance was dramatically altered by major external events such as reunification or the financial crisis. We also see that consolidation efforts are unevenly distributed, and happened under different types of governments. Finally, governments seemed to do more consolidation in the beginning of their respective terms, and especially once voted into office than in later years (Figure 3.1). These observations call for a more systematic inquiry into the determinants of German fiscal consolidation.

Kohl I and II: From Blaming to Fearing Opposition

Helmut Kohl's predecessor had a stressful life. Between 1974 and 82, Helmut Schmidt had to cope with the consequences of two oil crises and the end of a long period of high growth and fiscal stability. German gross public debt doubled from 17.85 to 36.49 percent of GDP, and the deficit of the CAPB reached 4.6 percent of GDP in 1975. During these years it was very obvious that the government could only control the expenditure side of the budget, as from 1976 onwards the Bundesrat was in the hands of the opposition[24] and made reforms of revenues more difficult. The second oil shock increased tensions in the government coalition between SPD and the liberal party (FDP). Stimulated by policy experiments like those of Thatcher and Reagan, the FDP increasingly pressed its coalition partner for monetarist solutions, mainly embodied by cuts in social transfers to spur private investment and budgetary consolidation. This generated conflicts with the SPD, which preferred ring-fencing the welfare state and placing the burden of adjustment on business and the upper part of the income distribution. The FDP defected from the coalition with the SPD, proposing a new alliance with the CDU/CSU.

A new coalition government between CDU/CSU and FDP was ushered in, initially without new elections. However, the new chancellor Helmut Kohl sought a stronger mandate and dissolved the parliament. New elections gave his government a comfortable, even if relatively short-lived electoral margin (Figure 3.3). In

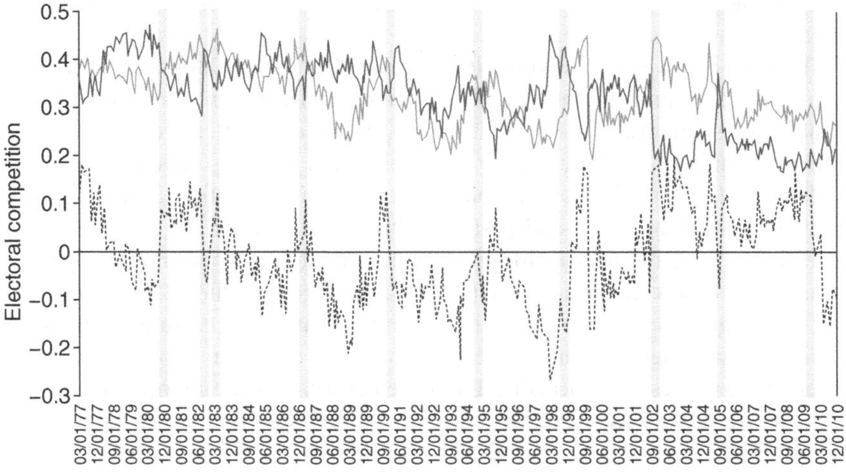

Figure 3.3 Public opinion (source: Authors' graph on basis of the "Sonntagsfrage" ("If there was an election next Sunday, which party would you vote for?"). Electoral competition is the difference between the shares of CDU+FDP and SPD+Greens. The source is Politbarometer, cumulative file (GESIS)).

the wake of Thatcher in Britain and Reagan in the United States, a change was expected to happen in the way fiscal retrenchment was to be conducted.[25] The new government wanted to first deal with deficits before embarking on a thorough tax reform.

The Kohl government dealt with the deficit on two fronts (Devries et al. 2011: 39): on one hand, Kohl let spending cuts fall on social programs (unemployment benefits, payments for retraining the unemployed, child allowances). In 1984, civil servant salaries were reduced and unemployment benefits cut down from 68 to 63 percent of net earnings, and unemployment assistance, similar to social assistance, decreased from 58 to 56 percent. However, we see clear limits how far Kohl could go. The strong political representation of (denominational) workers' interests in the CDU made it impossible for Kohl to go further.[26] In certain policy areas such as early retirement, the CDU even increased pension expenditure.[27]

On the other hand, Kohl strived to increase indirect taxation. It started with tax hikes on excises and on unemployment insurance and on pensions in 1982 and continued with VAT in 1983. As a whole, fiscal consolidation mainly concerned the lower part of the earnings distribution.[28] Expenditure cuts fell on expenditure items like the annual pension increase, income support programs, family allowances (but those were targeted mainly at the wealthier households), educational grants, unemployment benefits and fees in the healthcare system. The Bundesbank clearly supported these government cuts. In later years, the new government shifted its attention to other areas such as a major tax reform reducing the burden on firms and middle incomes as well as cuts in the trade tax.[29]

Fiscal consolidation became of secondary importance till reunification. Combating unemployment gained in political salience and led to a rise in passive transfers and rising pension debt.

The episode gives a relatively clear picture: The early 1980s were still dominated by the second oil shock and the spike in international interest rates, so problem pressure was an important issue, but the actual government efforts quickly subsided over time. In the beginning, a right-wing government indeed implemented reforms in the traditional logic of partisan politics: cuts in expenditure. The U-turn of the liberal party (FDP) from an SPD-FDP to a CDU-FDP government gave the new Kohl government a relatively comfortable margin in terms of electoral competition (see Figure 3.3). Moreover, the CDU ran its electoral campaign and its early years in government quite successfully blaming the previous government for the tremendous increase in public debt. Yet once the government parties started losing Länder elections and the margin shrank dramatically, reform efforts decreased and debt started accumulating again.

For this reason, the second Kohl consolidation (1991–97) was much less coherent ideologically: alternating stop-and-go policies in tax hikes and expenditure cuts in order to react to the deep recession of 1991 and the fundamental problems of financing German Reunification. The closer the deadline of EMU qualification, the higher the pressure of *drei punkt null* politics ("three point zero", i.e., the limit imposed by the Maastricht Treaty on deficits as percentage of GDP for the deadline of 1998) and the higher electoral competition was, the more hectic were the measures. The consolidation mix focused on expenditure cuts to areas such as subsidies to industries, unemployment compensation, reducing tax expenditures. Revenue measures included an increase in indirect taxation (VAT from 14 percent to 15 percent, especially on oil and gas—increase in the fuel tax in 1991–94—and tobacco), hikes in direct taxes, and measures to broaden the tax base and fight tax evasion. Later, the government shifted to a more balanced fiscal consolidation, including a solidarity pact in 1995–97. This pact between the Federal Government, the Länder, local governments, and the opposition of Social Democrats included tax hikes with an income tax surcharge of 7.5 percent and an increase in the wealth tax. On the spending side, cuts were made to defense, industrial subsidies, pay for civil servants, and the number of federal employees.

The biggest fiscal consolidation in Germany in one year (1.6 percent of GDP) was seen in 1997; it included the following expenditure cuts: wage restraints, spending limits on the level of the Länder, health insurance benefits, reducing the eligibility for unemployment benefits, freezing spending at the federal level. Tax hikes included raising social security contribution rates. Yet, despite these measures, in the end, Germany only qualified for EMU thanks to fiscal gimmicks, not unlike Greece.[30, 31]

Problem pressure, external restrictions, or partisan ideology are insufficient to explain the government's efforts of consolidation. One relevant factor of later years was the Bundesrat as a powerful veto player. For instance, the SPD in opposition vetoed Finance Minister Waigel's proposed tax hikes in other fields of taxation. Yet Waigel found new ways, for instance, by using revalued gold

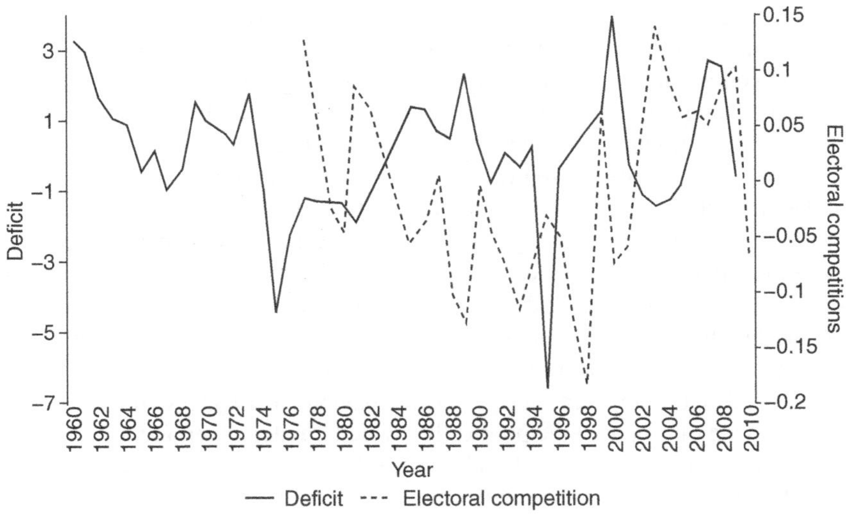

Figure 3.4 Electoral competition and budget deficits (source: Authors' graph. Primary annual budget deficit (source: OECD)).

reserves of the Bundesbank to repay federal debt, thus bringing the deficit under 3 percent of GDP. More promising is an explanation on grounds of electoral competition. Reunification gave a tremendous, but short-lived, boost for the CDU, which gave the government some electoral breathing space. However, the government had promised not only a relatively short and painless period of transition, but also that no tax increases were going to be necessary to finance reunification. Hence, in the medium run, blaming opportunities were limited, and consolidation efforts came at a tremendous electoral risk (see the narrow margins close to later elections in Figure 3.4). Once postponing consolidation became untenable in the late 1990s, it proved to be the straw that broke the camel's back. Whereas the Kohl government had dodged losing the elections by late turn-arounds in public opinion several times, its time was up in 1998.

Schröder I and II: From Experimentation to Gambling for Resurrection

Like the Kohl era, the Schröder era saw two fiscal consolidations. Yet, paradoxically, while the Kohl governments ended up implementing fiscal consolidations mainly based on taxes, the Schröder government behaved more like a Nixon going to China:[32] much of the consolidation took place on the expenditure side, with cutting unemployment benefits as the most notorious example.[33]

In its very beginning the coalition followed the expected partisan pattern and reversed some of the conservative retrenchment of previous years.[34] The coalition ended a spending freeze in 1998 and social spending increased by 12 percent (Hallerberg 2004: 99). But soon, reforms took a different path. In March 1999, finance minister Oskar Lafontaine resigned because of disputes in the cabinet and at the EU level over tax harmonization. His successor Hans Eichel changed course and increased VAT by one percentage point. The government's political situation worsened after it lost the majority in the Bundesrat, so that it became more difficult to implement tax-based consolidation. In 2000, the behavior of the coalition moved even further away from its political ideology: the consolidation package of 2000 had clear similarities to a right-wing consolidation, with a decrease in taxes (0.05 percent of GDP) and a cut in expenditures (0.75 percent of GDP). Those cuts concerned the social expenditures and the indexation of pensions, subsidies and the public sector wage bill. More surprising still was the fact that the government did this consolidation while at the same time implementing a major tax reform that relieved the tax burden on (large) companies. And it did so even against the opposition of a CDU-dominated Bundesrat, buying out some of the politically divided Länder governments.[35]

This reorientation of the fiscal consolidation strategy during the early Schröder government is mirrored in conflictive intra-party politics. In 1998, the SPD was split between "modernizers" and "traditionalists," the latters' preferences being strongly voiced by Oskar Lafontaine. As finance minister and chairman of the party, he had a strong influence on the shape of the consolidation package.[36] With the departure of Lafontaine, Schröder reorientated governmental policies towards new priorities satisfying what he saw as the core of the "new labour" electorate. Thus Schröder switched to a rhetoric accentuating individual values and focused less on the traditional values of equality (Harlen 2002: 6).

Hence, this episode was marked by the political consequences of the SPD's move to the middle of the political spectrum. But it is also the consequence of unresolved problems in the labour market. The traditional German solution, i.e., converting elderly unemployed people into retirees, had become impossible, and the specter of high non-wage labour costs was looming large (Kemmerling 2014). Due to high unemployment rates, the government's popularity plummeted (see Figure 3.4). The government responded with a more moderate stance on fiscal policy. Even though popularity recovered somewhat, the next elections seemed to be lost. Three events would come to rescue the government. First, the government took a very popular pacifist stance against the war in Iraq, whereas the leading opposition held to the US administration. Second, the flooding in Eastern Germany gave the Chancellor a boost. Third, the government started a political offensive: it used a scandal at the Central Agency for Jobs to commission a set of far-ranging labour-market reforms that would also affect social security.[37] While in the long run these measures would prove detrimental to the party, in the short run they contributed to just enough additional votes to guarantee a razor-thin majority in the 2002 elections.[38]

The second fiscal consolidation of the Schröder government was incoherent and mainly triggered because of concerns related to the Stability and Growth Pact. In 2003, the government increased taxes by 0.74 percent of GDP, trying to raise higher revenues from income, business and indirect taxes. In 2004, by contrast, the government relaxed the constraints on the revenue side of the budget and switched to an expenditure-based consolidation, making the cuts fall mainly on social transfers and subsidies, most which were summarized in the so-called "Agenda 2010." This agenda was the consequence of the electoral pledges two years earlier, but only now did the effects become clear to the people. The most important example of these cuts was in unemployment benefits (the so-called "Hartz IV reform"). Whereas, previously, unemployed people received unemployment benefits for an unlimited time, the government now introduced a maximum period of 12 months. Even if the net effect on expenditures was around zero in the short run, the long-run effects of the reform contributed to fiscal consolidation by lowering unemployment rates. The reform constitutes, therefore, an important example of an implicit measure to consolidate public budgets.

All in all, the Red–Green coalition first raised cyclically adjusted expenditures from 44.6 to 44.9 percent of GDP between 1998 and 2002, before reducing them to 44.1 percent of GDP later. The Schröder governments indeed turned away from traditional partisan politics. Problem pressure was a reason, but it was arguably more the rising levels of unemployment than of debt that made the government react. Once the government was in the domain of impending electoral losses it started gambling for resurrection. In doing so one may argue that its behavior is consistent with the forecasts of prospect theory.[39] However, whilst in the short run the strategy seemed to work, in the medium to long run it upset both traditional voters and allied trade unions. It was a rare occasion to judge the actual size of voter retaliation: the second Schröder government resigned early. Moreover, ever since then, the SPD's public support hovers around a level that is 5 to 10 percent lower than before.

Merkel I and II: From No Competition to No Need

An unexpected and unpopular Grand Coalition had to deal with the "crisis of fiscal democracy"[40] (Streeck 2007, 2009; Streeck and Mertens 2010). Given the poor state of German public finances (gross public debt increased to 68.6 percent of GDP in 2005), the situation was conducive to a fiscal adjustment. However, the government soon felt less pressure to undertake fiscal reforms. The business cycle became favorable and the outgoing government's Agenda 2010 had prepared the ground with drastically lower rates of unemployment, even if reforms came at the heavy price of increasing inequality and a huge low-wage sector.

This recovery partly explains why explicit fiscal adjustment of the Grand Coalition was mild at best. In general, grand coalitions are said to lack ambition when it comes to fiscal consolidation, not least due to programmatic differences.[41] Nonetheless, 65 percent of the consolidation efforts concentrated on the expenditure side. In 2006, the coalition enacted expenditure cuts estimated by the IMF to be at the level of 0.5 percent of GDP. In 2007, the expenditure cuts, which fell mainly on social transfers like allowances for job seekers (the aftermath of Hartz IV), were balanced with tax hikes. Those tax hikes continued the trend started in the 1980s to shift the tax mix to regressive taxation.[42] VAT alone saw a hefty increase by three percentage points from 16 to 19 percent.

As a result, the 2007 budget came close to being in balance. The cyclically adjusted balance fell from –3.3 percent of GDP in 2003 to –0.8 percent of GDP in 2007. Cyclically adjusted revenues actually fell from 45.0 percent of GDP in 2003 to 42.9 percent of GDP in 2007, but expenditures fell even more from 45.26 in 2003 to 40.95 in 2007. Moreover, the government did also tackle the long-term issue of implicit pension liabilities. The grand coalition was the first government to implement a substantial increase in the statutory retirement age to 67, which will reduce pension future liabilities considerably.

As mentioned before, the government also tightened its own "handcuffs" on fiscal policy, by introducing a new and tougher debt brake in 2009. In part this was a response to the 2002–06 budgets being unconstitutional according to German federal supreme court.[43] This legal reform and the introduction of the German debt brake seem to have curtailed public debt in the short and medium run since and imposed stringent limits on both federal and regional borrowing which should achieve a structural balance of –0.35 percent of GDP in 2016 and 2020.[44] Figure 3.1 suggests that the structural break in German public debt happening since 2009 can be assigned to the debt brake, but one should be cautious on this point. Past experience has shown that, if anything, stringent institutions like fiscal rules can also be overridden.

All in all, the episode shows that grand coalitions are not always as immobile as critics would argue. While electoral competition is still present, it is less problematic because blame sharing can reduce the reluctance to introduce unpopular reforms such as extending the retirement age. Also, the increase of VAT by 3 percentage points is easier to spread over both major parties. The grand coalition made sure that neither of the two partners alone had to take the blame for unpopular reforms. Similar considerations apply to reduced pension liabilities. Extending the retirement age had been an electoral taboo in post-war German public opinion and both major parties had waited for the chance to capitalize on a mistake by the other in this respect.[45]

In 2009, the voters decided against the grand coalition, but Merkel was able to run a minimum-winning coalition with the FDP. Fiscal policy was formulated in the shadow of the Great Recession of 2008. Germany opted for a more balanced fiscal consolidation than its European neighbors: it reduced cyclically adjusted expenditures by two percentage points between 2010 and 2012 and increased revenues on average by two percentage points between 2008 and 2012, in contrast to other countries.[46] The overall ambition of the coalition government between conservatives (CDU/CSU) and liberals (FDP) was limited. The government inherited a relatively large package of fiscal stimulus of about 3.0 percent of GDP implemented by the grand coalition in late 2008 and early 2009. This was in addition to the effect of automatic stabilizers—around 4.2 percent of GDP.[47] Much of this package consisted of permanent reductions in taxation and social security contributions that created a legacy for future consolidations.

One issue is, of course, that except for the huge and contingent bailout packages for other EMU members, the economic environment was surprisingly moderate. It is true that the first reductions in output were tremendous, but at the time the CDU/FDP took over, the effects of the stimulus seemed to have kicked in.[48] Moreover, in certain aspects, Germany benefited from the financial crises of its neighbors by becoming a safe haven for foreign capital and the negative real interest rates this provoked. Hence, while it is true that some observers saw German public finances in dire straights,[49] and even questioned democracy in a country in which only 17 percent of the public budget is left to discretionary spending (Streeck and Mertens 2010), this did not produce strong incentives for the government to react.

Electoral competition, however, has resurfaced as a political constraint. True, the CDU, and Merkel in particular, had a long honeymoon period in terms of public opinion, but electoral competition is fierce. The two major ideological camps are now quite close, and the communist PDS could tip the balance between right and left. Since the German finance minister can currently issue debt at negative interest rates, serious efforts of consolidation seem to be unnecessarily risky from an electoral perspective. The Merkel government seems to have opted for a strategy of "resting on its laurels." Nonetheless, the German mix of passive and active consolidation since 2010 has worked: Germany was, in 2012, the only EU Member State to post a surplus of its public finance (0.2 percent of GDP) and since then the structural balance is in positive territory. In the meantime, the upward path of public debt was broken and switched to a downward path instead.

Conclusion: The Art of Surviving Fiscal Consolidation

These six episodes of fiscal adjustments show us that several conditions need to hold to make fiscal consolidation politically feasible in Germany. The economic environment is an important contextual factor that explains part of the size and occurrence of fiscal consolidation. Institutional factors, such as the role of the Bundesrat in blocking tax hikes, also shape the nature of fiscal politics. The presence of an external constraint also matters, as the need to qualify for EMU led to a more balanced burden of adjustment and a social pact.

Other factors prominent in the literature seem to be less relevant for the German case. Explicit tripartite social pacts are less visible than in other countries (see Chapter 4 in this volume). For instance the Solidarity Pact of 1993–95 (which is formally still in place through the Solidarity Pact II until 2019) was a government initiative that brought together the federal government, the Länder and the political parties to finance the Reunification (with a Solidarity Surcharge on the income tax of 7.5 percent), but did not include social partners. And when the state does implement labor market reforms, such as in the case of the Schröder administration, often it does so against the will of trade unions.

Instead, the German case illustrates the importance of electoral competition and the politics of blame avoidance looming large behind governments' attempts of fiscal consolidation. Whereas the Kohl governments until 1994 and the Merkel governments after 2005 consolidated in environments of low electoral competition, the last Kohl government and, in particular, the Schröder governments show the fatal electoral and political consequences of consolidating public finances when electoral competition is high. In these rare circumstances we see the electoral price tag of fiscal consolidation in full swing.

Figure 3.4 shows the relationship between the electoral competition of the two major political camps and the annual deficits. A clear negative correlation between the two is visible: when deficits are high, electoral margins are low and vice versa. This is especially true before reunification, but also holds for the period thereafter.

The episodes have also revealed that a concentration on explicit efforts of fiscal consolidation is misleading. Most of the fundamental reforms are parametric or systematic changes in social expenditure. The Schröder reforms, the pension overhaul and the resulting very low unemployment rates relieved the pressure on the budget. Behind this may stand a political coalition agreeing that fiscal balance is good for the competitiveness of the export sector. From this follows that episodes of fiscal consolidation are subject to political and economic selection: only when economic pressure mounts, and only as much as political rationale would allow for. Otherwise, German governments are very cautious in their use of consolidation strategies.

Hence, the logic of political survival has important implications for fiscal performance. Successful episodes of consolidation will mainly happen if they are also successful politically. This creates selection bias. For instance, not all types of reforms are equally likely to happen, and they don't happen at all times of the electoral cycle. Few governments ever implemented the flip side of Keynes' deficit spending: reducing debt during periods of economic boom. But then it is hard to assess the success of (anti-)Keynesian fiscal consolidation without correcting for the possibility of non-reform. For instance, Alesina and Ardagna (2009) claim that anti-Keynesian reforms are successful economically, but they do not pose any electoral risk. This might be an artifact, since we can only observe those reforms in which governments were sufficiently sure to survive politically. This kind of a selection bias is an important area of future research.

Moreover, if the German case shows the political perils of fiscal consolidation, and Germany is a case of a relatively conservative fiscal and monetary culture, the situation in other countries may be worse. In other words, Germany is a least likely case and may underestimate the electoral consequences of fiscal consolidation. The German governments faced certain structural advantages that other governments do not have at their disposal. The constraint of European monetary integration had a different role in Germany compared to other countries. While Italy, for instance, anchored itself to a *vincolo esterno*,[50] Germany was the anchor itself and it entered the EMU with an overvalued exchange rate. From this point of view, one can see fiscal consolidations as a "fiscal devaluation." Increasing Value Added Tax (VAT) can have positive effects on exports by lowering social contributions, thus mimicking lower wages and a nominal devaluation that would be compensated with increased VAT.[51] Coupled with wage restraint and structural reforms, this is a sure a way to regain lost competitiveness. Hence, the tensions between political pressures and economic context are arguably much worse in other countries of the OECD, which makes political survival of fiscal consolidation all the more delicate.

This brings us, finally, to a normative implication: since successful fiscal consolidation only seems possible if it means economic as well as political success, internally or externally imposed debt rules might not work. They especially will not work if they create too much of a disadvantage for incumbent politicians in the race for reelection. Therefore, such rules need to adhere to some sort of political impartiality, i.e., they should neither benefit nor harm the government vis-à-vis the opposition. In that sense, fiscal pacts and other forms of inclusive, deliberative policies might work better than management by sterile institutionalization.

Notes

1 Holzmann et al. (2004).
2 Hall and Soskice (2001).
3 Genschel (2002); Ganghof (2006); Kemmerling (2010).
4 Adema (2001); Kemmerling (2004).
5 Manow and Seils (2000).
6 Kemmerling (2009, 2010).
7 Verdier (2000).
8 Domestic investors hold 38 percent (compared to a eurozone average of 28 percent), residents outside the eurozone hold 34 percent—see Artus (2012).
9 European Commission, "Fiscal Rules Index," *DG Ecfin*, 2012.
10 Data retrieved from the Fiscal Governance Database of the European Commission, available at http://ec.europa.eu/economy_finance/db_indicators/fiscal_governance/index_en.htm (accessed November 6, 2013).
11 Hallerberg et al. (2009).
12 Kastrop et al. (2009).
13 Streeck (2007).
14 Kastrop et al. (2009).
15 Hodson (2011).
16 Authors' own calculation based on the preventive and corrective arms of the SGP for the period 1998–2008. The SGP has a "preventive" and a "corrective" arm. The "preventive" arm has established country-specific budgetary objectives fixed by Member States themselves. Member States pursue these objectives through annually updated stability programmes. The "corrective" arm looks at the compliance with the Maastricht criteria concerning the deficit (maximum 3 percent of GDP).
17 Streeck and Hassel (2003).
18 According to the World Bank advanced economies had on average savings amounting to 17.53 percent of GDP for 2011, while Germany had 22.81 percent (http://data.worldbank.org/indicator/NY.GNS.ICTR.ZS).
19 Hallerberg and Wolff (2008).
20 Girouard and Price (2004); Romer and Romer (2007).
21 Devries et al. (2011).
22 Hallerberg (2004); Mulas-Granados (2006); Ganghof (2004); Zohlnhöfer (1999).
23 Compared to Breuer et al. (2011), we did not include the consolidation episodes of Helmut Schmidt in the 1970s, we split the Schröder episodes into two distinct ones and we include the German fiscal consolidation from 2010.
24 Scharpf (1991); Hallerberg (2004).
25 Zohlnhöfer (1999).
26 Zohlnhöfer (2001).
27 Streeck and Trampusch (2005).
28 As Zohlnhöfer argues the government did try to introduce a levy on the better off in the form of a forced loan *(Investitionshilfeabgabe)*. It was supposed to be a 5 percent surcharge on the income tax burden, similar to the solidarity surcharge after reunification, but unlike the latter, it was judged unconstitutional by the federal supreme court.

29 Ganghof (2004).
30 Savage (2008).
31 After reunification, intra-German *transfer flows* increased from 139 in 1991 to 189 billion DM in 1997, amounting to a total 1.37 trillion DM between 1991 and 1998. When it became clear that the transfers would become permanent, the government started to impose a solidarity surcharge in 1991 and re-imposed it again in 1995. Since PIT and CIT needed to stay internationally competitive, the burden fell largely on social security contributions. These changes de-correlated tax revenues from GDP growth, and thus made fiscal planning very difficult and incurred financing gaps (von Hagen and Strauch 1999).
32 Ross (2000).
33 Kemmerling and Bruttel (2006); Palier and Thelen (2010).
34 Egle and Zohlnhöfer (2007).
35 Ganghof (2004); Zohlnhöfer (2004).
36 Harlen (2002).
37 Kemmerling and Bruttel (2006).
38 Egle and Zohlnhöfer (2007).
39 Vis and van Kersbergen (2007).
40 Miskimmon et al. (2009).
41 Wagschal and Wenzelburger (2012); Zohlnhöfer (2011).
42 Kemmerling (2009).
43 Grasl and König (2010).
44 For an example of how this debt brake works, see the German Stability and Convergence Programme 2013, page 14, available at: http://ec.europa.eu/europe2020/pdf/nd/sp2013_germany_en.pdf (accessed November 23, 2013).
45 Kemmerling (2009).
46 The UK consolidated its public finance mainly on the expenditure side, while France did the opposite.
47 Egle and Zohlnhöfer (2010); Schelkle (2012); Cameron (2012).
48 Schelkle (2012).
49 Streeck (2007).
50 Dyson and Featherstone (1996).
51 Fahri et al. (2013); de Mooij and Keen (2012).

References

Adema, Willem. 2001. *Net Social Expenditure*. 2nd edition. OECD Labour Market and Social Policy Occasional Paper. Paris: OECD Publishing.

Alesina, Alberto and Silvia Ardagna. 2009. *Large Changes in Fiscal Policy: Taxes versus Spending*. National Bureau of Economic Research Working Paper No. 15438, Cambridge, MA.

Artus, Patrick. 2012. *The Effects of the Holding Structure of the Euro Zone's Public Debt*. Economic Research 834. Paris: Natixis.

Breuer, Christian, Jan Gottschalk, Anna Ivanova and Paulo Mauro. 2011. "Germany: Fiscal Adjustment Attemps with and without Reforms." In *Chipping Away at Public Debt: Sources of Failure and Keys to Success in Fiscal Adjustment*, 85–114. John Wiley.

Cameron, David R. 2012. "European Fiscal Responses to the Great Recession." In *Coping with Crisis Government Reactions to the Great Recession*, edited by Nancy Bermeo and Jonas Pontusson, 91–129. Russell Sage Foundation.

De Mooij, Ruud and Michael Keen. 2012. *"Fiscal Devaluation" and Fiscal Consolidation: The VAT in Troubled Times*. IMF Working Paper WP/12/85. Washington, D.C.: International Monetary Fund.

Devries, Pete, Jaime Guajardo, Daniel Leigh and Andrea Pescatori. 2011. *A New Action-Based Dataset of Fiscal Consolidation*. IMF Working Paper WP/11/128. Washington, D.C.: International Monetary Fund.

Dyson, Kenneth and Kevin Featherstone. 1996. "Italy and EMU as a 'Vincolo Esterno': Empowering the Technocrats, Transforming the State." *South European Society and Politics* 1(2): 272–299.

Egle, Christoph and Reimut Zohlnhöfer. 2007. "Projekt oder Episode—Was Bleibt von Rot-Gruen." In *Ende Des Rot-Grünen Projekts. Eine Bilanz der Regierung Schröder 2002–2005*, edited by Christoph Egle and Reimut Zohlnhöfer, 511–536. Wiesbaden: VS Verlag.

Egle, Christoph and Reimut Zohlnhöfer. 2010. *Die Zweite Große Koalition*. Wiesbaden: Springer.

European Commission. 2006. *Public Finances in EMU 2006. No. 3. European Economy*. Luxembourg: Office for Official Publications of the European Commission.

European Commission. 2009. *Public Finances in EMU 2009. No. 4. European Economy*. Luxembourg: Office for Official Publications of the European Commission.

European Commission. 2012. *Fiscal Rules Index*. DG Ecfin.

Fahri, Emmanuel, Gita Gopinath and Oleg Itskhoki. 2013. *Fiscal Devaluations*. Harvard and Princeton.

Ganghof, S. 2004. *Wer regiert in der Steuerpolitik? Einkommensteuerreform zwischen internationalem Wettbewerb und nationalen Verteilungskonflikten*. Frankfurt am Main; New York: Campus.

Ganghof, S. 2006. *The Politics of Income Taxation. A Comparative Analysis*. Colchester: ECPR Press.

Genschel, P. 2002. "Globalization, Tax Competition, and the Welfare State." *Politics and Society* 30(2): 245–275.

Girouard, Nathalie and Robert Price. 2004. *Asset Price Cycles, "One-Off" Factors and Structural Budget Balances*. OECD Economics Department Working Paper. Paris: OECD Publishing.

Grasl, Maximilian and Markus König. 2010. "Von außen getrieben. Die Finanzpolitik der großen Koalition 2005–2009." In *Die zweite große Koalition: Eine Bilanz der Regierung Merkel 2005–2009*, edited by Christoph Egle and Reimut Zohlnhöfer, 205–233. Wiesbaden: VS Verlag.

Hall, Peter A. and David Soskice. 2001. *Varieties of Capitalism: The Institutional Foundations of Comparative Advantage*. Oxford: Oxford University Press.

Hallerberg, Mark. 2004. *Domestic Budgets in a United Europe: Fiscal Governance from the End of Bretton Woods to EMU*. Ithaca, NY: Cornell University Press.

Hallerberg, Mark and Guntram B. Wolff. 2008. "Fiscal Institutions, Fiscal Policy and Sovereign Risk Premia in EMU." *Public Choice* 136(3–4): 379–396.

Hallerberg, Mark, Rolf Strauch and Jürgen von Hagen. 2009. *Fiscal Governance in Europe*. New York: Cambridge University Press.

Harlen, Christine M. 2002. "Schröder's Economic Reforms: The End of Reformstau?" *German Politics* 11(1): 61–80.

Hodson, Dermot. 2011. *Governing the Euro Area in Good Times and Bad*. Oxford: Oxford University Press.

Holzmann, Robert, Robert Palacios and Asta Zviniene. 2004. *Implicit Pension Debt: Issues, Measurement and Scope in International Perspective*. Social Protection Discussion Paper. Washington, D.C.: World Bank.

Kastrop, Christian, Helmut Herres, Jürgen Schneider, Bernd Hanke, Elke Baumann, Martin Snelting and Elmar Dönnebrink. 2009. *Reforming the Constitutional Budget*

Rules in Germany. Federal Ministry of Finance—Economics Department: Public Finance and Economic Affairs Directorate Deficit Rule Reform Team.

Kemmerling, Achim. 2004. "Die Messung sozialstaatlicher Leistungen—Brutto- und Nettosozialleistungsquote." In *Oekonomische Leistungsfaehigkeit Deutschlands. Bestandsaufnahme und statistische Messung im internationalen Vergleich*, 150–172. Wiesbaden: Statistisches Bundesamt.

Kemmerling, Achim. 2009. *Taxing the Working Poor. The Political Origins and Economic Consequences of Taxing Low Wages*. Cheltenham: Edward Elgar.

Kemmerling, Achim. 2010. "Does Europeanization Lead to Policy Convergence? The Role of the Single Market in Shaping National Tax Policies." *Journal of European Public Policy* 17(7): 1058–1073.

Kemmerling, Achim. 2012. "How Labour Ended up Taxing Itself and Why It Matters: The Long-Term Evolution of Politics in German Labour Taxation." *Journal of European Social Policy* 24(2): 150–163.

Kemmerling, Achim and Oliver Bruttel. 2006. "New Politics in German Labour Market Policy? The Implications of the Recent Hartz Reforms for the German Welfare State." *West European Politics* 29(1): 90–112.

Manow, P. and E. Seils. 2000. "The Employment Crisis of the German Welfare State." *West European Politics* 23(2): 138–160.

Miskimmon, Alister, William E. Paterson and James Sloam. 2009. *Germany's Gathering Crisis: The 2005 Federal Election and the Grand Coalition*. Palgrave Macmillan.

Mulas-Granados, Carlos. 2006. *Economics, Politics and Budgets: The Political Economy of Fiscal Consolidations in Europe*. Basingstoke; New York: Palgrave Macmillan.

OECD. 2010. *Revenue Statistics. 1965–2009*. Paris.

Palier, Bruno and Kathleen Thelen. 2010. "Institutionalizing Dualism: Complementarities and Change in France and Germany." *Politics and Society* 38(1): 119–148.

Romer, Christina D. and David H. Romer. 2007. *The Macroeconomic Effects of Tax Changes: Estimates Based on a New Measure of Fiscal Shocks*. National Bureau of Economic Research Working Paper No. 13264, Cambridge, MA.

Ross, Fiona. 2000. "'Beyond Left and Right': The New Partisan Politics of Welfare." *Governance* 13(2): 155–183.

Savage, James D. 2008. *Making the EMU: The Politics of Budgetary Surveillance and the Enforcement of Maastricht*. New York: Oxford University Press.

Scharpf, Fritz W. 1991. *Crisis and Choice in European Social Democracy*. Ithaca, NY: Cornell University Press.

Schelkle, Waltraud. 2012. "Policymaking in Hard Times: French and German Responses to the Eurozone Crisis." In *Coping with Crisis: Government Reactions to the Great Recession*, edited by Nancy Bermeo and Jonas Pontusson, 130–161. New York: Russell Sage Foundation.

Streeck, Wolfgang. 2007. *Endgame? The Fiscal Crisis of the German State*. Köln: Max-Planck-Institut für Gesellschaftsforschung.

Streeck, Wolfgang. 2009. *Re-Forming Capitalism: Institutional Change in the German Political Economy*. Oxford: Oxford University Press.

Streeck, Wolfgang and Anke Hassel. 2003. "The Crumbling Pillars of Social Partnership." *West European Politics* 26(4): 101–124.

Streeck, Wolfgang and Daniel Mertens. 2010. *An Index of Fiscal Democracy*. Köln: Max-Planck-Institut für Gesellschaftsforschung.

Streeck, Wolfgang and Christine Trampusch. 2005. "Economic Reform and the Political Economy of the German Welfare State." *German Politics* 14(2): 174–195.

Verdier, Daniel. 2000. "State and Finance in the OECD: Previous Trends and Current Changes." *Politics and Society* 28(1): 35–65.

Vis, Barbara and Kees van Kersbergen. 2007. "Why and How do Political Actors Pursue Risky Reforms?" *Journal of Theoretical Politics* 19(2): 153–172.

Von Hagen, Jürgen and Rolf R. Strauch. 1999. "Tumbling Giant: Germany's Experience with the Maastricht Fiscal Criteria." *In From EMS to Emu: 1979 to 1999 and Beyond*, edited by David P. Cobham and George Zis, 70–94. New York: St Martin's Press.

Wagschal, Uwe and Georg Wenzelburger. 2012. "When do Governments Consolidate? A Quantitative Comparative Analysis of 23 OECD Countries (1980–2005)." *Journal of Comparative Policy Analysis: Research and Practice* 14(1): 45–71.

Zohlnhöfer, Reimut. 1999. "Institutions, the CDU and Policy Change: Explaining German Economic Policy in the 1980s." *German Politics* 8(3): 141–160.

Zohlnhöfer, Reimut. 2001. *Die Wirtschaftspolitik der Ära Kohl. Eine Analyse der Schlüsselentscheidungen in den Politikfeldern Finanzen, Arbeit und Entstaatlichung, 1982–1998.* Opladen: Leske und Budrich.

Zohlnhöfer, Reimut. 2004. "Destination Anywhere? The German Red–Green Government's Inconclusive Search for a Third Way in Economic Policy." *German Politics* 13(1): 106–131.

Zohlnhöfer, Reimut. 2011. "Between a Rock and a Hard Place: The Grand Coalition's Response to the Economic Crisis." *German Politics* 20(2): 227–242.

4 Fiscal Performance in Italy

A Historical Institutionalist Approach

Benedicta Marzinotto

Introduction

There is a vast collection of political economy literature looking at the conditions under which fiscal stabilization is more likely to occur. Three broad categories of explanation can be isolated: (1) the role of pressures coming from markets, international/supranational organizations (i.e., the International Monetary Fund or the European Union), or both (Haggard and Kaufman 1992; Dyson and Featherstone 1996; Featherstone 2001) and the domestic motivation for accepting these pressures; (2) socioeconomic interests and preferences that include partisanship (Hibbs 1977; Mulas-Granados 2006), as well as the wider socioeconomic context at the time of adjustment (Giavazzi and Spaventa 1989; Boltho 1992; Bruno 1993); here, the constellation of preferences matters because it determines the extent to which it is possible to solve "wars of attrition" between socioeconomic interests that have divergent preferences over the composition of deficit reduction (Alesina and Drazen 1991); and (3) finally, acting as mediating factors, the constraints and opportunities coming from budgetary and/or political institutions (Alesina and Perotti 1994; Poterba and Von Hagen 1999; Hallerberg et al. 2009).

These perspectives are mostly applied in isolation or jointly to explain turning points in fiscal performance such as major fiscal consolidation episodes. Yet the habit of using these approaches to explain extraordinary circumstances misses the fact that turning points may just be the culmination of an incremental process of institutional change that has involved societies and institutions over a relatively long period of time. Purely quantitative approaches to studying the probability of fiscal adjustment are unfit to capture this long-term dimension. Moreover, whilst standard macroeconomic models describe fiscal policy as a fully exogenous shock, macroeconomics is embedded in domestic institutional arrangements as much as any other feature of economic systems and locked in with the other institutions of a country's political economy. All this justifies using a historical institutionalist approach to the analysis of macroeconomic stabilization. The study of the origins of institutions, their intrinsic path-dependency as well as their patterns of change, are at the heart of the historical institutionalist agenda. Extensively applied to welfare regimes, skill formation, financial systems, and, more generally, production regimes or varieties of capitalism (Hall and Soskice 2001; Thelen

2004), this perspective is in fact rarely used to understand the origins and evolution of domestic macroeconomic regimes.

This chapter applies a historical institutionalist perspective to the study of the macroeconomic stabilization Italy went through in the run-up to the Economic and Monetary Union (EMU), from roughly 1991 to 1997. It is argued that Italy's fiscal adjustment in the 1990s was of course critically conditioned by the prospect of EMU membership, but the external pressure would not have been sufficient without the macroeconomic regime change that started in the early 1980s. The transformation of the country's macroeconomic regime was initiated in 1981 when the Bank of Italy's obligation to monetize general government debt was eliminated. Even if the departure from fiscal dominance was piecemeal, this institutional innovation led to adjustments in the labor market and further reform in 1988, transforming its budget institutions from within. It also led to a slow process of repositioning of political and socioeconomic interests that explains why the fiscal stabilization of the 1990s was supported also by the social partners.

The historical institutionalist perspective is found to have superior explanatory power compared with some parts of the "short-term" theories of fiscal adjustment that have been identified above. External pressures coming from the fact that Italy was lining up for the EMU were certainly important but second-order with respect to the fact that Italy's macroeconomic regime had changed before the Maastricht process had even started; ultimately, the pressure to qualify for the EMU simply accelerated the adjustment process. Moreover, the country's high debt level was not such that national authorities were prompted into action against fear of a fiscal crisis of the state; such pressure should have been there also before the Maastricht Treaty, not to mention that the Maastricht debt criterion was not perceived as binding as the deficit criterion and, in fact, in the end, it was not respected. By contrast, and in accordance with some of the political economy literature evoked earlier, socioeconomic preferences were arranged in a way that allowed striking a social compromise over fiscal reform and avoiding a delay in stabilization (i.e., Alesina and Drazen 1991). It is important to bear in mind that the repositioning of socioeconomic interests vis-à-vis fiscal austerity had started much earlier and was a response to the slow transformation of the country's macroeconomic regime: hence, interests and preferences mattered but their content is part of the broad institutional change that took place in the 1980s. At the same time, it should be noted that during the 1990s the country's political instability was conspiring against fiscal reform. Here, efficient budget institutions after the 1988 Budget Reform did play an important role, including nullifying the potentially perverse effects of political instability. Again, though, the budget reform process and its outcomes were the by-product of the systemic transformation that had started almost a decade earlier.

The rest of the chapter is structured as follows. Section 1 describes Italy's fiscal adjustment in the 1990s explaining why it was indeed a well prepared turning point. Section 2 reviews the theories of successful fiscal consolidation and provides a primer for the historical institutionalist perspective on macroeconomic regimes proposed here. Section 3 applies this perspective to the study of Italy's fiscal consolidation in the 1990s, focusing on the importance that monetary policy reform eventually had on the form and direction of the country's fiscal regime and on interlinkages with other reform areas (i.e., labor markets and budget reform). In Section 4, the societal dimension is specifically addressed. It is argued that the macroeconomic regime change of the 1980s, whilst initiated by political elites, led to changing socioeconomic interests and preferences that could be reconciled effectively under the fiscal-discipline agenda of the 1990s; as a result, fiscal adjustment was not only possible but also relatively consensual. Section 5 uses the same historical institutionalist perspective to assess Italy's performance under the EMU.

Italy's Fiscal Adjustment in the 1990s

After a few failed attempts in the mid-1980s, and under pressure to participate in the first wave of European monetary integration, Italy succeeded in cutting the public deficit down in the 1990s. Figure 4.1 describes the evolution of Italy's fiscal balance as a percentage of GDP over the period 1970–2013, in comparison with that of Germany before and after unification. The contrast between the countries' fiscal performance is evident especially in the early 1980s when both were hit by recession. Italy started with a slow process of adjustment that became evident only starting in the early 1990s and going on until the outbreak of the euro debt crisis. The data distinguishes between the general government fiscal balance and the fiscal balance net of interest rate payments, where the gap

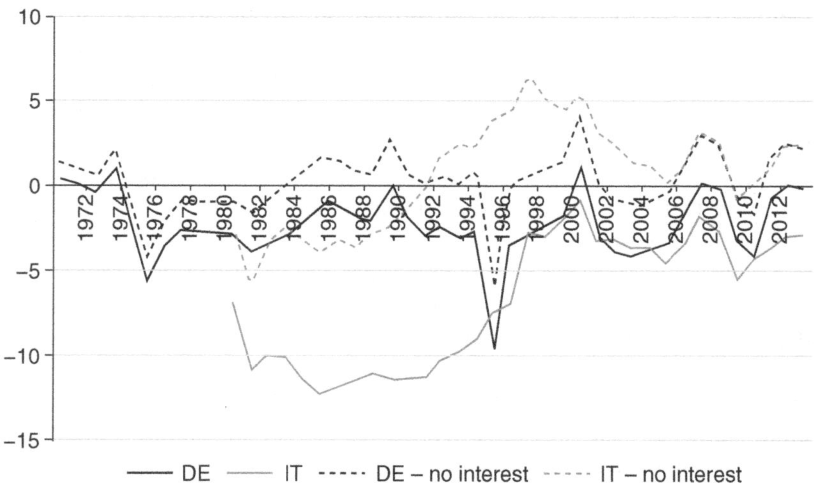

Figure 4.1 Fiscal balance with and without interests as percentage of GDP, 1970–2013 (source: AMECO database, European Commission. General government net lending (+) or net borrowing (+) as a percentage of GDP at market prices (including one-off proceeds relative to the allocation of mobile phone licenses)).

Note
DE Germany; IT Italy.

between the two indicators is representative of the economic significance of interests paid on the stock of debt. Interest payments are of course much greater for Italy, given the country's high public debt level, than they have ever been for Germany. The improvement in the fiscal balance net of interest rate payments, which is purged of the dynamics on financial markets beyond state control, started in the late 1980s, immediately after the 1988 Budget Reform. In fact, when Prime Minister Giuliano Amato made fiscal consolidation a top priority in 1992 in an effort to initiate the convergence process that would have brought Italy into the EMU, as agreed in the Maastricht Treaty, the country's fiscal stabilization process was already on the right footing. Nevertheless, the fiscal balance including interest payments continued to disappoint until the early 1990s because government bond spreads had been rising in anticipation of the elimination of capital controls in the 1990s and shortly thereafter.

The debt stock was on a downward trend starting in 1994, reflecting improvements on the deficit front. Figure 4.2 provides an impression of the evolution of the general government gross debt as a percentage of GDP in Italy and Germany over the period 1984–2013. Whilst high in a comparative perspective, Italy's public debt started clearly decreasing in the 1990s, but only until the 2008–09 recession and the subsequent euro debt crisis, when it began to rise again on the back of dismal economic growth.

The focus of this chapter is specifically on fiscal adjustment rather than the mere conduct of fiscal policy. Fiscal adjustment consists of the reduction in

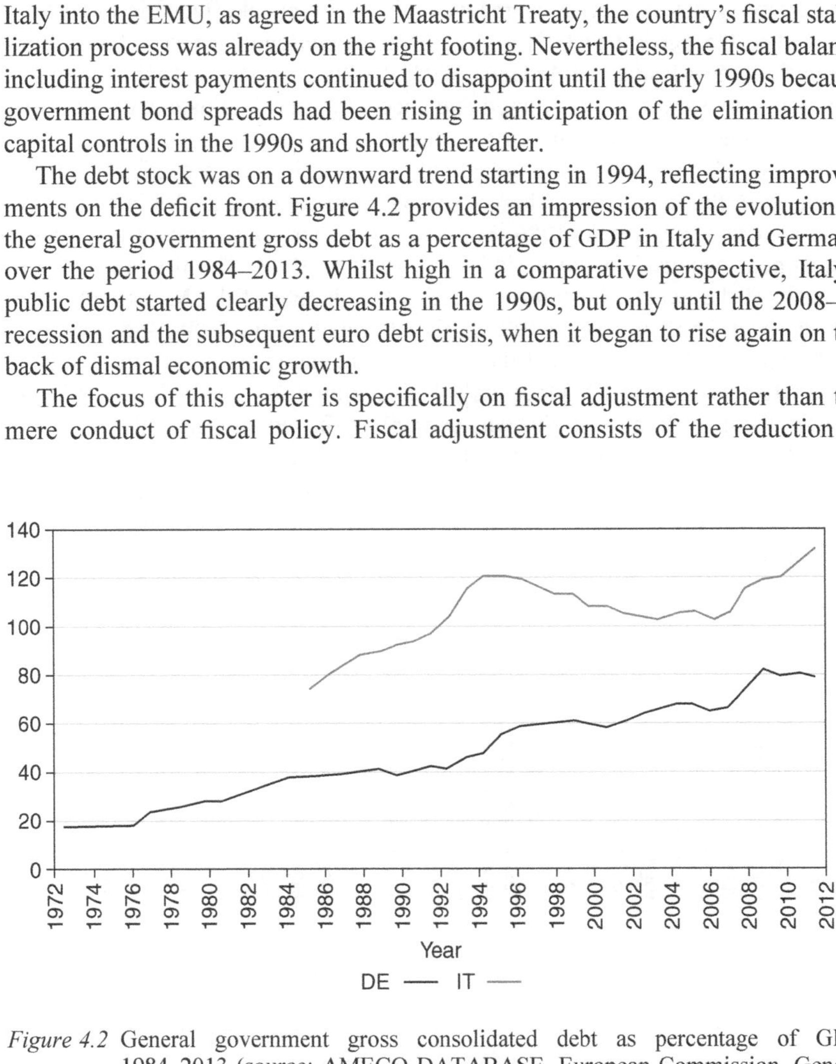

Figure 4.2 General government gross consolidated debt as percentage of GDP, 1984–2013 (source: AMECO DATABASE, European Commission. General government consolidated gross debt as a percentage of GDP at market prices (European System of Accounts (ESA) 1995 but former definition for West Germany)).

Note
DE Germany; IT Italy.

deficit levels beyond cyclical effects, hence without accounting for the operation of the automatic stabilizers. In turn, the attention is on discretionary fiscal measures implemented for the explicit purpose of achieving stabilization. Even if here fiscal consolidation is defined as the conscious effort to reduce deficits and debts, as it would emerge from existing narratives,[1] some measure of success is still needed to describe annual improvements in the balance. For illustrative purposes, a fiscal adjustment is here regarded as successful if it delivers a minimum benchmark change in the cyclically adjusted primary surplus (i.e., public lending or borrowing net of interest payments and net of cyclical effects) in the order of more than 0.5 percent of GDP in one or more consecutive years (for a similar definition, see Alesina and Ardagna 1998; Perotti et al. 1997). That way, the distinction between simply attempted and successful fiscal adjustments allows isolating the determinants of successful adjustment.

Figure 4.3 provides figures for annual changes in Italy's cyclically adjusted primary surplus since 1981. There are two consolidation episodes in 1982, 1983, and, to a lesser extent in 1986, but a much higher concentration of structural adjustment occurred in the period from 1990 to 1997. The first consolidation episode of the twentieth century preceded the signing of the Maastricht Treaty, having been implemented in 1989 in the aftermath of the 1988 Budget Reform, and after Italy had abandoned the policy of realignments within the Exchange Rate Mechanism (ERM). Once Italy had qualified for the EMU in 1997, the commitment to fiscal austerity was certainly softened and the only adjustment episodes were implemented in 2006—following the breach of the Stability Pact's target in the same year—and then in 2011 and 2012 in an effort to show to the rest of the EU Italy's commitment to discipline in the midst of the euro area debt crisis.

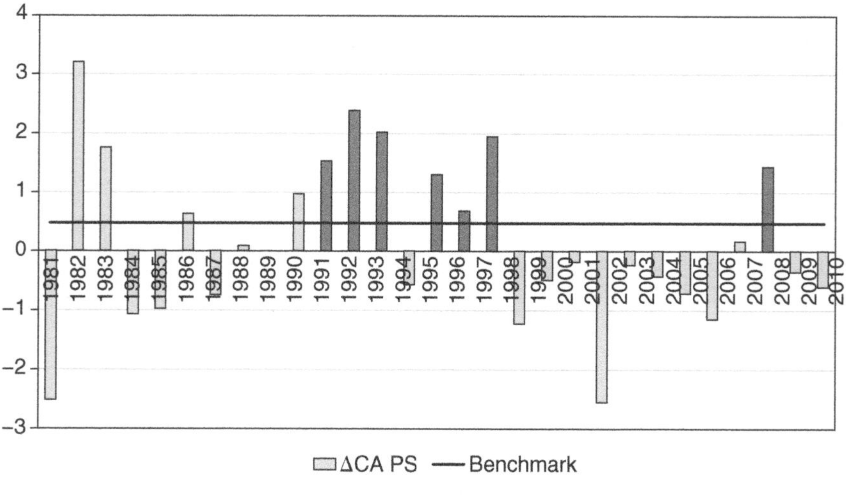

Figure 4.3 Successful, unsuccessful, and non-fiscal consolidations, 1981–2009 (source: AMECO database, DG ECFIN, European Commission and Devries *et al.* (2011). The indicator ΔCA PS is the change in the cyclically adjusted primary surplus as a percentage of GDP at market prices).

Next, fiscal consolidations identified by changes in fiscal variables are juxtaposed to adjustment episodes identified on the basis of narratives that capture authorities' explicit commitment to consolidation, independently of actual results.[2] From 1978 to 2009—the time span for which data are available—12 consolidation attempts have been identified. Table 4.1 provides figures on the size—and composition—of such episodes, reporting years in which public authorities officially committed to adjustment, and the figures for it as they appeared in official documents.[3] When juxtaposing this data with those in Figure 4.3, it is found that: (1) the adjustments in 1982, 1983, and 1986 cannot be qualified as fiscal consolidation episodes as the results are achieved independently of public authorities' commitment to do so, namely they were driven by favorable cyclical conditions; (2) successful fiscal reforms are those implemented in 1994, 1992, 1993, 1995, 1996, 1997, and 2007; (3) unsuccessful episodes are those of 1994, 1997, 1998, 2004, 2005, and 2006. The evidence therefore suggests that Italy's successful consolidation periods started with 1991 and followed for the whole European convergence process until 1996, with the exception of 1993.

An important dimension of consolidation is its composition, whether deficit reduction is mostly achieved on the revenue or the expenditure side of the budget. The quantitative literature indicates that fiscal adjustment is expenditure-based when spending cuts contribute to at least half of the total yearly deficit reduction or revenue-based if revenues increases contribute to at least half of the deficit reduction (von Hagen et al. 2001). Composition is important both because it signals distributional preferences and because an important strand of literature has suggested that expenditure-based adjustments tend to deliver superior results in terms of persistence (see, for example, Alesina and Perotti 1995). The preference for one consolidation strategy over another is likely to depend on an array of potential factors ranging from partisanship to institutions, as well as starting conditions. The insights from the existing literature are that left-wing governments would tend to

Table 4.1 Size and composition of "action-based" budget maneuvers 1978–2009 (percentage of GDP)

Year	*Δ Deficit*	*Δ Taxes*	*Δ Expenditure*
1991	2.77	1.69	1.08
1992	3.50	1.60	1.90
1993	4.49	2.00	2.49
1994	1.43	–0.27	1.70
1995	4.20	2.41	1.79
1996	0.34	–0.74	1.08
1997	1.82	0.89	0.93
1998	0.68	0.01	0.67
2004	1.30	0.67	0.63
2005	1.00	0.40	0.60
2006	1.39	0.50	0.89
2007	1.03	1.32	–0.29

Source: Devries et al. (2011).

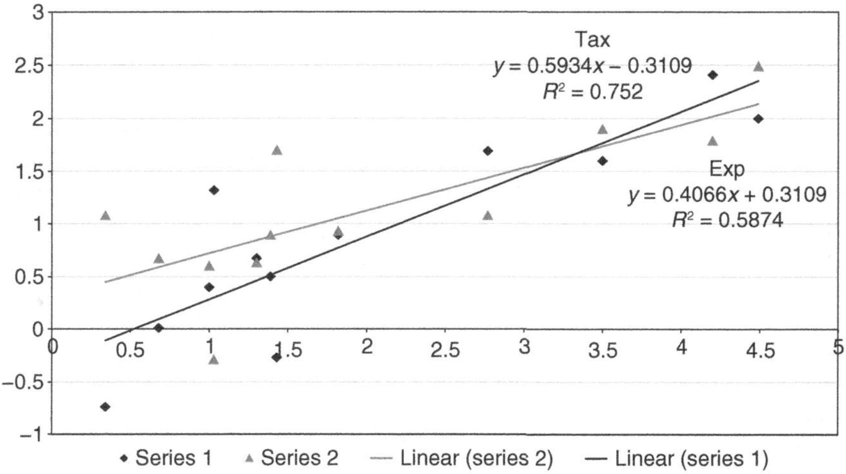

Figure 4.4 Correlation between size and composition, 1991–2007 (source: Author's elaboration based on Devries et al. (2011)).

prefer revenue-based adjustments (Fatás and Mihov 2003)—the same applies to fragmented governments and inefficient budgetary institutions where the high number of veto players makes it hard to target spending programs. Also, large deficit reductions are more revenue-based by default as most spending programs are relatively rigid. Finally, countries starting from small tax burdens tend to opt for revenue-based adjustment (Fatás and Mihov 2003). Figure 4.4 relates the size of budget maneuvers, as stated in official documents, to their composition or rather the planned change in revenues and expenditures, as stated in official documents. Obviously, the two lines are upwards sloping because a larger deficit reduction requires a larger contribution by both revenues and expenditures. It is noteworthy, however, that the correlation is stronger for the tax component (the bold line), implying that the larger the correction, the greater the reliance on the revenue side of the budget. The mechanistic explanation is that this is so because of the rigidity of expenditure programmes. Yet, as will be discussed below, in the case of Italy, there may also be a societal explanation behind the fact that large corrections mostly relied on the revenue side of the budget.

Theories of Successful Fiscal Adjustment

Theories of successful stabilization typically look at the conditions under which various kinds of constraints can be overcome. They differ, however, in that they each identify a different type of constraint, which may be of an institutional, political, or societal nature. They also differ in their view of the potential for overcoming these constraints, with some arguing that only external forces can trigger domestic change top-down, while others suggest that change may only come bottom-up from either political or societal forces that enable institutional reform and, eventually, regime change. Whilst pressures top-down or bottom-up are necessary they may not be sufficient in the presence of ill-functioning political and budgetary institutions. That is, political and fiscal institutions that either prevent or reduce collective action problems and free-riding are believed to be more conducive to successful fiscal stabilization policies.

The Role of External Pressures

In the accounts of the Maastricht convergence process that led to the introduction of the single currency, there is normally great emphasis on the importance of the commitment to the EU and EMU. Some stress the fact that fiscal discipline was imposed as a legal constraint upon which EMU membership depended. Others talk of an external constraint (or *vincolo esterno*) that supported reform efforts because national policy makers could make use of it to acquire legitimacy at home (Dyson and Featherstone 1996). Under this latter scenario, EMU-induced fiscal adjustment is more of a two-level game (Putnam 1988) by which national authorities tie their hands voluntarily in order to pave the way to efficiency-improving economic reforms.[4] But pressures may also come from markets and be fully internalized by national policy makers if they lead to the perception of an incumbent fiscal crisis of the state (O'Connor 1970).

Socioeconomic Interests and Preferences

Bottom-up explanations of fiscal adjustment emphasize the role of interests and preferences as factors that either facilitate or hinder macroeconomic adjustment. Preferences may be formed around partisanship so that governments of different ideological orientation would differ in their stance on fiscal reform (Hibbs 1977; Mulas-Granados 2006). Right-wing governments may be more interested in rigorous fiscal policy than left-wing governments, as their natural constituency sees fiscal discipline and low inflation as a means to preserve the value of financial assets. Left-wing governments would be slightly more in favor of fiscal expansion as a way to maintain full employment. At the same time, they would not fear inflationary pressures if there is a mechanism in place to defend real wages. Besides the general fiscal stance, it is likely that there are different ideological preferences concerning the composition of fiscal adjustment, as each consolidation strategy would come with a differentiated distributional impact (Mulas-Granados 2006).

Ideological preferences may go hand-in-hand with socioeconomic interests if parties of the right are representative of the owners of capital, and parties of the left are representative of wage earners. But reform coalitions are typically more complex than that. Socioeconomic interests cannot always be defined along the right-left continuum but might, for example, be more or less organized in cross-class coalitions that defend specific sectors, e.g., the export-oriented sector (Frieden 1991). There is also an institutional dimension to it because socioeconomic interests may represent veto points when they have some role in the fiscal policy making process or they are veto points because the fiscal preferences that cannot be reconciled give rise to a war of attrition that delays stabilization (Alesina and Drazen 1991). All in all, bottom-up studies normally stress the contents of fiscal preferences and try to identify the cleavages around which preferences and interests are organized.

Fiscal and Political Institutions

Fiscal institutionalism emphasizes the role of budget institutions as factors enabling fiscal reform. Strong fiscal institutions such as delegation or fiscal rules provide for better macroeconomic results than other institutional set-ups. The literature has developed composite qualitative indexes that aim to measure the relative strength of budgetary processes (Poterba and von Hagen 1999; von Hagen et al. 2001; Hallerberg 2004; Hallerberg et al. 2009).

Political institutionalism offers a similar angle but concerns the broader political system. At the core of this literature is the argument that proportional representation (PR) systems that tend to produce coalition governments are mostly associated with undisciplined fiscal behavior. In addition, in these systems, government tenure tends to be shorter, and short-sighted politicians do not have the incentive to put in place unpopular adjustment programs (Nordhaus 1975). By the same token, the proximity of a national vote—a condition more frequent where governments remain politically unstable—induces deficit spending with policy makers inclined both to increase spending and reduce fiscal pressure before an election, taking advantage of the fiscal illusion of misinformed voters (de Haan and Sturm 1994). By implication, countries with the opposite characteristics, namely majoritarian electoral systems that produce long-lived, single-party governments are deemed to be more disciplined spenders (Roubini and Sachs 1989; Grilli et al. 1991; Alesina and Perotti 1994; Alesina and Perotti 1996; Alesina and Ardagna 1998; Hallerberg and von Hagen 1997; Persson and Tabellini 1999; Poterba and von Hagen 1999; von Hagen et al. 2001). Behind these accounts is the rational-choice premise that the high number of bargaining actors creates collective action problems that make fiscal policy change extremely difficult.

Fiscal and political institutionalism has some limitations. First, they underestimate institutional choice (Iversen and Soskice 2006). Budgetary processes are often designed in a manner that reflects broader political and societal objectives. More generally, governments may well agree on budget reforms that, for example, improve centralization and thus reduce the scope for free-riding. However, they would do so only after having concurred that fiscal stabilization is a desirable output; in other words, political actors' consensus in favor of fiscal discipline precedes institutional adaptation. Second, fiscal and political institutions should not be treated separately. They are interrelated at the origins, as for example countries with proportional representation tend to have weak budgetary institutions. They also interact dynamically at each point in time; for example, they may neutralize each other, with strong politicians able to impose fiscal discipline in spite of poor fiscal institutions, or well functioning budget institutions may help ring-fence the budgetary process from political pressures, inefficiencies, or, indeed, veto points that stem from collective action problems in the political arena.

Historical Institutionalism and Macroeconomics

It is here suggested that fiscal regimes are as embedded in societies and their institutions as any other dimension of an economy. Thus, it seems plausible to study fiscal regime change from a historical institutionalist perspective. This approach has been rarely applied to macroeconomics. One notable exception is Soskice (2007), where the author explains the origins of institutional complementarities between macroeconomic regimes, labor market institutions, and the reasons why these two institutions are in a functional relationship. Whilst not explicit about the patterns of change in macroeconomic regimes, the work by Soskice (2007) is a good starting point for developing a tentative framework that explains institutional change as well.

Soskice (2007) suggests that each variety of capitalism—which is mostly defined along the nature of its domestic labor market institutions—is functionally linked with a specific type of macroeconomic regime, where the distinction is between rigid and flexible aggregate demand management regimes. So-called coordinated market economies (CME) tend to have rigid fiscal and monetary policies, whilst liberal market economies (LME) have flexible macroeconomic regimes. The explanation provided is as follows: there is a tight interaction between macroeconomic policy and labour market institutions, an idea that goes back to the corporatist literature of the 1970s, but that is developed in Soskice (2007) within a rigorous New-Keynesian macroeconomic framework. The argument is that loose fiscal and monetary policies may only coexist with decentralized wage setting systems in which there are small and numerous wage setters that are disciplined by the market. This allows fiscal and monetary authorities to open the purse strings without risking wage-price spirals and, in turn, ineffectiveness of their policy actions. By contrast, where there are few large wage setters, as in CMEs, that potentially affect inflation, fiscal and monetary regimes need be rigid to create an incentive structure in which wage setters refrain from free riding. Fiscal rigidity is preserved, for example, by the introduction of binding fiscal rules and/or by budget institutions that ring-fence fiscal policy making from political pressures—as when fiscal policy is fully or partially delegated to a strong finance minister or to an independent fiscal council.

Building on the premises of this historical institutionalist reading, four core tenets are isolated that also help account for regime change. First, as highlighted above, macroeconomic regimes should be considered as institutions themselves. Second, institutional change is informed by path-dependency and can only occur incrementally; fiscal regimes that have been typically flexible would become rigid only over time. Third, reform in one area triggers reforms in the areas that are functionally related to the reformed sector—so, for example, macroeconomic policies are tightly intertwined with labor market institutions. Fourth, for all the interlinked institutions to be eventually reformed so as to preserve the internal consistency of macroeconomic regimes, it is necessary that coordination problems are overcome, which can happen only when distributive issues are resolved and a coalition in favor of reform emerges.[5] Italy's experience with macroeconomic regime change is described with constant reference to these four analytical categories.

Historical Institutionalism Applied

Central Banking

Up to 1981, Italy was characterized by a flexible macroeconomic regime, with the Bank of Italy obliged to monetize all the public debt that was not bought at Treasury auctions. There was clear fiscal dominance, which led to intense inflationary pressures over the years, contributing to loosen real monetary conditions. This set-up was functional to putting minimal effort in public debt management: inflation was there to reduce the real value of the outstanding debt, whilst no risk of scaring foreign investors away was felt because foreigners were not interested in Italian public assets in the first place. At the same time the system was costly for competitiveness (Grilli et al. 1991), but this was typically recouped by means of successive devaluations. On the back of imported inflation, wage indexation was at the origin of price-wage spirals that further abated the real value of the stock of debt. Moreover, whilst the public debt was domestically owned, until the mid-1980s it was mostly in the hands of banks rather than households, hence the latter had no reason to fear the effects of inflation on their savings.

This setting was favorable to rapid and exponential debt growth. The strong rise in Italy's public debt started in the 1970s, mostly driven by the formation and expansion of the national welfare system, and continued through the 1980s on the back of the deep recession of the early 1980s. Moreover, public resources were also used for "political stabilization" by policy makers in the form of side payments to voters and the numerous potential veto players that animated the country's socioeconomic life. With current expenditures growing exponentially and revenues unable to keep pace, deficit and debt levels were rising without end in sight. The so-called divorce between the Italian Treasury and the Bank of Italy in 1981 interrupted the practice of monetizing large shares of public debt. This of course came with a tightening of the monetary stance. The Bank of Italy was less and less responsible for the creation of monetary base against Treasury Bills. Whilst the central bank was providing close to 50 percent of the public sector borrowing requirement just in 1970–76, this ratio dropped to 14 percent in the period around the divorce, and continued to fall, albeit slightly, in the post-reform period. The shift from an accommodating to a non-accommodating monetary regime was also evident in the evolution of real interest rates, which moved from negative to close to 4 percent in the years following the divorce (Table 4.2). Nevertheless, the end of fiscal dominance was not abrupt because the Treasury was still left with the option of expanding the monetary base through the overdraft account at the Bank of Italy, with a ceiling equivalent to 14 percent of public expenditure. This is also the period in which a secondary market for public debt became fully operational; owners of public debt were more and more households rather than banks (Tabellini 1988).

Table 4.2 Public debt and monetary aggregates

	Coefficient of deficit monetization	*Real interest rate*	*Monetary base creation*	*Overdraft*	*Rate of growth of monetary base*
1970–76	47.73	−1.27	4.72	2.73	17.7
1977–82	14.10	−1.47	1.32	4.25	16.9
1982–86	12.83	3.84	1.97	6.83	13.6

Source: Tabellini (1988): 93.

Notes
Coefficient of deficit monetization = creation of monetary base against Treasury liabilities, as a fraction of the public sector borrowing requirement; real interest rate = nominal interest rate on six-months Treasury bills minus CPI inflation rate; monetary base creation and overdraft are scaled to nominal GDP.

From being an instrument for competitiveness, fiscal discipline became a policy objective in its own right in 1983–84. The fiscal policy debate soon revolved around the identification of the most appropriate debt stabilization strategy (Morcaldo in Graziani 1988; Giavazzi and Spaventa 1989). However, observers note that the commitment to austerity remained superficial in those years. The country's high political instability and the inefficiencies in the budgetary process neutralized any attempt at correcting fiscal imbalances (Salvati 1984, 2000; Monorchio and Tivelli 1999). Failure to consolidate was even more disappointing if one considers that in the late 1980s high growth rates should have softened the recessive impact of fiscal austerity (Sartor 1998).

Labor Markets

The end to mandatory debt monetization disrupted the existing institutional equilibrium between the macroeconomic regime and labor markets and put fiscal authorities under a new hard constraint. The operation of labor markets, and in particular wage indexation, was no longer functional to the macroeconomic regime for two reasons. First, wage inflation was problematic because it undermined the country's credibility at a time when fiscal authorities had to start looking abroad to sell their debt. Second, households started to hold large amounts of government bonds. That came with the fact that aversion to inflation was slowly building in society. It is no coincidence that wage indexation was partially reformed in 1981 and 1983 to put a limit to wage-price spirals. The transformation of the monetary regime was progressively accompanied by a transformation of labor markets as well. Table 4.3 uses the same periodization adopted to account for the evolution of monetary policy and provides the number of social pacts signed between the government, the unions, and the employers over the three periods. The table indicates how many of the pacts concerned wage issues, and, in particular, provisions for changing the wage-setting system. No pact is signed in the

Table 4.3 Number of agreements to limit wage growth

	Tripartite social pacts	*Wage issues*	*Wage-setting procedures*
1970–76	0	0	0
1977–82	1	1	1
1982–86	2	2	0

Source: Visser (2013).

Notes
Tripartite social pacts = the tripartite social pact between the government, the unions, and the employers is signed in a specific year; wage issues = the pact signed is about wage issues; wage-setting procedures = the pact signed is about procedures for wage-setting (e.g., articulation of levels).

years of the loose fiscal regime, one social pact concerning wage-setting procedures is signed around the time of the divorce, and two attempting to limit wage growth are signed in the immediate subsequent period (Visser 2013). This evidence is indicative of the fact that the progressive abandonment of fiscal dominance and the ensuing need to control inflation more than ever before led to reform also in the areas that were functionally related to the monetary-fiscal policy mix.

The divorce between the Treasury and the Bank of Italy had a number of important consequences on Italy's macroeconomic regime: (1) financial markets started exercising direct influence over economic policy; (2) exchange rate stability was used to gain international credibility, with the consequence that disinflation remained the only instrument to support cost competitiveness; (3) households began to hold large amounts of public debt and to fear default and inflation; (4) wage indexation was adjusted so as to limit its inflationary potential with, to some extent, limited redistributive effects—all else equal—as wage earners had become owners of government bonds. This was a process of incrementally embracing a new culture of stability. One other effect from the change in the monetary regime was making fiscal imbalances clearly visible and fiscal authorities directly accountable (Tabellini 1988). Italy's first extensive budget reform was implemented in 1988. It was not motivated by the prospect of accessing the EMU, but stemmed endogenously from the transformation of the country's fiscal regime and the recognition that the new macroeconomic regime required supportive fiscal institutions. It is no coincidence that in the same year as the reform the Bank of Italy started a rather restrictive monetary course, which allowed the lira to remain in the ERM until the early 1990s (Giovannini 1990).

Until the late 1970s, Italy's budget process consisted of the mere elaboration of a "formal law," the so-called *Legge di Bilancio* (Budget Bill). It was termed "formal" because neither the government nor the parliament had the power to prescribe new expenditures and/or revenues. Their task was limited to acknowledging the budgetary impact of previous legislative decisions. The two oil shocks in the 1970s induced Italian public authorities to desire control capacity over public resources (Verzichelli 1999). In 1978, the country engaged in a significant restructuring of the country's public finance legislation. The 1978 Financial Law established the mandatory estimate of the net borrowing requirement within the newly created *Legge Finanziaria* (Finance Bill). In contrast to the Budget Bill, the new Finance Bill provided room for concrete fiscal interventions (and corrections). The jargon was that the older one was the "budget of bureaucracy" and the new one the "budget of politics" (Lower House, September 19, 1996).

By itself, the 1978 legislation was, however, not sufficient to guarantee fiscal discipline. Poorly designed institutional arrangements continued to compromise Italy's fiscal performance. First, the finance minister did not play a strong supervising role. Second, the parliament enjoyed extensive amendment powers over government proposals. Third, budget documents lacked transparency; this implied that efficient financial planning was compromised, with fiscal decisions being mostly taken on an incremental basis (Morcaldo 1993; Alesina and Perotti 1995; Monorchio 1996; Giavazzi et al. 1998). Fourth, the process was open to pluralist interest groups (Cotta and Isernia 1996) and public authorities were inclined to distribute public resources in areas far from traditional redistributive tasks (Ferrera 1992).

It is against this background that, in the late 1980s, a widespread consensus emerged around the need to improve the institutional foundations of fiscal policy making (Bernardi 1990). The 1988 Budget Reform emerged out of this reform process and endogenously from the fact that the macroeconomic regime had been under a piecemeal but significant transformation since the year of the divorce between the Treasury and the Bank of Italy. The reform introduced a new medium-term financial planning document as well as so-called "accompanying provisions" which contained measures in specific areas, not subject to parliamentary scrutiny, whose use would significantly speed up the parliamentary passage of the budget as they could not be amended by parliament. In addition, on August 8, 1988, the government issued a directive imposing limits on spending by the individual ministries. For the first time, spending centers were subject directly to a legal constraint. Whilst in the past limits had been imposed on expenditure items, limits were now imposed on decision makers (Bernardi 1990).

But one has to wait until the early 1990s to see institutional reforms having a concrete impact on Italy's fiscal performance. The 1988 Budget Reform started to be implemented in all its parts, so that fiscal authorities continued an incremental process of institutional adaptation. It was only after 1992 that the government required the strict application of one of the provisions contained in the 1988 Budget Law: parliamentarians, submitting an amendment to the government budget proposal, had to indicate the corresponding financial coverage for the entire period of application and not just for the following year (Degni et al. 2001). Governments in the 1990s also exploited the option of making use of the "accompanying provisions" with the purpose of ring-fencing entire sections of the budget from parliamentary amendments, thereby speeding up the approval of yearly budgets. All these measures ultimately strengthened the role of the executive over parliament and created the necessary, albeit not sufficient, conditions for Italy's successful fiscal adjustment prior to the launch of the EMU.

Political Institutions

In the theoretical debate, government instability and political fragmentation of the party system are associated with larger public deficits and debts. In the post-war period, Italy experienced the most numerous government change-overs of all OECD countries (Lijphart 1984). Fiscal imbalances were strategically employed in a war of attrition between alternating governing party coalitions, where the incumbent would purposely leave large debts to its successors. Weak, short-sighted, executives proved unable and/or unwilling to adjust public finances (Morcaldo 1993; Verzichelli 1999).

The 1990s are no exception to Italy's record of instability. In the wake of a vast institutional crisis after most politicians had been accused of corruption in the 1992 *Mani Pulite* scandals, Italy's political parties found it difficult to forge long-lasting parliamentary coalitions. Between 1992 and 1998, five different governments undertook the troublesome task of leading the country to the ambitious goal of deficit and debt reduction. Yet political instability was no constraint on the country's capacity to succeed in fiscal stabilization. The presence over those years of two technocratic governments under Ciampi in 1994 and Dini in 1995 may have reduced the scope for inter-party electoral competition. Nonetheless, two elections took place in 1994 and 1996, which could have potentially kick-started a vicious game between alternating coalitions. Still, deficit reduction was achieved—and was most intense—under the fragile multi-party Prodi government in 1996. Reform of the budgetary process and of budgetary institutions were important because they ring-fenced the budget process from the side effects of political instability; they serve the primary function of minimizing and counterbalancing the weakness of political institutions by centralizing the budgetary process around pivotal institutions (see also Fabrizio and Mody 2006).

Interestingly enough, the two smallest corrections were implemented in 1993 and 1995 under two technocratic governments, whilst the three largest deficit reductions took place under elected, and hence more legitimate, governments.[6] The regular juxtaposition of small interventions and non-elected governments is indication of the fact that the lack of an electoral base and support somehow functioned as a constraint on the size of fiscal policy measures. This suggests that sociopolitical consensus from the bottom, whether formally or informally channeled, plays an important role in Italy's adjustment.

Social Consensus for Fiscal Reform

In 1991, the year in which the Maastricht Treaty was signed, Italy was in a much different situation than it had been a decade earlier. The Bank of Italy had been on a relatively restrictive course of action for about a decade: it stood in the third year of strict adherence to exchange rate stability; it was about to be given full independent powers to set official rates, and a law in force since 1992 was to prohibit the State from financing itself by account overdrafts with the Bank. Highly politicized labour unions had accepted successive adjustments to automatic wage indexation in the 1980s, and were about to give their consent—in

1992 and 1993—to the complete elimination of automatic indexation and to a transformation of wage setting into a two-tier system that should have given a role to firm-level bargaining. Finally, following the 1988 Budget Reform, fiscal institutions were in a much better shape than they had ever been. Nevertheless, whilst the institutional environment had dramatically improved from the early 1980s, political instability was not eradicated and was more intense than ever, with five different governments—following one after the other between 1992 and 1998—during the Maastricht convergence process.

A common view of Italy's fiscal adjustment in the 1990s is that the prospect of EMU membership was sufficient to silence political struggles and interparty competition, as all contending, albeit fragile, political parties were equally in favour of bringing the country into the monetary union. There is no doubt that the "beauty contest" by which the country had to show itself fit for the monetary union had an impact on the commitment to fiscal reform and on the speed of adjustment, but the extensive fiscal stabilization of the 1990s required more than political consensus on the opportunity of adopting the euro. Possibly, even macroeconomic institutions that were significantly more efficient than they had been in the late 1970s and early 1980s, whilst necessary, may have not been sufficient. This is because of the nature of any stabilization exercise. Independently of how it is pursued, fiscal consolidation involves social costs. Inasmuch as (benevolent) governments find it difficult to distribute them evenly, deficit reduction is about the debate over which socioeconomic category should prevail. The model of reference is that of the "war of attrition" in which fiscal stabilization is depicted as a redistributive struggle between competing economic interests. Delay in stabilization entails the same costs for all; therefore the process will be unavoidably delayed when a specific social group is bound to bear a disproportionate share of the adjustment burden (Alesina and Drazen 1991). Stabilization succeeds when coordination problems between actors and institutions are solved, making it possible for the whole political economy system to move consistently towards the same objective. Seen through these lenses, Italy's successful stabilization of the 1990s would have not been possible without societal consensus over the ultimate aim—fiscal sustainability and EMU membership—but *in particular* over the distribution of the burden of adjustment.

Arguably, more fragmented and divisive societies are a less favorable context for stabilization than cohesive societies. But cross-coalition deals may also be struck on an ad hoc basis, independently of the underlying structure of the society, provided each group extracts comparable benefits from the agreement. The early 1990s have been characterised in Italy by a historically high number of social pacts. These social pacts followed from those of the 1980s and mostly included provisions on wage-setting practices and systems. At the same time, as in other European countries, tripartite pacts were implicitly tied to the broader measures that successive governments had been undertaking over those years with the more or less explicit purpose of reducing deficits and debts (Ebbinghaus and Hassel 2000; Hancké and Rhodes 2005). An important institutional aspect then was that the Italian government was obliged to consult social partners on fiscal policy issues even if not forced to take their preferences and proposals into account. Partners participating in the consultations included the Italian Confederation of Industry (CONFINDUSTRIA)—which is at the same time the employers' and the business association—and the three largest trade unions, CGIL (Confederazione Generale Italiana del Lavoro), CISL (Confederazione Italiana Sindacati Lavoratori), and UIL (Unione Italiana del Lavoro). The modus operandi was semi-corporatist in the end, prompting some observers to label Italy's adjustment in the 1990s as a perfect example of "consensual stabilization" (Cella and Treu 1998).

Besides the existence of a formal framework for the consultation of social partners, what favored social agreement on fiscal reform making it possible to overcome coordination failures between actors and institutions? The argument developed here builds on two propositions. First, in high-debt countries, reaching consensus on fiscal reform is generally easier than in low-debt countries provided the issue of financial credibility is relevant: in fact, large deficit reductions send positive signals to markets allowing for lower spreads, which implies that expenditures are cut with no distributional effects; all groups will thus tend to agree on large and "credible" deficit reductions. But also, large deficit corrections imply that, more or less, all have to pay, even if eventually the distribution of costs is not perfectly symmetric. That way, high debts foster fruitful coordination and cooperation between competing interests. Second, as the informal participation of social partners in fiscal policy making is not sufficient to deliver consensus, a compromise is to be reached over contents, hence what matters are the preferences of social partners over both the size and the composition of fiscal adjustment. Preferences may be reconcilable or not depending on the external environment. Contingent macroeconomic conditions have a bearing on fiscal preference formation. So, for example, the exchange rate regime may soften the costs of adjustment for some categories of actors, making them more compromise-prone vis-à-vis contending groups' reform proposals. The section that follows provides a description of the fiscal preferences of the societal actors that were involved in fiscal policy making in the 1990s: CONFINDUSTRIA and the three unions CGIL-CISL-UIL, which sat at the negotiating table as a single actor. Fiscal preferences are also summarized in Table 4.4.[7]

CONFINDUSTRIA was typically in favor of fiscal discipline as this was associated with small government. Behind it was the embracement of neo-liberal

Table 4.4 Ordering of fiscal preferences, 1991–97

	Employers/business	*Trade unions*
High intensity	Large deficit reduction	Large deficit reduction
Moderate intensity	Support for welfare cuts and opposition to tax rises (1995–97)	Support for tax rises and opposition to welfare cuts (1992–95)
Low intensity	Opposition to tax rises (1992–95)	Opposition to welfare cuts (1995–97)

Source: Author's elaboration based on content-analysis and interviews.

economics, and a strong belief in the crowding out of private investment by government spending. Since the late 1970s, Italian producers have been blaming the national government for jeopardizing the country's competitiveness on two fronts. First, an excessively generous and badly organized welfare state pushed non-wage labor costs upwards, of which an average of 75 percent was paid by employers. Moreover, compensation for public employees was extremely high and exercised pressure on wages in the private sector as well, through mechanisms of spill-over. Second, the Italian state had failed to provide proper infrastructure. Their inadequacy increased logistics and transportation costs to which high compliance costs had to be added as a result of various administrative inefficiencies. Whilst working against domestic producers, such deficiencies were also compromising Italy's attractiveness as a business location. In a nutshell, producers would welcome a balanced budget insofar as this signified a more efficient allocation of national resources.

The plea for a small and less interventionist government became much stronger in the 1990s with an "obsession" for international competitiveness following the intensification of competitive pressures after the planned completion of the Single European Market (SEM) in 1992. In use from the late 1970s to the late 1980s, competitive devaluations had outlived their usefulness, and Italian business grew sceptical of their capacity to generate growth in the long run. Fiscal discipline and wage moderation in the form of the elimination of the national indexation system—which had been introduced in 1975—had remained the only tools available to improve competitiveness. As to fiscal discipline, CONFINDUSTRIA thought that it was necessary to reduce public expenditures so as to create sufficient room to lessen fiscal pressure, and thus generate opportunities for private investment. With regards to wage restraint, employers believed that wage moderation would guarantee more immediate benefits than debt stabilization. By controlling inflation, slow wage growth would end up reducing interest rates, making money less costly. Easier availability of credit was not only supportive of investment initiatives and thus of economic growth as a whole, but it also exercised a positive impact on the state budget by reducing the cost of servicing the debt and potentially alleviating the output costs from fiscal consolidation. The fact that CONFINDUSTRIA represented both national producers and employers explains why wage moderation was never put forward in a vacuum but always connected to major issues, such as fiscal pressure, welfare reform, and public investment.

All in all, extensive budget consolidation was producers' most intensive fiscal preference. The Bank of Italy played a relatively smaller role in setting monetary conditions and had, in fact, proved slow in reacting, in spite of some improvement in price and wage developments after 1992. Rather, austerity was a means to lower long-term interest rates. It was believed that successful budget consolidation would send a credibility message to financial markets, which would allow for an externally induced reduction of long-term interest rates. The preferences in favor of large deficit reductions were even more intense in 1992 and 1994, when, in the wake of a vast political and financial crisis, markets turned pessimistic about the future of the Italian economy—reflected in the significant expansion of the spread between Italian and German government bonds.

CONFINDUSTRIA's second most intense preference was the support for welfare cuts, namely for an expenditure-based budget consolidation that tackled excessive spending in the areas of public employment, pension, and healthcare (Pininfarina 1992). Relatively lower primary expenditures would create room for tax alleviation,[8] thereby supporting the country's export performance.

In contrast—at least from 1992 to 1995—the opposition to higher fiscal pressure was the least intensive preference. Even if high taxes were perceived as being an impediment to competitiveness improvements, the currency regime was still providing producers with export opportunities. Whilst it is true that CONFINDUSTRIA had been conscious of the limits of competitive devaluation since the 1980s, the shift from a relatively fixed to a de facto flexible exchange rate—after the lira's exit from the European Monetary System (EMS) in September 1992—was opening up new export opportunities,[9] thereby partly muting the organization's opposition to tax increases. Most interestingly, under this currency regime, the need for rapid fiscal consolidation became an absolute priority since persistently high interest rates may have inverted the lira's trend of depreciation (Walsh 1999), reducing the initial benefit of devaluation for the trade balance. In this respect, business actors were well aware of the interlock between fiscal and exchange rate policies. After 1995, the Confederation would oppose greater fiscal pressure more strongly than in the previous years, especially when this took the form of increased social security contributions and/or direct taxes. This happened because after the revaluation of the lira at the end of 1996—a move required by the EU as spelled out in the Maastricht convergence criteria—"business-friendly" fiscal policy and structural reform had remained the only competitiveness-boosting tools available. The change in the ordering of preferences after 1995 thus confirms that compromise between socioeconomic actors was achieved because contingent macroeconomic conditions created room for an agreement and ultimately for coordination between all the actors involved.

CGIL, CISL, and UIL were interested in fiscal consolidation at least as much as CONFINDUSTRIA during the 1990s, and for similar reasons. High public indebtedness was responsible for high interest rates, which, by dampening private investment, implied significant employment costs. Budget consolidation was not only welcome as it anticipated a reduction in the cost of money, but also because it was deemed to soften inflationary pressures. Inflation was an issue to which labor unions were particularly sensitive because relatively higher inflation compromised international competitiveness with employment costs concentrated in export-oriented sectors. But also, inflation was an evil following the elimination of the national indexation system. The cancellation of the so-called *scala mobile* in July 1991, which did not occur without intense internal confrontation (CGIL, *NRS 36*, 12/10/1992), aimed to prevent the devaluation of the lira, under pressure from international speculators (CGIL, *NRS* 8, 28/9/1992), even it did not prove sufficient. But the end result was that inflation would after 1991 partly reduce workers' purchasing power in all sectors and was, as such, negatively perceived by workers' representatives. The opposition to welfare retrenchment was moderately intense. Having already had their arms twisted into wage moderation, Italian labor unions had no intention of tolerating a curtailment in welfare benefits, primarily because they had played a significant role in the formation of the national welfare state just as in other Western European countries. Whilst, in the past, they had accepted wage restraint in exchange for additional social transfers, in the 1990s unions were generally in favor of the preservation of the status quo or, when prone to compromise, in favor of welfare reform that would rationalize spending without reducing social rights. Welfare reform had to be implemented against a vision that would take sustainability into consideration (CISL, *CdL*, 30/9/1994; 24–26/9/1996); this view was mostly welcomed as a long awaited rationalization of public expenditures since it meant eliminating unjust and unfair practices locked in the system, securing greater equality (Salvati 2000; Treu 1994).

By default, CGIL/CISL/UIL supported a revenue-based fiscal consolidation; hence their least intensive preference was the fight against mounting fiscal pressure. They would insist on the need to create a more equitable tax system where the self-employed were subject to the same fiscal duties as dependent workers and where tax evasion and elusion were eradicated. While they did not oppose increases in direct taxation, if these were progressive, they were less inclined to accept a rise in indirect taxation fearing possible inflationary pressures (CGIL, *NRS 29*, 27/7/1992; CISL, *CdL*, 15/9/1992; 22/9/1992; 25/9/1992).

As to the process of preference formation, two variables seem of interest: the debt level and the currency regime. Regarding debt levels, high-debt countries seem better able to consolidate public finances than low-debt countries, especially under a short time frame. This circumstance has not gone unnoticed in previous research. There are numerous econometric calculations that show that deficits decrease in increasing starting levels, an association consistent with the "crisis hypothesis" for which fiscal consolidation is not delayed any further once all actors concerned have become aware of fact that the fiscal path is on an unsustainable path (Ardagna 2004; Alesina et al. 2006). Such an explanation is surely convincing, but does not seem sufficiently detailed. By contrast, Italy's case shows that high-debt countries enjoy a peculiar comparative advantage that is not necessarily related to the idea of a fiscal crisis.

First, when the size of the necessary adjustment is significant, the expectation is that all have to pay and this makes sacrifices acceptable to the society/electorate as a whole. In other words, there is less scope for free riding. Such a perception should be there independently of the number of actors in the society (or more strictly of those involved in the fiscal consolidation game). This implicitly indicates that the number of veto points is probably less important than initially thought and that some political institutionalist interpretations have limited explanatory power if used in isolation from the qualitative socioeconomic context in which fiscal consolidation takes place.

Second, part of the adjustment can stem from credibility gains once financial markets are persuaded by a government's deficit reduction efforts, or even by their mere announcement. During the EMU convergence process, in Italy, implicit interest rates fell by 7.2 per cent, thus allowing impressive savings on interest payments. This is confirmed by econometric calculations showing that the effects of fiscal reduction on long-term interest rates are amplified where the debt burden is large to start with (Ardagna 2004). This deficit reduction strategy does not have a tangible distributional impact and is thus fairly feasible from a political point of view.

Third, high-debt countries tend to suffer from unfavorable price and wage developments. Once market conditions change—as they did in the years in which the SEM was being completed—business actors in high-debt countries will more vehemently oppose large interest rate and inflation differentials. The Italian Confederation for Industry was strongly in favor of fiscal adjustment in the expectation that the Bank of Italy might have relaxed monetary policy, and thus contributed to more favorable investment conditions after the completion of the single market. But inflation would also damage workers after unions had agreed to give up on automatic wage indexation.

The exchange rate regime is the second macroeconomic feature that appears capable of affecting fiscal preference formation. Socioeconomic interests form their preferences after having taken tradeoffs between different policy areas into account (i.e., fiscal, exchange rate, and wage policies). For instance, where the exchange rate offers a pressure valve to preserve or even boost competitiveness, business leaders may be open to strike compromises with the unions over the composition of budgetary interventions, provided these are significant in size and such that financial markets believe that deficit reduction is really possible. Figure 4.5 shows the evolution of Italy's real effective exchange rate (REER) based on unit labor costs relative to other EU countries and to all industrialized countries that traded with Italy over 1970–2013. It is juxtaposed to Germany's REER so as to stress divergences. The adjustment has been impressive starting with 1972, driven by Italy's participation in the European Monetary System (EMS) since 1979, and by the monetary policy shift in the 1980s (Figure 4.5a). But the early 1990s were accompanied by a significant devaluation that lasted until 1995 (Figure 4.5b). Italy's industrial sector agreed to a largely revenue-based adjustment just because the depreciated lira, from September 1992 to late 1995, continued to fuel exports in spite of the rise in fiscal pressure. Reinforcing this view is the fact that all soft-currency candidates to the euro consolidated their public finances mainly relying on the revenue side of the budget (e.g., Ireland, Italy, Portugal, Greece). And greater fiscal pressure did not nullify the benefits from a depreciated exchange rate as they all posted comparatively strong export performances during those years. Moreover, the advantage of a flexible and relatively low exchange rate is more manifest where voluntary wage moderation prevents currency depreciation from creating inflation. In Italy, the elimination of wage indexation in 1992, just before the lira exited the EMS, was providential insofar as it created a domestic cushion against the risk of imported inflation.[10]

So, all in all, socioeconomic preferences had started changing already during the 1980s when a broad societal coalition against inflation slowly emerged. Once devaluation stopped being a policy option already in 1988 and after automatic wage indexation had been eliminated in 1992, socioeconomic interests were

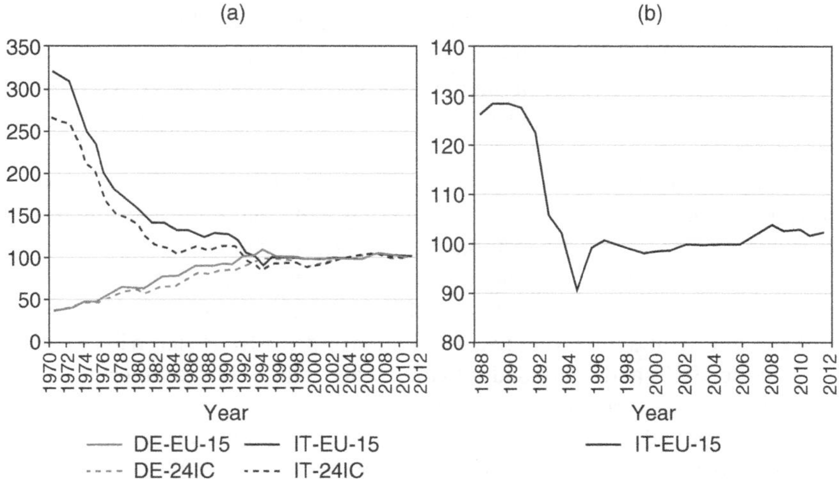

Figure 4.5 Real effective exchange rates based on unit labor costs (total economy): relative to groups of countries double export weights (2005 = 100), 1970–2013 (source: AMECO database, DG ECFIN, European Commission).

Note
DE Germany; IT Italy.

eventually allied on the need to achieve macroeconomic stability, with low inflation believed able to support not only competitiveness but also jobs and workers' purchasing power. Nevertheless, whilst consensus on the ultimate objective was there, the possibility of reaching an agreement on the distribution of the adjustment burden, that is on the composition of deficit reduction, was importantly conditioned also by contingent factors and, more specifically, by the fact that the devaluation of 1992–95 softened the opposition of business actors to (progressive) tax increases, whilst allowing unions to defend the budget's welfare chapters.

Italy under EMU

The core idea developed in this chapter is that the divorce between the Bank of Italy and the Treasury in 1981 paved the way to macroeconomic regime change, with Italy abandoning fiscal dominance, albeit not all at once, and embracing exchange rate stability and, more generally, a culture of macroeconomic stability before these became requirements imposed from outside with the 1992 Maastricht Treaty. Absent the option of monetizing public debt, the idea of a comprehensive budget reform that would make the Italian budgetary process more efficient and better able to deliver on fiscal discipline started to take shape. An extensive budget reform was in fact approved in 1988 and enforced progressively until the early 1990s, exactly at the time when Italy was faced with the challenge of meeting the fiscal convergence criteria laid down in the Maastricht

Treaty. True, the prospect of EMU membership was important in accelerating Italy's fiscal adjustment, but the results achieved in the 1990s would have not been possible without the macroeconomic regime that was initiated in the early 1980s, which also created the momentum for later reforms in areas that were not necessarily fiscal but functional to the new emerging fiscal regime, including labor markets.

Italy's performance in the post-Maastricht period offers an ideal context for testing the validity of this reading considering that each euro area member is now subject to an external constraint in the form of the Growth and Stability Pact (SGP), just as EMU candidate countries were subject to the Maastricht convergence criteria in the early 1990s.[11] If the historical institutionalist perspective is correct, one should observe a fiscal course that is mostly in line with what had started in the 1980s and continued into the 1990s, with EU fiscal rules impacting on the country's performance only at the margins.

The EMU period is one in which the momentum for adjustment appears to be interrupted, but in fact the time after 1999 implies a stabilization of the macro results achieved in the 1990s, with the deficit never plunging to the levels of the preceding decade. Whilst the presence of the SGP may be used to account for relatively contained deficit levels, it would be at the same time unrealistic and irrational for a country to flip upside down a macroeconomic regime that had been constructed over time and could rely on relatively efficient budget institutions in the period from 1999 to the euro debt crisis. This is not to deny that the SGP has helped contain deficits, but its effectiveness in imposing fiscal discipline is certainly also a function of domestic institutions. Domestically, institutional reform was not discontinued after 1999. Italy approved a new budget reform in 2009. The 2009 Reform essentially altered the structure, timing of presentation, and modes of adoption of budgetary documents. It was decided that the Economic and Fiscal Planning Document known as DPEF needed to be presented before Parliament by September 15 instead of June 30 so as to concentrate the discussion of multi-annual and annual budget documents in a shorter time span. Under the same logic, the annual budget session was restricted to just two months from October 15 through December 31 following the successful experience of other countries. So, policy learning was important but there was also clear path-dependency with the 1988 Budget Reform, whose main weaknesses were indeed addressed by the reform of 2009. The launch at the EU level of the European Semester process forced the amendment of the 2009 Budget Reform in 2011.[12] In particular, the presentation of the Economic Planning Document was brought forward to April 10 to make it possible for the government to submit to the EU both the Stability Programme and the National Reform Programme by April 30. This came directly from the EU but it was a cosmetic institutional change, not something that is likely to alter in any way the domestic political economy of fiscal stabilization.

The second institutional innovation was the Fiscal Compact signed in 2012 (formally, the Treaty on Stability, Coordination and Governance) to which EU countries agreed on a voluntary basis.[13] By ratifying the Fiscal Compact, each participating country was committing to introducing a budget balance rule either in their constitutions or an equally binding piece of law and to create independent fiscal councils. Compared with the SGP, which was in fact strengthened in 2011, the Fiscal Compact put greater emphasis on structural deficits (i.e., nominal deficit corrected for the impact of the business cycle and for one-off measures). Since 2012 the new Article 81 in the Italian Constitution makes it thus mandatory for every tier of government to achieve a balanced budget and an independent fiscal council was created to provide analysis to Parliament. Whilst the crystallization of a balanced budget rule in the Constitution is potentially revolutionary, the following weaknesses remain: (1) the new rules impose an automatic correction of deviations in the structural balance from the declared objective, but there is no automatic correction in the case of deviation of the debt ratio; (2) the rules have no memory—the first deviation is corrected automatically but if the objective is still not achieved a new correction is defined (i.e., there is no consideration of cumulative deviations over time, whether positive or negative); (3) the correction is not designed with an eye at the cycle (i.e., there is no stronger correction in good times); (4) the balanced budget does not include the balance sheets of publicly owned enterprises. Ultimately, the Fiscal Compact seems rather embedded in the institutions of Italy's political economy and informed by the opportunities and constraints that domestic institutions pose. As its operationalization varies from country to country, so should its effectiveness.

As was stressed throughout the account of Italy's stabilization in the 1990s, societal consensus in favor of fiscal discipline was strong in the early 1990s and an important success factor. Successive Italian governments signed social pacts with trade unions and employers' associations gaining their support in favor of fiscal reform. Italian unions got away with their preference for a largely revenue-based fiscal adjustment. The business and employers' association did not object to it, at least in the period from 1992 to 1995, because the competitiveness lost through tax increases was in fact more than recouped through the lira's devaluation over that period. Contingent macroeconomic conditions should also condition fiscal adjustment after 1999. Looking at the micro aspects of Italy's fiscal performance under EMU, there were a number of failed consolidation attempts: in 2004, 2005, and 2007. Fiscal adjustment was successful in 2006, probably because the country risked being sanctioned by the EU for an excessive deficit, and then in 2011 and 2012 when the deterioration of the euro debt crisis forced the new technocratic government under Mario Monti to make an extraordinary fiscal effort to gain market credibility. Generally, consensus over adjustment was more difficult to achieve than in the early 1990s, arguably for three reasons. First, at least until the euro debt crisis, there was little room for credibility gains on markets as long-term interest rates on Italian government bonds were very low to start with. Second, a massive fiscal regime change had taken place in the 1990s; in turn, the yearly adjustments necessary to comply with the Stability Pact were relatively small in size, which probably made potential distributional effects more visible. Third, there were no compensations available to losers from fiscal adjustment in the same way that devaluation had been a form of compensation in the 1990s; in other words, the war of attrition over the composition of fiscal consolidation was hard to solve. These factors may help account for the fact that three times after 1999 successive Italian governments attempted at deficit reduction plans, without succeeding.

Conclusion

In conclusion, whilst EU fiscal rules had certainly a role in directing Italy's fiscal efforts after 1999 by favoring urgent corrective measures when the deficit was in dangerous territory and by forcing some institutional adaptation, domestic factors continue to play an important role. That said, Italy is not completely immune to external pressures. Yet most of the pressure seems to come from markets, which is hardly surprising in a high-debt country. The adjustment strategy of the 1990s consisted, among other things, of a signalling game with the markets, which eventually made it possible for Italy to save on interest payments and approximate the target of a deficit below 3 percent of GDP. This tool of adjustment disappeared after 1999, a period in which Italy enjoyed historically low interest rates and the potential for credibility gains was absent. Credibility effects became prominent again only in the midst of the euro debt crisis. Sizeable deficit reductions were implemented in 2011 and 2012 when market sentiment was turning against Italy, with the potential of precipitating a fiscal crisis in a self-fulfilling manner. What this seems to suggest is that, in high-debt member countries, the market has potentially a stronger disciplining role than EU fiscal rules. Yet it comes with critical side effects: one is that it can actually force government default once pressures have become excessive and the other is that it obliges governments to choose between the market and domestic politics.

Notes

1 The reference here is to a growing body of literature that used government documents to isolate years in which the political establishment is explicitly committed to fiscal consolidation, so as to distinguish between periods in which the adjustment is (1) successful but unintended, (2) successful and planned, and (3) unsuccessful but planned, a categorization that offers degrees of freedom for assessing the true determinants of successful fiscal consolidation.

2 To systematically account for "action-based" adjustments we rely on a dataset recently developed by the IMF, which collects fiscal consolidation measures taken by the governments of 17 OECD countries to reduce deficits in the period 1978–2009 (Devries et al. 2011).

3 The year represents the year of implementation.

4 The "tying one's hands" theory is often used to explain European countries' enthusiastic embracing of the European Monetary System (EMS) project in 1979.

5 This argument is akin to those developed by rational institutionalism; in this respect, the analysis uses a hybrid historical institutionalist approach.

6 At the same time, external pressures should by no means be underestimated. Prime Minister Amato had to respond, in 1992, to a dramatic financial crisis. In 1996, Prodi aimed to secure Italy's accession to EMU.

7 The evidence has been collected on the basis of content analysis of newspapers and union confederations' newsletters and of interviews, including *Conquiste del Lavoro* (CdL), *Nuova Rassegna Sindacale* (NRS), *Financial Times*, *The Economist*, *Corriere della Sera*, *Il Mondo*, *La Repubblica* and *Il Sole 24 Ore*.

8 From a long-term perspective, producers believed that financial markets would have perceived structural reform as a sign of serious commitment to adjustment. The appreciation from financial markets would have initiated a virtuous circle, reducing the country's risk premium, and thus long-term interest rates.

9 Even government authorities recognized that the devaluation, while not intentionally induced, ended up offering some leeway (Ciampi 1996).
10 From a political economy perspective, the abolition of wage indexation can accelerate the conclusion of a political agreement on stabilization insofar as the costs of inflation result increased (Alesina et al. 2006).
11 This is not to deny the two constraints are very different in nature. Failure to convergence prior to 1999 was punished with exclusion from EMU, whilst the sanction for not complying with the SGP is pecuniary and generally easier to circumvent than the threat of being left out of the monetary union.
12 The European Semester is a cycle in economic policy coordination at the EU level characterized by a precise schedule. National governments are under the obligation to submit their European plans jointly to the European Commission by April 30 every year. These documents include the Stability or Convergence Plans, laying down each country's strategies for respecting the SGP and the National Reform Programs, which describe structural reform plans.
13 Of 28 EU countries, 25 adopted the Fiscal Compact.

Bibliography

Alesina, Alberto and Silvia Ardagna. 1998. "Tales of Fiscal Adjustment." *Economic Policy* 27, October 1998: 489–545.

Alesina, Alberto and Allan Drazen. 1991. "Why are Stabilizations Delayed?" *American Economic Review* 81(5): 1170–1188.

Alesina, Alberto and Roberto Perotti. 1994. *The Political Economy of Budget Deficits*. National Bureau of Economic Research Working Paper 4637, Cambridge, MA.

Alesina, Alberto and Roberto Perotti. 1995. *Fiscal Expansions and Fiscal Adjustments in OECD Countries*. National Bureau of Economic Research Working Paper 5214. Cambridge, MA.

Alesina, Alberto and Roberto Perotti. 1996. *Budget Deficits and Budget Institutions*. National Bureau of Economic Research Working Paper 5556. Cambridge, MA.

Alesina, Alberto, Silvia Ardagna, and Francesco Trebbi. 2006. *Who Adjusts and When? On the Political Economy of Reforms*. National Bureau of Economic Research Working Paper 12049. Cambridge, MA.

Ardagna, Silvia. 2004. "Fiscal Stabilizations: When do They Work and Why?" *European Economic Review* 48: 1047–1074.

Bernardi, Luigi. 1990. *La Finanza Pubblica Italiana. Rapporto 1990*. Bologna: Il Mulino.

Boltho, Andrea. 1992. *Il Disavanzo Pubblico in Italia. Natura strutturale e politiche di rientro*. Milan: E. Einaudi.

Bruno, Michael. 1993. *Crisis, Stabilization, and Economic Reform. Therapy by Consensus*. Oxford: Oxford University Press.

Budge, Ian and Hans-Dieter Klingemann. 2001. *Mapping Policy Preferences: Estimates for Parties, Electors, and Governments 1945–98*. Oxford: Oxford University Press.

Cella, Gian Primo and Tiziano Treu, eds. 1998. *Le Nuove Relazioni Industriali. L'Esperienza italiana nella prospettiva europea*. Bologna: Il Mulino.

Ciampi, Carlo Azeglio. 1996. *Un Metodo per Governare*. Bologna: Il Mulino.

Cotta, Maurizio and Pierangelo Isernia, eds. 1996. *Il Gigante dai Piedi di Argilla. Le Ragioni della Crisi della Prima Repubblica: Partiti e politiche dagli Anni Ottanta a Mani Pulite*. Bologna: Il Mulino.

Degni, Mario et al. 2001. *Il Riequilibrio della Finanza Pubblica negli Anni Novanta*. Siena: Monte dei Paschi di Siena.

de Haan, Jakob and Jan-Egbert Sturm. 1994. "Political and Institutional Determinants of Fiscal Policy in the European Community." *Public Choice* 80(1–2): 157–172.

Devries, Pete Jaime Guajardo, Daniel Leigh, and Andrea Pescatori. 2011. *A New Action-Based Dataset of Fiscal Consolidation*. International Monetary Fund Working Paper 11(128).

Dyson, Kenneth and Kevin Featherstone. 1996. "Italy and EMU as 'Vincolo Esterno': Empowering the Technocrats, Transforming the State." *South European Politics and Society* 1(2): 272–299.

Dyson, Kenneth and Kevin Featherstone. 1999. *The Road to Maastricht: Negotiating Economic and Monetary Union*. Oxford: Oxford University Press.

Ebbinghaus, Bernard and Anke Hassel. 2000. "Striking Deals: Concertation in the Reform of Continental European Welfare States." *Journal of European Public Policy* 7(1): 44–62.

Fabrizio, Stefania and Ashoka Mody. 2006. *Can Budget Institutions Counteract Political Indiscipline?* International Monetary Fund Working Paper 6(123): 1–49.

Fatas, Antonio and Ilian Mihov. 2003. "Fiscal Policy and EMU: Challenges of the Early Years," in *EMU and Economic Policy in Europe*, ed. Marco Buti and Andre Sapir. Cheltenham, UK: Edward Elgar.

Featherstone, Kevin. 2001. *The Political Dynamics of the* Vincolo Esterno*: the Emergence of EMU and the Challenge to the European Social Model*. Queen's University of Belfast.

Ferrera, Maurizio. 1992. "La Logica delle Scelte Pubbliche: Il Caso delle Politiche Distributive," in *Dentro la Politica*, ed. Giovanni Urbani. Milan: Il Sole 24 Ore.

Frieden, Jeffry A. 1991. "Invested Interests: The Politics of National Economic Policies in a World of Global Finance." *International Organization* 45(4): 425–451.

Giavazzi, Francesco and Luigi Spaventa. 1989. *High Public Debt: The Italian Experience*. Cambridge: Cambridge University Press.

Giavazzi, Francesco, Alessandro Penati, and Guido Tabellini. 1998. *La Costituzione Fiscale*. Bologna: Il Mulino.

Giovannini, Alberto. 1990. *The Transition to European Monetary Union*. Princeton, NJ: Princeton University Press.

Grilli, Vittorio, D. Masciandaro, and G. Tabellini. 1991. "Political and Monetary Institutions and the Public Financial Policies in Industrialised Countries." *Economic Policy* 13: 342–392.

Graziani, Augusto, ed. 1988. *La Spirale del Debito Pubblico*. Bologna: Il Mulino.

Haggard, Stephen and Robert R. Kaufman, eds. 1992. *The Politics of Economic Adjustment: International Constraints, Distributive Conflicts, and the State*. Princeton, NJ: Princeton University Press.

Hall, Peter A. and David Soskice. 2001. *Varieties of Capitalism: The Institutional Foundations of Comparative Advantage*. Oxford: Oxford University Press.

Hallerberg, Mark. 2004. *Domestic Budgets in a United Europe: Fiscal Governance from Bretton Woods to EMU*. Ithaca, NY: Cornell University Press.

Hallerberg, Mark and Jürgen von Hagen. 1997. *Electoral Institutions, Cabinet Negotiations, and Budget Deficits within the European Union*. Centre for Economic Policy Research Discussion Paper No. 1555, London.

Hallerberg, Mark, Rolf Rainer Strauch, and Jürgen von Hagen. 2009. *Fiscal Governance in Europe*. Cambridge: Cambridge University Press.

Hancké, Bob and Martin Rhodes. 2005. "EMU and Labor Market Institutions in Europe: The Rise and Fall of National Social Pacts." *Work and Occupations* 32(2): 196–228.

Hibbs, Douglas A. 1977. "Political Parties and Macroeconomic Policy." *American Political Science Review* 71(4): 1467–1487.

Iversen, Tobern and David Soskice. 2006. "New Macroeconomics and Political Science." *Annual Review of Political Science* 9: 425–453.

Lijphart, Arend. 1984. *Democracies: Patterns of Majoritarian and Consensus Government in Twenty-One Countries*. New Haven, CT: Yale University Press.

Monorchio, Agostino. 1996. *La Finanza Pubblica Italiana dopo la Svolta del 1992. I Nodi strutturali ed istituzionali della politica di bilancio del nostro paese: approfondimenti e proposte*. Bologna: Il Mulino.

Monorchio, Agostino and Luigi Tivelli. 1999. *Dove Va l'Italia? Democrazia, Economia e Stato Sociale*. RAI-ERI.

Morcaldo, Giancarlo. 1988. "Le Politiche del Bilancio e del Debito Pubblico," in *La Spirale del Debito Pubblico*, ed. Augusto Graziani. Bologna: Il Mulino.

Morcaldo, Giancarlo. 1993. *La Finanza Pubblica in Italia (1960–1992). Il Ruolo e le Dimensioni del Settore Pubblico nell'Economia Italiana dell'Ultimo Triennio. Analisi e linee di riforma*. Bologna: Il Mulino.

Mulas-Granados, Carlos. 2006. *Economics, Politics and Budgets: The Political Economy of Fiscal Consolidations in Europe*. London; New York: Palgrave Macmillan.

Nordhaus, William D. 1975. "The Political Business Cycles." *Review of Economic Studies* 42: 169–190.

O'Connor, James. 1970. *The Fiscal Crisis of the State*. Piscataway, NJ: Transaction Publishers.

Perotti, Roberto, Rolf Strauch, and Jürgen von Hagen. 1997. *The Sustainability of Public Finances*. Centre for Economic Policy Research Discussion Paper No. 1781, London.

Persson, Torsten and Guido Tabellini. 1999. "The Size and Scope of Government: Comparative Politics with Rational Politicians." *European Economic Review* 43: 699–735.

Pininfarina, Sergio. 1992. *L'Impegno dell'Industria tra l'Italia e l'Europa. Discorsi e interventi in quattro anni di presidenza Confindustria 1988–1992*. SIPI.

Pisauro, Giuseppe. 2003. *The Central State Budget Process in Italy*. Bologna: Prometeia.

Poterba, James M. and Jürgen von Hagen, eds. 1999. *Fiscal Institutions and Fiscal Performance*. Chicago: Chicago University Press.

Putnam, Robert D. 1988. "Diplomacy and Domestic Policies: The Logic of Two-Level Games." *International Organization* 42: 427–460.

Roubini, Nouriel and Jeffrey Sachs. 1989. "Government Spending and Budget Deficits in Industrial Countries." *Economic Policy* 8: 99–132.

Salvati, Michele. 1984. *Economia e Politica in Italia dal Dopoguerra ad Oggi*. Milan: Garzanti.

Salvati, Michele. 2000. *Occasioni Mancate. Economia e politica in Italia dagli Anni Sessanta ad oggi*. Rome: Laterza.

Sartor, Nicola. 1998. *Il Risanamento Mancato. La politica di bilancio italiana 1986–90*. Rome: Carocci.

Sestito, Paolo. 2002. *Il Mercato del Lavoro in Italia. Com'è. Come sta cambiando*. Rome: Laterza.

Soskice, David. 1990. "Wage Determination: The Changing Role of Institutions in Advanced Industrialised Countries." *Oxford Review of Economic Policy*, 6(4): 1–23.

Soskice, David. 2007. "Macroeconomics and Varieties of Capitalism," in *Beyond Varieties of Capitalism*, ed. Robert Hancké, Martin Rhodes, and Mark Thatcher. Oxford: Oxford University Press, 89–121.

Tabellini, Guido. 1988. "Monetary and Fiscal Policy Coordination with a High Public Debt," in *Surviving With a High Public Debt: Lessons from the Italian Experience*, ed. Francesco Giavazzi and Luigi Spaventa. Cambridge: Cambridge University Press.

Thelen, Kathleen. 2004. *How Institutions Evolve: The Political Economy of Skills in Germany, Britain, the United States, and Japan*. Cambridge: Cambridge University Press.

Traxler, Franz, Sabine Blaschke, and Bernhard Kittel. 2001. *National Labour Relations in Internationalised Markets*. Oxford: Oxford University Press.

Treu, Tiziano. 1994. "Procedures and Institutions of Income Policy in Italy," in *The Return to Income Policy*, ed. Ronald Philip Dore, Robert Boyer, and Zoe Mars, 161–174. London: Pinter.

Verzichelli, Luca. 1999. *La Politica di Bilancio*. Bologna: Il Mulino.

Visser, Jelle. 2013. *Database on Institutional Characteristics of Trade Unions, Wage Setting, State Intervention and Social Pacts in 34 countries between 1960 and 2012.* Amsterdam Institute for Advanced Labour Studies.

von Hagen, Jürgen, Andrew Hughes Hallett, and Rolf Strauch. 2001. *Budgetary Consolidation in EMU*, European Economy—Economic Papers 148, Directorate General Economic and Monetary Affairs (DG ECFIN), European Commission.

Walsh, J. 1999. "Political Bases of Macroeconomic Adjustment: Evidence from the Italian Experience." *European Journal of Public Policy* 6(1): 66–84.

5 Explaining Japan's Fiscal Performance

Why has it Become an Outlier?

Masayuki Takahashi and Takaharu Shimada

Introduction: Taking Distinctiveness Seriously

Japan's public sector debt has reached an unprecedented level (Figure 5.1). After a 20-year rise, outstanding general government debt has surpassed 200 percent of GDP, making Japan a clear outlier among major industrialized countries.

What is behind Japan's chronic deficits and accumulating level of public debt? This is the central question that we deal with in this chapter. This is not an easy task; conventional theories of fiscal outcomes do a poor job of explaining the Japanese case. Looking at Japan's fiscal performance in a snapshot, one might assume that drastic changes in institutions or political behavior must be behind the major turn in fiscal outcomes during the 1990s, namely the rapid increase in government debt. In reality, the essential characteristics in Japanese fiscal policy making have largely been unchanged, and we argue that political lock-in of these patterns is in fact behind Japan's current fiscal dilemma.

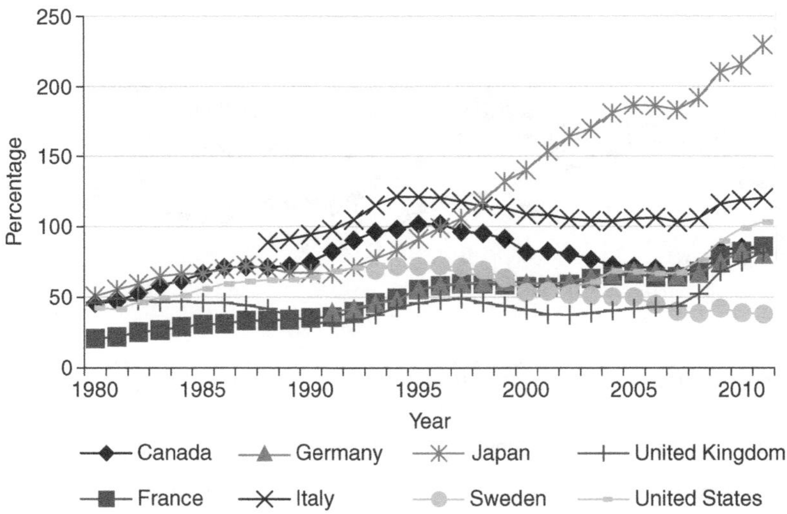

Figure 5.1 General government gross debt outstanding (percentage of GDP) (source: IMF, *World Economic Outlook*).

Focusing on the Japanese case, this chapter attempts to contribute to our understanding of fiscal performance by illuminating political and institutional factors that have not often received adequate attention in the existing quantitative studies on fiscal consolidation. Our analysis highlights the underlying historical and institutional context in explaining Japan's fiscal pattern.

In section 2, we discuss limitations of the existing literature in explaining Japan's fiscal performance since the 1990s, by looking at the role of party politics, electoral reform, and reforms to budget making institutions. Sections 3 and 4 focus on two enduring historical institutional factors which have had a decisive impact on long-term fiscal performance to date: the evolution of close coordination between fiscal and financial policies in and after the 1990s and the historically entrenched pattern of Japanese taxation and budget expenditures. Section 5 concludes by identifying the implications of the Japanese case for future studies on the determinants of fiscal performance.

Fiscal Trend and Explanatory Factors

Fiscal Trend

Japan's level of public expenditure has been low although it has been expanding recently (Figure 5.2). Despite Japan's limited government size, it is the most heavily indebted nation.

The Japanese government has made three concerted efforts at fiscal consolidation in recent decades. In the 1980s, the government pursued spending cuts with the slogan of "fiscal consolidation without tax increase." This strategy succeeded

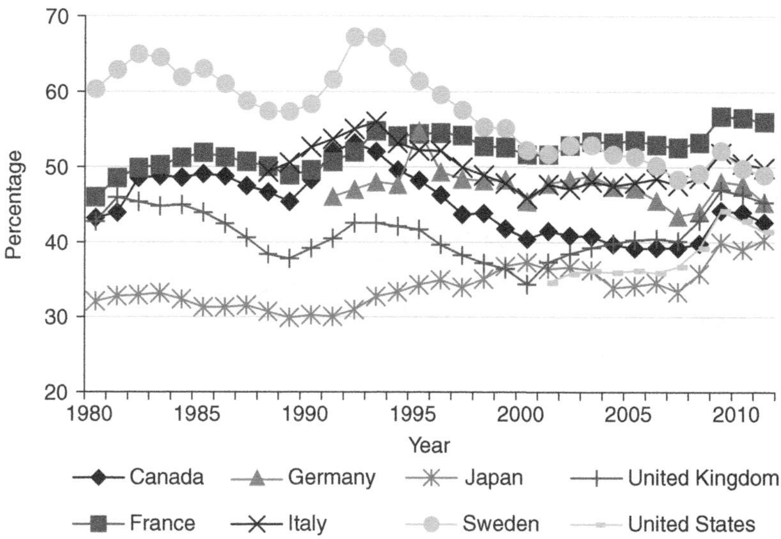

Figure 5.2 General government expenditure (percentage of GDP) (source: IMF, *World Economic Outlook*).

partly, allowing the government to cover general current account expenditures in 1990 without bond issues.[1] After the bubble economy collapsed in 1991 and Japan's fiscal condition deteriorated, there was a second attempt at fiscal consolidation in the late 1990s. This time, the VAT (referred to as the "consumption tax" in Japan) rate was raised from 3 to 5 percent, but an attempt to introduce rule-bound fiscal consolidation ended in failure shortly thereafter. The third period of consolidation began in 2001 and lasted until 2006 under the Koizumi administration. Koizumi focused on slashing expenditures, which resulted in a moderate decline in both general government expenditure relative to GDP (Figure 5.2) and central government (general account) expenditure (Figure 5.3).

Looking at the overall trend of revenue and expenditure, the problem appears to be on the revenue side (Figure 5.3.) Although there was a steady increase in spending in the 1990s, the pace of expenditure increase was roughly in line with or below that of the successful consolidation period in the 1980s. Furthermore, spending declined as a share of GDP from 2001 to 2006, reflecting the aforementioned austerity under Koizumi administration.

On the revenue side, the downward trend has been clear and consistent. In terms of budget balance, revenue shortfall was the main contributor to ballooning debt. Although the decline of tax revenue was partly due to prolonged recession starting in the early 1990s, it should be noted that tax reduction measures (mainly in individual and corporate income taxes) were repeated during this period with no major attempt to increase revenue throughout the decades after 1990. Even the introduction of the VAT in 1989 and upward revision of its rate in 1997 (from 3 to 5 percent) were accompanied by reductions in individual and corporate income taxes. In recent decades, the government consistently failed or

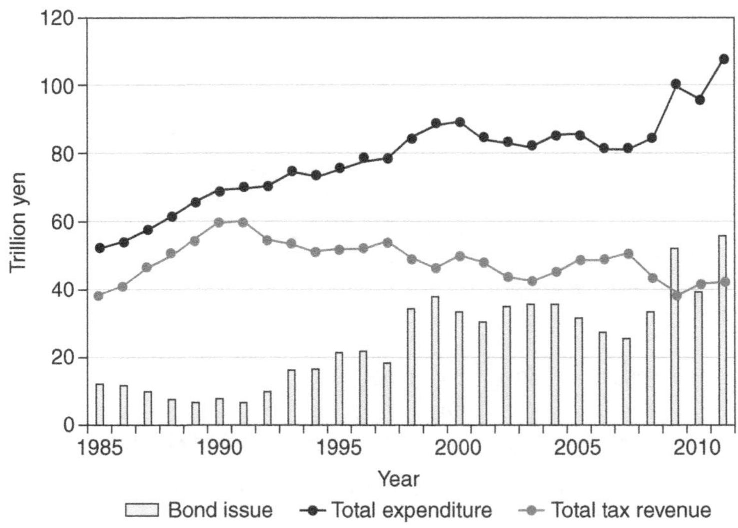

Figure 5.3 Fiscal trend of the central government (general account) (source: Japanese Ministry of Finance).

avoided to raise enough revenues to finance its relatively modest level of expenditures.

While revenue growth has been stagnant, demand for social security and welfare provision has grown significantly in recent decades. Demographic change—especially the rapid aging of the population—has driven increases in expenditures for welfare programs. As shown in Figure 5.4, Japan had the least aged population among major countries until the 1970s, but exhibited the highest pace of aging ever since, becoming the country with the most aged population in the late 2000s. This demographic shift has pushed up expenditures for public pension benefits, medical care, and elderly care services.

The decline of the fertility rate has made the situation worse. The fertility rate plunged to the lowest level among countries (Figure 5.5), hitting bottom at around 1.25. The decline of the share of working age population is not only a problem for social insurance plans but also for economic growth.

Demography, however, is only part of the story. Just as in other industrialized countries, job and income insecurity (caused in part by a stagnant economy but also labor market deregulation) and diversification of the composition of households (more people living alone, single-parent households, or households with aged people only) resulted in the prevalence of various forms of "new social risk."

Although these are tendencies commonly observed in industrialized countries, their impact stands out in Japan. The poverty rate rose to levels close to that of the United States. Rapid aging of the population (i.e., the decline of the share of working people) only partly explains this trend, as poverty is prevalent regardless of age category (Table 5.1.) The economic situation of the working age population worsened substantially. Furthermore, income insecurity of workers,

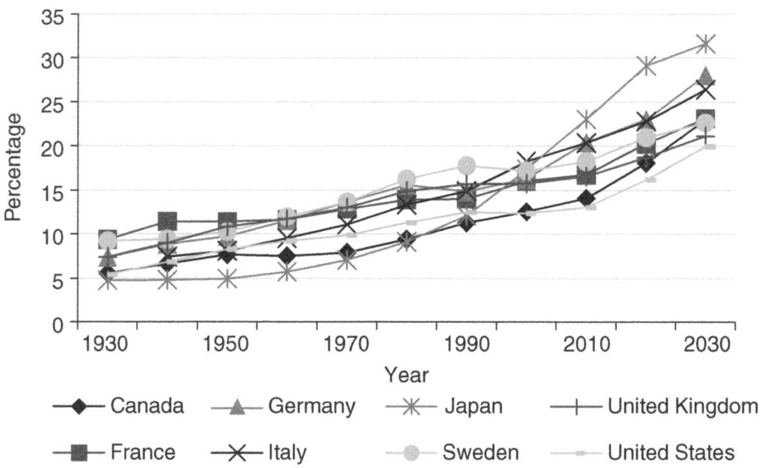

Figure 5.4 Share of population aged 65+ (source: Kokuritsu Shakai Hoshou, Jinkou Mondai Kenkyusho (National Institute of Population and Social Security Research), Jinkou Toukei Shiryoushuu (Population Statistics Factbook)).

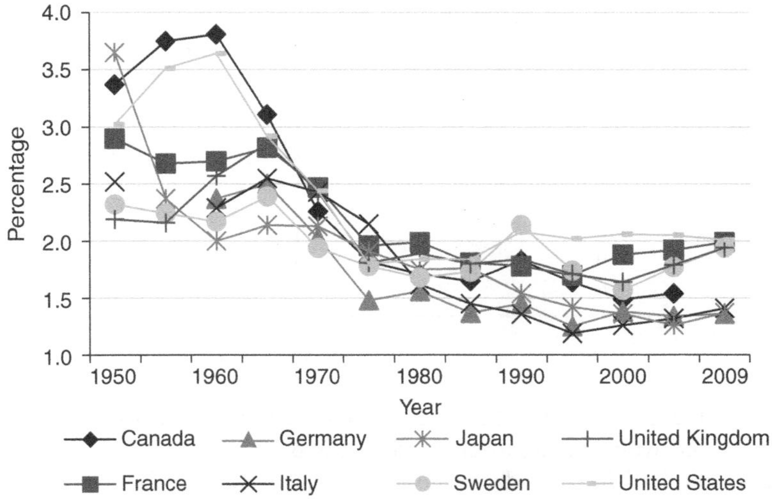

Figure 5.5 Total fertility rate (source: Kokuritsu Shakai Hoshou, Jinkou Mondai Kenkyusho (National Institute of Population and SocialSecurity Research), Jinkou Toukei Shiryoushuu (Population Statistics Factbook)).

Table 5.1 Poverty rate (disposable income), by age category (around 2000)

	Age category		
	65+	*18–64*	*Total*
Canada	4.3	10.3	10.3
France	10.5	6.0	7.0
Germany	8.5	9.2	9.8
Italy	15.3	11.5	12.9
Japan	21.1	13.5	15.3
Sweden	7.8	5.1	5.3
United Kingdom	14.4	8.7	11.4
United States	24.6	13.7	17.1

Source: OECD, Social Expenditure Database and Family Database.

many of whom are parents, contributed to growing child poverty. More than half of single-parent families in Japan live below the poverty line (Table 5.2.).

The last two decades have witnessed a growing public perception of the worsening situation. The public demand for social policy intensified especially in the mid-2000s. It culminated in an overwhelming victory of the Democratic Party of Japan (DPJ) in the 2009 lower house election, terminating the dominance of the conservative Liberal Democratic Party (LDP) since the 1950s (interrupted only by a non-LDP administration in 1993–94, which did not last for a year.) The reluctance of the LDP-centered coalition government to respond to social issues,

Table 5.2 Poverty rate of individuals living in families with children (disposable income, the mid-2000s)

	All households with children	*Lone-parent*	*Two parents*
Japan	12.5	58.7	10.5
United States	17.6	47.5	13.6
Canada	12.6	44.7	9.3
Germany	13.2	41.5	8.6
Italy	14.3	25.6	14.0
United Kingdom	8.9	23.7	6.1
France	6.9	19.3	5.8
Sweden	3.6	7.9	2.8

Source: OECD, Family Database.

especially in the 2000s under the Koizumi administration, led to this upset, something no one would have expected a decade ago.

However, the DPJ largely adhered to the persistent policy mix of financing the government without increasing tax. At the 2009 election, they claimed to improve welfare provision not by taxing more but slashing expenditure items with lower priority. After having failed to secure adequate fund through expenditure cuts, they turned to raising the consumption tax rate, against their election promise. The government formulated a "Combined Reform of Social Security and Tax" proposal, which passed the legislature in 2012. Although the reform was presented as the revision of the consumption tax rate (from 5 to 8 percent in 2014, and to 10 percent in 2015) to raise revenues needed to improve social security programs, a major part of the accruing additional revenue was planned to be allotted for debt reduction. This move by the DPJ to raise consumption tax rate received a strongly negative public perception and helped the LDP regain overwhelming majority in the 2012 general election.

The LDP administration led by Shinzo Abe further diluted the original intention of the Combined Reform by increasing public works spending and planning to lower the effective corporate income tax rate from the current 38.01 percent to less than 30 percent. As for improving budget balance, they rely heavily on the possibility of economic recovery by so-called "Abenomics," consisting of extraordinary monetary easing with expansionary fiscal policy (and market deregulation measures, most of which are yet to materialize). Thus the rare revenue-enhancing measure of the aforementioned consumption tax revision seems likely to end up as a compensation for corporate income tax reduction and expansionary public works spending, not for fiscal consolidation or upgrading welfare provision.

In sum, the recent decades have witnessed a relative emphasis on controlling (especially social, not public, works) expenditures and less focus on revenue enhancement, despite growing demand for a larger government role in meeting social needs. This is the overall fiscal pattern that we seek to explain. Before elaborating on the question, we examine the Japanese case in light of existing literature on fiscal performance.

Political and Institutional Factors

Studies on the determinants of fiscal performance have identified a number of key political and institutional factors. To what extent are they relevant to understanding the Japanese case in recent decades?

First, there was a significant change in partisan politics in the 1990s. The dominance of the conservative LDP, since the mid-1950s, ended in 1993 when a broad coalition of non-LDP parties was able to build a ruling coalition. This was an epochal political change. The LDP recovered, but since then have been unable to maintain a majority without forming coalitions with moderate or in some cases left parties.

Multiple studies have suggested that coalition governments are more prone to expansionary fiscal policy than single-party governments (e.g., Alesina and Perotti 1995, Persson et al. 2007). The rapid development of a budget deficit in Japan in the 1990s under coalition governments seems to fit in with this pattern. However, it should be noted that budget deficits started to expand before FY1994, when the budget was passed by the non-LDP coalition government. As for the composition of fiscal expansion and consolidation, no government—be it LDP-led or not—resorted to tax increases to finance expanded expenditures or correct budget imbalance until the very recent decision to raise the VAT rate from 5 to 8 percent in FY2014. In sum, partisan politics did not have a clear impact on Japan's fiscal policy pattern.

Second, there was a major reform in the parliamentary election system. Lower House (House of Representatives) members had been elected in multiple-member districts (non-transferable vote) until 1994, when it was replaced by a combination of single-member districts and proportional representation (in which 62.5 percent of the members are elected by single-member districts). The first election under the new system took place in 1996.

As summarized in the introduction of this volume, the findings of comparative studies on the effect of electoral systems on fiscal discipline have been mixed. As far as the Japanese case is concerned, however, Estévez-Abe (2008) argues that the old multiple-member district system had led to political fragmentation by giving candidates incentives to respond to particularistic (local and business) interests. This argument conforms to the conventional view that a single-member district system promotes a centralized party system, making party goals more important than the particularistic interests of candidates and reducing the number of competing parties through winner-take-all elections. In fact, the reform in Japan was motivated by such a logic. Centralization of decision-making could have increased the likelihood of successful fiscal consolidation. What in fact happened?

The electoral reform certainly changed the political landscape. It triggered the merger of opposition parties, culminating in the formation of the DPJ in the 2000s, which then ruled from 2009 to 2012. Both the conservative LDP and new center-left DPJ attempted to develop a more centralized intra-party decision making structure, which might plausibly have enabled them to pursue fiscal consolidation more easily.

The outcome, however, was not clear-cut. Among the three government fiscal consolidation packages mentioned in the beginning of this section, the second one was attempted in 1997 by an LDP administration (in coalition with two small, center and leftist parties). They enacted a Fiscal Structural Reform Law ("Zaisei Kouzou Kaikaku Hou") with a long-term debt reduction target. However, within a year, the another conservative LDP administration, after the replacement of the Prime Minister Ryutaro Hashimoto by Keizo Obuchi, effectively cancelled the law and turned back to massive public works projects to mitigate the negative impact of the Asian financial crisis.

The third episode of consolidation, again under an LDP administration with Prime Minister Junichiro Koizumi, was relatively successful as they managed to constrain expenditures mainly in the area of public works, social security and welfare, and transfers to local governments. It should be noted that Koizumi, backed by high popularity, succeeded in the centralization of the budget making process by utilizing the newly created Council on Economic and Fiscal Policy (CEFP), which was established in 2001. With the prime minister as the chair, key cabinet members, the president of the central bank (Bank of Japan, BOJ), representatives from the corporate sector, and academics as members, the CEFP discusses and formulates the basic policy direction for the budget.

There are debates over the extent to which this institutional change facilitated fiscal consolidation efforts under the Koizumi administration. Indeed, the Koizumi administration, which lasted from 2001 to 2006, utilized the CEFP effectively in slashing expenditures. He successfully mobilized the mandate of CEFP to set baseline general account primary balance fiscal targets, to articulate policy directions, and to protect the budget making process from particularistic demands from LDP backbenchers to some degree. Institutional reforms from the late-1990s aimed at enhancing the power of the cabinet vis-à-vis bureaucracy enhanced his leadership. However, we cannot make easy generalizations. While centralization should have had an effect on fiscal outcomes, since the turn of the century there has been considerable variation (Figure 5.6). The economic downturn from the global

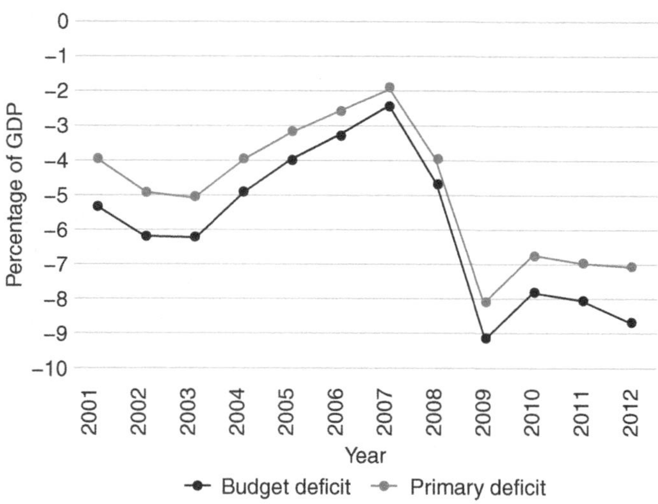

Figure 5.6 Budget balance, consolidated central government (source: Japanese Cabinet Office).

financial crisis (GFC) obviously affected budget management after 2008, and no decisive conclusion can be drawn about the impact of the centralizing effect of CEFP and other provisions on fiscal performance within the limited time span of its existence, especially since some subsequent cabinets abandoned using the CEFP.

We should take into account the fact that informal practices, rather than formal institutions such as CEFP, continue to affect the degree of centralization or fragmentation in policy making. In post-war Japanese politics, informal ties between the cabinet, bureaucracy, and ruling party have functioned as the core mechanism of policy making. Iio (2004) depicts this close relationship between the cabinet, bureaucracy, and the ruling party (which has long been LDP) as consisting of two aspects. First, the "bureaucratic cabinet system," in which cabinet members act more as agents of ministerial bureaucracies than of the prime minister. Second, the "dual system of government and ruling party," in which the ruling party retains considerable power by being allowed to intervene in the policy making process. These aspects point to the weakness of the cabinet vis-à-vis bureaucracy and the ruling party politicians in policy making. These characteristics were nurtured during more than 30 years of LDP dominance in post-war Japanese politics and have become a firmly entrenched tradition.

In this respect, the Koizumi administration was exceptional. He retained high popularity throughout his term, and that enabled him to overcome bureaucratic and political resistance. He gained popular support by fiercely accusing traditional LDP politicians (although he was from the LDP himself) of sticking to particular, personal, interests and blocking policies in the collective interest of citizens. He advocated neo-liberal goals, such as cuts in redistributive spending. In this way, he had relative success in restoring some degree of fiscal discipline.

However, after Koizumi's departure in 2006, for subsequent LDP administrations, the relative influence of the prime minister and cabinet eroded, due mainly to declining popular support and loss in parliamentary seats. In addition, when the DPJ became the ruling party in 2009, they focused heavily on concentrating policy making power in the cabinet but failed both to contain party influence and do away with dependence on the bureaucracy. This implies that although there have been some centralizing reforms in formal institutional arrangements, whether the leader in office successfully overcomes political opposition still depends much on the strength of his popular support base.

To summarize, the Japanese case is not necessarily inconsistent with some existing theories of fiscal performance, but as the foregoing discussion suggests, existing theories do not fully account for Japan's rapidly rising debt. The following sections draw attention to two distinct aspects in the Japanese case. One is the evolution of fiscal and monetary policy since the 1990s, which mitigated the danger of fiscal crisis and allowed the government to rely on debt financing. The other is a distinct pattern of fiscal and social policy mix that emerged in the high growth period from the 1950s to the early 1970s. This mix greatly affected the choice of fiscal policy tools and weakened the ability of the government to maintain fiscal balance in the following decades. We also suggest that the fact that recent fiscal management tended to concentrate more on restraining expenditures than enhancing revenue—while failing to meet social needs—should be understood within this historically specific institutional context.

Debt Financing and Management after the 1990s

Overview

Japan enjoyed high economic growth from the mid-1950s to the early 1970s, with average annual growth around 10 percent. Even after the Nixon shock and two oil crises in the 1970s, the Japanese economy enjoyed steady growth until the end of the 1980s (Figure 5.7). After a short-lived asset and stock market bubble in the late 1980s collapsed, the Japanese economy fell into severe recession in the 1990s. The balance sheets of financial institutions turned red with huge amounts of non-performing loans and depreciating collateral; some financial institutions, including major banks, went bankrupt in the mid- and late 1990s. Furthermore, this crisis coincided with increasing competition from Japan's Asian neighbors. Major manufacturers, which used to boast their international competitiveness, faced stagnant domestic demand and cost competition from other Asian countries.

Such severe circumstances compelled the Japanese government to react to three major challenges. First, the government used expansionary fiscal policy to respond to long-lasting economic stagnation. In the 1990s, the government launched several major fiscal stimulus packages, the common core of which was large-scale public works spending financed by bond issues. Expansionary monetary policy by the central bank (BOJ) complemented fiscal stimulus.

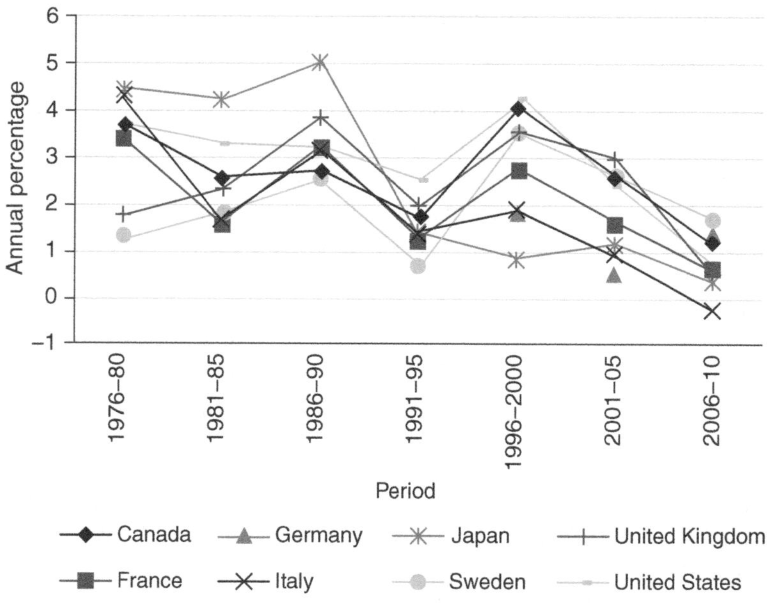

Figure 5.7 Nominal GDP growth rate (source: OECD.Stat).

Second, the moribund financial sector had to be revived by forcing banks to dispose of bad assets through painstaking restructuring and government assistance. Despite government efforts, it took more than a decade for banks to restore their balance sheets.

Third, fiscal conditions deteriorated as tax revenues shrank due to recession and expenditures (especially capital expenditures) rose in the 1990s. As already mentioned, however, the government did not attempt to enhance revenue but repeatedly reduced taxes, mainly those on individual and corporate incomes. Tax reductions were legitimized as a part of fiscal stimulus, even though the deficit was rapidly growing with no reasonable prospect of full economic recovery.

Put simply, the government reacted to a dire economic situation with a policy mix of public works spending, tax reduction, and monetary easing. How could such a policy mix be sustained financially? The simplest answer is that the government succeeded in keeping the long-term interest rate extremely low, which made it easier for the government to borrow massively. As shown in Figure 5.8, the long-term interest rate on Japanese government bonds has consistently been lower than that of other major economies throughout decades. It stands out as an exceptional case in the sense that a worsening fiscal balance commonly pushes up the interest rate. Italy in the 1990s (see Chapter 4 in this volume), for example, could never resort to excessive debt financing since it would have inevitably resulted in an interest rate hike and harmed fiscal sustainability. Thus budget consolidation was the only viable choice in the case of Italy. So how was it possible for Japan to keep the long-term interest rate exceptionally low, without successful fiscal consolidation?

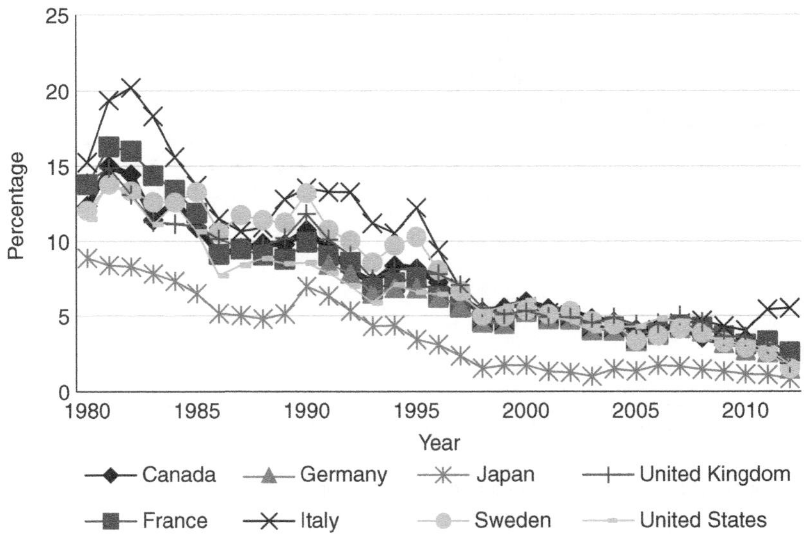

Figure 5.8 Long-term interest rate on government bonds (source: OECD.Stat).

Creation of Favorable Environment

There are four keys to solving this puzzle. First, since the first half of the 1990s, the private non-financial sector maintained a financial surplus—see Figure 5.9. Consequently, it was highly unlikely that any increase in government spending would hinder private investment and thereby raise the interest rate.

The second key is the development of the financial market. A low interest rate environment, the introduction of stricter accounting standards (e.g., BIS regulations), and the absence of safe investment alternatives all encouraged the holding of government bonds as a low-risk asset by private financial institutions (including the Postal Savings Bank, which used to be a public corporation until the mid-2000s). The global financial crisis also helped keep long-term interest rates low by creating the flow of money to safer assets.

The third key is the bond holding structure of the financial market. On one hand, as Table 5.3 demonstrates, the foreign holdings of government bonds are low. Thus, a Greek-style crisis with foreign investors dumping bonds is very unlikely in Japan. Domestic financial institutions, holding large amounts of public bonds as safe assets on their balance sheets, do not want the price of bonds to decline rapidly. Accordingly, domestic institutional bondholders and the government have a common interest in keeping interest rates low and stable.

The fourth key is the existence of governmental entities—the Fiscal Investment and Loan Program (FILP) and the BOJ—that play a significant role in absorbing public bonds (Kimura 2013). The FILP is a "government-run financial system that mobilizes and allocates savings in the form of investments and loans that serve public policy purposes" (Park 2011). Before its fundamental reform was implemented in April 2001, funds from postal savings and public pension reserves were transferred to the Trust Fund Bureau Fund (TFBF) controlled by the Ministry of Finance. The government used the TFBF extensively to absorb

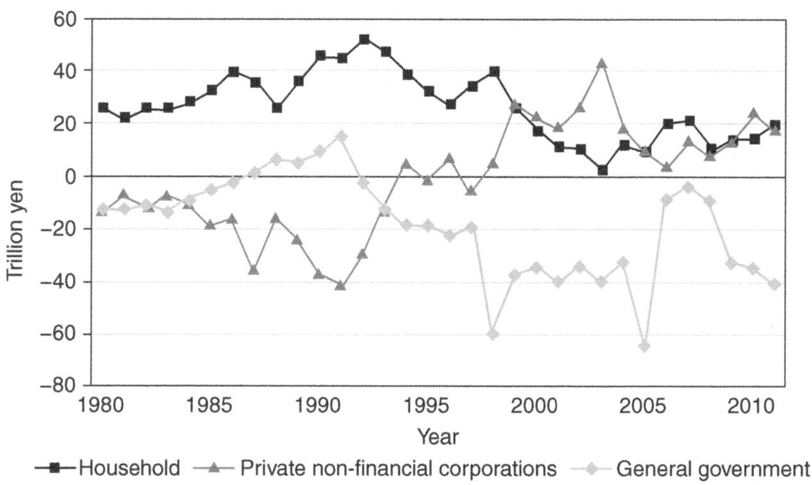

Figure 5.9 Financial surplus/deficit by sector (source: Bank of Japan (www.stat-search.boj.or.jp)).

Table 5.3 Holders of national government bonds (end of June 2013)

Holder		*Bond held (trillion yen)*	*Percent of total*	*Percentage change from preceding year*
Financial intermediaries		604	62.3	–3.9
	Institutions for SME lending	169	17.4	–4.4
	Insurance companies	189	19.5	5.3
	Domestic banks	137	14.2	–14.2
	Pension funds	31	3.2	5.1
General government and public financial institutions		95	9.8	2.5
	Of which; public pension	69	7.1	1.8
Bank of Japan		150	15.4	55.5
Overseas		81	8.4	–0.4
Household		23	2.4	–15.3
Others		17	1.7	7.7
Total		969	100.0	3.0

Source: Bank of Japan, *Shikin junkan toukei: sankou zuhyou* (Money Circulation Statistics (2nd Quarter of 2013), reference tables).

Note

Postal Savings Bank is included in ‘Institutions for SME lending.’ ‘Others’ consists of non-financial private corporations, non-profit bodies, etc.

public bonds. In 1989, the TFBF held 39.6 percent of total domestic government bonds.

The FILP reform in 2001 disconnected postal savings and public pension reserves from FILP. The TFBF was reorganized as the Government Investment and Loan Fund and shrunk substantially from 77.3 trillion yen in 2000 to 23.9 trillion yen in 2006. The decreased government bond absorption, however, was partly offset by direct bond purchases by the Postal Savings Bank and the public pension system.

Meanwhile, the BOJ adopted a quantitative easing policy (hereafter QE) in April 2001 and started to purchase huge amount of public bonds.[2] As Kimura (2013) notes, the BOJ operation effectively compensated for the downsizing of FILP. The amount of public bonds held by the BOJ increased from 47.7 trillion yen in 2000 to 92.1 trillion yen in 2004. Although the BOJ ended its first QE in March 2006, the basic policy pattern did not change. The BOJ continued to support the purchase of newly issued government bonds by private banks and investors, by absorbing public bonds with less liquidity in open market operations.

Furthermore, as a means to combat prolonged recession after the recent international financial crisis, in conjunction with Prime Minister Abe's economic policy ("Abenomics"), the BOJ decided to ease monetary policy further by implementing quantitative and qualitative monetary easing (QQE) in 2013.[3] The amount of public bonds held by the BOJ grew by 55.5 percent, compared to the same quarter of the preceding year, and reached 15.4 percent of the total bond holdings in the financial sector in June 2013 (Table 5.3). It should be noted that as the BOJ purchases more public bonds, it increasingly shares a common interest with domestic institutional bondholders and the government for smooth absorption of public bond issues. The BOJ has increasingly become closer to a policy instrument of the government, rather than an independent monetary authority.[4]

The combination of macroeconomic and financial market conditions, the availability of policy finance tools (FILP), and mobilization of the central bank for debt management created an environment highly favorable to debt financing in the 1990s and thereafter. Whereas the debt growth in this period has certainly been a concern for the government, they did not face up to the need to rebalance the budget.[5] Instead, they successfully created financial market conditions that allowed for massive debt financing by employing policy finance and central banking.

Fiscal Policy Pattern, Welfare Regime Type, and Institutions

Japanese Welfare Regime Reconsidered

The core suggestion of this chapter, to articulate again, is that we cannot explain Japan's unprecedented degree of indebtedness in and after the 1990s adequately if we focus only on the political and institutional factors emphasized in the existing literature. As already discussed, although electoral and institutional reforms appear to have changed the political landscape, the extent and durability of fiscal consolidation efforts remained limited. Even under the strong leadership of the Koizumi administration, the government only managed to restrain expenditures and left the issue of inadequate revenue untouched. The end of the Koizumi administration marked a return to massive debt financing.

The discussion above identified two key aspects of Japan's fiscal path in and after the 1990s, namely, the continuous failure to enhance tax revenue in spite of its clear necessity, and the ability of the government to create a debt-friendly financial environment by mobilizing policy finance (FILP) and the BOJ. These aspects are closely connected to each other and have deep roots in the postwar evolution of Japan's fiscal and social policy.

Borrowing from Esping-Andersen's conceptualization of welfare regime types (Esping-Andersen 1990), Japan can be viewed as liberal in terms of its modest social expenditures, but conservative in such aspects as the prevalence of a "male-breadwinner" family model with relatively persistent familism, and occupation-based social insurance schemes. In a similar vein, Japan has been categorized as part of an "East-Asian model," characterized by small social spending, emphasis on economic development and important role of family in welfare delivery (Goodman and White 1998; Kwon 2005).[6] In other studies, Japan has been referred to as a "construction state" (Kitayama 2003). In this framework, regional redistribution of wealth by means of public works projects (rather than redistribution by income strata by means of progressive taxation and welfare provision) is regarded as the core of the Japanese welfare regime.

These formulations depict certain features of Japan's fiscal policy pattern. However, they do not adequately explain the origins of the Japanese model. In this sense, the work by Estévez-Abe (2008) is noteworthy as it not only identified public works spending, selective industrial policy, and corporate welfare for employees as "functional equivalents" of public provision of social protection, but offered an explanation that heavily emphasizes electoral incentives, offering what she calls a "structural logic approach" (Estévez-Abe 2008).

Building on this work, others have explored the connection between Japan's welfare model, its fiscal policies, and high level of debt. By tracing the evolution of fiscal politics and policies in postwar Japan, Ide (2012) argues that the erosion of tax consent (or growing tax resistance) among the middle class, the largest potential source of tax revenue, is the biggest factor behind huge public debt accumulation in contemporary Japan. Park and Ide (2014) identifies Japan's postwar "tax-welfare mix" as the root cause of Japan's weak extractive capacity and indebtedness. More specifically, they argue that this mix has three interlocking pillars: an underdeveloped formal welfare state, a tax system with targeted tax reductions as part of its system of social protection, and redistributive public investment. The following discussion draws on their framework, albeit with varying points of emphasis.[7]

Entrenchment of Basic Policy Pattern

Viewed historically, two basic elements of institutional and political context have been critical to Japan's fiscal evolution. First, in postwar Japan, the concept of "budget balance" was regarded by politicians and bureaucrats alike as referring only to the general account of the national budget. This habitual understanding originates from fiscal austerity imposed in the postwar occupation period (so-called "Dodge Line"), which strictly required a balanced budget within the general account of the national government. This led to the proliferation of special (earmarked) accounts and the extensive use of the FILP, which was established in 1953. The FILP provided loans to government affiliated financial institutions and public investment corporations, and they implemented concessional loan programs for SMEs, small farmers, the individual purchase of houses, and infrastructure projects. The extensive use of the FILP was the key to maintaining general account balance and pursuing selective industrial policy, social protection, and infrastructure provision simultaneously.

Since the annual plan of the FILP was formulated by the Ministry of Finance (MOF) in parallel with the budget proposal, its use was closely coordinated with the tax-financed budget. As a policy instrument that did not rely on taxes, there was a strong incentive for the government to use FILP extensively (Park 2011).

Second, under high economic growth from the mid-1950s to the early 1970s, the government repeatedly reduced the individual income tax by revising the tax code almost every year. Conservative LDP-led governments worried about a rapid rise in the progressive income tax burden as income levels kept rising as a consequence of rapid economic growth. The policy was also intended to encourage individual economic self-sufficiency by allowing middle-class citizens to retain enough disposable income. With a booming economy, the government could enjoy substantial natural increases in tax intake in spite of continual tax reductions. It should also be noted that the low individual income tax burden not only allowed people have higher disposable income and the government to minimize social expenditures, but that it also contributed to high household savings, a substantial part of which were absorbed by postal savings and transferred into FILP.

These two aspects of Japan's tax and social policy helped form a distinct policy pattern in high growth periods. Funds poured into FILP, tax revenues for the general budget increased naturally, and the government emphasized infrastructure development and the provision of concessional policy loans for both economic and social purposes. Furthermore, income tax cuts supplemented modest formal welfare provisions. This was the core of the fiscal mechanism behind the Japanese welfare regime.

With regard to debt financing, the role of the FILP and the BOJ should be highlighted. The MOF not only controlled the FILP directly, but also retained a relatively strong position vis-à-vis the BOJ, exerting influence on the BOJ's operations. Ever since the government started issuing bonds in the latter half of the 1960s, the FILP and BOJ were mobilized to absorb bonds (Kimura 2013).

Following the Oil Crisis in 1973, Japan faced significant social and economic challenges, including an economic downturn and rising demand for formal welfare. Japan was on the verge of transitioning to a European-style welfare state with high social expenditure, but it never materialized. The growth of tax revenue slowed down, and the government was unable to raise the income tax on a population heavily accustomed to tax reduction.

Concerned with limited tax revenue and obsessed with restoring general account balance, politicians and bureaucrats had strong incentives to utilize the FILP, which could fund public works and loan programs but not current expenditures, such as welfare (especially care services) programs. The 1970s witnessed the intensification of pork-barrel politics with the government relying heavily on FILP to finance it. As a result, the FILP grew more rapidly than tax-financed budget expenditures including social spending (Figure 5.10).

The mobilization of the off-budget FILP only partly made up for on-budget expenditure needs, so the budget deficit soared in the latter half of the 1970s (Figure 5.11). The government faced strong opposition to increasing individual income taxation, and the business sector increasingly resisted corporate income taxation under volatile economic conditions. As a consequence, discussion of a general consumption tax, essentially a VAT, emerged on the agenda in the late 1970s. In 1978, Prime Minister Ohira announced his general consumption tax plan, but was forced to withdraw it in the face of opposition. It was, however, too late to avoid a bitter defeat in a lower house election, after which Ohira resigned.

This political setback paved the way for a new formula and political slogan in the 1980s: "fiscal consolidation without tax increase." To give a full picture of politics behind this policy shift, however, we must take a close look at the position taken by the business sector around this period. Corporate income tax rate had been revised upwards in 1970 and 1974 mainly to compensate for the loss of revenue due to individual income tax cuts. As economic conditions deteriorated after the Oil Crisis, Keidanren (Keizai Dantai Rengoukai), the peak-level big business association, increasingly demanded a corporate income tax cut and implicitly supported the introduction of a general consumption tax.[8]

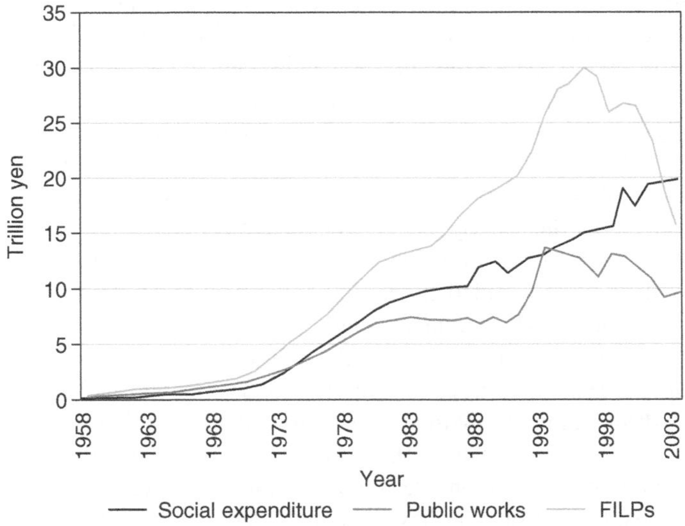

Figure 5.10 Annual outlays of public works, social expenditure, and FILP (source: Japanese Ministry of Internal Affairs and Communications, Statistics Bureau).

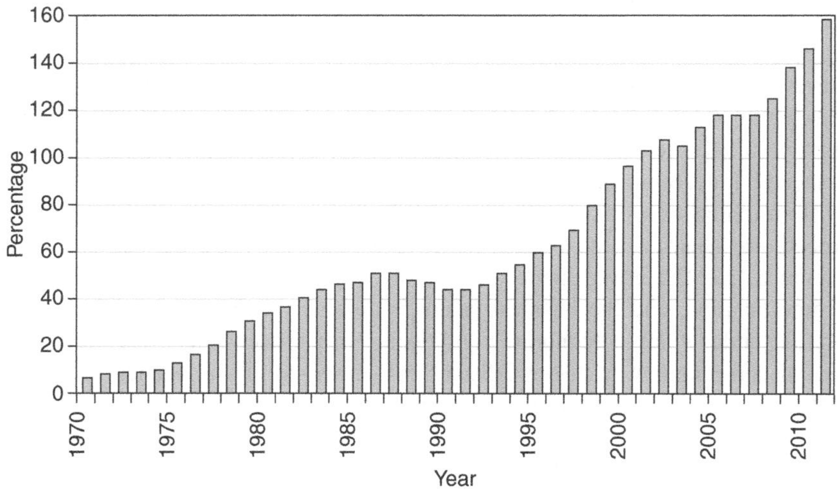

Figure 5.11 National government long-term debt outstanding, as percentage of GDP (source: Japanese Ministry of Finance).

However, given the failure to introduce a general consumption tax and persistent public resistance to the individual income tax burden, MOF had no choice but enhance corporate income taxation which, as a result, reached the statutory rate of 43.3 percent, the highest in postwar Japan to date, in 1984. "Fiscal consolidation without tax increase" was the product of the compromise between the government and the business sector. In return for accepting the increased corporate tax burden, the former chairman of Keidanren was appointed to the chair of the Provisional Council for Administrative Reform (Rinji Gyousei Chousakai) with the task of public sector rationalization and spending cuts. It was in the first report of this council that the phrase "fiscal consolidation without tax increase" was officially used (Ishi 2008, 348–349.) The council formed the baseline of measures to slash expenditures in the 1980s by proposing such major reforms as the restructuring of pension and medical insurances and privatization of state-run enterprises, including the heavily indebted national railways.

The 1980s witnessed an entrenchment of the basic pattern of Japanese fiscal policy. Tax hikes were avoided time and again because of strong tax resistance.[9] The FILP and BOJ were increasingly mobilized to absorb public debt, which was a clear precedent for how the domestic bond market structure developed in the 1990s and beyond (Kimura 2013). General budget expenditures were restrained mainly by limiting social welfare spending[10] and offloading capital expenditures to the FILP. All these efforts, combined with a favorable economic environment, resulted in a smaller general account deficit in the late 1980s, but the same policy pattern created huge deficits in the 1990s onward as depicted in the previous sections of this chapter.

To summarize, the efforts to maintain fiscal discipline (in the general account of the national budget) throughout the decades leading up to the 1980s created a distinct institutional context and policy pattern, which ironically tended to induce fiscal indiscipline later. The ever-worsening fiscal performance in and after the 1990s is deeply rooted in this historical development of institutions and policies.

Erosion of Tax Consent

The policy development described above also had a long-term impact on state–society relations, that is, the erosion of tax consent (Ide 2012; Takahashi 2012; Park and Ide 2014).

Public opinion in contemporary Japan captures this problem. Taro Miyamoto cites the result of an opinion survey in his discussion on welfare politics in Japan. The survey, conducted in 2007, asked two questions. One was about the future direction of Japanese society: 58.4 percent of respondents chose "welfare society like in Nordic states," while 31.5 percent of them chose a "society centered in lifetime employment protection like Japan in the past." A mere 6.7 percent wanted a "competition- and efficiency-centered society like the United States." However, when the same respondents were asked how to finance government provisions of services and benefits, only 17.8 percent of them answered "we should accept an increase in the consumption tax rate," while 46.4 percent answered "we should reduce tax burden by the restructuring of government activities" (Miyamoto 2009). In other words, people demand improved social policy but are unwilling to bear the burden for it.

This pattern is more than the impulse of wanting more for less. Cross-national surveys show that more middle-class citizens feel that their tax burden is heavy in Japan than in other countries with a higher tax burden. Japanese taxpayers believe that they are taxed heavily, although they are actually not (Ide 2011).

There are a number of potentially plausible explanations, though they need to be tested further. To mention one, there is a perception among Japanese people that they are not getting enough for what they pay in taxes. Rational choice theorists have emphasized the importance of this link between taxation and public services (Lindert 2004; Timmons 2005). One implication is that small governments, which leave services to markets and individual households, face a dilemma in gaining tax consent from their citizens. The fact that fiscal performance (in terms of budget balance) is relatively better in Nordic countries with "big governments" (see Chapter 7 in this volume) than in countries like Japan and the US with small governments suggests support for this argument.

In the Japanese case, however, the current situation is more complex than what this snapshot comparison tells us. There has been a long history in Japan that has contributed to a very powerful form of fiscal illusion. Utilizing the off-budget FILP for infrastructure provision, the development of financial market structure highly favorable for large-scale debt financing, and continual tax reductions have reduced the perceived costs of the benefits they receive from public services.

Another promising research avenue could focus on the relationship between patterns of social policy types (i.e., universalism and selectivism), social trust among people, political trust, and tax consent. Some argue that the universal provision of welfare benefits nurtures tax consent since it covers a broader population, whereas selective social protection divides society: upper- and middle-class populations receive little but low-income populations benefit with little or no tax burden (Rothstein 1998; Steinmo 2010). Furthermore, selectivism tends to hinder social trust (the strength of trust among citizens) and trust in government, because targeting welfare benefits to low income citizens entails discrimination and cannot correct income inequality effectively (Korpi and Palme 1998; Rothstein and Uslaner 2005). On the other hand, Hinnfors (2008), elaborating on this work, points to fact that the key for tax consent is not just the distinction between universalism and selectivism, but the sense of fairness that a certain social policy arrangement may nurture or hinder.

In light of these discussions, the "tax-welfare mix" in postwar Japan could have had strongly negative long-term impacts on the tax consent of citizens (Park and Ide 2014). Pensions and medical insurance schemes have long been based on occupational categories with different levels of benefits and contributions. It has triggered a deep sense of unfairness but no effective reform has materialized to date, as the divisiveness of the system itself created conflicting interests between people covered by different insurance schemes. Family benefits, childcare, and elderly care services have long been relatively selective. Attempts were made in recent decades to make them more universal, but lack of funds has limited improvement in coverage, and an emphasis on the role of the family in providing domestic care persists as a legacy of prolonged domination by the conservative LDP (Takahashi 2012). Thus, the combination of tax-cutting, small government, and selective, discriminatory welfare provisions has likely contributed to a state–society relationship characterized by low tax consent and more demand for services.

Conclusion

What we find in Japan in the last two decades is the deterioration of fiscal performance, observable not only quantitatively as ballooning deficit but also qualitatively with the erosion of tax consent. Currently, Japan has not succeeded in getting out of a vicious circle. Historically entrenched institutional settings and policy patterns support debt financing and allow the government to circumvent tax resistance. This, in turn, results in further erosion of tax consent. Inability to tax not only adds to fiscal stress but also makes fundamental policy change harder. Thus institutional and policy patterns exhibit strong "institutional stickiness" (Pierson 2001).

That is not to say that there has been no meaningful change in recent decades. We have already discussed electoral reform and reforms to centralize the budget making process. As for fiscal policy tools, the FILP was reduced significantly in size and the postal savings corporation was privatized in 2007. This change has effectively limited the possibility of off-budget funding of infrastructure projects and the absorption of public-issued bonds. One consequence, however, is heavier reliance on the BOJ's operations in both stimulating the economy and absorbing public debt. We can see this pattern in the BOJ's latest monetary easing as part of Abenomics (as already discussed in section 3 of this chapter.)

Another sign of change can be found in the recent decision to raise the consumption tax. The rate was raised from 5 to 8 percent in April 2014, and may be raised further to 10 percent in April 2017. With the record-high deficit and ever more pressures from financial markets, the consumption tax increase is increasingly perceived as inevitable by politicians, bureaucrats, business sector, and the general public.

However, a question remains as to whether these two episodes imply significant changes in Japan's historically entrenched fiscal policy patterns. Restructuring of the FILP and heavier reliance within the paradigm on the BOJ's operations seem to represent a shift but not a departure from it. If the consumption tax rate is raised to 10 percent, it will be a result of reluctant acceptance by the public threatened by the looming fiscal crisis and by the business sector supporting consumption tax increase to enable reductions in corporate (tax and social insurance) burdens, not of tax consent based on people's perceptions of the benefit from public expenditures or trust in government.

Thus, in a short run, we do not see a fundamental break from the fiscal and social policies that have contributed to Japan's high level of debt. Although the ongoing changes may be signs of "gradual transformation" leading to future discontinuity (Streeck and Thelen 2005, 8–9), any significant departure from the enduring, debt-prone fiscal policy patterns would likely be triggered by factors external to political institutional arrangements, such as the increasing financial market risk or the deepening mismatch between societal needs and policy responses.

Notes

1 In Japan's central government budget, there is no distinction between current and capital budget. There is the "general account" for tax-financed items, and numerous "special accounts" for specific programs with earmarked source of funds, such as public pension, public works, transfer to local governments, etc. See also section 4 of this chapter.

2 The QE was implemented from March 2001 through March 2006 to combat deflation. See Ugai (2007).

3 For details, see *Introduction of the "Quantitative and Qualitative Monetary Easing"* (www.boj.or.jp/en/announcements/release_2013/k130404a.pdf).

4 This has happened in spite of BOJ reform in 1997, which enhanced BOJ's independence from the government. It can be viewed as another case in which the impact of changes in formal institutional settings was effectively nullified by informal political processes.

5 It should also be noted that the situation faced by Japanese government in this period obviously differed from that in euro area countries because of the existence of the conversion rule in the latter.

6 Peng (2005) argues that the concept of the developmental welfare state (welfare state in East Asia) can offer only a partial explanation of the recent development of the Japanese welfare state (welfare expansion in the 1990s).

7 See Ide (2012), Kimura (2013), and Park and Ide (2014) for more detailed treatment of discussion here.

8 Keidanren did not openly support the introduction of a general consumption tax because such a move by the business interest group would likely have provoked public demand for an increased corporate tax burden (Keidanren 1999, 112).

9 In contrast to the period up to the mid-1980s, even the corporate tax rate has been revised downward multiple times in the latter half of the 1980s and thereafter. Throughout the period, the only significant exception was a temporary provision of special corporate income tax earmarked for rehabilitation projects after the great earthquake in 2011. A growing concern for international competitiveness and prolonged recession were the two main factors behind the trend.

10 In the 1980s, the government adopted the slogan of "Japanese Welfare Society" with emphasis on the role of the family in care provision. The slogan appeared first in the late 1970s and had served as a rationale for a number of reforms, mainly in the areas of individual income taxation and old-age pension scheme, with the clear intention to reinforce the male-breadwinner family model. In retrospect, the government's effort for the "re-familialization" (as opposed to "de-familialization") of the welfare regime in the 1980s, despite such irreversible trends as rapid population aging, diversification of family structure and the rise of dual-earner families being already evident, created the basis for the lagging social policy development from the 1990s to date.

References

Alesina, Alberto and Roberto Perotti. 1995. "The Political-Economy of Budget Deficits." *International Monetary Fund Staff Papers* 42(1): 1–31.

Esping-Andersen, Gøsta. 1990. *The Three Worlds of Welfare Capitalism.* Cambridge: Polity Press.

Estévez-Abe, Margarita. 2008. *Welfare and Capitalism in Postwar Japan.* New York: Cambridge University Press.

Goodman, Roger and Gordon White. 1998. "Welfare Orientalism and the Search for an East Asian Welfare Model." In *The East Asian Welfare Model: Welfare Orientalism and the State*, edited by Roger Goodman, Gordon White, and Huk-Ju Kwon. New York: Routledge.

Hinnfors, Jonas. 2008. "The Puzzling Lack of a Social Dilemma." *Scandinavian Political Studies* 31(1): 69–90.

Ide, Eisaku. 2011. "Chowa no toreta shakai to zaisei" (Harmonized Society and Public Finance: Applying Social Capital Theory to Fiscal Analysis). In *Kokyo suru shakai: "Jiritsu to chowa" no seijikeizaigaku* (Creating a Harmonious Society: Political Economy of Social Configuration), edited by Eisaku Ide, Tau Kikuchi, and Tau Handa. Kyoto: Nakanishiya Shuppan.

Ide, Eisaku. 2012. *Zaisei akaji no engen* (The Origins of Government Deficit). Tokyo: Yuhikaku.

Ide, Eisaku and Sven Steinmo. 2009. "The End of the Strong State? On the Evolution of Japanese Tax Policy." In *The New Fiscal Sociology: Taxation in Comparative and Historical Perspective*, edited by Isaac William Martin, Ajay K. Mehrotra, and Monica Prasad, 119–137. New York: Cambridge University Press.

Iio, Jun. 2004. *Zaisei katei ni okeru nihon kanryousei no futatsu no kao* (Two Faces of Japanese Bureaucracy in Fiscal Process). RIETI Discussion Paper Series 04-J-007. Tokyo: Research Institute of Economy, Trade, and Industry,.

Ishi, Hiromitsu. 2008. *Sengo zeisei kaikaku shi* (Postwar History of Tax System). Tokyo: Toyo Keizai Shinpo Sha.

Keidanren (Keizai Dantai Rengoukai). 1999. *Keizai dantai rengoukai goju-nenshi* (Fifty-Year History of Keizai Dantai Rengoukai). Tokyo.

Kimura, Yoshihiro. 2013. "Gendai nihon ni okeru seifu saimu no juyou kouzou" (Absorption Structure of Public Debt in Modern Japan). In *Kiki to saiken no hikaku zaiseishi* (Comparative Fiscal History of Crisis and Consolidation), edited by Eisaku Ide. Kyoto: Minerva Shobou.

Kitayama, Toshiya. 2003. "Doken kokka nihon to shihonshugi no shoruikei" (Japanese Construction State and Varieties of Capitalism). *Leviathan* 32: 123–146.

Korpi, Walter and Joakim Palme. 1998. "The Paradox of Redistribution and Strategies of Equality: Welfare State Institutions, Inequality, and Poverty in the Western Countries." *American Sociological Review* 63: 661–687.

Kwon, Huck-Ju. 2005. "An Overview of the Study: Developmental Welfare State and Policy Reforms in East Asia." In *Transforming the Developmental Welfare State*, edited by Huck-Ju Kwon. London: Palgrave.

Lindert, Peter H. 2004. *Growing Public: Social Spending and Economic Growth since the Eighteenth Century*. New York: Cambridge University Press.

Miyamoto, Taro. 2009. *Seikatsu hoshou: haijo shinai shakai e* (Security of Living: Towards an Inclusive Society). Tokyo: Iwanami Shoten.

Park, Gene. 2011. *Spending without Taxation: FILP and the Politics of Public Finance in Japan*. Stanford: Stanford University Press.

Park, Gene and Eisaku Ide. 2014 "The Tax-Welfare Mix: Explaining Japan's Weak Extractive Capacity." forthcoming in *The Pacific Review* 27(5): 675–702.

Peng, Ito. 2005. "The New Politics of the Welfare State in a Developmental Context: Explaining the 1990s Social Care Expansion in Japan." In *Transforming the Developmental Welfare State*, edited by Huck-Ju Kwon. London: Palgrave.

Persson, Torsten, Gerard Roland, and Guido Tabellini. 2007. "Electoral Rules and Government Spending in Parliamentary Democracies." *Quarterly Journal of Political Science* 2(2): 155–188.

Pierson, Paul. 2001. "Coping with Permanent Austerity: Welfare State Restructuring in Affluent Democracies." In *The New Politics of the Welfare State*, edited by Paul Pierson. Oxford: Oxford University Press.

Rothstein, Bo. 1998. *Just Institutions Matter*. Cambridge: Cambridge University Press.

Rothstein, Bo and Eric M. Uslaner. 2005. "All for All: Equality, Corruption, and Social Trust." *World Politics* 58: 41–72.

Steinmo, Sven. 2010. *The Evolution of Modern States: Sweden, Japan, and the United States*. New York: Cambridge University Press.

Streeck, Wolfgang and Kathleen Thelen. 2005. *Beyond Continuity: Institutional Change in Advanced Political Economies*. New York: Oxford University Press.

Takahashi, Masayuki. 2012. *Fukkou to nihon zaisei no shinro* (Recovery from Disaster and Future Direction of Japan's Fiscal Policy). Tokyo: Iwanami Shoten.

Timmons, Jeffrey F. 2005. "The Fiscal Contract: States, Taxes and Public Services." *World Politics* 57: 530–567.

Ugai, Hiroshi. 2007. "Effects of the Quantitative Easing Policy: A Survey of Empirical Analyses." *Monetary and Economic Studies* 25(1): 1–48.

6 Fiscal Performance in South Korea (1970–2012)

Budgetary Reforms with Growing Non-Budgetary Indiscipline

Myung-koo Kang

Introduction

This chapter explores South Korea's[1] fiscal performance[2]—patterns of deficits and debt—in the historical and comparative contexts. During Korea's high economic growth period, lasting from the early 1960s to the late 1980s, Korea established a strong tradition of keeping a balanced budget. Fiscal discipline was also buttressed by an institutional arrangement that depoliticized the fiscal policy making process. Key to this was the dominance of the executive over the legislature in the budgetary process. Under Korea's presidential system, the powers of the legislature in budget drafting, execution, and oversight were very limited—unlike the United States (Lienert 2005; Stapenhurst et al. 2008). The strong presidency, which was established during the military dictatorship (1961–87), insulated the Korean economic bureaucracy, which was hierarchically organized with the Economic Planning Board (EPB) at the top (Choi 1991). The EPB, established in 1961, could influence every important economic policy making process by monopolizing the budget planning and implementation process. During the high economic growth period, the EPB developed the tradition of maintaining a balanced annual budget.

The situation changed with the democratic transition in 1987. Since the transition, the power balance in fiscal policy making gradually shifted from the executive to the legislature, with the shift accelerating in the 2000s, as Korean politics experienced repeated changes in government. The EPB was dismantled in 1994,[3] causing the fiscal bureaucracy to lose its policy autonomy gradually. This power shift coincided with a series of neo-liberal economic reforms, which the Korean government pursued since the early 1990s and then gained momentum after the Asian financial crisis of 1997. The series of neo-liberal reforms contributed to deepening the social and economic gaps of Korean society. Worsening socioeconomic polarization increased the demand for expanded social welfare programs.

With the 1987 democratic transition, the balanced budget tradition was gradually dismantled and the government consistently ran budget deficits, particularly after the Asian financial crisis of 1997. As a result, public debt has mounted over the past decade. But importantly, as non-budgetary fiscal indiscipline increased the government attempted to bypass the growing legislative oversight over the budgetary process. The Korean government has used public corporations or extra-budgetary funds in response to the growing fiscal reforms to enhance the powers of the National Assembly on the budgetary process. By the end of 2013, the debt held by public corporations exceeded the debt held by the government.

This chapter is organized into five sections. The first section reviews the historical trends of fiscal performance from the early 1970s to 2012. The second looks at the distinctive features of Korea's tax and expenditure structure, and reviews how the balanced budget was institutionalized during the high economic growth period from the early 1960s to the early 1990s—specifically with the establishment of the EPB in 1962 and its abolition in 1994. The third section explores the budgetary politics, with special attention to the evolving relations between the executive and legislative branches of the government. The fourth section discusses fiscal challenges that the Korean government needs to tackle in the near future due to an aging population and dualistic employment structure. The chapter concludes with a discussion on comparative implications and policy lessons we can learn from the Korean case.

Trends in Fiscal Performance

Overview

Korea's fiscal performance has varied since the early 1970s. While the fiscal balance of the Korean government consistently fluctuated during the 1970s, it improved significantly from the early 1980s to 1996. Since then, primarily due to the Asian financial crisis of 1997–98, it has consistently worsened.

From the early 1970s to early 1980s, fiscal balance fluctuated as the Korean economy was hit by the shock of the collapse of the Bretton Woods system, in 1971, and two oil crises, from 1972 to 1974 and 1978 to 1981. During these periods, fiscal deficits ranged from 3.5 percent of Gross Domestic Product (GDP) to 4.5 percent. The Korean government launched the Heavy and Chemical Industrialization (HCI) strategy, which focused on developing steel, petrochemicals, automobiles, shipbuilding, machinery, and electronics. This HCI strategy required massive investments. The Korean government not only created various investment-related funds, but also a priority-loan program in which the government applied lower interest rates toward the loans for big companies (*chaebols*), which were engaged in developing those strategic industrial sectors (Cho and Kim 1997; Kim 2004). The HCI strategy decreased the savings-investment imbalances, and the expansionary fiscal spending for increasing investments aggravated the fiscal balance of the government (Bahl et al. 1986; Choi 1992).

It should also be noted that the two periods of 1972–74 and 1979–81 were periods of political instability. In 1972, a series of presidential emergency decrees were announced due to the mounting public demonstrations against the constitutional revision—the *Yushin* constitution, which gave permanent dictatorial power to Park Chung Hee (Lee 2005). But Park was assassinated in October 1979, followed quickly by a military coup. As a result, an interim military government was established by Chun Doo-hwan, under martial law, which lasted until 1981. Massive demonstrations against Chun Doo-hwan's coup and his interim government intensifed in early 1980. Chun's interim government tried to quell the demonstrations by using the special forces of the Korean military, which resulted in a massacre in the Kwangju area, the capital city of the Southwest province in May 1980 (Katsiaficas 2012). As a consequence of this social and political instability, exports plummeted and inflation mounted in the early 1980s.

The budget remained largely in balance from the early 1980s to 1996—as Figure 6.1 shows—while the savings–investment imbalance decreased. During this period, the Korean economy boomed, while accumulating current account surpluses. Furthermore, the Korean government tightened its monetary and fiscal policies. It attempted to slow down the annual growth rate of money supply to target the inflation caused by the oil crises and the subsequent political turmoil in 1979 and 1980, and restrain government spending. In 1982, the government set up the Budget Review Committee (BRC)—within the budget office—which reviewed the ministerial budget requests with the goal of containing spending increases and establishing fiscal discipline (Koh 2007).

In the late 1980s, the Korean economy reaped the economic benefits of low oil prices, low interest rates, and a weak dollar in international markets. From 1986 to 1988, Korea's exports and current account surpluses increased remarkably. Exports rose 28.3 percent in 1986, 36.4 percent in 1987, and 29.0 percent

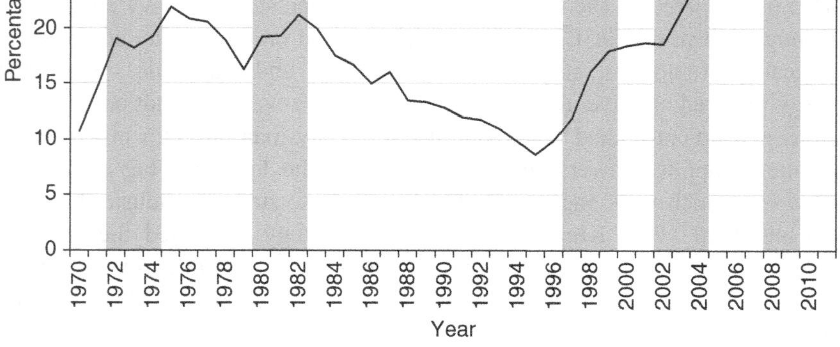

Figure 6.1 Percentage of government debt to GDP, 1970–2011 (source: MOSF, *Digital Budget and Accounting System portal* (www.digitalbrain.go.kr)).

Note

1 The grey area highlights the period of economic or financial crises. Specifically, those periods are from 1972 to 1974; from 1979 to 1981; the Asian financial crisis from 1997 to 1999; the credit card companies crisis from 2002 to 2003; the global financial crisis of 2007 to 2009.

in 1988. Meanwhile, account surpluses increased from US$4.6 billion in 1986 to US$14.1 billion in 1988. As a result, the fiscal debt level decreased greatly. As Figure 6.1 highlights, from 1982 to 1996, the percentage of government debt-to-GDP fell continuously, going below 10 percent of GDP by the end of 1996. It can safely be said that until the mid-1990s, Korea's fiscal performance was positively balanced.

This trend, however, has changed since 1997. The Korean government has consistently had a budget deficit and its fiscal performance has continuously declined. The government debt level has increased from 10 percent of GDP in 1997 to 34 percent of GDP in 2012. During this period, the Korean economy went through three financial crises: the Asian financial crisis of 1997–98, the crisis of credit card companies in 2002–04, and the global financial crisis of 2007–09. These financial crises, and ensuing fiscal measures to cope with them, have contributed greatly to the sharp increase of Korean government debt. For instance, during the Asian financial crisis of 1997–98, the Korean government launched fiscal stimulus packages, including the usage of government money for financial restructuring. The government used a large amount of funds again to resolve the crisis of credit card companies in 2002–04. This pattern was repeated during the global financial crisis of 2007–09.

The fiscal balance worsened with the increasing demand for social protection as well. Since the Asian financial crisis, the Korean government has pushed several liberalization agendas in the financial, corporate, and labor sectors which have contributed to deepening socioeconomic polarization, reflected in the widening income gaps. To cope with the polarization, the Korean government tried to expand its spending for social security, specifically expanding the social safety net. However, despite the mounting demand for social welfare, the incumbent and opposition parties have not raised taxes to pay adequately for the expanding social welfare programs. Consequently, the increased rate of spending for social security has continuously exceeded the rate of tax revenue growth.

Despite the increase of government debt, Korea's debt level has been much lower than most Organization of Economic Cooperation and Development (OECD) countries for the past decade. As of the end of 2011, Korea's government debt-to-GDP ratio was less than 34 percent, while the average for OECD countries was 75 percent. Other fiscal indicators, such as structural budget deficits and net public debt, also suggest that Korea's fiscal condition is in much better shape than most OECD countries (OECD Economic Outlook No. 92).

It should be noted, however, that the data provided by the International Monetary Fund (IMF), OECD, and other international organizations, does not yet show comparable consolidated information[4] on public sector debt. In most cases, IMF or OECD data on public debt covers only the general government sector,[5] and does not include other subsectors of the public sector, such as nonfinancial public corporations and financial public corporations. As a result, we cannot capture the consolidated debt situation of the entire public sector. In this context, the World Bank and the IMF jointly launched in December 2010 the Public Sector Debt Statistics (PSD);[6] the quarterly PSD provides information covering both the general government sector and financial and nonfinancial public corporations.[7]

Because the Korean government has yet to provide the consolidated public sector debt to the PSD, we cannot do a real cross-country comparison on Korea's public sector debt level. Still, we get a sense of the recent trend by investigating the outstanding debt of nonfinancial public corporations in Korea. The level exceeded the outstanding general government debt, reaching more than 38.7 percent of GDP in 2013 (MOSF, April 9 2013), and it has increased 8.4 times since 1998, with particularly rapid growth during the last five years. Thus Korea's national debt level, including the debt in the public sector, may not be particularly low compared with that of other OECD countries, as is often believed.

Tax Structure

Korea's tax revenues have increased greatly during the past decades; more than 430 times from KRW492 billion in 1971 to KRW212 trillion in 2008. In particular, from the 1970 to the late 1980s, the proportion of national taxes levied and operated by the central government was about 90 percent of total tax revenues. But with the growing fiscal decentralization since the late 1980s, the proportion of local taxes had grown gradually to more than 20 percent of the total tax revenues in the early 1990s. Since then the proportion of local taxes has continued to rise.

One of the more interesting aspects of Korea's tax structure is that the tax rate has been one of the lowest in the OECD area. Table 6.1 shows the ratio of the total tax revenue of major OECD countries to GDP. Korea's aggregate tax level was far lower than the OECD average from the 1970s to the 1990s. In particular, during the 1980s Korea's rate was about half the OECD average. But, with the increasing social security contributions, the rate increased to 25.1 percent by 2010, reaching a similar level as the United States and Japan.

Table 6.1 Total tax revenue[1] as percentage of GDP, selected countries, 1980–2010

	1975	*1980*	*1985*	*1990*	*1995*	*2000*	*2005*	*2010*
France[2]	35.5	40.2	42.8	42.0	42.9	44.4	44.1	42.9
Germany[3]	34.3	36.4	36.1	34.8	37.2	37.5	35.0	36.3
Italy	25.4	29.7	33.6	37.8	40.1	42.2	40.8	43.0
Japan	20.7	25.1	27.1	29.0	26.8	27.0	27.4	27.6
Korea	14.9	17.1	16.1	19.5	20.0	22.6	24.0	25.1
Korea without social security	14.8	16.9	15.8	17.5	17.6	18.8	18.9	19.3
United Kingdom	34.9	34.8	37.0	35.5	34.0	36.3	35.7	35.0
United States	25.6	26.4	25.6	27.4	27.8	29.5	27.1	24.8
OECD (total)	29.4	30.9	32.5	33.1	34.6	35.3	35.0	33.8

Source: OECD, *Revenue Statistics 1965–2011* (http://dx.doi.org/10.1787/888932720302).

Notes
1 Total tax revenue includes social security contributions.
2 Total tax revenues have been reduced by amount of any capital transfer that represents uncollected taxes.
3 Unified Germany beginning in 1991.

This lower level of tax burden reflects the long tradition of the benevolent state in Korea, resulting not only from a Confucian political culture, but also from the legacy of past authoritarianism. In Confucian tradition, the state was placed in the highest status of the hierarchical social order, and a good state—or a virtuous leader—was expected to be benevolent to the people. Moreover, due to the weak political foundation of legitimacy, authoritarian governments—lasting from 1961 to 1987—tried to compensate for coercive and oppressive rule by maintaining lenient tax policies. This prolonged history of lower taxes makes it more politically difficult to increase taxes to meet the growing demand for expanding social welfare.

By contrast, Korea's indirect tax proportion has been much higher than the OECD average, primarily because of a high proportion of consumption taxes. Of total tax revenues, the indirect tax to direct tax ratio declined from the early 1970s to the mid-1980s. It then began to rise in the mid-1980s, a trend that has continued. For the past decade, the indirect tax proportion has been consistently over 50 percent of total tax revenues. Of those indirect taxes, the value-added tax (VAT)—which was introduced in Korea in 1978—has been a primary source of indirect tax revenues, exceeding over 30 percent of the total tax revenue since its introduction.

Indeed, taxes on specific goods and services in Korea have been much higher than those in other OECD nations on average since 1980. For example, the proportion of taxes on goods and services was 62.6 percent in 1980, almost twice as high as the OECD average at the time. The proportion started to decline sharply under the Roh Tae Woo administration (1988–93)—as the Korean government began to introduce more social security taxes—and stayed around 40 percent of the total tax revenue from the early 1990s to the early 2000s. It has declined for the past decade, but was over 33 percent of total tax revenue in 2010 (OECD Revenue Statistics 2012). This high proportion of indirect taxes highlights how the Korean tax structure has been institutionalized favoring the rich or high income earners.

Meanwhile, Korea's social security contributions as a share of total taxation have been much lower than the OECD average. Social welfare programs were introduced in Korea far later than other European welfare states or Japan. For instance, the National Pension System was introduced in Korea in December 1973 under Park Chung Hee (1961–79). In the original pension plan, the contribution rate was low and mandatory coverage was narrow. Furthermore, the original pension scheme was introduced, not for improving the pension system per se, but for mobilizing domestic capital for investment in the heavy and chemical industries (Kim and Stewart 2011). The national pension scheme was not fully implemented until the enactment of the National Pension Act in 1988.

As Table 6.2 shows, in 1985, the proportion of social security contributions to total tax revenues was about 1.5 percent. But with the democratic transition in 1987, specifically during the Roh Tae-Woo administration (1988–93), additional social welfare programs were introduced. As a result, the proportion of social security contributions jumped to 10.1 percent in 1990, and grew continuously thereafter. By the end of 2010, it was at 22.8 percent of the total taxation, slightly

Table 6.2 Social security contributions as percentage of total taxation

	1975	*1985*	*1990*	*1995*	*2000*	*2007*	*2010*
France	40.6	43.3	44.1	43.0	36.1	37.1	38.7
Germany	34.0	36.5	37.5	39.0	39.0	36.6	39.0
Italy	45.9	34.7	32.9	31.5	28.5	29.9	31.3
Japan	29.0	30.3	26.4	33.5	35.2	36.5	41.1
Korea	0.9	1.5	10.1	12.1	16.7	20.7	22.8
United Kingdom	17.5	17.8	17.0	17.8	17.0	18.4	19.0
United States	20.5	25.2	25.2	24.9	23.4	23.3	25.7
OECD (total)[1]	22.0	22.1	22.0	25.1	24.6	24.6	26.4

Source: OECD, *Revenue Statistics, 2012 Edition* (www.oecd.org/tax/taxpolicyanalysis/revenuestatistics2012edition.htm).

Note
1 Unweighted average.

lower than the OECD average of 26.4 percent. Considering the recent rate of increase in social security contributions, it looks obvious that social security contributions will continue their growth in Korea in the near future, converging with the general pattern of other advanced OECD countries.

Expenditure Structure

The Korean government has traditionally used the majority of its spending on national defense and education. However, defense spending has been in steady decline since the early 1980s, while the spending for education has remained at the same proportion of total government spending, as Figure 6.2 shows.

It should also be noted that government spending for social protection has remained minimal until recently, unlike the advanced economies of Europe. Of the total government expenditure, spending for social protection has been below 7.5 percent until 2010. Indeed, Korea's public social spending has been the lowest among OECD countries. For instance, as of the end of 2009, the average gross public social expenditure in OECD countries was 22.4 percent of GDP. In Korea, however, it was only 9.4 percent of GDP. Mexico was the only OECD country whose public social expenditure was lower than Korea's (OECD, Revenue Statistics 2012). As noted in the previous section, the Confucian tradition remained strong in Korea and, in that context, family members were often socially expected to take care of individual family member's welfare necessities. Moreover, the public welfare system was introduced much later than in most OECD countries. As a result, Korea's public spending for social security has been an outlier among OECD countries (Yang 2013).

Government spending on healthcare, however, has increased remarkably over the past two decades. In 1988, the total spending for healthcare was only KRW1 trillion, but it increased to KRW38.1 trillion in 2010. In 2010, the proportion of the government spending for healthcare was larger than that of defense, education, and general public services, as Figure 6.2 shows. This increased government

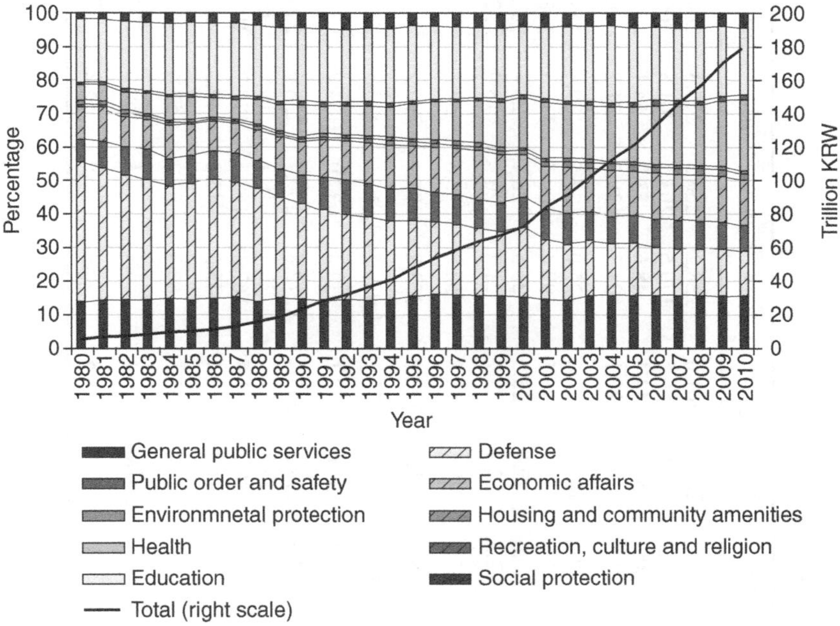

Figure 6.2 General government final consumption expenditure, 1980–2011 (source: Bank of Korea, *Economic Statistics System* (https://ecos.bok.or.kr)).

spending for healthcare was mobilized through social security funds, which are managed and operated by the government. Between 1990 and 2007, Korea's public social spending increased at an 11 percent annual rate in real terms, which was the fastest in the OECD (OECD 2012). Between 2007/08 and 2011/12, Korea's real social spending increased by 29 percent, the largest increase among OECD countries (OECD 2012, chart 2).

Meanwhile, fiscal spending by local governments grew rapidly. Local governments in Korea did not have any fiscal autonomy until 1995, as the military dictatorship suspended it from 1963. Local autonomy was restored only after a long political struggle following the democratic transition in 1987. However, even after the restoration of local autonomy in 1995, local governments had only a limited degree of fiscal autonomy.[8] Nonetheless, fiscal decentralization has gradually progressed over the recent decade. In 2003, the total budget of local governments was approximately 40 percent of the total budget of the central government, but it increased to about 53.4 percent by 2011 (see Table 6.3). For the past decade, the share of the local tax revenue in the local budget has declined, and the fiscal condition of local governments has worsened as spending of local government has often been swayed by local special interests.[9] To remedy this, the Korean government passed, in 2005, the Local Finance Act. With the Act, the Minister of Public Administration and Security came to be able to intervene in the operation of the budget by local governments (Article 5 of Local Finance Act).

Table 6.3 Budget of central and local governments, type of accounts, 2003–11 (unit: trillion KRW, %)

		2003	*2004*	*2005*	*2006*	*2007*	*2008*	*2009*	*2010*	*2011*
Central government	Subtotal (A)	191.9	187.9	195.8	204.2	201.0	228.2	256.5	255.3	264.1
	General account (a)	118.1	120.1	135.2	147.0	156.5	179.6	203.5	201.3	209.9
	Special accounts (b)	73.8	67.8	60.6	57.3	44.4	48.6	53.0	54.1	54.2
	(b)/(a) (%)	38.4	36.1	31.0	28.0	22.1	21.3	20.7	21.2	20.5
Local government	Subtotal (B)	78.1	87.3	92.4	101.4	112.0	125.0	137.5	139.9	141.0
	General account (c)	60.5	66.6	71.8	78.7	86.5	98.4	109.5	113.4	108.5
	Special accounts (d)	17.7	20.6	20.6	22.7	25.5	26.5	28.1	26.4	32.5
	(d)/(c) (%)	22.6	23.6	22.3	22.4	22.7	21.2	20.4	18.9	23.0
Local budget to central budget: (B)/(A) (%)		40.7	46.5	47.2	49.6	55.7	54.8	53.6	54.8	53.4
Total National Budget (C): (A)+(B)		270.0	275.2	288.2	305.6	312.9	353.2	394.1	395.2	405.1
Nominal GDP: (D)		767.1	826.9	865.2	908.7	975	1,026.5	1,065	1,173.3	1,237.1
Total National Budget/GDP: (C)/(D) (%)		35.2	33.3	33.3	33.6	32.1	34.4	37.0	33.7	32.7
Tax revenue	Subtotal (E)	147.8	152	163.4	179.3	205	212.8	209.7	226.9	244.7
	Tax burden ratio: (E)/(D)	19.3	18.4	18.9	19.7	21	20.7	19.7	19.3	19.8
	National tax (F)	114.7	117.8	127.5	138	161.4	167.3	164.5	177.7	192.4
	Local tax (G)	33.1	34.2	36	41.3	43.4	45.5	45.2	49.2	52.3
Total tax revenue to total National Budget: (E)/(C) (%)		54.7	55.2	56.7	58.7	65.5	60.3	53.2	57.4	60.4
National tax/central government budget: (F)/(A) (%)		59.8	62.7	65.1	67.6	80.3	73.3	64.1	69.6	72.9
Local tax/local budget: (G)/(B) (%)		42.4	39.2	39.0	40.7	38.8	36.4	32.9	35.2	37.1

Source: MOSF, KOSIS and Bank of Korea, *Statistics Portal*.

Evolution of Budgetary Politics

The historical vicissitude of Korea's fiscal performance and its relatively low level of public debt beg some comparative questions; whether Korea's fiscal performance is an outlier case among OECD countries or only a transitory phenomenon resulting from an economic development that occurred later than other advanced economies. One interesting issue in the Korean case is the impact of fiscal institutions in the Korean context. To answer this question, we need to understand how the strong tradition of a balanced budget was established, and then how it has been gradually dismantled with the democratization and economic liberalization beginning in the early 1990s.

Korea's balanced budget tradition was founded upon the supremacy of the executive branch over the legislature in regards to the budgetary process. However, with the transition from a military dictatorship to a democratic regime—first in 1987 and again in 1992—popular demand for social welfare soared. Nonetheless, it took time for the increasing demand to have real effects on government's tax revenue and expenditure structure. Fiscal policy making was still under the heavy influence of the balanced budget principle until 1996. The turning point came with the Asian financial crisis and the subsequent regime change in 1998. The crisis and the regime change triggered a power shift between the executive and the legislature in fiscal policy making, with various fiscal reforms being taken to strengthen legislative power in budgetary planning and oversight.

Weak Veto Power of the Legislature

Korea's fiscal policy making was long dominated by the executive branch of the government.

It reflects the long tradition of a strong presidency, which originated from the military dictatorship lasting from 1961 to 1987.[10] Park Chung Hee set up and consolidated this strong presidency during his dictatorial rule from 1961 to 1979. He claimed that "democracy should be established by administrative (fiat), not by political means (popularly determined)" (Park 1962, 208). He asserted that the state, especially the executive branch of the government, should "guide" democratization given the retarded social and economic conditions of the nation, calling it an "administrative democracy." With the notion of "administrative democracy," he laid out an institutional foundation that enabled the supremacy of the executive over the legislature and political parties in the national agenda-setting process in general, and in fiscal policy making in particular.

Park set up the Economic Planning Board (EPB) in July 1961. The EPB wielded monopolistic power on budget planning and allocation until 1994 when it was merged with the Ministry of Finance; it then was integrated into the Ministry of Finance and Economy. The EPB was placed at the top of the economic bureaucracy, and the head of the EPB, as a deputy prime minister, was in charge of orchestrating and coordinating the macroeconomic policies of the government. With the power of controlling the budget, as well as approval power for foreign loans, the EPB, until 1993, was able to implement their five-year economic plans without hindrance (Choi 1991).

A "Planning and Control Office" (PCO) was established within the EPB from its creation in July 1961, a model that gradually extended to other ministries. Placed under the Office of Planning Coordination in the Prime Minister's office, the PCOs monitored and evaluated the status of the implementation of economic projects assigned to each ministry in quarterly reports. This controlling mechanism provided the Prime Minister, and ultimately the President, with an independent channel of information (Lee 1968, 144–145). As a result, during its existence the EPB's fiscal policy making process was fully insulated from any political interference from party politics. Without interference, the EPB was free to pursue their goal of an annual balanced budget (Kim 1992).

The supremacy of the executive in fiscal policy making continued even after the democratic transition, with multiple factors contributing to its sustenance. One key factor was the fiscal rules in the Constitution. According to the revised Constitution of 1987, "the legislative power is vested in the National Assembly" (Article 40) with the National Assembly holding final authority in deciding the government's budget. The president could not veto the budget bill, once it passed the National Assembly. However, the power of the National Assembly in the budgetary process was very limited by the fiscal rules stipulated in the Constitution.

One such rule was that the National Assembly could not increase the amount of fiscal money for any programs in the budget bill, submitted by the executive, without the consent of the executive (Article 57 of the Constitution).[11] The National Assembly was therefore only empowered to cut the budget for specific fiscal programs. Moreover, the Korean Constitution (Article 54) stipulates that:

> (1) The National Assembly deliberates and decides upon the national budget bill, while (2) The Executive formulates the budget bill for each fiscal year and submits it to the National Assembly within ninety days before the beginning of a fiscal year.

As a result, only the executive can introduce budget bills to the National Assembly.

More importantly, the National Assembly had limited institutional capacity for budget audit and oversight. It did not have power to audit and oversee the operation of budgetary expenditure of executive agencies. Such functions belonged to the Board of Audit and Inspection (BAI), which served (and still does) as the government's principal auditing and evaluation agency.[12] This pattern is strikingly different from those countries in which the auditing functions and power belong to the legislature—often called the Westminster model—in which the legislature authorizes expenditure and revenue, and receives audit reports from an independent audit agency (Lienert 2005).[13] It was only after 2003, when the National Assembly Budget Office (NABO)[14] was established, that the National Assembly came to have a regular organizational structure for budget auditing and oversight.

Before the establishment of the NABO, annual budget reviews were done by the Special Committee for Budget and Accounts, which was composed of 50 National Assembly members. But the Committee was an ad hoc committee until 2000, and the turnover ratio of the Committee members was very high. In the Korean National Assembly, it is commonplace to reshuffle the Assembly members on the Special Committee for Budget and Accounts every year. As a result, those Special Committee members often suffered a lack of expertise on fiscal issues. Moreover, the total time for budget deliberation is limited to three months, curbing the budgetary review power of the National Assembly. In Korea, as the new fiscal year begins on January 1st, the budget must be passed before the end of the year. In practice, however, the real regular session for budgetary review often lasts less than a month.

Political party structure and practices, consolidated during the authoritarian regimes, also limited the power of the National Assembly against the executive. Until 2004, the president could dominate the legislative process in the National Assembly. The Korean president was not only the executive leader of the government, but also chairman of the ruling party. The president, as a ruling party boss, could wield almost absolute power over the nomination of district representatives for the National Assembly elections. Thus, personal loyalty to the president was a critical factor for politicians in being nominated and re-elected.[15] This institutional setting installed a president-centered, highly personalized and centralized structure in the ruling party, and it enabled the president to dominate in the legislative process in general, particularly in budgetary politics. With the exception of 1987 to 1989, the ruling party held majority status in the National Assembly, and the president could control the budgetary process without complications.

Shift in Executive–Legislature Relations and Budgetary Reforms

Despite various institutional constraints, the power of the National Assembly has grown gradually with democratic consolidation. Since the democratic transition in 1987, there have been six presidential elections every five years, from the thirteenth in December 1987 to the eighteenth election in December 2012, and seven elections for the National Assembly members every four years, from the thirteenth in April 1988 to the nineteenth in April 2012. Of those six presidential elections, right-leaning conservative party candidates were elected four times, and conservatives parties won six out of seven legislative elections—the exception being the seventeenth legislative election in April 2004. These election results clearly demonstrate Korean voters have consistently supported right-leaning conservative parties.

It should be noted, however, that in the Korean political context, ideological positions of political parties have not usually aligned with their policy orientations (Kim 2000, 2002). Electoral politics are not typically determined by parties' ideological positions on certain economic policies or the role of the government in the economy. Likewise, political parties are not organized based on articulated interests of different social groups. Instead, most Korean parties are catch-all parties, based on certain regional power bases. Until the regime change through the presidential election of December 1997, all incumbent ruling parties were based in *Kyungsang* (Southeastern) Province. During the military dictatorship, all three former dictatorial leaders—Park Chung Hee (1961–79), Chun Doo-hwan (1980–87), and Roh Tae-woo (1988–93)—were from the North *Kyungsang* Province, and the succeeding first civilian President, Kim Young-sam (1993–98), was from South *Kyungsang* Province.

Major opposition parties were also region-based. Indeed, in every election since the democratic transition in 1987, a region-oriented voting behavior pattern has determined the election results. This has prevented a policy or ideology-based party system from developing (Choi et al. 2014; Lee and Brunn 1996; Kwon 2004).

In a western political context, conservative parties prefer a smaller government. Partisan politics with diverging ideological orientations are one of the critical determinants in fiscal policy making (Ljungman 2009; Wehner 2009; Klarner et al. 2012). But in the Korean context, the conservative–liberal ideological divide has not been a guiding principle in determining political parties' fiscal policy orientations. Indeed, public debt increased at a much faster rate under the recent conservative Lee Myung-bak administration (2008–13). And in the presidential election of December 2012, both conservative and liberal candidates—Park Geun-hye from the conservative *Saenuri* Party and Moon Jae-in from the liberal Democratic United Party—commonly insisted that they should make every effort to improve, and increase public spending for, the social welfare system.[16]

A far more important factor in determining a government's fiscal policy orientation lies in the legislature–executive relationship. The first turning point came with presidential election of 1997. After a long-held dominance of conservative political parties, the victory of the left-leaning center-liberal political leader, Kim Dae-jung, paved way for a shift in fiscal policy. Former ruling parties from the military dictatorship put more emphasis on the growth of the economy than on redistribution or social welfare issues. But during the Kim Dae-jung administration, the focus of fiscal policy shifted from a growth-driven paradigm toward a more redistributary role. Indeed, Kim Dae-jung tried to spend more fiscal money on expanding social welfare and strengthening the social safety net.

However, a real tipping point of change in the legislature–executive relationship came with the establishment of a left-leaning liberal party, the Open Woori Party, and its victory in the presidential election of 2002. As a result of the election, the Roh Moo-hyun administration (2003–08) was inaugurated. Roh's ruling party, the Open Woori Party, shared a similar political orientation with Kim Dae-jung's New Millennium Democratic Party, but Roh's party was more progressive than that of Kim's in terms of making efforts to eradicate the institutional legacy from the past authoritarian regimes or strong presidency. In particular, Roh, as a presidential candidate, accepted his own party's request to introduce a division of power between the president (or presidential candidate) and chairpersonship of the party. As a result, for the first time in Korea's party politics, Roh did not keep the chairpersonship of his incumbent ruling party while he was president. He felt that the dominance of the executive in policy making, and even in the legislation process, is a legacy from the past that had to be overcome in the course of consolidating democracy. From this, the incumbent Open Woori Party launched a series of reforms concerning the existing budgetary process with the aim to enhance the power of the National Assembly against the executive.

One such reform measure was to introduce a consolidated budget system. The Korean government traditionally maintained three fiscal categories—one general account, special accounts, and public funds (see Table 6.4). For example, as of 2001, about 31 percent of government spending was covered by 18 extra-budgetary funds. These funds were not included in the consolidated fiscal balance of the central government and were not subject to an ex-ante approval by the National Assembly, although they used tax revenues or just in case contingent liabilities should occur the government had to take fiscal responsibility (IMF 2001). As a result, it was difficult to identify the consolidated fiscal balance of the central government. To reform the situation, the ruling Open Woori Party initiated the National Finance Act, which came into effect in January 2007. With this Act, the government was required to manage all fiscal accounts by integrating them into the national finance account.

Furthermore, the Open Woori Party took measures to strengthen the budget oversight power of the National Assembly. One such measure was to make the Special Committee on Budget and Accounts—which was only an ad hoc committee until 2000—a standing committee, composed of 50 National Assembly members from the ruling and opposition parties. In 2008, the Special Committee organized the Adjustment Subcommittee, composed of 15 National Assembly members, for the purpose of deliberating the proposed budget plan.

Meanwhile, the Open Woori Party tried to enhance transparency in fiscal management by reforming the existing fiscal accounting system. The National Assembly enacted the National Accounting Act in October 2007 and changed the fiscal accounting system from a cash-based, single-entry bookkeeping practice into an accrual-based, double-entry bookkeeping one[17] for fiscal accounts, and this change came to be effective in 2009. As a result, from 2009, the government records every financial activity of the government (both central and local) at every stage of budget formulation, execution, and account settlement by applying double-entry bookkeeping and accrual accounting and reports it to the National Assembly. The government also came to be obligated to formulate and submit a medium-term (at least five years) Financial Management Plan to the National Assembly, in addition to the annual budget plan.

In short, the ascending power of the National Assembly against the executive has contributed to introducing more disciplinary measures in the budgetary policy making process. A series of fiscal reform measures were taken with an aim of enhancing transparency by integrating all fiscal processes including budget formulation, execution, account settlement, and performance management, while strengthening the power of the National Assembly in the budgetary process.

Table 6.4 Characteristics of general account, special accounts, and funds (end of 2011)

	General account	*Special accounts*	*Funds*
Objective	Supporting general fiscal activities	Supporting specific programs	Supporting specific programs
Revenues	General-purpose taxes[1] and nontax revenues	Ear-marked taxes, mandatory contributions, transfers from other accounts and funds, etc.	Mandatory contributions, transfers from other accounts and funds, etc.
Expenditures	Unrequited expenditures	Unrequited expenditures and loans	Unrequited expenditures and loans
Linkages between revenues and expenditures	None	Clear linkages	Clear linkages
Authorization and execution of expenditure plans	Voted on in the National Assembly Controlled and monitored during execution as mandated by the Constitution	Same as general account	Same as general account but with greater flexibility[2]
Items		18 accounts: corporate-related special accounts (5), others (13)	65 funds: project funds (44), social security funds (6), finance-related funds (10), others (5)
Total Revenue (planned)	209.9 trillion KRW	45.7 trillion KRW	369.3 trillion KRW

Sources: Koh (2007), table 9.6 and MOSF, *Fiscal Statistics Portal* (www.mosf.go.kr/lib/lib02.jsp).

Notes

1 Domestic taxes, composed of 14 taxes: customs, transportation–energy–environment tax, educational tax, and comprehensive real estate tax.

2 Central agencies which operate funds can change fund expenditures within 30 percent of the planned amount without notice to the budget authorities and the National Assembly. Cash flows are managed independently by the central agencies in charge and do not go through the treasury single account held in the Bank of Korea. Unlimited carry-overs of used cash are allowed.

Table 6.5 Debt trend of general government, 2007–12 (unit: trillion KRW, %)

	2007	*2008*	*2009*	*2010*	*2011*	*2012*
GDP (a)	975.0	1,026.5	1,065.0	1,173.3	1,235.1	1,272.5
Total debt (b)	299.2	309	359.2	392.2	420.5	443.1
(b)/(a)	30.7	30.1	33.8	33.4	34.0	34.8
General Budget Account (c)	55.6	63	97	119.7	135.3	148.6
(c)/(b)	18.6	20.4	27.0	30.5	32.2	33.5
Public funds	52.7	49.2	49.5	47	45.7	45.7
Monetary Stabilization Fund (d)	89.7	94	104.9	120.6	136.7	153
(d)/(b)	30.0	30.4	29.2	30.7	32.5	34.5
National Housing Fund	43.6	45.2	48.5	49.3	48.9	49.6
Others	57.6	57.6	59.7	55.6	53.9	46.2

Source: KOSIS *Statistics Portal.* (http://kosis.kr).

To date, however, budgetary discipline has not materialized, primarily because of the expansionary fiscal measures used to cope with the global financial crisis of 2008–10. As Table 6.5 shows, the total general account debt has been on the rise since 2007, reaching 34.8 percent of GDP at the end of 2012. During this period, there was no substantial change in the outstanding amount of public funds, national housing funds, or other categories of the general government account. However, the debt in the general budget account and monetary stabilization fund sharply increased. This sharp increase resulted from a variety of fiscal stimulus measures to reverse the economic downturn—which had a net effect on fiscal balance of minus 6.1 percent of GDP (OECD 2010, 50)—and from government intervention in the money and currency markets in an attempt to stabilize interest rates and foreign exchange rates (Tsutsumi et al. 2010).

Considering the effects of the global financial crisis and the short timeframe in which those reform measures have been implemented, it looks too early to identify the medium- or longer-term effects of these reform measures. Still, we are able to see a newly emerging feature in Korea's fiscal politics: non-budgetary government spending has sharply increased, as more reform measures have been taken to strengthen the government's budgetary discipline.

Mounting Non-Budgetary Debts in Public Corporations

In response to growing oversight from the National Assembly, the government has tried to find an alternative way of increasing government spending, bypassing the approval and oversight of the National Assembly. For this purpose, the Korean government has mobilized public corporations—especially during the Lee Myung-bak administration (2008–13)—to carry out various social overhead capital (SOC)[18] projects over the past decade.

At the end of 2012, there were 295 public corporations, whose management and operations were controlled and supervised either by the central or local governments. As Table 6.6 shows, at the end of 2012, the total outstanding debt of the 295 public corporations was KRW493.3 trillion, which amounts to about

Table 6.6 Debt composition of public corporations, 2007–12 (trillion KRW, %)

	2007	*2008*	*2009*	*2010*	*2011*	*2012*
GDP (a)	975.0	1,026.5	1,065.0	1,173.3	1,235.1	1,272.5
Total debt (b)	249.2	290.0	336.8	397.0	459.0	493.3[1]
(b)/(a) (%)	25.6	28.3	31.6	33.8	37.2	44.5
Top 12 corporations (c)	186.9	227.7	267.4	324.4	378.7	412.3
(c)/(b) (%)	75.0	78.5	79.4	81.7	82.5	83.6

Source: KIPF (December 2013).

Note

1 This amount varies, depending on the scope of public corporations.

38.8 percent of GDP. This amount was larger than the total outstanding debt of the general government for the year (see Table 6.5). From 2007 to 2012, the outstanding debt amount of public corporations increased more than KRW244 trillion, which amounted to almost 50 percent of the total outstanding debt of all public corporations. Considering the fact that if public corporations cannot pay back their debt, all contingent financial liabilities are the government's responsibility, the growing debt of public corporations can result in a massive increase in public sector debt.

The debt of public corporations is concentrated in 12 major public corporations,[19] which primarily undertake government-directed economic activities such as SOC-related projects or energy development activities. As of the end of 2012, the share of those 12 major corporations was about 83.6 percent of the total outstanding debt of all 295 public corporations, reaching a total of about KRW412 trillion. The total debt of these major public corporations was only KRW59.4 trillion in 1997, but it increased roughly seven times in 15 years (KIPF 2013, 2). Moreover, the debt increase rate of these same public corporations grossly accelerated from 2007 to 2012, as Table 6.6 highlights. During this period, their total debt increased more than 2.2 times, from KRW186.9 trillion to KRW412.3 trillion. This increase rate of debt is much faster than the overall debt growth rate of the general government—as Table 6.5 shows—and the GDP growth rate.

While there might be other economic reasons for the mounting debt in the twelve major public corporations, one of the primary reasons is that the government has tried to use public corporations to bypass the approval or oversight of the National Assembly by launching various SOC projects. Indeed, according to an investigation by the BAI regarding the causes of mounting financial liabilities among public corporations from 2007 to 2011, more than half of the financial liabilities occurred as public corporations undertook government policy-related projects (mostly SOC projects), or the government repressed the public price levels for items—such as electricity and water—of public corporations despite the mounting prices of energy resources in the national markets (KIPF 2013).

The Four Major Rivers Restoration Project under the Lee Myung-bak administration represents one such case of bypassing the budgetary process. President Lee originally planned to build an inland canal, linking two major rivers—the

Hankang river and *Nakdong* river—but when he attempted to undertake the inland canal plan, many political opposition groups, including opposition political parties, and civic and environmental organizations united against the plan. Although President Lee was elected with a platform to build an inland canal, most popular polls[20] showed that the majority of the people opposed the inland canal project not only because of its cost or economic ineffectiveness, but also because of environmental concerns.

Under the continued popular protests and the overwhelming popular disapproval against the project, the Lee administration changed the original inland canal plan into the Four Major Rivers Restoration Project. The budget of about KRW22.2 trillion (approximately US$17.3 billion), however, was not enough to carry out the project in four major rivers simultaneously. Under the circumstances, the Lee administration forced the Korea Water Resources Corporations (KWRC) to participate in the Restoration Project. Indeed, KWRC's debt was only KRW1.75 trillion in 1997, but increased to KRW13.8 trillion by 2012, with its debt growing by 62.4 percent annually, from 2008 to 2012 (KIPF 2013, 26).

The mounting debt of the Korea Land and Housing Corporation (LH) also highlights the government's attempts to avoid formal budgetary oversight from the National Assembly. For example, LH's debt was only KRW14.7 trillion in 1997, but it increased to KRW138.1 trillion by 2012, which was about 33.5 percent of the total debt of the 12 major public corporations. From 1997 to 2012, LH's debt increased about 8.4 times with a 17.2 percent annual growth rate (KIPF 2013, 28). One of the primary reasons for such a rapid growth of LH's debt lies in the fact that the government has used LH for massive SOC projects, such as constructing big rented houses and new city building projects, during both the Roh and Lee administrations. Such politicized investment can create losses that the government must bear, as the case of Japan's system of SOC—the Fiscal Investment Loan Program—illustrates (Park 2011).

The mounting debt in public corporations highlights a couple of distinctive features developing in Korea's fiscal politics. First, the leadership factor matters for fiscal discipline. As reviewed, since the early 2000s the National Assembly has introduced a series of reform measures to enhance fiscal transparency and discipline. But such efforts were not effective—they were even futile—in checking and balancing the top leader's decision of using public corporations for fiscal purposes, bypassing the oversight of the legislature. This pattern indicates that not only fiscal institutions or rules, but also political elite commitment to fiscal discipline, are essential elements for successful fiscal consolidation.

Second, rising non-budgetary debt highlights that it is necessary to focus fiscal consolidation on both general government and non-financial/financial public corporations. The fiscal consolidation efforts in Korea, which were reviewed in the above section, have primarily focused on consolidating the various budgetary accounts into one.

Conventional fiscal politics has also centered on the budgetary process. However, the debt level of public corporations has already become larger than the debt of the government. Considering the fact that debts in public corporations can ultimately be a fiscal liability for the government, inter-sectorial fiscal consolidation is a necessary step for successful fiscal discipline, with more efforts needed to consolidate the entire public sector debt, covering both public corporations and the government.

Future Fiscal Challenges

The Korean government has faced, or will confront, many fiscal challenges resulting from economic and demographic changes. Of the various challenges, two critical issues need to be emphasized: Korea's dualistic employment structure and the aging population—specifically issues of poverty among the elderly population and mounting healthcare costs. To cope with these fiscal challenges, the Korean government has relied more on issuing public bonds, and those public bonds have been issued especially related to special government fiscal accounts.

Dualistic Employment and Industrial Structure

As of 2012, Korea's public spending on social security was the lowest among OECD countries. Likewise, employer contributions for social securities have been lower than those of other OECD countries. One of the primary reasons that makes it difficult to enhance employers' contributions is Korea's dualistic employment and industrial structure. In Korea, the proportion of irregular or part-time workers has sharply increased since the Asian financial crisis of 1997–98, as the Korean government has adopted aggressive labor market liberalization policies. Before the financial crisis it was difficult for employers to fire employees, but after the crisis regulations to preserve job security were lifted in the name of enhancing labor market flexibility. As a result, the number of irregular workers greatly increased.

As Table 6.7 shows, in 2004, out of a total 14.8 million wage and salary workers, more than five million workers (34.1 percent) were irregular workers, and 2.1 million workers were daily workers. This dualistic (or polarized) employment structure slightly improved between 2004 and 2011, but, due to a lack of job security, many irregular or daily workers could not participate in national pension, health insurance, or employment insurance through their companies. As a result, from 2004 to 2011, on average, only 40 percent of irregular workers could participate in these social insurance programs. Moreover, the percentage of self-employed workers is very high among Korea's economically active population. By 2011, of those 24.2 million economically active citizens, Korea's self-employment percentage was 28.8 percent, while the OECD average was 15.9 percent. Of those, 39.6 percent (9.6 million workers) were working in companies that have less than four employees (KOSIS portal). It is likely that this aggravating employment and industrial structure will increase pressures to expand social security programs for those who are not protected properly by the existing welfare programs.

Table 6.7 Social insurance subscribers, status of employed workers, 2004–11 (unit: %, 1,000 persons)

		Year[1]							
		2004	*2005*	*2006*	*2007*	*2008*	*2009*	*2010*	*2011*
National pension subscribers (%)	Regular	72.5	75.7	76.1	76.3	77.3	78.9	78.4	79.1
	Irregular	37.5	36.6	38.2	40.0	39.0	38.2	38.1	38.2
Health insurance subscribers (%)	Regular	73.8	75.9	76.1	76.7	78.0	79.8	79.5	80.9
	Irregular	40.1	37.7	40.0	42.5	41.5	43.4	42.1	44.1
Employment insurance subscribers (%)	Regular	61.5	63.8	64.7	64.3	65.8	67.6	75.7	77.4
	Irregular	36.1	34.5	36.3	39.2	39.2	42.7	41.0	42.3
Wage and salary workers (total)		14,894	15,185	15,551	15,970	16,206	16,454	16,971	17,397
Regular employees		7,625	7,917	8,204	8,620	9,006	9,390	10,086	10,661
		51.2%	52.1%	52.8%	54.0%	55.6%	57.1%	59.4%	61.3%
Temporary employees		5,082	5,056	5,143	5,172	5,079	5,101	5,068	4,990
		34.1%	33.3%	33.1%	32.4%	31.3%	31.0%	29.9%	28.7%
Daily workers		2,188	2,212	2,204	2,178	2,121	1,963	1,816	1,746
		14.7%	14.6%	14.2%	13.6%	13.1%	11.9%	10.7%	10.0%

Source: KOSIS. *Statistics Portal.* (http://kosis.kr).

Notes

1 The figures for workers who participate in national pension, health insurance, and employment insurance are based on the census data of August of each year.

2 The number of regular, temporary, and daily workers is the end of the year figure.

Aging Population: Poverty and Healthcare

An aging population is already posing a pronounced fiscal challenge to the Korean government. The proportion of the elderly population—people 65 years of age or over—in Korea reached 7.2 percent of the total population in 2000, and increased to 11.3 percent by the end of 2011. It is projected that the proportion will be over 20 percent by 2026, and close to 40 percent by 2050. As Table 6.8 shows, the aging index total dependency ratio, old-age dependency ratio, and working population to the old age group will grow rapidly in the coming decades. Indeed, as of the end of 2010, Korea's fertility rate—number of children born to women aged 15 to 49—was the lowest of all OECD countries, at 1.24, while the OECD average was 1.7 (OECD 2014, 17). In Korea's case, the demographic structure is being transformed too rapidly for social institutions to adjust. Population aging in Korea is projected to be faster than any other OECD nation. For instance, in Japan, it took 24 years for the elderly population to reach the level of 14 percent of total population, from 7 percent, and then took another 12 years to rise from 14 to 20 percent. However, in Korea, it took 18 years, and will take only 8 years, respectively, to make the same percentage jump.

The poverty rate among elderly people is much worse than that of other OECD countries—with the exception of Mexico and Chile—making fiscal management plans more challenging. As Figure 6.3 shows, in Korea, the Gini coefficient score—after taxes and transfers—in the working age group (18–65 years), is similar to the OECD average, 0.3, but the the Gini coefficent of the retirement age population (above 65 years) is 0.405. In other words, inequality is much worse in the retirement age population in Korea. More notably, the score gap

Table 6.8 Projection of aging population, 1980–2050

	Year								
	1980	*1990*	*2000*	*2010*	*2016*	*2020*	*2030*	*2040*	*2050*
Total dependency ratio[1]	60.7	44.3	39.5	37.3	37.2	40.7	58.6	77.0	89.8
Old-age dependency ratio[2]	6.1	7.4	10.1	15.2	18.5	22.1	38.6	57.2	71.0
Aging index[3]	11.2	20.0	34.3	68.4	99.5	119.1	193.0	288.6	376.1
Working population to old-age[4]	16.3	13.5	9.9	6.6	5.4	4.5	2.6	1.7	1.4

Source: KOSTAT 2011.

Notes
1 The total dependency ratio is the number of persons under age 15 plus persons aged 65 or older per 100 persons 15 to 64 years old.
2 The old-age dependency ratio is the number of persons 65 years and over per one 100 persons 15 to 64 years.
3 The aging index is calculated as the number of persons 65 years old or over per 100 persons under age 15.
4 The working population ratio is the number of persons 15 to 64 years divided by the number of persons aged 65 or over.

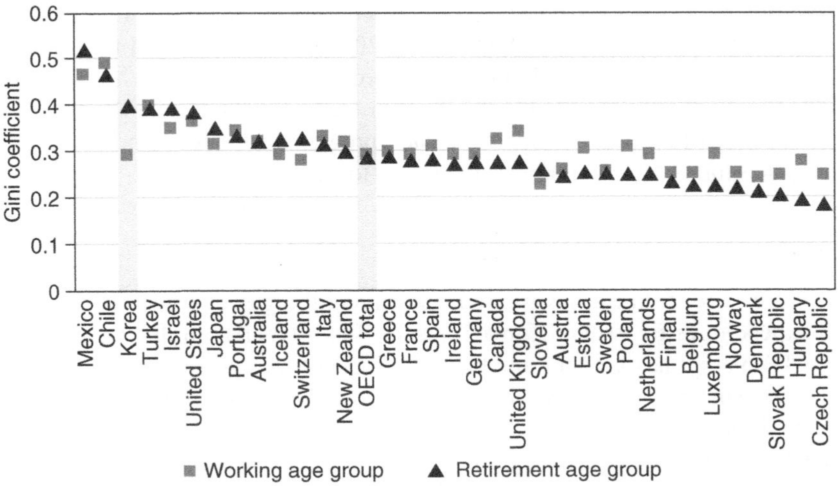

Figure 6.3 Gini coefficient (after taxes and transfers), OECD countries, late 2000s (source: OECD, *Database on Income Distribution Inequality* (www.oecd.org/els/social/inequality)).

(inequality) between these two age groups is much worse than any other OECD country. It implies that many retirement age Koreans are not financially prepared for their retirement life. Nonetheless, as of 2010, of those people who are 65 years or over, only 28.7 percent had jobs, while 71.3 percent were unemployed (KOSTAT 2011). With that said, public spending on old-age benefits was 1.6 percent of GDP in 2007, a quarter of the OECD average, resulting in only one-fifth of the elderly receiving pensions (OECD 2012a).

The poverty rate among the elderly population is already a social and fiscal problem. One of the most serious fiscal challenges is increasing medical costs for the elderly. For instance, as of 2011, the total medical fees paid by the National Health Insurance Service was KRW460 trillion, which was larger than the total annual budget of both the central and local governments. Of these fees, the cost for the elderly (65 year or above) was KRW148 trillion (32.2 percent). Considering the alarming growth of the aging population in Korea, the social and political demand for public social spending—especially for healthcare—will increase greatly in the near future.

To tackle these challenges, the Korean government needs to improve its public pension programs. As of 2012, there were three occupational pension plans—Government Employees' Pension Plan (GEPP), Private School Teachers' Pension Plan (PSTPP), and Military Personnel Pension Plan (MPPP)—and one universal pension program—National Pension Plan (NPP). These pension plans are no longer sustainable, as two of them already have deficits; MPPS has posted a deficit for over 10 years and requires government support of about KRW1 trillion each year. GEPP posted a deficit in 2001. The pension benefits of NPP are a defined-benefit program, which is not influenced by the investment performance of pension reserves, but by the level of inflation-adjusted monthly income of its pension participants. The current replacement rate is 50 percent, but it is scheduled to drop to 40 percent by 2028. The reserve fund for the NPP is projected to peak around 2043 but is forecast to be completely depleted by 2060 (Kim and Stewart 2011). To cope with these challenges, the Korean government needs to reform its public pension programs very soon and it is likely that such efforts will add more fiscal burdens to Korea.

Increasing Reliance on Public Bonds

The Korean government has tried to supplement the gap between tax revenues and expenditures by issuing Korea Treasury Bonds (KTB). For the past decade, the KTB market has grown remarkably in terms of its size and liquidity. As of 2011, the outstanding KTB reached a net worth of KRW340.1 trillion, representing 47.7 percent of GDP, while the annual trading volume increased to KRW3,045 trillion. The Korean government issues KTB on a regular basis, with the approval of the National Assembly, in five fixed maturities—3, 5, 10, 20, and 30 years—at the market interest rate through public tender. The demand for KTB has been on the rise, as the bid-to-cover ratio—a ratio that compares the number of bids received in a Treasury security auction to the number of bids accepted—indicates, while the KTB financing rate has been in decline. Moreover, the average term to the maturity of KTB has become longer—from 4.04 years in 2004 to 5.56 in 2011—as the Korean government has recently increased the issuance of 10-year bonds (Baek 2012).

Indeed, the current status of the KTB market is in good shape. Its turnover ratio—which is often used as a measure of bond market liquidity—is higher than that of other Asian government bonds markets, except Japan. The percentage of the KTB market to GDP stood at only 47.7 percent as of June 2012, while Japan's ratio of government bonds to GDP is 194.1 percent. The KTB is the most actively traded bond in Korea, and it is used as the benchmark and base rate in formulating the interest rate policy in the financial markets as in advanced economies where public bonds markets are well developed. Considering the short history of the KTB market, this must be seen as a remarkable development.

It should be noted, however, that the Korean government has issued increasing volumes of KTB as various kinds of funds, whose management has more flexibility over general or special accounts. As Figure 6.4 shows, the government's bond issuance for the special account of budgets has been in decline since 2002, but issuance for funds has sharply increased during the past years. Originally, the Korean government issued various kinds of KTB in the course of restructuring the financial sector after the Asian financial crisis (Kang 2009). Financial restructuring was a driving motivation for the Korean government to launch a plan for stimulating the KTB market. However, the Korean government has issued more KTB recently, not to supplement the deficits in the general or special accounts—which are more tightly monitored and reviewed by the National Assembly—but to benefit various public funds, in which the government has far more flexibility regarding management and operation.

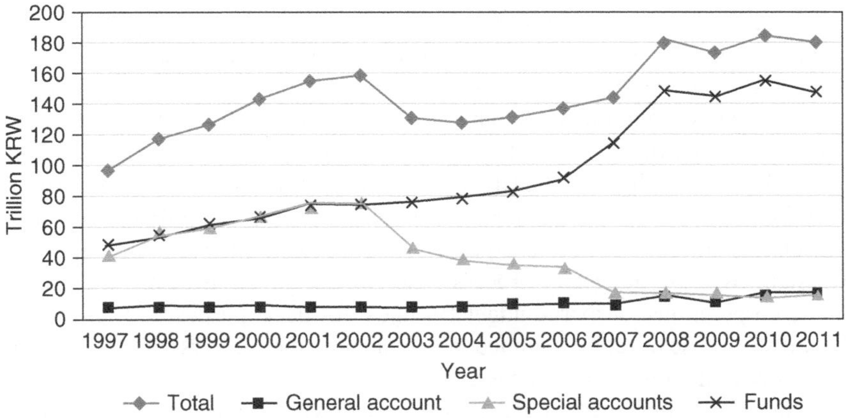

Figure 6.4 Government bonds issuance, type of fiscal accounts, 1997–2011 (source: MOSF, *A Report on the Gross Total of Government Bonds* (2012)).

Indeed, the National Finance Act (Article 70) allows the central agencies that operate funds to revise the amount of expenditures without submitting the revised expenditure plan to the National Assembly. They only need to get an approval from the National Assembly on their annual fund management plans, after which they can be far more flexible. As Figure 6.4 shows, the Korean government has sharply increased the issuance of funds-related government bonds from 2009 to 2012, but the detailed spending of those newly mobilized funds was beyond the oversight of the National Assembly. Despite the growing size of the KTB market, a "crowding out" effect—which drives down the spending/investment in the private sector—has yet to occur. However, the recent trend indicates that the Korean government may be tempted to use KTB to further meet the growing demand for social securities.

The new president, Park Guen-hye (2013–present), promised to aggressively increase social welfare spending as part of her campaign platform. She promised that her government would generate KRW27 trillion of tax revenue a year, or KRW135 trillion over the next five years, to expand various welfare programs. The political environment is favorable to the incumbent government—of which President Park is a member—as for the first time since the democratic transition in 1987, the ruling party gained the majority of seats in the legislative election in April 2012, and the president's popular vote exceeded 50 percent in the presidential election in December 2012. However, both the ruling party (*Saenuri* party) and the Park administration insisted that the government should expand more social welfare programs without increasing taxes. Under such circumstances, a viable option for the new government will be to issue more KTB. However, it is doubtful whether the Korean government can meet the mounting demand for public spending for social welfare programs without tax hikes, or undertaking substantive tax reforms.

Conclusion

The Korean case shows a similar pattern of growing fiscal indiscipline. Korea's fiscal indiscipline has worsened with growing political influence in fiscal policy making, growing political demands for social welfare spending, and aggravated macroeconomic conditions, as other cases of fiscal indiscipline have shown (Alesina and Perotti 1995; Alt and Lassen 2006; Fabrizio and Mody 2006; Eslava 2011; Blöchliger et al. 2012). However, we can find some distinctive features in Korea's recent fiscal performance as well. First, non-budgetary fiscal indiscipline has been strengthened as a way of bypassing the growing legislative oversight over the budgetary process. The Korean government has tried to use public corporations, or extra-budgetary funds, for fiscal purposes in response to the growing fiscal reforms aimed at enhancing the powers of the National Assembly in the budgetary process. We do not yet know whether it is a temporary phenomenon occurring only during the Lee Myung-bak administration, but at the very least, this phenomenon highlights that it is necessary to consolidate the fiscal accounts and debts covering both the general government sector and both financial and non-financial public corporations. In particular, in a country where the share of public corporations are high in the national economy, such efforts look essential for fiscal consolidation. Enhancing transparency and discipline in the budgetary process is critical for successful fiscal consolidation, but non-budgetary fiscal venues should be properly monitored and included in the fiscal consolidation agenda.

Second, unlike advanced welfare states, the tax-welfare nexus has not been developed fully in Korean fiscal politics. As reviewed, Korea's tax rate is much lower than the OECD average, and the share of indirect tax in total tax revenue is lopsidedly high. But the demand for expanding social welfares has been noticeably on the rise. Nonetheless, fiscal politics have not been centered around tax reforms or broadening the tax revenue. Instead, political conflicts have focused on the expenditure side, concentrating on how to allocate government budgets. This reflects the shallow tradition of the welfare state, and the short history of partisan and ideological fights concerning fiscal sustainability and accountability, unlike cases in advanced economies where partisan politics with diverging ideological orientations determine the fiscal politics. But considering the fiscal challenges the country faces, it appears essential for Korea to create a new kind of social pact concerning taxes and social welfare. In particular, the Korean government needs to broaden the tax base in those areas where proper taxes have not been levied, such as capital gain taxes and social security contributions by employers.

Third, the Korean case shows that rigorous fiscal rules concerning ceilings on the deficits of the government's fiscal accounts, or the debt level, can be necessary for better fiscal discipline, while minimizing political discretions and indiscipline. As to achieving fiscal consolidation effectively, the debate remains, especially as to the European Union case, whether fiscal institutions or fiscal rules matter more (Wyplosz 2005, 2011). In the Korean case, fiscal institutions have gradually changed. From the dominance of the executive to the legislature, and other reform measures aimed at enhancing fiscal transparency. Nonetheless, annual budget deficits have remained, and the public debt level has been on the rise. In this context, institutionalizing more clear fiscal rules as to the government's expenditures—either by legislation or creating a more neutral independent oversight agency—may be helpful in maintaining fiscal discipline. In the end, reforms for better fiscal governance in expenditure practices need reforms in both fiscal rules and institutions, and better governance will be essential for achieving fiscal discipline and meeting Korea's longer-term social needs.

Notes

1 Hereafter Korea/Korean will refer exclusively to South Korea.

2 For more details on the definition of fiscal performance and why we focus more on the long-term fiscal performance than overall short-run fluctuations of fiscal debt and consolidations, see the Introduction of this volume.

3 The EPB and the Ministry of Finance were merged and the Ministry of Finance and Economy was established in December 1994.

4 The IMF's manual for government finance statistics defines consolidation as "a method of presenting statistics for a set of units as if they constituted a single unit, and it involves the elimination of all transactions and debtor-creditor relationships that occur among the units being consolidated" (IMF 2001, 33).

5 The IMF's guide book on public sector statistics defines that "the general government sector comprises all government units and all nonmarket nonprofit institutions that are controlled by government units" (IMF 2013, 6).

6 For more details on the background of launching the PSD, see the official website (see following endnote 7).

7 Data are available at the PSD website (available at http://web.worldbank.org/WBSITE/EXTERNAL/DATASTATISTICS/EXTQPUBSECDEBT/0,,contentMDK:22720531~menuPK:7409953~pagePK:64168445~piPK:64168309~theSitePK:7404473,00.html) and the World Bank website.

8 Korea has adopted a two-tier local government system. There are 16 upper-level local governments (seven metropolitan and nine provincial governments) and 232 lower-level local governments: 91 counties (rural local bodies), 72 cities, and 69 urban districts.

9 All the local governments in Korea have chief executives (governors, mayors, county executives, and district executives) and local councils. Chief executives of both upper- and lower-level local governments are elected by direct popular vote for a four-year term. Lower-level council members are also elected by direct popular vote for a four-year term, and the upper-level council members are elected in a mixed form: While 10 out of 11 are elected by the popular vote, the remaining one is selected through a proportional representation system that was adopted just before the 1995 election. However, due to party nominations for those candidates for these elections, local elections have become an extension of the political struggle of political parties at the national stage.

10 The Roh Tae-woo administration (1988–93) is often treated as a continued regime of the past military dictatorship, as Roh Tae-woo himself was a general in the military and participated in the December 12 military coup. But it was established through a direct presidential election in December 1987 after the official democratic transition, so this chapter does not count it as a military dictatorship.

11 Article of 57 of the Constitution stipulates the changes in the budget bill as follows: "The National Assembly shall, without the consent of the Executive, neither increase the sum of any item of expenditure nor create any new items of expenditure in the budget submitted by the Executive."

12 Article 97 of the Constitution stipulates that:

> The Board of Audit and Inspection shall be established under the direct jurisdiction of the President to inspect and examine the settlement of the revenues and expenditures of the State, the accounts of the State and other organizations specified by Act and the job performances of the executive agencies and public officials.

13 The Westminster model has been adopted by most Commonwealth countries, a few European countries like Ireland and Denmark, and some Latin American countries, such as Peru and Chile.

14 The organizational capacity of the NABO is still limited. For instance, as of 2011, the NABO has 116 full-time employees, and its Program Evaluation Bureau has only 28 full-time employees, while the BAI has 1,035 full-time employees (Kim 2012.)

15 An extreme example is the revised Constitution (*Yushin*) in 1972. According to the revised constitution, the President was empowered to nominate one-third of the National Assembly members.

16 The Saenuri Party claimed a tailored lifelong welfare system that encompasses both universalism and selectivism, while the Democratic United Party campaigned for a universal welfare system. But in terms of the scale of public spending for social welfare, there were no significant differences between the two parties. Both parties promised to offer free child-care services for children under five, free education for high-school students, regardless of income level, and half college tuition and others.

17 Accrual accounting provides better information about government assets and liabilities, and the full costs of a government's fiscal activities. For more details on the benefits of accrual-based accounting over cash-based accounting and those countries that have adopted a full accrual accounting standard, see Khan and Mayes (2009).

18 The concept of "social overhead capital" (SOC) refers to transportation, communication, and power facilities in a narrow sense, but it also refers to facilities for such things as education and health, for maintenance of law and order, and for research. For more details, see Bruton (1968).

19 They are Korea Gas Corporation, Korea National Oil Corporation, Korea Electric Power Corporation, Korea Coal Corporation, Korea Resources Corporation, Korea Expressway Corporation, Korea Water Resources Corporation, Korea Railroad Corporation, Korea Land and Housing Corporation (LH), Korea Rail Network Authority, Korea Deposit Insurance Corporation, Korea Student Aid Foundation.

20 The support rate for the Four Major Restoration Project was 50:50 when the Lee Myung-bak administration was established, but it decreased continuously, in opposition to the Project. For instance, only 5 percent of the people supported carrying out the Project as President Lee had campaigned during the presidential election, according to a public poll conducted 100 days after the estabishment of the Lee administration (*Kukminilbo*, June 1, 2008).

References

Alesina, Alberto and Roberto Perotti. 1995. "The Political Economy of Budget Deficits." *International Monetary Fund Staff Papers* 42(1): 1–31.

Alt, James E. and David Dreyer Lassen. 2006. "Fiscal Transparency, Political Parties, and Debt in OECD Countries." *European Economic Review* 50: 1403–1439.

Baek, In Seok. 2012. "Changes in the Ktb Market after the Crisis and Challenges Ahead." *Capital Market Opinion*. Korea Capital Market Institute.

Bahl, Roy W., Chuk Kyo Kim, and Chong-gi Pak. 1986. *Public Finances during the Korean Modernization Process*, Harvard East Asian Monographs 107. Cambridge, MA: Council on East Asian Studies, distributed by Harvard University Press.

Bank of Korea, *Economic Statistics System.* (https://ecos.bok.or.kr).
Blöchliger, Hansjörg, Douglas Sutherland, and Dae-Ho Song. 2012. *Fiscal Consolidation: Part 4. Case Studies of Large Fiscal Consolidation Episodes.* OECD Economics Department Working Papers.
Bruton, Henry J. 1968. "Capital, Social Overhead." *International Encyclopedia of the Social Sciences.* (www.encyclopedia.com/doc/1G2-3045000162.html).
Cho, Yoon Je and Joon Kyung Kim. 1997. *Credit Policies and the Industrialization of Korea.* Seoul: Korea Development Institute.
Choi, Byung-sun. 1991. *Economic Policymaking in Korea: Institutional Analysis of Economic Policy Changes in the 1970s and 1980s.* Seoul: Chomyung Press.
Choi, Joon Nak, Myung-koo Kang, and Gi-wook Shin. 2014. "Democratic Transition and Intraparty Politics: The Distribution of Key Party Positions in Democratizing South Korea." *Journal of Korean Studies* 19: 7–36.
Choi, Kwang. 1992. *Public Finance in Korea.* Seoul: Seoul National University Press.
Eslava, Marcela. 2011. "The Political Economy of Fiscal Deficits: A Survey." *Journal of Economic Surveys* 25: 645–673.
Fabrizio, Stefania and Ashoka Mody. 2006. "Can Budget Institutions Counteract Political Indiscipline?" *Economic Policy* 21: 689–739.
IMF (International Monetary Fund). 2001. *Government Finance Statistics Manual.* Washington, D.C.
IMF (International Monetary Fund). 2013. *Public Sector Debt Statistics: Guide for Compilers and Users.* Revised second printing. Washington, D.C.
Kang, Myung-koo. 2009. "The Sequence and Consequences of Bank Restructuring in South Korea, 1998–2006: Too Fast to Adjust." *Asian Survey* 49: 243–267.
Katsiaficas, George N. 2012. *Asia's Unknown Uprisings (Vol. 1): South Korean Social Movements in the 20th Century.* Oakland, CA: PM Press.
Khan, Abdul and Stephen Mayes. 2009. *Transition to Accrual Accounting.* Washington, D.C.: International Monetary Fund (www.imf.org/external/pubs/ft/tnm/2009/tnm0902.pdf).
Kim, Byung-kook. 2000. "Party Politics in South Korea's Democracy: The Crisis of Success." In *Consolidating Democracy in South Korea*, ed. L. Diamond and B.K. Kim, 53–86. Bouder, CO: L. Rienner Publishers.
Kim, Choong-soon. 1992. *The Culture of Korean Industry: An Ethnography of Poongsan Corporation.* Tucson, AZ: University of Arizona Press.
Kim, Hyung-A. 2004. *Korea's Development under Park Chung Hee: Rapid Industrialization, 1961–79*, RoutledgeCurzon/Asian Studies Association of Australia (ASAA) East Asia Series. New York: RoutledgeCurzon.
Kim, Kun-oh. 2012. *Fiscal Consolidation and Budget Reform in Korea: The Role of the National Assembly.* RAND, Occasional Paper.
Kim, Sunhyuk. 2002. "Party Politics in South Korea." In *Korea in Transition: Three Years under the Kim Dae-Jung Government*, ed. Chung-in Moon and David I. Steinberg, 45–66. Seoul: Yonsei University Press.
Kim, Woochan and Fiona Stewart. 2011. *Reform on Pension Fund Governance and Management.* OECD Working Papers on Finance, Insurance and Private Pensions 7.
KIPF (Korea Institute of Public Finance). 2013. *Kongkongkikwan boochaewi woninkwa daechaek* (The Causes and Solutions of Mounting Debt in Public Corporations). Seoul.
Klarner, Carl E., Justin H. Phillips, and Matt Muckler. 2012. "Overcoming Fiscal Gridlock: Institutions and Budget Bargaining." *The Journal of Politics* 74: 992–1009.
Koh, Youngsun. 2007. "Reforming the Fiscal Management System in Korea." In *Fiscal Policy and Management in East Asia*, ed. Takatoshi Ito and Andrew K. Rose. Chicago, IL: University of Chicago Press.

KOSIS (Korean Statistical Information Service). *Statistics Portal*. (http://kosis.kr).

KOSTAT (Statistics Korea). 2011. *Jangraeinguchugye: 2010–2060* (The Prospect of Future Population: 2010–2060). Seoul.

Kwon, Keedon. 2004. "Regionalism in South Korea: Its Origins and Role in Her Democratization." *Politics and Society* 32: 545.

Lee, Byeong-cheon, ed. 2005. *Developmental Dictatorship and the Park Chung-Hee Era: The Shaping of Modernity in the Republic of Korea*. Paramus, NJ: Homa & Sekey Books.

Lee, Dong Ok and Stanley D. Brunn. 1996. "Politics and Regions in Korea: An Analysis of the Recent Presidential Election." *Political Geography* 15: 99–119.

Lee, Hahn-Been. 1968. *Korea: Time, Change and Administration*. 1st edn. Honolulu: East-West Center Press.

Lienert, Ian. 2005. *Who Controls the Budget: The Legislature or the Executive?* IMF Working Paper 05/115.

Ljungman, Gösta. 2009. *Top-Down Budgeting: An Instrument to Strengthen Budget Management*. IMF Working Paper 09/243.

MOSF (Ministry of Strategy and Finance). April 9, 2013. *2012hoegyeyundo kukkagyulsan gyulkwa* (Result of the Operation of State Fiscal Accounts in 2012). Seoul.

MOSF (Ministry of Strategy and Finance). 2012. *A Report on the Gross Total of Government Bonds*. Seoul.

MOSF (Ministry of Strategy and Finance). *Fiscal Statistics Portal*. (www.mosf.go.kr/lib/lib02.jsp).

OECD (Organisation for Economic Co-operation and Development). 2010. *Economic Survey of Korea 2010*. Paris.

OECD (Organisation for Economic Co-operation and Development). 2012a. "Social Spending after the Crisis." In *Secondary Social Spending after the Crisis*. Reprint. Paris.

OECD (Organisation for Economic Co-operation and Development). 2012b. *OECD Economic Outlook No. 92*. (www.oecd-ilibrary.org/economics/data/oecd-economic-outlook-statistics-and-projections_eo-data-en).

OECD (Organisation for Economic Co-operation and Development). 2012c. *Revenue Statistics 2012*. (www.oecd-ilibrary.org/taxation/revenue-statistics_19963726).

OECD (Organisation for Economic Co-operation and Development). 2014. "Fertility", in *OECD Factbook 2014: Economic,Environmental and Social Statistics*, OECD. (http://dx.doi.org/10.1787/factbook-2014-2-en).

OECD (Organisation for Economic Co-operation and Development). *Database on income distribution inequality*. (www.oecd.org/els/social/inequality).

Park, Chung Hee. 1962. *Our Nation's Path: Ideology of Social Reconstruction*. Seoul: Dong-a Publishing Company.

Park, Gene. 2011. *Spending without Taxation: FILP and the Politics of Public Finance in Japan*. Stanford, CA: Stanford University Press.

Stapenhurst, Rick, Riccardo Pelizzo, David M. Olson, and Lisa von Trapp, eds. 2008. *Legislative Oversight and Budgeting: A World Perspective*, WBI Development Studies. Washington, D.C.: World Bank.

Statutes of the Republic of Korea. 2010. *Local Finance Act*. (http://elaw.klri.re.kr/kor_service/lawView.do?hseq=24720&lang=ENG).

Statutes of the Republic of Korea. 2011. *National Finance Act*. (http://elaw.klri.re.kr/kor_service/lawView.do?hseq=22015&lang=ENG).

Tsutsumi, Masahiko, Thomas Cargill, and Randall Jones. 2010. *The Korean Financial System: Overcoming the Global Financial Crisis and Addressing Remaining Problems*.

OECD Economics Department Working Papers, No. 796. OECD Publishing. (http://dx.doi.org/10.1787/5kmbhk6d24ln-en).

Wehner, J. 2009. "Institutional Constraints on Profligate Politicians: The Conditional Effect of Partisan Fragmentation on Budget Deficits." *Comparative Political Studies* 43: 208–229.

Wyplosz, Charles. 2005. "Fiscal Policy: Institutions versus Rules." *National Institute Economic Review* 191: 64–78.

Wyplosz, Charles. 2011. "Fiscal Discipline: Rules rather than Institutions." *National Institute Economic Review* 217: R19–R30.

Yang, Jae-jin. 2013. "Parochial Welfare Politics and the Small Welfare State in South Korea." *Comparative Politics* 45: 457–475.

7 Fiscal Performance in Sweden

Jonas Edlund and Morinao Iju

Introduction

When the national economy collapsed in the early 1990s, Sweden experienced negative economic growth from 1991 to 1993, which resulted in large budget deficits as shown in Figure 7.1. The social democratic government, which came back to office in September 1994, announced the first fiscal consolidation plan in November the same year. By implementing the consolidation programs which combined with both expenditure cuts and tax increases, the government achieved budget surplus in 1998.

While implementing the fiscal consolidation programs, the government also reformed the budget system with the introduction of the State Budget Act in

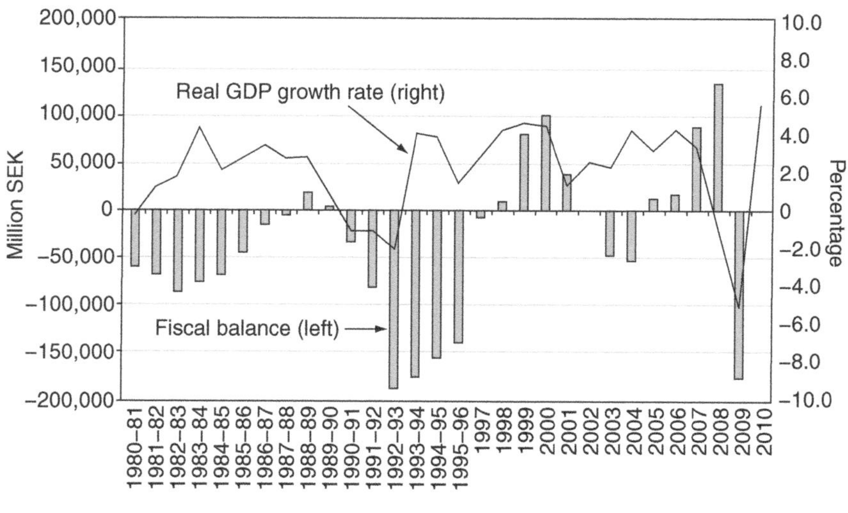

Figure 7.1 Fiscal balance for Swedish central government (source: *Statistisk Årsbok för Sverige*).

Note
The former fiscal year was from July to June (FY 1980/81) starts on July 1, 1980 and ends on June 30, 1981. The new fiscal year was changed to calendar year from 1997. Accordingly, only FY 1995/96 shows 18 months from July 1, 1995 to December 31, 1996. Real GDP growth rate is shown on a calendar-year basis.

1996, in which a new "three-year budget framework" was established. With the new budget system, Sweden succeeded in maintaining a comparatively high level of fiscal discipline even through the new century.[1]

The Swedish case is rather unique. The change from a situation characterized by negative economic growth, a huge budget deficit, an increasing gross debt, and an unemployment level around 10 percent to a situation with stable economic growth, a budget in balance, stable gross debt, low inflation, and an unemployment level around 5 percent took less than six years.

This chapter has two objectives. First, since Sweden has proven to be successful in achieving and maintaining fiscal consolidation, it is of interest to examine the key reforms in-depth, both for descriptive and informative purposes. Second, the chapter identifies the driving economic and political factors that made it possible to implement the reforms leading to fiscal consolidation and the construction of the current Swedish fiscal policy framework.

The chapter is structured as follows. First, the characteristics of the Swedish fiscal system are described. This is followed by a content-analysis of the consolidation programs that were implemented in response to the economic crisis. Next, the chapter takes a closer look at the Swedish budget system: a short historical overview is followed by an in-depth examination of the 1996 State Budget Act and the reformed budget process. The chapter closes with an analysis of the principal political actors' motives and behavior in relation to the consolidation policies as well as to the reformed fiscal policy framework.

The Swedish Fiscal Structure and its Characteristics

Tax and Expenditure Structure and Intergovernmental Relations

Table 7.1 shows the tax structure of the Swedish general government. Total tax revenue including social security contributions amounts to 1,422 billion SEK, equal to 54.9 percent of GDP in 2006. The main revenue sources for the central government are indirect taxes (VAT and excise duties) and social security contributions. Other revenue sources, of comparatively less significance, are taxes on property and corporations. The personal income tax is divided between central and local governments. For local governments, the proportional income tax, which has an average tax rate of approximately 31 percent, is the main tax revenue. On incomes above a certain limit, an additional tax is added by central government.[2]

Figure 7.2 shows the revenue and expenditure of the Swedish general government in 2006. Total revenue amounts to 1,756 billion SEK, of which tax revenue equals 1,422 billion SEK as shown in Table 7.1. The central government expenditure of 850 billion SEK consists largely of transfers (65 percent) and consumption (25 percent). The consumption expenditure covers areas such as defense, diplomacy, tax collection authorities, law and order, justice, higher education, and labor market policy. Half of transfer payments are allotted to social insurance payments to households such as sickness benefit, parents benefit, etc., which are managed separately from the social security fund for the

Table 7.1 Tax structure in Sweden, 2006

Tax items	*Tax revenue (SEK million)*	*Share (%)*	
State Income Tax	42,756	3.0	
of which Tax Reduction	–82,379	–5.8	
Capital Income Tax	37,423	2.6	Central Government
Corporation Tax	99,044	7.0	→ 810 billion SEK
Value Added Tax	265,151	18.6	57%
Excise Duties	112,283	7.9	
Others	89,065	6.3	Local Government
			450 billion SEK
Local Income Tax	454,117	31.9	32%
Social Security Contributions: employers	328,052	23.1	Social Security Fund
			→ 160 billion SEK
Social Security Contributions: employees	77,329	5.4	11%
Total	1,422,841	100	

Source: Skatteverket.

Note
Tax revenue for the state income tax shows negative due to tax credits.

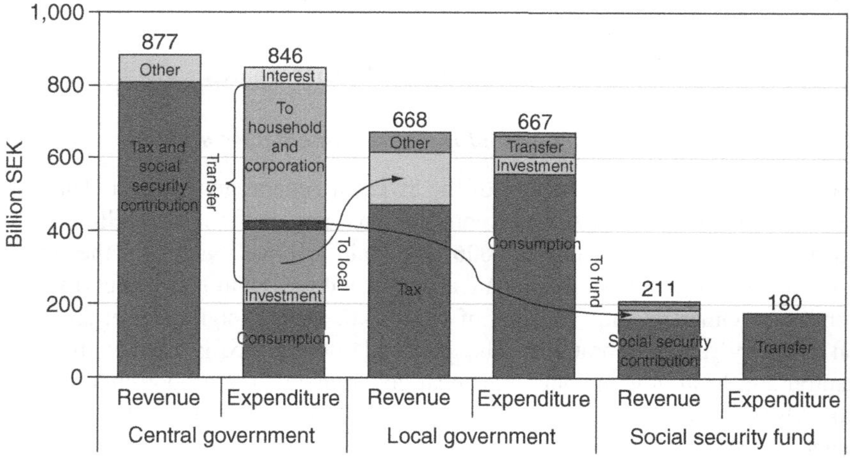

Figure 7.2 Revenue and expenditure of Swedish general government, 2006 (source: SCB, *Nationalräkenskaper*).

old-age pension. Transfer payments also include transfers to local governments, most of which are composed of general grants for equalizing the difference in fiscal power capacity of local governments.

Local government revenue mostly comes from taxes and general grants. The share of local income tax to local revenue is approximately 70 percent. Together with the general grant, most local government revenue is not ear-marked by the central government. As for the expenditure side, 85 percent of local expenditure is disbursed as consumption and the share of investment and transfer is limited. This means that while local governments are not engaged much in public works or cash payments to households, resources are distributed heavily to social services such as education, healthcare, welfare services.

Table 7.2 shows the expenditure structure of local governments. As seen in the table, the characteristic of expenditure assignment in Sweden is a clear division of responsibilities between municipalities and county councils. Municipalities take responsibility mainly for basic and secondary education and social services such as elderly care and child care, while county councils are responsible mostly for healthcare. There is no hierarchical relationship between both tiers of local governments because of this clear separation of the responsibilities (Elander and Montin 1990: 2).

Figure 7.3 shows the change of the general government expenditure excluding the social security fund as a percentage of GDP. The final consumption expenditure of the central government stayed around 10 percent after the late 1960s and then tended to decrease after the 1980s, though it increased temporarily at the beginning of the 1990s due to the increase in unemployment allowances and the expansion of labor market policy following the recession. Local governments' expenditures increased rapidly, especially after the late 1960s, and continued to increase until the beginning of 1980s, when it was stabilized at around 20 percent.

It should be pointed out that the trend of final consumption expenditure of local governments played a very important role in the development of the Swedish welfare state. While cash transfer to households by both the central government and the social security fund reached the level of 17–19 percent of GDP in the 1980s, the size of local expenditure increased to 20 percent of GDP in the early 1980s (SCB 2007: 18). During this period, in addition to the housing program, called the "million housing program," the construction of high schools and nursery schools strongly influenced local expenditures. Thus the expansion

Table 7.2 Expenditure structure of local governments in 2000

Municipalities			*County councils*		
	million SEK	*%*		*million SEK*	*%*
Education	98,707	32	Health care Social	135,860	88
of which Basic education	59,712		activities Mental	262	0
High school education	23,055		Health care Education	205	0
Elderly- and handicapped Care	95,092	31	and culture	5,183	3
Child care	39,862	13	Administration	4,193	3
Care for individuals and families	24,071	8	Others	19,617	6
Infrastructure, defense, etc	22,711	7			
Culture and recreation	16,906	5			
Immigrant, labor market policies	7,022	2			
Others	6,770	2			
Total	311,141	100	Total	156,320	100

Source: Den Offentliga Sektorns Finanser Verksamhetsåret 2000.

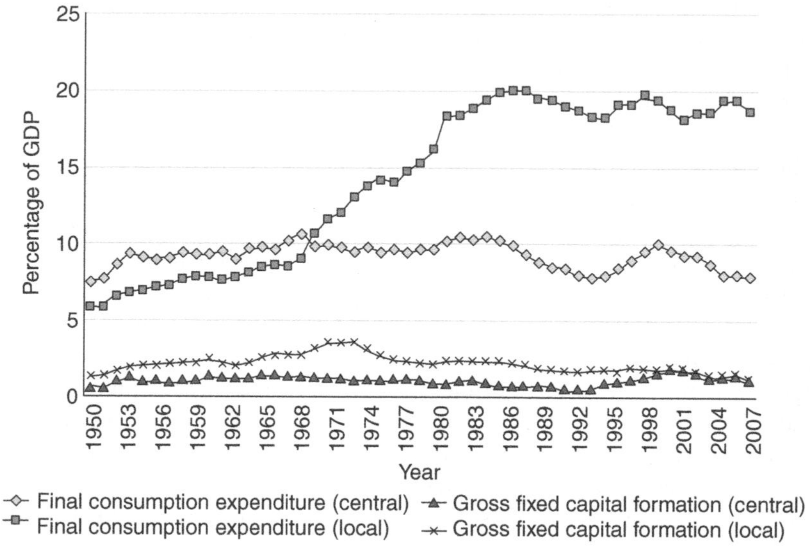

Figure 7.3 General government expenditure (percentage of GDP).

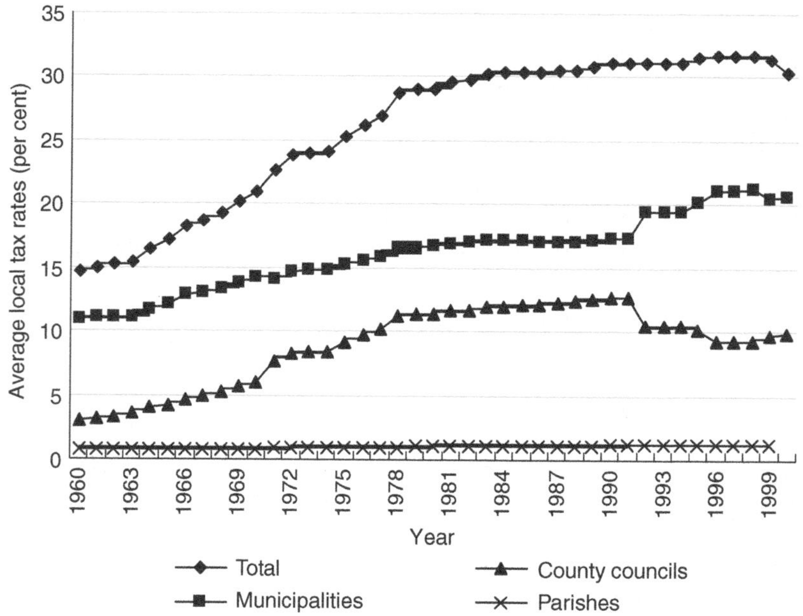

Figure 7.4 Average local tax rates (source: SCB (www.scb.se) and *Statistisk Årsbok för Sverige*).

Note
The local tax, which had been levied as parish tax, has been defined as charge after the parishes were excluded from local governments in 2000.

of the public sector in Sweden after World War II has been achieved largely by that of local governments since the late 1960s, in which the expenses for social services and healthcare increased rapidly.

How was the expansion of local governments financed? Figure 7.4 shows the change in average local income tax rates. The total average rate was around 15 percent in the early 1960s. It rose after the mid-1960s corresponding to the expansion of expenditure and reached over 30 percent in 1983. Each local government has the right to decide its own income tax rate since the local government ordinance in 1862 (Häggroth 2000: 13).[3] Here we can observe the important expenditure/revenue relationship. That is to say, while the Swedish municipalities and county councils rapidly increased the expenditures based on their own assignments to satisfy citizens' needs, they increased their own tax rates year by year so that the expansion of services could be financed.

Responses to the Economic Crisis: Fiscal Consolidation Policies 1994–98

The real GDP growth rate turned negative from 1991 to 1993, and the unemployment rate increased rapidly from less than 2 percent in 1990 to nearly 10 percent in 1993. As a result, the fiscal deficit of the general government reached 11.9 percent of GDP in 1993, and the gross debt reached 77.9 percent of GDP in 1994. It was recognized that the fiscal situation, where one-third of expenditure in the central government budget was borrowed and approximately one-third of expenditure was appropriated for interest payment, was not sustainable in the long term, and that a high interest rate due to the lack of trust in public finance would further delay economic recovery (Swedish Ministry of Finance 2001: 27).

During this severe situation, a parliamentary election was held in September 1994. The public concern was concentrated on economic problems, and the central issue was which party's fiscal consolidation plan would be the most effective for solving the situation (SCB 1995: 118).

The then bourgeois bloc coalition government had already presented its fiscal consolidation plan of 100.5 billion SEK in 1993 and 1994 (Table 7.3).[4] The fiscal consolidation plan put an emphasis on spending cuts such as the reduction of government consumption mainly on personnel expenses, and cutting transfer payments to households. It also aimed to reinforce tax increases through environmental taxes and excise duties. As to the reduction of transfer payments, the plan included the abolishment of partial pension, raising the pension age, lowering pension compensation rates, unemployment insurance, and parents insurance, and the abolition of the state subsidy for medical insurance (Finansdepartmentet 1993: 28). In contrast, the Social Democrats (SAP) highlighted that its approach was different from the government. In its campaign pledge, the Social Democrats emphasized consideration for income distribution, including reinforcement of capital income taxation and the maintenance of net wealth tax as revenue reinforcement, while asking a wide spectrum of the population to bear the burden of expenditure cuts.[5]

The new social democratic government announced the fiscal consolidation plan in November 1994 and carried out the programs that combined tax increases with expenditure cuts. In spite of being a minority government, the Social Democrats secured cooperation from the Left Party, as well as from the Center Party, which wanted to keep its distance from a Moderate Party that insisted on the fiscal consolidation solely through expenditure cuts (Swedish Ministry of Finance 2001: 28).

Three basic principles were adopted to prepare the fiscal consolidation plan: first, timing the program so as not to adversely influence demand; second, requiring a larger burden for higher-income groups from the viewpoint of income redistribution; third, focusing spending cuts on transfer payments to households, rather than benefits in-kind such as education, medical care, or social welfare services (Swedish Ministry of Finance 2001: 27).

In the fiscal consolidation plan which was announced in November 1994, the Social Democrats proposed to stabilize the gross debt of GDP by 1998 at the latest. The plan covered 56.4 billion SEK in addition to 18.3 billion SEK that had been already decided by the center-right government. In the budget bill of January 1995, the government raised the goal and added another reinforcement plan of 19.3 billion SEK to stabilize the gross debt of the central government by 1996 and achieve the fiscal balance of the general government by 1998.[6] Furthermore, 3.6 billion SEK was added in the revised budget bill of April 1995, 7.8 billion SEK in the revised budget bill of April 1996, and 20 billion SEK for EU contribution.[7] As a result, the fiscal consolidation programs amounted to 125.5 billion SEK in total, corresponding to 8 percent of GDP, and achieved the fiscal surplus in 1998 as targeted.

According to the government, the total amount of 125.5 billion SEK as shown in Table 7.3 was divided between expenditure cuts amounting to 66.1 billion SEK (52.7 percent) and 59.4 billion SEK (47.3 percent) in revenue reinforcements (Finansdepartmentet 1997a: 26).

As to the expenditure cuts, transfer payments in the social security area were the main targeted items, including the abolition of the at-home childcare allowance, reduction of child benefit, the reduction of pension payment, the reduction of compensation rates in social insurance such as unemployment benefits and medical insurance.

For the revenue reinforcement, the tax burden was increased mainly for high-income earners including the increase in the state income tax rate, reinforcement of capital income taxation, the maintenance of the net wealth tax, and increasing real estate and payroll taxes, as well as raising employees' burden for medical insurance. The income distribution analysis in the budget bill for 1998 suggested that 43 percent of the total amount for fiscal consolidation would be placed on the highest income quintile while 11 percent would be carried by the lowest (Finansdepartmentet 1997b: 30–31).

The Swedish fiscal consolidation programs in the 1990s were implemented by the Social Democrats on a large scale both in terms of expenditure reductions and revenue enforcements. According to the government, the choice behind the selection of expenditure and revenue areas was guided by the goal of fast economic recovery and the maintenance of services in-kind, but also to distribute the burden disproportionally towards higher-income groups. Moreover, based on

Table 7.3 Comparison of fiscal consolidation plans (billion SEK)

	Center-right coalition		*Social Democrats*	
Expenditure cut		76.8		71.2
	Transfer payments to households, etc.	36.8	Transfer payments to households, etc.	34.6
	Additional pension	5	Subsidies	8.1
	Government consumption	35	Government consumption	6.8
			Others	21.7
Revenue reinforcement		23.7		69.0
	Rationalization of tax collection	6	Self burden for medical insurance	23.7
	Base-broadening of VAT	2	Strengthening of capital income tax	7.5
	Environmental taxes and excise duties	14.7	Income tax to high income earners	4.2
	Reassessment of real estate	1	Production tax	6.1
			Others	27.5
Revenue cut		–		–14.7
			VAT	–7.6
			Others	–7.1
Total		100.5		125.5

Source: Finans Departmentet 1994: 49 and Swedish Ministry of Finance 2001: 28.

Note
The numbers show cumulative amounts to 1998.

the understanding that the former budget system in itself had brought structural fiscal problems ever since the 1980s, the government suggested that these consolidation programs should not be seen as a temporary measure, but should be complemented with policies directed towards sustainable fiscal management in order to achieve continuous economic recovery with employment recovery. With this recognition, a series of budget system reforms were implemented along with the fiscal consolidation plans (Swedish Ministry of Finance 2001: 27).

The Swedish Budget System: A Short History[8]

In the 1930s, Sweden adopted an economic stabilization policy ahead of other countries, under the influence of the Stockholm school such as Myrdal, Ohlin, and Lindahl, and introduced the double budget system in 1937, which consisted of the current budget and the capital budget. The current budget was based on the idea that the balance of budget should be achieved in the long term by utilizing the budget equalization fund for the purpose of fostering economic stabilization.

After World War II, the state budget expanded rapidly under the principle of long-term balance, and the social security system made progress. Supported by the high economic growth, there was not much criticism against the expansion of the state budget, but there were already arguments for a more rational budget process and cash management.

Influenced by the Planning, Programming, and Budgeting System (PPBS) in the United States, a program budget was introduced experimentally at the civil and military affairs administration for the first time in Europe in 1968. This budget reform, which aimed at more effective policy making and resource use—by systematizing policy planning, goal setting, budget compilation, budget execution, audit and policy evaluation—led to the introduction of the database of the accounting system and administrative audit by the national audit agency (RRV).

In the 1970s, the fiscal balance deteriorated rapidly due to the oil crises, and the budget equalization fund faced continuous shortage. The government committee for investigating the budget system had already urged the abolition of the double budget system in the report of 1973 since the budget system deviated from the traditional budget principles, such as the principle of comprehensiveness or gross budgeting, and the economic stabilization function did not work well. Following the recommendation, the double budget system was replaced by the current single budget system in 1980/81.

In addition, the attempt for more effective budget management, such as the program budget, made progress as a means for restraining expenditure at that time. In the budget compilation for 1979/80, every government agency was required to reduce the initial budget request to its ministry by 2 percent against the expenditure for the previous year.[9] However, only around one-third of the total followed this requirement. The reason for failure was that time was inadequate for agencies to prepare initial budget requests after the end of the previous fiscal year and that it was difficult to reflect policy results of the previous year since they needed to start budget preparation before the fiscal year ended. To solve this problem, a new reform was introduced in 1985, where an agency was required to reduce administrative expenses, excluding transfer expenses, by 5 percent over a three-year term. Following this attempt, the three-year budget compilation was applied to all expenses at government agencies in 1988. The model of the "three-year budget framework" was formed here, which became a main pillar of the budget system reform in the 1990s.

The introduction of three-year budgets gave government agencies discretion for efficient cash management. Directors of agencies were given comprehensive authority to decide personnel or equipment expenses that had before been closely controlled by the government (ESV 2001: 5). Following this, a new process of budget preparation within the government started from 1992, which estimated total expenditure and allocated it to each ministry within the three-year framework, though it did not having binding force in budget execution (SOU 2000: 50).

Furthermore, the discretion of agencies to execute appropriations was also expanded at the same time. The traditional appropriations had been comprised of estimated appropriation (*förslagsanslag*), multi-year appropriation (*reservationsanslag*) and fixed appropriation (*obetecknade anslag*). As for estimated appropriation, excess spending was possible without the approval of parliament while carry-forward of unused appropriation was not allowed. More than 80 percent of total expenditure was allocated as estimated appropriations. In multi-year appropriation, excess spending was not allowed while carry-forward to the following year was possible. This had been utilized mainly for infrastructure investment, where spending could not be completed within a year. In fixed appropriation, neither excess spending nor carry-forward was allowed. It had been usually used for subsidies to organizations such as museums, which did not belong to the public sector.

Flexible appropriation (*ramanslag*) was newly added to the traditional appropriations in 1988 at certain agencies in order to expand their discretion over cash management and was fully adopted from 1993. In this appropriation, both excess spending and carry-forward were accepted, and the excess spending was deducted from the appropriation of the following year. The conventional idea of input management switched to the new approach of outcome management. As a result, improvement of financial and administrative reports was required to increase accountability of agencies' outcome.

In 1993, accrual basis accounting was introduced at all the agencies, and consolidated financial statements of the central government came to be made from 1993/94. In addition, interest payment costs were distributed across each agency by the introduction of internal loans by the National Debt Office for agency investment, which enabled more accurate cost distribution and cost accounting. In other words, it was intended to establish outcome management through the accrual based cost and administrative accounting (ESV 2001: 7).

Budget System Reform with Introduction of the State Budget Act in 1996

Problems of the Former Budget System

In the early 1990s, two reports on the Swedish budget system were submitted. One was a report from an expert group of the Ministry of Finance, and the other was a report by a governmental economic committee (Lindbeck Committee) which was organized mainly with well-known Swedish economists and political scientists during the economic crisis.[10]

The expert group report of the Ministry of Finance evaluated fiscal discipline in Sweden, applying the same method as von Hagen's study that investigated the budget systems and the fiscal disciplines of 12 European countries for the introduction of European Monetary System (EMS). The report suggested that the Swedish budget system was weak, only above that of Italy, from the viewpoint of budget compilation, parliamentary control, transparency of budget, flexibility in execution, and long-term prospect (Molander 1992: 28).

In concrete terms, the report pointed out the following problems. First, as there was no base value at the budget preparation stage, budget demands from agencies became the starting value. Second, no one was able to know the total amount of the budget until it was finally decided because the budget bill was increased without limitation in budget deliberations in parliament. Third, budget documents lacked transparency because expenditure appropriations to the budget were insufficient about loans to off-budget funds and non-governmental corporations, and the classification of the budget did not correspond with that of the National Accounts. Fourth, both the Ministry of Finance and the parliament lacked a supervisory role over the budget execution process. Fifth, there were stringent limits for the transfer of appropriations between fiscal years. The long-term prospect of the budget was evaluated positively because of the three-year budget (Molander 1992: 25–28).

In order to solve these problems, the report proposed the following: first, expansion of the flexibility of appropriations; second, expansion of the coordination function of the Prime Minister's Office and the Budget Bureau of the Ministry of Finance in budget compilation; third, the application of the principle of comprehensiveness to budget documents; fourth, the adoption of a new parliamentary deliberation system (frame-decision model); fifth, reinforcement of policy evaluation and audit function of the parliament as its central role (Molander 1992: 30–32).

In addition to these reports, the parliament itself implemented an examination about its budget deliberation. A report submitted in 1993 by the parliamentary committee pointed out several problems, many of which overlapped with the remarks in the government reports. Based on these points, the report suggested the following: first, application of the principle of comprehensiveness; second, adoption of the frame-decision model in the parliamentary deliberation; third, shift of fiscal year to calendar year; fourth, two-step parliament deliberation in the spring and the autumn; fifth, reinforcement of the coordination function of the parliamentary finance committee (SOU 2000: 51).

The State Budget Act in 1996 and New Budget Process

The system reform was carried out in the mid-1990s, with reform proposals coming from several directions. It should be noted when we examine the reform that the budget compilation by the government and the budget deliberation at the parliament are regulated respectively by two different laws.

The parliament approved the parliamentary committee's proposals and amended the Parliament Act (Riksdagsordningen). The main contents of the amendment are the change of fiscal year to calendar year, the two-step budget deliberation of fiscal policy plan in the spring and government budget bill in the autumn, the adoption of the top-down frame-decision model, the change of classification of appropriations, and the extension of parliament's mandate period from three to four years.

As shown in Table 7.4, it was six months before the start of the next fiscal year when the government submitted a budget bill to the parliament in the former budget making process and the government submitted a revised budget bill based on modifications at parliamentary committees. The new process consists of a spring fiscal policy bill and a government budget bill. The spring fiscal policy bill, so-called "spring budget," is submitted nine months before the

Table 7.4 Change of budget-making process in Sweden

Fiscal year	*Periods to year beginning*	*Former Process*		*New Process*	
		Calendar	*Contents*	*Calendar*	*Contents*
N-1	11 months ago		Budget proposals inside agencies	early February	Each ministry's three-year revenue/ expenditure estimation to MoF annual reports (22 February) and budget demands (1 March) from agencies
	10 months ago	1 September	Budget demands from agencies to ministries	mid-March	Original budget bill by MoF
			Budget demands from ministries to the ministry of finance (MoF)	end March	Cabinet budget meeting: three-year ceiling for total expenditure and limits for 27 expenditure areas
	9 months ago			15 April	Spring fiscal policy bill to Parliament
	8 months ago		Coordination between MoF and other ministries	mid-May	Each ministry distributes to each appropriation
					Coordination between MoF and other ministries
	7 months ago	early December	Original budget bill by MoF	15 June	Parliament decision on Spring bill
			Coordination inside Government based on fiscal and economic situations		
	6 months ago	10 January	Government budget bill to Parliament	July	(EU budget making)
	4 months ago		Deliberation at each parliamentary committee	20 September	Government budget bill to Parliament
					Finance committee deliberates limits for 27 expenditure areas
					Each committee deliberates each appropriation
	2 months ago	end April	Revised budget bill to Parliament		
	1 month ago			end November	Parliament decision on limits for 27 expenditure areas
		end June	Decision in Parliament and Government	end December	Parliament decision on each appropriation
					Government decision
			Letter of instruction		Letter of instruction
N		1 July	Execution of Budget	1 January	Execution of Budget

Sources: Lane and Back 1989: Chapter 3 and Finansdepartmentet 2008.

following fiscal year and functions as a guideline for economic and budgetary policies, while the government budget bill is submitted four months before. The government can submit a revised budget bill only for special reasons, and accordingly the former process of submitting a revised budget bill was abolished.

Next, the frame-decision model means that the parliament deliberates the budget bill in two phases. In the first phase, the finance committee decides total expenditure and the upper limits of 27 expenditure areas, and in the second phase each committee in charge of each expenditure area decides each individual appropriation. With this model, the finance committee has a stronger coordination function and the Pay-As-You-Go principle has been applied to the budget allocation to expenditure areas as well as the deliberation in the individual committee (SOU 2000: 57). In addition, appropriations, which had been classified according to ministry, were changed to a classification among 27 expenditure areas corresponding to parliamentary committees. At the same time, the number of appropriations decreased from approximately 1,000 to 500. Furthermore, the fiscal year, which ran from July 1 to June 30, was changed to a calendar year in order to easily link budget compilation with various economic statistics from the viewpoint of macroeconomic management.

These changes to budget deliberation in the parliament have been applied since the budget compilation for 1997. While the former budget making process weakened fiscal discipline due to many modifications made at parliament level, the new process has contributed to improving discipline with the top-down decision model (Wehner 2007: 324). However, the Parliament Act never limits parliament's authority to increase the amount of the budget bill. In other words, the parliament reserves the authority to increase expenditure by its own decision. Therefore, it is the "three-year budget framework" introduced by the State Budget Act in 1996 which plays a key role in securing the fiscal discipline through the budget process based on the Parliament Act.

The legal framework related to the former budget system was limited to the Constitution (*regeringsformen*), the Parliament Act, and the State Borrowing Act (*lagen om statens upplåning och skuldförvaltning*). Although the parliament was responsible for deciding basic matters about the state budget—and it had actually made many decisions on budget matters—the processes and the distribution of responsibilities between the parliament and the government lacked clear guidelines (SOU 1996: 104–106). Accordingly reform aimed at making clear the responsibilities of the government for budget compilation by introducing a budget act to cover the decisions which had already been made.

The State Budget Act (Budgetlagen), enacted in 1996, clarified the responsibility of the government for the budget compilation. It contained the provisions concerning effective administration and outcome management of government activities, expenditure and revenue appropriations, range of budget, financing of investment, sale of state properties, financial prospects and ex-post evaluations, accounting and audit, and delegation to agencies. In addition, it also provided that the government set the multi-year budget framework to strengthen the frame-decision model in parliament and to enable long-term budget policy. This act, as well as the amendment of the Parliament Act where the three-year budget framework was established, started to be applied from the budget compilation for 1997.[11] As for expenditure appropriations, estimated appropriations, in which carry-forward was not allowed, were abolished because it would be difficult to combine them with an expenditure ceiling. Instead, appropriations were composed mainly of flexible appropriations.[12]

The characteristics of the new budget making process are shown in Table 7.4.[13] In the new budget making process with the new fiscal year, the Ministry of Finance updates the three-year framework from January to March, based on the latest economic data and budget demands from ministries and agencies. This process comprises three phases. First, the Ministry sets the general government's fiscal surplus target of GDP. Second, it sets the amount of upper limit of total expenditure, i.e., expenditure ceiling, to realize the surplus target. Third, it presents the distribution of total expenditure into the 27 expenditure areas under the expenditure ceiling. The fiscal surplus target, which was introduced from the budget compilation for 1997, and fully applied from 2000, aims at maintaining the general government's fiscal surplus of 1 percent of GDP through a business cycle.[14] Although the target was set mainly to reduce the gross debt when it was introduced, now it has several purposes such as securing trust in the fiscal policy from the nation, corporations and financial markets; maintaining the fiscal discipline to implement an active fiscal policy during economic recession; achieving fairness between generations in the context of an aging society; and avoiding a rising tax burden ratio (Boije et al. 2010: 204).

The expenditure ceiling includes not only central government expenditure but also expenditure for the old-age pension.[15] In mid-March, the Ministry of Finance prepares a draft for the new budget framework and submits it to the cabinet budget meeting. The budget framework lists the ceilings of total expenditure and 27 expenditure areas for the three coming years. As the numbers for the first two years are already decided, the government only adds the numbers of the third year unless it intends to revise the first two.

While each amount of the 27 expenditure areas is distributed under the expenditure ceiling, the difference between the total expenditure ceiling and the sum of 27 expenditure areas is defined as a budget margin. This functions as a buffer to maintain the total expenditure, when the expenditure changes due to modifications in economic forecasts, etc. The budget margins are usually set with 1.5, 2, and 3 percent of total expenditure from the first to third year.

The cabinet budget meeting in late March approves the budget draft from the Ministry of Finance, where the argument is focused mainly on additional budget demands from ministers. As the Pay-As-You-Go principle is also applied here, each minister must demand the redistribution of resources from another expenditure area or redistribute within his/her own area when he/she requests an increase in some appropriation. The spring fiscal policy plan is prepared based on the decision at the cabinet meeting and is submitted to the parliament by April 15.[16]

Each ministry prepares to draft the government budget bill for the next fiscal year while the parliament deliberates the spring fiscal policy bill. In August, the Ministry of Finance prepares budget-related documents while revising economic forecasts and making technical corrections to the budget bill. Thereafter, the government, after the cabinet decision, submits the budget bill to the parliament by September 20, and the parliament deliberates the bill according to the above-mentioned model and makes the final decision.

Thus, the new budget making process is comprised of the budget compilation by the government based on the three-year budget framework and the budget deliberation in parliament according to the frame-decision model. In particular, compared with the former process, which led to the loosening of fiscal discipline, under the new system the Ministry of Finance has an overarching responsibility for the budget process.

Evaluation of the New Budget System

Let us first consider the effects that the new budget making process has on the maintenance of fiscal discipline. Table 7.5 shows fiscal surplus target and its average, original expenditure ceiling, ex-post budget margin, and its proportion to expenditure ceiling since 2000 when the fiscal surplus target came to be fully applied. The fiscal surplus target, particularly when we see its average, stayed around 1 percent in the mid-2000s, which means that it did not achieve the original target of 2 percent, while some recovery can be observed in recent years. However, as the National Audit Office and the Fiscal Policy Council point out, the definition of the business cycle as a basis for numerical targets is uncertain and accordingly some evaluations prove to be incorrect. Therefore, the setting of indices toward long-term fiscal sustainability is being considered (Boije et al. 2010: 213).

The second point is concerned with the setting of expenditure ceiling by the government. Although it is possible to change the original ceiling for other than technical reasons, such changes have been made only twice before 2009, in which cases ceilings were actually reduced (ibid.: 206). We can also check if the expenditure ceiling is in practice respected by the ex-post budget margin. As seen in Table 7.5, the ex-post budget margin is positive every year, and its proportion to the ceiling shows a tendency of increasing in the latter half of the 2000s.

Overall, it seems that the three-year budget framework has functioned well (Boije et al. 2010; Swedish Government Office 2011). Next, let us examine the influence of the new system on the budget deliberation in parliament. The new process has decreased considerably the number of modifications of the budget bill at the parliament (Wehner 2007: 323–324).

A comparison of the average number of modifications to the budget, pre- and post-reform shows the following. In the period 1985/86 to 1995/96 (pre-reform), there were 33 modifications per year on average. In the 1997 to 2005 period (post-reform) the average number decreased to six. Wehner argues that this is a huge decrease even considering that the number of appropriations was reduced to half. In addition, this change becomes even clearer when we observe the change of the modified amounts. Modifications of the budget bill before the reform almost always led to an increase of the total expenditure. In contrast, after the reform until 2005, the parliament only increased the bill once.

Table 7.5 Changes of fiscal surplus, expenditure ceiling, and budget margin

	2000	*2001*	*2002*	*2003*	*2004*	*2005*	*2006*	*2007*	*2008*	*2009*
Fiscal surplus of GDP	3.7	1.7	−1.4	−1.2	0.6	2.0	2.4	3.8	2.5	−0.8
Average since 2000 (cyclically adjusted)	2.5	2.3	1.4	1.0	0.9	1.1	1.1	1.2	1.4	1.4
Expenditure ceiling (billion SEK)	765	791	812	822	858	870	907	938	957	989
Budget margin (billion SEK)	5.0	4.7	0.4	2.9	2.4	5.7	11.8	27.9	13.6	24.4
Proportion of budget margin (%)	0.7	0.6	0.0	0.4	0.3	0.7	1.3	3.1	1.4	2.5

Source: Boije et al. 2010: Table 1, 2.

Under the hard budget constraint of the expenditure ceiling based on the parliamentary decision, some loopholes have been created in some countries (Hansson Brusewitz and Lindh 2005: 677–678). In the new Swedish budget system, the principle of gross budgeting is applied, and all revenue and expenditure are to be appropriated to the budget as a general principle.

Moreover, the multi-year fiscal plan calls for accurate economic forecasts because optimistic forecasts would enable the government to make excessive revenue estimates. In Sweden the National Debt Office, being independent from the Ministry of Finance, makes an estimate of borrowing required; the National Financial Management Authority presents a mid-term revenue/expenditure prospect for the central government; the National Institute of Economic Research announces a mid-term fiscal prospect for the general government; and the Fiscal Policy Council works on evaluation of the government's fiscal policy. Through these attempts, the government tries to secure objectivity and accuracy of the economic forecasts by the Ministry of Finance.

In conclusion, evidence suggests that the reformed Swedish budget system functions effectively. In terms of democratic control, it is clear that the power has further moved to the Ministry of Finance at the expense of the parliament. While there are external agencies monitoring the goal fulfillment of the government's fiscal policy objectives, a well functioning apparatus of parliamentary control over the budget process has not been constructed.

Consolidation Policies and Current Fiscal Policy Framework: A Short Political History

In order to make sense of the Swedish political history behind the fiscal consolidation programs as well as the current fiscal policy framework, it is necessary to move back to the 1980s as some of economic policies from that period significantly contributed to an overheated economy and, eventually, to the economic collapse in the early 1990s. During this period, the Social Democrats and two parties within the bourgeois bloc—the Liberal Party and the Center Party—moved closer together in terms of fiscal policies and paved the way for critical political deals. This collaboration laid the foundation for future agreements on both consolidation and fiscal policies.

Social Democratic Government 1982–91

When the Social Democrats returned to office in 1982, most key statistics regarding the national economy signaled that it was in a poor state. By identifying the export industry as the main vehicle for economic recovery, the Social Democrats designed a "stimulus-package" including a significant devaluation of the krona (16 per cent) and a fixed krona exchange rate. Boosted by the devaluation, the export industry soon began to flourish and other sectors of the economy were positively affected. However, these measures involved a substantial redistribution of income from labor to capital, which led to frictions within the labor movement.

In 1985, known as the November revolution, the Swedish central bank in cooperation with the Social Democrats decided to deregulate the credit and banking systems (Feldt 1991; Carlsson 2003). These two factors—a prosperous economy and the liberalization of the financial markets—in combination with the breakdown of controlled centralized wage-bargaining would in a few years lead to a grossly overheated economy. However, in the latter part of the 1980s, most actors and scholarly commentators on the subject did not recognize the ominous signs of a forthcoming crisis. Quite the contrary, the dominant view suggested that the Swedish economic recovery—especially the ability of the state to bring down a huge budget deficit while still maintaining full employment—was a success story and, in a European context, Sweden should be seen as a role model (Pfaller et al. 1991 and works cited therein).

During 1988–89, the social democratic inner circle became increasingly aware that measures needed to be undertaken to cool down the booming economy (Feldt 1991; Carlsson 2003). However, when attempting to persuade different parts of the labor movement as well as their main ally in the parliament—the Left Party Communists—about the necessity to take strong actions to slow down the overheated economy and decrease inflation, the social democratic leadership ran into substantial problems, largely because the previous measures undertaken by the government had involved a massive redistribution of income and wealth to capital at the expense of ordinary citizens' real wages. On top of that, the social democratic leadership was in the process of changing the tax system in cooperation with the Liberal Party (Edlund 1999). The "tax reform of the century" included significant cuts in marginal income tax rates and would, in the words of the then finance minister Feldt (1991: 385), "demand exceptional pedagogical and agitatorial efforts [...], since the new tax system at first glance could be perceived as a violation of every social democratic idea of how justice is done".[17]

The period between 1988 and 1991 can be described as a gradual decline of mutual understanding between the social democratic cabinet and its traditional allies—the rank-and-file members of the party and the labor unions—regarding the design of both implemented and planned economic policies (Elmbrant 1993). The internal frictions within the labor movement as well as the reluctance of the Left Party Communists to support the governing party, forced, more or less, the Social Democrats to negotiate with two parties within the bourgeois bloc, the Center Party and the Liberal Party.

Together with the Liberal Party, the Social Democrats signed the "tax reform of the century" deal and together with the Center Party, a policy package designed to cool down the economy was signed in 1989. In 1990, after several unsuccessful attempts to close major binding agreements between the social partners on the labor market, the social democratic government decided to implement further policies in order to cool down the economy. Here, it is important to note that a number of traditional policies and agreements to control the economy were not available due to the deregulation of the credit and banking systems, the fixed currency exchange rate, and the breakdown of centralized wage bargaining. The tools chosen by the government were non-traditional social democratic policies, such as wages and price freezes and restricting rights to strike (Elmbrant 1993). The Social Democrats did not receive support for these measures and as they had framed this as a "cabinet question" they had to resign in February 1990.[18] However, the parties within the bourgeois bloc were not able to come up with a realistic government alternative, and the Social Democrats returned to office. The Social Democrats had lost their faith in the Left Party Communists as a reliable partner and turned once again to the Liberal Party. Together they designed a "crisis-package" aiming at reducing cost further, which was passed by the parliament. This collaboration further helped to strengthen the ties between the Social Democrats and the Liberal Party leaderships.

Bourgeois Coalition Government 1991–94

In 1991, general elections were held, and the Social Democrats lost power by a large margin. The policies initiated by the Social Democrats, such as the interventions in the wage-negotiation process, the deregulation of financial markets, and the reformation of the tax system, gradually disillusioned traditional left voters from the party, since the government seemed to have tremendous difficulties controlling the economy (Korpi 1993; Åberg 1993).

The parliamentary situation after the election was complicated. A new right-wing populist party, New Democracy, gained parliamentary representation, preventing a traditional majority government solution. While some of the four parties within the bourgeois bloc were open to negotiations with New Democracy, the Liberal Party was strongly against it, and preferred cooperation with the Social Democrats. However, due to the long tradition of bloc politics, the four bourgeois parties formed a minority government, headed by the Moderate Party.

Coincident with the change of government, the signs of an emerging economic crisis became increasingly apparent: large capital outflows, an increasing budget deficit, increasing unemployment, and large bank credit losses. The Moderate Party-dominated government attempted to solve the situation by implementing policies along the neo-liberal formula: capital friendly tax cuts to promote economic growth. However, the budget deficit continued to increase, and confidence in the Swedish economy among major financial market actors declined, as manifested by continuing large capital outflows and speculation against the krona. During the fall of 1992, an internally divided government invited the Social Democrats to negotiate. The Social Democrats had mixed feelings. In their view, the Moderate Party leadership had behaved arrogantly ever since in office; moreover, the Moderate Party had refused to help them during the previous decade when the Social Democrats were in trouble. But due to the previous successful collaboration with the Center Party and, in particular, the Liberal Party, the Social Democrats accepted the invitation and together the five parties designed two "crisis-packages" in order to bring down the budget deficit, which was considered to be the main cause behind the lack of confidence in the Swedish economy among financial market actors. However, these measures did not solve the situation, capital outflows and currency speculations continued, and, finally in November 1992, the central bank was forced to abandon the fixed currency exchange rate. The value of the krona immediately dropped substantially (Elmbrant 1993; Isaksson 1994).

While many considered the agreements between the Social Democrats and the bourgeois government as an historical event where the five parties cooperated across the bloc border, it did not have any lasting effect regarding the design of the policies enacted by the government for the rest of the mandate period. However, the mutual understanding and similar frames of reference between the Social Democrats on the one hand, and the Center and the Liberal Parties on the other hand, were intact and strengthened.

Seen in retrospect, Swedish politics was in a state of emergency. Rapidly increasing unemployment, from less than 2 percent in 1990 to nearly 10 percent in 1993, and a huge budget deficit put the welfare state under severe pressure. The profound economic crisis was perceived as a national matter of utter importance and acted as such as a uniting force between the major political party leaderships. While it was a matter of disagreement about the roots of the crisis, it was commonly agreed that the solution of the crisis was to be found in policies to bring the state finances in balance. In short, at the end of the mandate period, the Swedish voters were confronted by a political message backed up by nearly all major organized interests arguing that if Sweden failed to get the budget in balance, things would get even worse.

Social Democratic Government 1994–2002

The recession cast its dark shadow over the 1994 general elections. The campaign was rather unique in the sense that there was political consensus across the major parties on the necessity to get the budget in balance (Gilljam and Holmberg 1995). According to the election result, the Social Democratic campaign, which emphasized both spending cuts and revenue enforcements, was rather successful. Compared to the 1991 election, the Social Democrats went from 37.6 to 45.3 percent, while the electoral support for the bourgeois coalition dropped considerably, from 46.6 to 41.4 percent.

When seeking mandate to form a government, the Liberal Party was open to form a coalition government with the Social Democrats. The Center Party was not interested in being part of a formal coalition, but was open to cooperation regarding the economic policies for restoring the public finances. The friendly ties between the Social Democrats and the Liberal Party and Center Party at this time are rooted in the previous behavior of the Moderate Party. As a leader of the coalition government from 1991 to 1994, the Moderate Party exercised heavy influence on the design of the economic policies enacted by the government, and the heavy-handed leadership of the Moderate Party was not only felt by the Social Democrats, but also by their coalition parties, in particular the Center and the Liberal Parties.

After some deliberation, the Social Democrats eventually turned down the invite from the Liberal Party. As a result, the Liberal Party's leader resigned. The new Liberal Party leadership was not interested in cooperating with the Social Democrats. The Social Democrats formed a single party government relying on the support from the Left Party but kept in mind the Center Party's willingness to cooperate. As promised during the Social Democratic campaign, getting the public finances in order topped the agenda. This was seen as the key in order to bring down the high interests rate, which would facilitate economic growth thereby reducing unemployment.

In the spring of 1995, a few weeks before the Social Democrats were going to present their analysis of the economic situation and present the necessary policies that should be implemented, the Moderate Party asked for a special debate regarding the unhealthy state of the Swedish economy. This action annoyed both the Social Democrats and the Center Party as it was considered to be a break against normal procedure and a selfish politically tactical action that jeopardized further the commitment to assure the financial market. It was also viewed as sign of ingratitude for the help from the Social Democrats in carrying the crisis packages through the parliament in the fall of 1992 (Carlsson 2003).

In effect, however, this and previous actions of the Moderate Party helped to secure a far-reaching and close collaboration between the Center and Social Democratic Parties throughout the mandate period. Together these two parties accomplished several radical changes in welfare programs in order to bring down costs and increased virtually all available taxes. These measures, in particular the cutbacks in welfare programs, could be seen as quite non-social democratic in character. From the perspective of the Social Democratic leadership, a review of the economic situation over the last decade suggested that a balanced budget would be central to secure state independence from the pressure from financial markets. The deal with the Center Party and the policies they implemented, however, led to internal frictions within the labor movement. The cutbacks in welfare programs as well as the continuing high level of unemployment were the main causes behind the internal cleavages within the movement.

Similar to the situation in 1990, when the Social Democratic government eventually had to resign, the policies promoted by the Social Democratic leadership again alienated them from their traditional allies. However, this time they had a trusted partner in parliament to rely on. The main components of the first broad agreement between the Center Party and the Social Democrats were: (1) lowered consumption taxes on food, (2) lowered replacement rates in social insurance programs, (3) a new system for redistributing financial resources across municipalities, and (4) an expenditure ceiling. The finance minister—and later prime minister—Göran Persson admits that it was tremendously helpful that these four components were designed into a single package to get carried through the parliament. The chances for successfully carrying each one in isolation through the parliament would have been close to zero. According to Persson, the most difficult component to agree upon was the design of the system for redistributing financial resources across municipalities, both between the two cooperating parties as well as within the Social Democratic Party. The reason why this issue caused so much disagreement and heated discussion has to do with the substantial proportion of politicians active at the municipal level in Sweden, which far outnumber those in parliament. However, as soon as an agreement on the new system was accomplished, it was not difficult to carry the package through parliament (Persson 2007: 89). During this period, the Social Democrats received support for introducing a budget surplus target that would complement the expenditure ceiling policy. Both would be brought into force in 1997. In addition, the wish of EU friendly party elites within the parliament that Sweden would successfully meet the requirements set out by the European Union's "Stability and Growths Pact," which regulates the permitted size of the budget deficit, helped secure parliamentary support.

For the Social Democratic government, in order to secure the goal that a balanced budget would be permanent, it was important to complement the budget surplus target and the expenditure ceiling with a more stringent top-down budget process. These additional policies would strengthen the power of: (1) the cabinet vis-à-vis the parliament, (2) the Ministry of Finance vis-à-vis other ministries and (3) central government vis-à-vis local governments.[19] In the late 1990s political environment, where unemployment and welfare cutbacks dominated the public debate and political rhetoric, the reformation of the budget process rules did not cause any headline news.

In 1998 general elections were held and both the Center Party and, in particular, the Social Democrats lost electoral support. While the policies enacted by the Social Democrats together with the Center Party had resulted in a substantial annual reduction of the budget deficit, ending the mandate period with a budget in balance, many left voters were disappointed with the implemented cutbacks in welfare programs. Another important issue was the continuing high level of unemployment. The Center Party changed leadership and the period of close cooperation with the Social Democrats ended. With the support of the Green Party and the Left Party, the Social Democrats did, however, manage to secure government. During the mandate period from 1998 to 2002, the Swedish economy performed rather well: stable economic growth, a budget in balance, a substantial reduction of the national debt, and a low inflation rate. On top of that, the unemployment rate decreased, from about 10 percent in 1997 down to about 5 percent in 2001. As the economy improved, the Social Democratic government introduced measures to compensate for previous welfare cutbacks and tax increases. These measures, however, were not extensive enough to restore the welfare state to something similar to the pre-crisis level.

Conclusion

The current Swedish fiscal policy framework consists of the following components: a three-year budget framework; a surplus target for both central and local governments; an expenditure ceiling for central government combined with a stringent top-down budget process; a budget-balance requirement on local governments; and agencies for external monitoring. As a system for maintaining fiscal discipline, the framework has served its purpose well.

Which were the main drivers behind the implementation of the fiscal policy framework? First, the most decisive factor was the economic turbulence Sweden experienced in the early 1990s, culminating with the deep and long economic crises that hit the country in 1992. The crisis helped to foster a political alliance between the Social Democrats and two parties within the bourgeois bloc: the Liberal and the Center Parties.[20] Second, some of the key fiscal reforms, such as the expenditure ceiling, were brought to the parliament as part of a package, a strategy that greatly improved the conditions for carrying the motion through parliament. Third, this was a turbulent time in Sweden and the consolidation policies dominated both public and political debates. In such an environment, the fiscal policy reforms, having a more "technical-administrative" character attached to them, received comparably less attention.

From a democratic perspective, the politics preceding the implementation of the consolidation and the fiscal policies deserve a few comments. First, the political story told in this chapter is largely a story of successful agreements between different inner-circle political elites, where the negotiations took place behind closed doors, preventing any active involvement of their fellow-party members in parliament. Second, the results of these agreements were often presented to the parliament in the form of a policy-package, making them considerably less vulnerable to suggestions about modifications or outright rejection. Third, the policy reforms that created the current fiscal framework have substantially strengthened the decision-making power of the Ministry of Finance versus both other ministries as well as the parliament.

While there may be disagreement whether or not efficiency should triumph democracy in times of economic turmoil, it is clear that the policies directed towards improved fiscal consolidation enacted in the latter half of the 1990s were successful, both in the short term—by transforming a huge budget deficit into a budget surplus—and in the long term—by providing the necessary tools for stable fiscal performance.

Notes

1 Although previous research points out that the severe economic crisis in the early 1990s promoted the fostering of political consensus to implement a series of system reforms leading to the introduction of the State Budget Act of 1996 (Lindström 2007; Tanaka 2001, 2011), it should be noted that the budget reform process had already begun in the 1980s due to the expansion of the fiscal deficit after the oil crises.
2 The state income tax with progressive tax rates of 20 and 25 percent is to be imposed mainly on high-income earners. Approximately 70 percent of full-time workers pay income tax only to local governments (Skatteverket 2012: 75).
3 This autonomous right of taxation has been guaranteed by the 1974 constitution (Häggroth 2000: 13).
4 The "bourgeois bloc" refers to a group of center and right-wing parties: the Center Party, the Liberal Party, the Moderate Party, and the Christian Democrats.
5 See Svensk Nationell Datatjänst (http://snd.gu.se/sv/vivill) for each party's pledge for the 1994 election.
6 In the Swedish Convergence Program, which was prepared based on this revised budget bill and submitted to EU, it was specified that Sweden would reduce the fiscal deficit of the general government by 1997 to under 3 percent of GDP, which is the condition for joining EMU (Swedish Ministry of Finance 2001: 28).
7 By joining EU in 1995, the burden for EU contribution was calculated to amount to 20 billion SEK to 1998. It was planned to finance 16 billion SEK by increases in real estate tax and environmental and energy related taxes and 4 billion SEK by expenditure cuts, so that the additional burden for EU contribution would not worsen state finances (Finansdepartmentet 1995: 32).
8 This section owes much to Lane and Back (1989).
9 The Swedish central government consists of small-sized ministries and approximately 300 agencies. While ministries are in charge of policy planning, agencies play a role in policy implementation. Agencies are characterized by strong independence from ministries for policy implementation.
10 The report from the Lindbeck Committee included comprehensive policy proposals to solve the structural problems that Sweden faced at that time. It dealt with not only economic issues but also political and constitutional issues. Per Molander, who wrote the expert group report, also joined the committee and made similar proposals to the expert group report about the budget system (Lindbeck et al. 1994).
11 While the three-year budget framework started practically by the introduction of the State Budget Act in 1996, the "three-year" term was provided clearly at the amendment of the Act in 2009.
12 Furthermore, multi-year and fixed appropriations were abolished as well by the amendment of the State Budget Act in 2011. Accordingly, appropriations have consisted only of flexible appropriations.
13 See Blöndal 2001 and Tanaka 2001, 2011 for details of the new budget making process.
14 While the target was set as 2 percent of GDP when it was introduced, it was reduced to 1 percent in 2007 after Eurostat decided that savings of the premium pension system are not included in fiscal surplus (Swedish Government Office 2011: 19).
15 In order to maintain the sound fiscal management of the general government, the balanced budget principle for local governments was introduced in the Local Government Act (*kommunallagen*). It provides that a local government which falls into deficit needs to recover the fiscal balance within three years while no penalty clause is provided (Lindström 2007: 4).
16 When the new process was introduced, the parliament was to make decisions on the three-year budget framework proposed by the spring fiscal policy bill. However, as it was criticized that the contents of budget deliberation in parliament in the spring and the autumn overlapped, the parliament decided in 2002 that it would no longer make decisions on the budget framework in the spring (Lindström 2007: 6).

17 Empirical evidence suggests that the tax reform enjoyed support mainly from professionals, managers, and high income earners; a demographic profile that strongly deviates from the traditional Social Democratic voter (Edlund 1999).

18 A "cabinet question" means that the government asks for support from parliament for the suggested actions. If the government does not receive support from parliament, it resigns. If this happens, the *talman* (speaker of parliament) contacts the party leaderships within the parliament, in order to clarify support for different alternative governments. If it is not possible to find support for an alternative government, new general elections are announced.

19 In order to have better control over the local public sector's expenditures, all local governments were, from 2000, required by law to have a balanced budget.

20 The proportional Swedish political system opens up for cross-party agreements. However, before 1989, cross-party agreements were usually kept within the socialist or the bourgeois bloc, not across blocs.

References

Åberg, Rune. 1993. *Århundradets skattereform?* (The Tax Reform of the Century?). Stockholm: Fritzes.

Blöndal, Jon R. 2001. "Budgeting in Sweden." *OECD Journal on Budgeting* 1(1): 27–57.

Boije, Robert, Albin Kainelainen, and Jonas Norlin. 2010. "The Swedish Fiscal Policy Framework." *Nordic Economic Policy Review* 1: 199–217.

Carlsson, Ingvar. 2003. *Så tänkte jag* (That is the Way I Thought). Stockholm: Hjalmarson & Högberg.

Edlund, Jonas. 1999. *Citizens and Taxation: Sweden in Comparative Perspective*. Doctoral Thesis at the Department of Sociology, No 11, Umeå University, Department of Sociology.

Elmbrant, Björn. 1993. *Så föll den svenska modellen* (The Fall of the Swedish Model). Stockholm: T. Fischer.

ESV (Ekonimistyrningsverket). 2001. *Accrual Accounting in Swedish Central Government. Stockholm*. ESV 2001: 8. Stockholm.

Feldt, Kjell-Olof. 1991. *Alla dessa dagar ... I regeringen 1982–1990* (All These Days ... in the Government 1982–1990). Stockholm: Norstedts.

Finansdepartmentet 1993. Förslag till Slutlig Reglering av Statsbudgeten för Budgetåret 1992/93, m.m., Regeringens proposition 1992/93: 150.

Finansdepartmentet 1994. Förslag till Slutlig Reglering av Statsbudgeten för Budgetåret 1993/94, m.m., Regeringens proposition 1993/94: 150.

Finansdepartmentet 1995. Förslag till Slutlig Reglering av Statsbudgeten för Budgetåret 1994/95, m.m., Regeringens proposition 1994/95: 150.

Finansdepartmentet 1996. Ekonomisk Vårproposition med Förslag till Riktlinjer för den Ekonomiska Politiken, Utgiftstak, Ändrade Anslag för Budgetåret 1995/96, m.m., Regeringens proposition 1995/96: 150.

Finansdepartmentet 1997a. 1997 års Ekonomiska Vårproposition, Regeringens proposition 1996/97: 150.

Finansdepartmentet 1997b. Budgetpropositionen för 1998, Regeringens proposition 1997/98: 1.

Finansdepartmentet 2008. Den Statliga Budgetprocessen, Fi 2008.07.

Gilljam, Mikael and Sören Holmberg. 1995. *Väljarnas val* (The Voters' Choice). Stockholm: Fritzes.

Häggroth, Sören. 2000. *Local Governance: The Case of Sweden*. Stockholm: Hjalmarson & Högberg.

Hansson-Brusewitz, Urban and Yngve Lindh. 2005. "Expenditure Ceilings and Fiscal Policy: Swedish Experiences," paper presented at Banca d'Italia Workshop on Public Finance, Perugia, March 31–April 2, 2005.

Isaksson, Christer. 1994. *Världens bästa regering* (The Best Government in the World). Stockholm: Norstedts.

Korpi, Walter. 1993. "Politik och väljare bakom valutgången 1991" (Politics and Voters and the 1991 Elections Result). *Sociologisk forskning* 30(1): 3–28.

Lane, Jan-Erik and S. Back. 1989. *Den Svenska Statsbudgeten.* SNS Förlag.

Lindbeck, Assar, Per Molander, Torsten Persson, Olof Petersson, Agnar Sandmo, Birgitta Swedenborg, and Niels Thygesen. 1994. *Turning Sweden Around.* MIT Press.

Lindström, E. 2007 *Regulating Public Spending: Some Swedish Experiences.* Riksrevisionen.

Molander, P. 1992. Statsskulden och Budgetprocessen, Ds 1992:126. Stockholm: Allmänna förlaget.

Persson, Göran. 2007. *Min väg, mina val* (My Road, My Choices). Stockholm: Bonniers.

Pfaller, Alfred., Gough, Ian. and Therborn, Göran. (eds.) 1991. *Can the Welfare State Compete?* London: Macmillan.

SCB (Statistiska Centralbyrån). 1995 *Allmänna Valen 1994: Del3. Specialundersökning.* Örebro.

SCB (Statistiska Centralbyrån). 2007. *Sveriges ekonomi-statistiskt perspektiv.* Stockholm.

Sedigh, Per. 2008. "Svenska folket om finansiering av välfärden," *Synovate.* www.skl.se/vi_arbetar_med/ekonomi/publikationer-ekonomi/framtidens_utmaning.

Skatteverket. 2011. *Skatter i Sverige 2011. Skattestatistisk Årsbok.* Stockholm: Elanders.

Skatteverket. 2012. *Skatter i Sverige 2012. Skattestatistisk Årsbok.* Elanders.

SOU (Statens Offentliga Utredningar). 1996. Budgetlag—Regeringens Befogenheter på Finansmaktens Område. 14.

SOU (Statens Offentliga Utredningar). 2000. Utvärdering och Vidareutveckling av Budgetprocessen. 61.

Swedish Government Office. 2011. *The Swedish Fiscal Policy Framework.* Skr. 2010/11: 79.

Swedish Ministry of Finance. 2001. "An Account of Fiscal and Monetary Policy in the 1990s." Government Bill 2000/01: 100, annex 5.

Tanaka, Hirokazu. 2001. "Sweden; Radical Reform to Maintain the Welfare State." In *Budget and Fiscal Management Reform with the Private Sector's Management Ideas or Measures*, Ministry of Finance, Policy Research Institute.

Tanaka, Hirokazu. 2011. *Fiscal Discipline and Budget System Reform: Why has Japan Failed in Fiscal Reconstruction.* Nihon-Hyoronsha.

Wehner, Joachim. 2007. "Budget Reform and Legislative Control in Sweden." *Journal of European Public Policy* 14(2): 313–332.

8 Long-Run Fiscal Consolidations in the United States

The History at the Federal Level[1]

W. Elliot Brownlee

Introduction

This chapter surveys the history of long-run fiscal consolidation by the federal government of the United States.[2] The primary goal is to understand the possibilities for, and constraints on, adopting policies that would be effective in addressing the federal government's long-term debt, structural deficits, and unfunded future obligations.[3] In this chapter I am not concerned with an evaluation of the economic and social effects of either successful or unsuccessful programs of long-run consolidation. At times such programs have had unfortunate consequences for economic growth and stability, employment, and social welfare.[4] But analysis of these consequences is secondary in this essay. My focus is on (1) identifying the major successes and failures in long-term fiscal consolidation, (2) understanding the reasons for the successes or failures in terms of underlying political, economic, and social forces, and, based on this understanding, (3) speculating on the chances of the future success of consolidation efforts in the United States. To help ferret out the deeper forces that have shaped consolidation policies I survey the history of the nation's seven major consolidation programs, beginning with the one intimately associated with the origins of the republic.[5]

Post-Revolution Consolidation and the Hamiltonian Model

The founding of the modern government of the United States—the movement that resulted in the drafting and adoption of the Constitution in 1789—was, to a significant extent, a project in fiscal consolidation. On a more general level, the movement sought to enhance the power of the federal government and create a national government that would replace and improve upon the British government that the American Revolution had removed from power. But it was in the realm of fiscal performance that the Articles of Confederation were exposed as pathetically and disastrously weak. Under the Articles, the new states had the power to snub the requisitions of the federal government or block national taxes while they themselves lacked, or were unwilling to employ, the power to raise sufficient tax revenues. The result during the Revolution was soaring deficits and debt, and runaway inflation.[6] Then during the severe deflation of the 1780s, defaults ensued on the debt accumulated during the Revolution.

The leadership in coping with these defaults fell to national interest groups that emerged in the 1780s and had a direct stake in the flourishing of international commerce or valued its indirect benefits. A central goal of these interest groups was the funding of the foreign debts that the Confederation and its constituent states had inherited from the Revolutionary war, and to do so in a way that would win the confidence of the international and domestic financial markets to which both government and private enterprise in the new nation would have to turn for capital in a relatively capital-scarce economy. This goal was more than economic in character, however. It was also an assertion of civic virtue. In the process of funding the debates, the new government would both nurture and demonstrate to the authoritarian European world the fiscal integrity and strength of the citizens of a republic. From the outset of the reformed nation, fiscal consolidation acquired the civic aura associated with the victors of the American Revolution. From the standpoint of fiscal discipline, this was an auspicious beginning for the new nation.

Alexander Hamilton provided key leadership for both the movement on behalf of a new Constitution and, as the nation's first Secretary of the Treasury, for the subsequent implementation of a program of fiscal consolidation. His cosmopolitan education, including the close study of Adam Smith and other leading political economists of his day, coupled with his high-level of military and legal experience, had prepared him well for financial leadership. He drew his financial model from the successful political economies of Great Britain and the Netherlands, and, in the process, imported the elements of the modern fiscal state to the United States. Under this model, the federal government imposed taxes on either domestic consumption or international trade, collected the taxes indirectly (through third parties), established those taxes as the primary source of federal revenue, and leveraged the new tax revenues in long-term borrowing. The new tax revenues and long-term loans became the central funders of the modern state, enabling it to meet the nation's social agenda in a flexible fashion, especially in the face of international threats. Under this financial model, the national debt was not a structural problem but rather an instrument that could advance the interests of society. This modern fiscal state was much more than the "tax state," as described by economist Joseph Schumpeter in the early twentieth-century. Tax revenues would fund public projects and, perhaps even more importantly, provide the means for acquiring even greater resources for both short- and long-term projects through borrowing in the emerging financial markets of international capitalism.[7]

Hamilton's specific innovations that he used to implement the model of a modern fiscal state are well known and much studied, but worth summarizing here because they constitute the founding consolidation of the United States.[8] During 1790, beginning with his "Report on the Public Credit," Hamilton prepared and led in negotiating a complex financial plan through Congress. As adopted, it included provisions to pay off the loans that foreign governments, primarily France and the Netherlands, had made to the Continental Congress during the Revolution; to redeem the obligations that the Continental Congress and the Confederation government had incurred by borrowing domestically; and to assume most of the debts that state governments had accumulated during the Revolution. Measurement of Gross Domestic Product (GDP) is extremely difficult for this period, but a reasonable guess is that in 1790 these foreign and domestic loans constituted about 30 percent of GDP.[9] Under Hamilton's program, the United States would retire the foreign loans but trade the complicated morass of domestic notes and bonds of varying durations and interest rates for new, long-term federal bonds and maintain this new debt, assisted by a central bank (the first Bank of the United States) as a permanent feature of the fiscal landscape. On one hand, this program would, Hamilton hoped, establish the credit of the United States and its citizens in European markets. On the other hand, the program would create in the United States a class of wealthy citizens who would provide capital to meet the needs of an expanding economy and, because they were long-term creditors of the new national government, would be loyal to it and be willing to help finance wars or fund major national projects.

The lynchpin of Hamilton's financial program was taxation. The Constitution provided the new government with the power to tax effectively and, on July 4, 1789, even before Congress had created the Treasury, President Washington signed into law a tariff act that would raise revenues for the new government. The act established a complex set of duties on imports, rebates for re-exported goods, and special favors for imports carried on American vessels. The act yielded more than $1 million per year, but this was far less than the $3 million that Hamilton estimated would be required each year for interest payments to the holders of federal debt. Therefore, in 1790 Hamilton recommended—and Congress subsequently adopted—both an increase in tariffs and the introduction of an internal tax: an excise tax on distilled spirits.

Hamilton's economic policies established a fiscally strong federal government, just as he had planned. In 1793, under Hamilton's tax regime, the federal government collected enough revenue to pay off interest on the public debt ($2.8 million in 1793), fund the army and navy (over $1 million in 1792), and still balance the federal budget. By 1795 the regular payment of interest enabled the Treasury to float new loans in the Netherlands and pay off its debts to Spain and France. Meanwhile, Hamilton redeemed the domestic debts, including the debts of state government, and the new securities circulated at close to par value. Vigorous capital markets, in turn, along with vibrant exports, contributed to a dramatic economic expansion that began in the early 1790s and continued for a decade, reducing the burden of the national debt relative to GNP from 30 percent in 1790 to 15 percent in 1800.[10]

Throughout the nation's subsequent history a remarkable endowment of natural resources, lucrative markets in the metropolitan areas within the United States and around the world, the desire to attract international capital, and a commitment to the discipline of the international market would work hand-in-hand with the kind of economic policies Hamilton had established. For the next two centuries, Hamilton's model of a vigorous central government, including his policies of careful debt management, would heavily influence the development of the federal government as an integral part of American capitalism and help unleash the nation's economic energies. Indeed, subsequent creators of federal debt often looked to Hamilton and his career for guidance. In 1917, as the United States entered World War I, Congress commissioned a statue of Alexander Hamilton which stands prominently in front of the Treasury. The inscription on the statue reads: "He smote the rock of the national resources and abundant streams of revenue gushed forth. He touched the dead corpse of the public credit and it sprang upon its feet."

The Jefferson–Gallatin Alternative, New Debt, and a Second Consolidation

Hamilton's economic policies stimulated the development of organized opposition to the administration of George Washington and the formation of what became the Republican Party led by Thomas Jefferson and James Madison. They worried in particular about the size of national debt and how it risked encouraging the development of a new financial class whose influence and special privileges might corrupt the new republic just as such privileges had corrupted the British constitution. With the electoral victory of Jefferson and his Republican Party (later to spawn the Democratic Party) in 1800 came an intensified restraint with regard to deficits and debts. Jefferson's Secretary of the Treasury, Albert Gallatin, who had grown up in an aristocratic circle in the financial center of Geneva, worked more aggressively than had Hamilton to contain and reduce the national debt, which stood at about $83 million, or about 13 percent of GDP, by the time Jefferson took office in 1801. Gallatin's plan was to devote $7.2 million of revenue a year to paying principal and interest on the debt, and reduce the debt to $38 million by 1808 (when Jefferson would leave office if reelected in 1804). A continuation of the policy, he projected, would pay off almost all of the debt by 1817 (Myers 1970, 64).

Gallatin, like the other leaders of his party, was much more skeptical than Hamilton about an active role for the federal government, and worked harder than Hamilton had to make federal programs transparent to members of Congress and the voting public. But Gallatin was not narrowly ideological. He valued, as did Hamilton, the role of central banking and Gallatin favored at least one major spending program. He had built his early political career in the wilds of undeveloped western Pennsylvania and was an enthusiastic champion of the ambitious construction of roads and canals. Gallatin himself designed such a program, and Jefferson supported one important piece of it—the building of the National Road, funded by both customs duties and grants of public land. But he was unwilling to undertake most of what Gallatin had proposed in part because of two expensive enterprises of his own.

The first was a war over commercial rights with Tripoli (one of the Barbary States of North Africa) that began in 1801 and continued until 1805. It required the first wartime tax increase in US history. Jefferson's second spending project was the purchase of the vast Louisiana Territory from France in 1803, almost doubling the size of the United States and amounting to the single largest expansion of the landed domain of the United States. This completely derailed, at least for a time, Gallatin's financial strategy. The government paid off $3.75 million of the $15 million purchase price by erasing American mercantile claims on the French government (a legacy of an undeclared naval war during the late 1790s) and the rest by bond-like instruments bearing a 6 percent interest rate and payable to two British and Dutch financial houses that were the assignees of the French government. As a result, by the end of 1803, the percentage of US national debt held by foreigners climbed to 56 percent—a level not challenged until the twenty-first century. Gallatin responded by maintaining the wartime tax increases, scaling back his public works ambitions, and extending his time-line for debt-reduction. By 1812 Gallatin's "super-balanced" budgets, which had continued during the administration of President James Madison, reduced the national debt to $45.2 million (about 7 percent of GDP, half of the level in 1803) and paid off all the debt denominated in foreign currencies. However, British and Dutch investors still retained some of the remaining debt owed in dollars (Wilkins 1989: 35–36, 53; Adams 1884, 37).

The War of 1812 further disrupted Gallatin's plans, but he adapted and under his financial leadership the Madison administration revived excise taxation, chartered the Second Bank of the United States, and even initiated an unprecedented program of direct taxation, including taxes on houses, land, and slaves.[11] At the very end of the war, President Madison's new Secretary of the Treasury, Alexander J. Dallas, proposed an inheritance tax and a tax on incomes. But the war ended before Congress acted, and spared the Republican administration further departures from ideological purity. All in all, taxation had financed more than 40 percent of the wartime expenditures, and the war ultimately proved so popular that there was no significant political backlash against the temporarily high tax levels (Bank et al. 2008: 13–21).

As a consequence of the War of 1812, the federal debt more than doubled, increasing from $45.2 million (7 percent of GDP) at the beginning of 1812 to $119.6 million (10 percent of GDP) at the end of the war in 1815. Borrowing had been expensive, particularly at the beginning of the war when the metropolitan commercial centers of the nation opposed a fight with their British trading partners, but the US government continued to meet its obligations, including the interest payments which it owed to British investors, who were the largest foreign holders of US public debt. After 1815, over the next two decades, administrations and congresses followed the policies of Jefferson and Gallatin, consistently agreeing on super-balanced budgets and reducing the debt even while continuing to fund internal improvements. This process of consolidation intensified during the 1820s—the first decade in which the Industrial Revolution exercised a powerful influence on American society—and during the early 1830s—when cotton exports to Britain further accelerated the process of economic growth and indirectly stimulated customs revenues. In 1835 the federal government completed the total liquidation of its debt, both domestic and foreign—the first and only time in US history when this was accomplished (or attempted). The next year it allowed the charter of the second Bank of the United States to expire. In 1837 the tariff revenues continued to flow as trade increased, and the federal government distributed surplus revenue ($28 million that year) to the states for internal improvements.

During the next 25 years, the deficits and debts at the national level posed almost no problems in the United States. Tariff rates were low but vibrant international trade throughout most of the period meant solid growth in customs revenues. The expansion of federal programs was modest, limited by the fear of pro-slavery politicians, particularly within the dominant Democratic Party, that the growth of federal power would ultimately bring about the destruction of slavery. Consequently, the national government ran deficits and borrowed only during the depression of the early 1840s, the war with Mexico (1846–48), and the depression of 1857–58. (The Mexican war was the only major war, until the wars of the early twenty-first century, in which the United States did not raise taxes.) From 1850 through 1857 the federal government ran surpluses, cutting its debt in half. In 1860 its debt was minuscule, only about 2 percent of GDP. The American Civil War (1861–65), however, transformed much of this placid financial landscape.

The Civil War and the Third Consolidation

The Civil War was the nation's first modern war in the sense of requiring an enormous amount of capital, and the war costs drove up federal spending to an average of 31 percent of GDP. With an experimental mélange of new tariffs, excise taxes, and income taxation, the Union government managed to fund about 20 percent of wartime expenditures.[12] In addition, the government revived the movement toward national banking to expedite wartime borrowing. By the end of the war, the borrowing required to cover wartime spending drove the level of federal debt up to the level of about 31 percent of GDP. In a sense, the obligation was even greater, counting the issuance of "Greenbacks," a fiat currency that paid for about 10 percent of the wartime spending. During the war, the Republican Party not only successfully prosecuted the war but also instituted its wide-ranging program of national economic development. After the war, the expansion and continuation of this economic program received a huge impetus from the aura of victory, coupled with significant economic and social benefits for Americans living in the North and—temporarily—for the slaves and other supporters of the Union in the Southern states. At the same time the Republican architects of this program self-consciously and explicitly integrated a serious program of fiscal consolidation within the party's larger strategy. What followed constituted one of the most deliberate and stunning episodes of fiscal consolidation in American history.

For nearly a generation, a central part of this program was the creation of sustained budgetary surpluses and reductions of national debt. Beginning in 1866 and continuing through 1893, the federal government produced a surplus in every year, reducing its debt from \$2.8 billion to about \$1 billion, or from roughly 31 percent of GDP in 1866 to just 7 percent in 1893. The fiscal effort was impressive because the Union had found it necessary to pay high interest rates to compensate lenders for the high risk that borrowers faced throughout much of the war, because the era was deflationary (increasing the real value of outstanding debt), and because the Union government fulfilled its promise to pay interest in gold. Until the early 1880s payment of interest on the debt routinely took at least one-third of the regular expenditures of the federal government.

In order to produce the sustained surpluses the Republican leadership retained the high tariff duties and the high taxes on alcohol and tobacco products that they had imposed during the war. The tariffs provided some protection but Congress did not set the rates high enough to choke off trade. In an economy that grew at accelerated rates, particularly during the 1880s, these taxes provided a dynamic source of revenue. And, the tariffs continued to work politically, despite their regressive incidence. Part of the reason was that the United States Senate was insulated to some degree from democratic pressures by virtue of the election of its members by state legislatures. But the new tax regime had, in fact, acquired a surprising degree of popular acceptance, in large part because the debt repayment program had won significant support among the wealthy and middle-class victors in the Civil War who held the vast majority of the war's debt (perhaps as much as 90 percent). The domestic creditors also profited from a program of deflation that accompanied a decision in 1875 to resume full convertibility of the currency into gold in 1879. While wealthy citizens held much of the American debt, the Civil War program of war finance had included promotional campaigns that successfully persuaded many middle-class citizens to buy debt and save at higher rates. Between 1862 and 1865, the Union government had contracted with private banker Jay Cooke, who pioneered in mass-marketing techniques, including newspaper advertisements and employment of thousands of agents, to sell bonds in small denominations. Cooke's strategy was based, in part, on a desire to avoid foreign entanglements, particularly with the British. In 1863 he wrote: "We are free from foreign debt now. I count it as one of the many blessings to offset the miseries of this war." He went on to declare that the United States "had better not put a whip into the hands of foreigners to punish us whenever they see fit to go to war with us" (quoted in Oberholtzer 1970: 286).

The consumption-tax regime funded other programs that commanded a great deal of public support, and their popularity also gave the Republican Party greater flexibility in relying on consumption taxation. These programs included military efforts: the early phases of the Reconstruction of the former Confederacy, the continuing warfare with Native American tribes, and the initiation of a modern navy. The regime also funded broadly popular new programs of public works—the projects of the annual Rivers and Harbors Bill and the building of the transcontinental railroad—and transfer payments, including the nation's first system of social insurance: an ambitious program of pensions and disability benefits for Union veterans and their dependents. The federal government also used land grants to subsidize railroad construction and the creation of land-grant state universities.

The federal consumption taxes had other effects that proved popular. High tariffs seemed to benefit industrial workers, who often feared competition from lower-wage labor in Europe, Latin America, and Asia. Manufacturers also welcomed the protection the tariffs afforded them against foreign competitors, and many farm groups also supported protectionism. Bankers were less enthusiastic but liked the way substantial taxes on consumption coupled with debt repayment forced increases in the nation's rate of saving by transferring resources from lower-savers to higher-savers, and encouraged flows of investment capital from Europe.

The Republican economic system, however, aroused significant political opposition, led by the national Democratic Party, which became stronger as the states of the former Confederacy resumed participation in the national government. President Andrew Johnson (who had been a Democrat before teaming with Abraham Lincoln in the 1864 election) reflected the views of many Democrats when he declared: "An aristocracy based on nearly two and one half billion of national securities has risen in the northern states to assume that political control which was formerly given to the slave oligarchy" (quoted in Macdonald 2003: 391). In Johnson's view, by extensively borrowing, the Republican Party had traded the slave master for the capitalist master. The resurgent Democratic Party toned down this claim but charged that Republican programs created islands of privilege, enabling wealthy individuals to buy favors from the federal government and allowing the Republicans to buy support from the people that their programs served. The result, Democrats asserted, was an increasing concentration of wealth and corruption of the core values of the Republic. The appeal of the message helped the Democratic Party to engage in close competition with the Republicans. However, because they hated the debt, the Democrats found themselves in agreement with the Republicans on the virtues of consolidation. For example, the Democratic President, Grover Cleveland, who won election in both 1884 and 1892, scorned deficit spending and debt and harbored "hard money" views. In power, he and his Congressional supporters reinforced the efforts at financial consolidation that the Republicans had launched during the 1860s.

World War I, the Great Depression, and the Fourth and Fifth Consolidations

During the 1890s a prolonged depression weakened tax revenues. That, along with the Spanish–American war, produced the longest string of budget deficits since the Civil War. But even so, during the 1890s the national debt stood at only $1.4 billion, about 8 percent of GDP at its peak in 1896. It was about the same absolute size in 1916, when the United States had already launched its preparedness for entry into World War I, but inflation and economic growth had reduced its share of GDP to about 3 percent. The swift mobilization for World War I, coupled with an inflationary spike during the latter phase of the mobilization, rapidly increased the budgetary deficit to more than $13 billion in 1919 and the national debt to $25.5 billion, or about 33 percent of GDP.

During World War I, the level of debt relative to GDP could have been much higher, attaining the levels that prevailed in all the major belligerent nations. Among them, the United States financed the highest percentage of its war costs—more than one-third—out of current tax revenues. In doing so, President Woodrow Wilson took advantage of two Constitutional amendments adopted in 1913—the sixteenth, which authorized federal income taxation, and the seventeenth, which provided for the direct election of Senators. The new, and highly progressive, income tax focused on the incomes of the wealthiest families through its individual component and the wealthiest corporations through a rigorous excess-profits tax. With these taxes, President Woodrow Wilson and Congress struggled to keep down deficits and the national debt, and to minimize reliance on borrowing from the nation's wealthiest citizens, lest control of the state pass to a small class of capitalists. As Wilson's Secretary of the Treasury William Gibbs McAdoo put the matter, "In a democracy, no one class should be permitted to save or to own the nation" (McAdoo 1917). McAdoo sounded more like Thomas Jefferson or Albert Gallatin than like Alexander Hamilton, and in 1917 McAdoo lobbied Congress to erect a statue of Jefferson as well as Hamilton outside the Treasury building.[13] Wilson and McAdoo preferred to borrow from individuals rather than corporations, especially large banks, and to borrow as much as possible from middle-class Americans. The victories of progressive Democrats in 1912 and 1916 had not opened the door to greater deficit spending; in fact, it was quite the opposite. If the Republican Party had controlled the federal government and managed wartime finance, the United States no doubt would have relied more heavily on a Hamiltonian model—greater reliance on deficit finance and taxation of consumption during and after the war.

To embark on this borrowing program, the Wilson administration utilized the central, democratic control that Wilson had imposed on the new Federal Reserve System (established in 1913). He turned it into a source of easy finance for those, especially middle-class Americans, who wanted to lend money to the federal government by purchasing Liberty Loan bonds. The administration succeeded in placing the Liberty Loans deep within the American middle class. Also, Wilson's tax policy put his administration at odds with business leaders, especially Wall Street bankers, who wanted the federal government to borrow at even higher levels and later pay the costs of the war from taxes. They hoped that postwar administrations and congresses would be less inclined to tax progressively (Brownlee 1993; 2004: 58–72; 2008: 57–89).

After the conclusion of the war, the leaders of the Republican Party lashed back. They seized on popular concern with inflation and blamed the wartime tax program for causing it. In the battleground states of the Northeast, they successfully charged that the Wilson administration, with its Southern orientation, had been responsible for foisting high taxes on the rest of the nation. This campaign helped turn the Democrats out of power and won popular support for the repeal, in 1921, of the excess-profits tax, and for significant tax cuts in individual rates, including a reduction of the top marginal rate from 73 percent to 25 percent. The cuts in income taxation, coupled with the hostility of the public to any tax increases, reduced the ability of the Republican administrations of the 1920s to reduce the debts carried over from the war. But the progressive income tax survived, in part because Andrew Mellon—the secretary of the Treasury from 1921 to 1932—pragmatically cast his support behind preservation of the progressive income tax. Mellon valued this revenue for the major economic benefits that he believed came from both debt reduction and the expansion of the federal government in the realms of national defense, highway construction, public lands and national parks, education, hydroelectric projects, the regulation of immigration and commerce, and law enforcement. As a consequence of Mellon's intentional efforts—and those of the Wilson administration after the war—to consolidate the national debt, it shrank steadily for ten years, declining from $25.5 billion in 1919 to $16.1 billion in 1930. The decline relative to the rapidly increasing GDP was even greater, from 33 percent to about 16 percent during the same period.

In addition to resisting further tax cuts and thus maintaining tax revenues, two other policies of the early post-war period designed to contain debt and promote debt consolidation are worthy of mention. One was Mellon's imposition, for the first time, of budgetary controls. In 1910 President William Howard Taft had appointed a Commission on Economy and Efficiency that in 1912 delivered a report, *The Need for a National Budget*. Because of its identification with a Republican president who was seen as hostile to progressivism, the Wilson administration moved only slowly toward embracing the report, even though Wilson and his administration agreed with the basic thrust of the report toward budget coherence. The war had further delayed budget reform, although during the early phase of American involvement Benjamin Strong, the Governor of the New York Federal Reserve Bank, vigorously advocated adoption of the British model by giving a group of chairs of congressional committees and administration officials the sole power to initiate appropriate bills. After the war, Wilson's Treasury Department advanced the more moderate 1912 reforms and Congress enacted them in 1921, once the Republicans—including Andrew Mellon—had taken office. The resulting Budget and Accounting Act of 1921 required the President to establish an executive budget. Under the legislation, each year the President had to provide Congress with formal estimates of budgets, including tax revenues, for all federal programs. To assist the president in preparing the budget and strengthening his control over his departments, the act created the Bureau of the Budget within the Treasury Department. The act also created the General Accounting Office under the Comptroller General in hopes that this agency would be independent of the president and protect legislative intentions. The act was not dramatic in its effects but it made the setting of budgetary priorities more coherent. Political scientist Charles Stewart has concluded that the 1921 reforms "served as potent symbolic foci for retrenchment," and that "some retrenchment would have come without reform, but the reforms provided new mechanisms to effect it."[14]

Another self-conscious and effective consolidation policy during the 1920s was President Calvin Coolidge's insistence on the repayment of the loans (funded by the wartime Liberty Loans) that the Wilson administration had extended to the governments of its Allies. Through a debt commission set up under the leadership of Secretary Mellon, the US government scaled down the war debts according to each nation's ability to pay. Even so, Europeans paid back about $200 million of the debts per year until 1931, when the administration of Herbert Hoover declared a moratorium on the debt payments. Altogether, the United States received repayment of about 20 percent of its wartime loans in flows that helped Mellon conduct his consolidation program. The immediate beneficiaries of the program, as was the case in the Civil War, were the vast number of Americans—many of them middle-class—who held the bonds issued under the Liberty Loans. Mellon's fiscal consolidation was popular but it came at an economic price, increasing the instability of the international economy that contributed to the severity of the Great Depression.

In 1931, as a consequence of the Great Depression gathering force (following the Federal Reserve's dramatic contraction of the money supply), the federal budget moved into deficit territory for the first time since World War I and did not emerge until the late 1940s. Meanwhile, the national debt rose relentlessly. By 1940, even before mobilization spending for World War II took hold, the national debt had risen from $16.1 billion in 1930 to $43 billion in 1940, or—in relative terms—from 16 percent to 43 percent of GDP. Most of these deficits and increases to the national debt—except in 1939 and 1940—were incidental, a result of a depressed tax base rather than deliberate policy (Brown 1956). In fact, for much of the depressed 1930s, the federal government engaged in a fiscal consolidation effort designed to reduce the deficit spending and contain the increases in debt. Indeed, this consolidation program contributed heavily to what were the most significant peacetime tax increases in US history. The most dramatic of these measures was the Revenue Act of 1932. The revenue it produced came mainly from raising personal and corporate income-tax rates across the board and reducing income-tax exemptions. The top marginal rate increased from 25 to 63 percent, thus returning to the level reached during World War I. President Herbert Hoover recommended the measure as one that could reduce the deficits, decreasing what he believed was excessive pressure on capital markets that forced increases in interest rates, ultimately worsening the depression.

In late December 1931, while building the case for the increase, Undersecretary of the Treasury Ogden Mills told the Economic Club of New York that financial weakness "reflects the response of the investing public to the possibility that we may be confronted with a rapid increase in the public debt, and in the volume of Government securities outstanding" (quoted in Stein 1969: 34). In 1932 Franklin Roosevelt campaigned for the presidency in part by claiming that he was more willing than Hoover to balance budgets and, in fact, until late in the 1930s, he consistently tried to raise taxes to cover the expenses of New Deal programs. It was not until he decided that his efforts to balance the budget had helped cause the severe recession of 1937–38 that he began to accept Keynesian enthusiasm for supporting demand via deficit spending. Economic historians now tend to view the consolidation efforts by Hoover and Roosevelt as counterproductive, hampering economic recovery and the strengthening of the tax base. The experience of Hoover in 1932 and Roosevelt in 1937 should serve as a cautionary tale for policy makers who contemplate serious consolidation programs during a depression or its immediate aftermath. The fifth consolidation was not completed until after World War II (Brownlee 1979: 418–420, 424–426).

Consolidations, 1940–2000: Completing the Fifth and Undertaking the Sixth and Seventh

World War II marked the great watershed in the history of deficits and debt in twentieth and twenty-first century America. Once again, by international standards, the United States financed its wartime mobilization by a high degree of reliance on tax revenues, undertaking the creation and enormous expansion of mass-based income taxation. However, the unprecedented scale of the mobilization for global war, even when funded to an impressive extent by taxation, produced huge deficits. Figure 8.1 shows that they increased the national debt held by the public from $43 billion in 1940 (43 percent of GDP), which was largely the legacy of Great Depression spending, to $269 billion (roughly 113 percent of GDP) in 1945.[15]

In contrast with the Civil War and World War I, World War II was followed by only a modest effort at fiscal consolidation. The post-war administration of Harry S. Truman curtailed deficit spending and managed to balance the federal budget in 1947–49 and 1951. But a massive reduction of the national debt was not a priority. Truman, his economic advisers, and other leading Democrats had embraced Keynesian economics and feared that large budgetary surpluses would undercut demand and return the nation to the depressed conditions of the 1930s. Partly as a consequence, World War II was the first major American war that was not followed by a significant deflation. Also easing the financial pressure was the fact that the American government had been able to "capitalize patriotism" during the war by borrowing from the public at relatively low rates. In addition, the Truman administration wanted to cut taxes, which it did in 1948, in order to relieve the "bracket-creep" problem that post-war inflation had created.

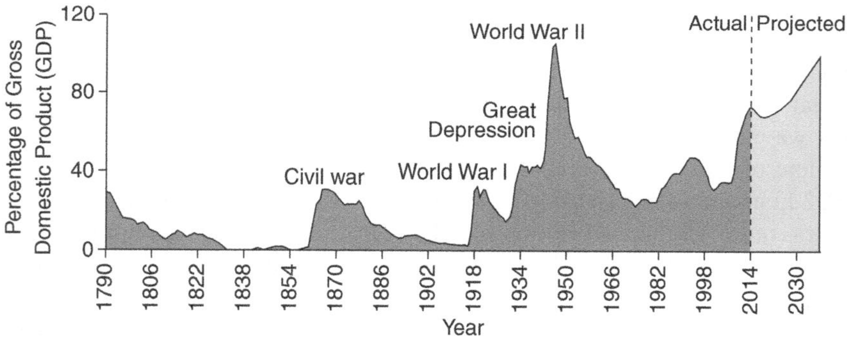

Figure 8.1 Federal debt held by public under CBO's extended baseline (source: Congressional Budget Office. For details about the sources of data used for past debt held by the public, see Congressional Budget Office, *Historical Data on Federal Debt Held by the Public* (July 2010) (www.cbo.gov/publication/21728)).

Notes

The extended baseline generally adheres closely to current law, following CBO's 10-year baseline budget projections through 2023 and then extending the baseline concept for the rest of the long-term projection period. The long-term projects of debt do not reflect the economic effects of the policies underlying the extended baseline. (For an analysis of those effects and their impact on debt, see Chapter 6.)

Data from 1929 onward reflect recent revisions by the Bureau of Economic Analysis to estimates of gross domestic product (GDP) in past years and CBO's extrapolation of those revisions to projected future GDP.

Nonetheless, Truman's early efforts to balance budgets did reduce the national debt from $269 billion in 1946 to $253 billion in 1949, its lowest level during the post-World War II era (Stein 1969: 197–280). But the 1949 level was still high by historic peacetime standards, about 81 percent of GDP. The administration of Dwight D. Eisenhower that followed Truman's had even less interest in debt reduction, despite relying heavily on the advice of Joseph Dodge, the Detroit banker who had imposed a draconian, super-balanced budget on Japan in 1949. The Eisenhower administration produced balanced budgets in 1956–57 and 1960 but failed to reduce the nominal value of the debt over the administration's eight years, primarily because the Eisenhower administration cut taxes. Nonetheless, Eisenhower did not cut taxes as significantly as many corporate leaders wished. He believed it was necessary to go beyond balancing the budget and adopt fiscal policies that allowed some reduction of the national debt and an increase in the funds available for private investment. His fiscal restraint was enough to contain the growth of the debt and allow its relative size to decline. By 1960, as a consequence of both Eisenhower's restraint in cutting taxes and a strong record of economic growth, the debt to GDP ratio fell to 45 percent (McClenahan and Becker 2011: 29–36, 65–73, 103–106, 194–195; Stein 1969: 346–371).

During the 1960s and 1970s, the growth of federal spending and the size of the federal government accelerated relative to the growth of GDP. The most significant surge was an increase in federal spending on domestic programs. The federal highway program, increases in Social Security coverage, the introduction of Medicare, and the diverse programs of the "Great Society" of President Lyndon B. Johnson all contributed. From the beginning of the administration of John F. Kennedy through 1980, the federal budget was in the black in only one year (1969). While the extreme Keynesian view that deficit spending was permanently necessary to attain full employment had not prevailed, Keynesian perspectives gained ground during the Kennedy and Johnson administrations, helping to reduce enthusiasm for budget surpluses that could help reduce the debt, particularly when recessions threatened. But the Keynesian revolution had failed to provide policy makers with a clear and compelling standard for budget balancing. Economist Herb Stein accurately described the intellectual disarray that began within the fiscal policy community during the 1960s as the "disintegration of fiscal policy." By this he meant the increasing resistance "of the specific instruments of budget policy to any general rules" coupled with the decline of all of the three previously leading "budget-balancing strategies"—rigorous balancing, the balancing of high-employment or full-employment budgets over time, and the extreme view of structural Keynesians like Alvin Hansen and Walter Heller. The bottom line for Stein was that policy makers became unwilling "to subordinate their desires for specific tax and expenditure programs to any aggregate goal" (Stein 1996: 196–201).

The way was open for sustained funding of an expanding federal government through moderate deficits accompanied by accelerated growth of national debt. Between 1960 and 1980 the national debt increased from $291 billion 1960 to $914 billion in 1980. But, because of economic growth, the nearly $1 trillion of debt was only about 26 percent the size of GDP—in fact, a major decline from the 45 percent level in 1960. Consequently, the national debt posed increasingly less difficulty for either capital markets or the Treasury, and popular fears of national debt eased.

When Ronald Reagan took office as President in 1981 with an anti-government agenda, the size of the national debt represented less of a problem, in both reality and public perception, than it had at any time since the 1930s. Nonetheless, the weakening during the 1960s and 1970s of the traditional centrist consensus opposed to increasing the national debt during peacetime helped set the stage for a subsequent reversal of the previous success in reducing the relative size of that debt. That loss of consensus, a severe recession, and Reagan's major tax cut in the Economic Recovery Tax Act of 1981 all worked together to produce what Herbert Stein called the "Big Budget Bang." In 1983 the budget deficit approached $200 billion, roughly four times the size of the deficits in the last half of the 1970s. By the time Reagan left office in 1989, the gross national debt compared with GDP had risen swiftly from 26 percent at the outset of his administration to 41 percent—an increase in both the nominal value of the debt and its relative size that was without precedent in peacetime except for the decade of the Great Depression.

In 1995, Stein wrote that Reagan's "Big Budget Bang ... ballooned the deficit up to levels never seen before" and fiscal policy became "dominated by efforts to deal with the consequences of that event" (Stein 1996: 266). What Stein referred to was a prolonged effort at fiscal consolidation that began, ironically, during the Reagan administration and continued through the administrations of George H.W. Bush and Bill Clinton. In response to the weakening of the revenue base, an increase in military expenditures, continued demographic pressure on entitlement spending in the form of Social Security and Medicare, and the deficit explosion, three successive administrations—those of Reagan, H.W. Bush, and Clinton—adopted major consolidation measures. First, they stabilized the growth in discretionary spending on domestic programs. Second, this bipartisan group of presidents collectively enacted the largest string of peacetime hikes in the income taxes since the New Deal. Reagan's increases in income taxation took the form of base-broadening through the reduction of various deductions and exemptions in 1982, just one year after the 1981 tax cut, and again in 1984. In addition, in 1983 Reagan accelerated scheduled increases in Social Security taxation. Bush and Clinton each signed off on increases in the highest marginal rates on individual incomes. Bush reluctantly approved an increase from 28 percent to 31 percent, and Clinton enthusiastically supported a further increase to 39.6 percent. Third, the Bush and Clinton administrations accepted the peace dividend that followed the Persian Gulf War and the Clinton administration made further, substantial, cuts in defense spending. The tax increases from Reagan's in 1982 to Clinton's in 1993, accompanied by the reductions in discretionary domestic spending and military spending, and by resumed economic expansion, allowed President Clinton to submit, in January 1998, the first balanced federal budget in three decades, or essentially a generation. At the same time, the tax increases, coupled with the strong economic performance of the nation, had begun to reduce the relative size of its public debt. By 2000, the debt had declined from 49 percent of GDP in 1995 to 34 percent (Brownlee and Steuerle 2003; Brownlee 2004: 147–216).

Policy Lessons from the Seven Consolidations, 1789–2001

My survey of fiscal consolidations proposes that through the twentieth century the United States established a remarkable record of success in financial discipline. The founding consolidators, most notably Alexander Hamilton and Albert Gallatin, established a model of fiscal probity, which American governments usually attempted to emulate during both war and peace. Wars produced the largest accumulations of debt but three of the successful consolidations—those following the Louisiana Purchase, the New Deal (completed after the conclusion of World War II), and the "Big Fiscal Bang" of the early 1980s—addressed significant increases in debt created by domestic spending.[16] In short, the history of American public finance has been that of a successful "modern fiscal state." Through the twentieth century, debt was almost always present but taxes were held at levels that allowed the federal government to manage its debt in ways that permitted the financing of major national projects, including wars, without unduly stressing either the government or the society at large.[17]

The key measure of the outcome of fiscal consolidation in the preceding survey is the ratio of publicly held debt to GDP. There are problems, however, in using this measure as a tool for assessing debt-management policy. One is that long-run consolidations, measured by declines in the ratio, can result from economic growth as well as fiscal policy. In fact, the burden of debt can decline even though policy moves in the opposite direction, increasing deficits and moving away from consolidation. One of the best examples of that was the tax cutting by the Truman and Eisenhower administrations after World War II. Another problem is that an increasing debt-GDP ratio may have significantly positive economic effects. For example, enormous debt creation may be required to break out of, or prevent long periods of economic stagnation during Keynesian liquidity-traps. However, none of the successful consolidations occurred during "liquidity-trap" situations and cannot therefore be faulted for deepening economic contractions. The same cannot be said, however, of the unsuccessful consolidation efforts during the 1930s. The Revenue Act of 1932 almost certainly worsened the great monetary contraction of 1931–33, and the enactment of Social Security taxes in 1935 may have impeded economic recovery. It should also be noted that large programs of debt creation may have positive developmental effects on capital markets. One of the most important examples of this was the creation and stimulation of fledgling institutions for capital formation by Alexander Hamilton's program for monetization of the huge national debt (*pace* Thomas Jefferson). Deficit financing of public investments in domestic projects can have high rates of social return (and low private returns); examples abound in US history. Perhaps the most profound in its long-run benefits was the Louisiana Purchase, which Jefferson and Albert Gallatin financed through public debt despite their ideological reservations.[18]

Assuming that fiscal consolidation is desirable, what lessons should we draw from the history of successful American consolidations? In answering, I would begin with a key political lesson: the consequences for the architects of long-term consolidators were minimal. The consolidation during the early republic may have weakened political support for Alexander Hamilton and the Federalist party, but that loss of support was just one factor among many in a much larger democratic transformation of the political parties that killed the Federalist Party, and the loss of support for the party had less to do with the fiscal dimensions of consolidation than with the public's view that Hamilton and the Federalists had enlarged special privilege and enhanced monopoly power. In fact, Jefferson and Gallatin continued Hamilton's fiscal policies and the success of their consolidation efforts reinforced the popularity of what became the Democratic Party. That party continued to advocate for small government throughout the nineteenth and into the early twentieth century. Like Jefferson and Gallatin, Democratic Party leaders resisted financial policies that threatened to create or favor a privileged financial class. The Democratic leadership hated the Civil War debts even more than Republicans did and, consequently, Democrats did not challenge the Republican commitment to fiscal consolidation after the Civil War. The bipartisan support for debt reduction had much to do with the striking success of the post-Civil War consolidation. The massive electoral victory of the Republican Party in 1896 established it as the dominant party until 1932 and, in a sense, ratified the Republican consolidation of the Civil War debts as well as its program of high tariffs and adherence to the gold standard. During the next two major consolidation efforts, those during the 1920s and 1930s, neither of the two presidents (Herbert Hoover and Franklin Roosevelt) nor their congresses appears to have paid any price for their leadership. It is possible that Hoover's sponsorship of the Revenue Act of 1932 may have damaged him in 1932 but the election of that year brought about a major voter realignment in which a single tax measure probably played a minor role. The victor in that election, Franklin Roosevelt, campaigned on the promise of being a more aggressive budget-balancer than Hoover. After World War II, the moderate consolidation policies of Eisenhower did not interfere with his re-election in 1956 although the increases in unemployment that they produced over his eight years in office may well have enhanced the candidacy of John F. Kennedy in 1960 (Richard Nixon certainly believed that to have been the case). The only consolidation that damaged its advocates was the process of tax increases and expenditure limitation between 1982 and 1993. President Reagan's personal popularity and reputation, however, seems to have emerged undiminished by his post-1981 series of tax increases. But this may well have been largely a consequence of the continuing utility to the Republican Party of his image—based on his rhetoric and the Economic Recovery Tax Act of 1981—as a slayer of pro-tax dragons. To subsequent Republicans, his agreement to three major tax increases was an inconvenient, but easily forgotten, reality. George H.W. Bush's endorsement of tax increases no doubt cost him support among the Republican base, but he was undoubtedly partly responsible for this by making an inept tactical error: the "Read my lips: No new taxes" pledge prior to his tax increase. Although factors other than fiscal policy contributed to his re-election defeat to Bill Clinton. The latter's tax increase of 1993 may have had aided the forces of Newt Gingrich in the mid-term elections of 1994, but Clinton won re-election in 1996 with a campaign that leaned heavily on his record of success in economic management.

A central reason for the low political costs paid by architects of successful consolidations, and also for the success of consolidation, was that all of these consolidations took place during periods of "easy finance" when economic growth increased tax revenues along with the economy's ability to carry debt. This element was lacking during the Great Depression when the federal government, under the leadership of both Hoover and Roosevelt, began an effort at fiscal consolidation. It was not until the Great Depression was over, and after World War II, that the federal government was able to reduce the debt accumulated during the 1930s and complete the process that Hoover and Roosevelt had begun.

Another important reason for the low political costs of successful consolidations was that "peace dividends" made major contributions to each of them. All of the successful consolidations occurred during immediate post-war periods—the periods after the American Revolution, the Civil War, World War I, World War II (offset in part temporarily by the Korean War), and the Cold War. Peace-dividends, as well as economic prosperity, were lacking during the 1930s when Hoover and Roosevelt attempted to consolidate. As many scholars have noted, wartime mobilizations in industrial democracies have often exercised a kind of upward-ratchet effect on public expenditures, pushing them up to levels higher than those that had prevailed before the war.[19] Scholars applying this model have often emphasized a concomitant increase in domestic spending. However, a significant portion of the increase in post-war domestic spending consisted of the payoff of both wartime debt and, as in the World War II consolidation, pre-war debt as well. In other words, post-war governments consolidated in part by foregoing or postponing cuts in wartime levels of taxation. Consolidation was certainly easier, in a political sense, if the consolidation via taxation involved simply moderation of tax cuts rather than increasing taxes over current levels. This was the case, for example, for World Wars I and II. Eisenhower's restraint in tax cutting provides an excellent example of the financial and political success of this approach, which his administration applied to both the New Deal and World War II debts.[20]

The consolidations also enjoyed political success because the consolidators, at least until the 1980s, avoided the retrenchment of domestic programs. In fact, during each of the consolidations before the 1980s the federal government expanded its domestic responsibilities and spending programs. In the less popular post-1981 consolidation, however, a policy of at least stabilizing domestic spending took hold. While overall domestic spending remained relatively constant as a share of GDP, the relative size of discretionary domestic spending declined. In effect, the Reagan, H.W. Bush, and Clinton administrations all undertook consolidation in part by choosing to reduce less popular spending in the discretionary categories rather than to cut back on more popular increases in Social Security and Medicare spending or adopt additional tax increases.

The history of successful fiscal consolidations through the twentieth century reveals that tax policy played a more important role than did government retrenchment. How was this possible without significant consequences for those who raised taxes? What were the reasons for their successes?

One of the reasons was that in every consolidation effort, successful and unsuccessful, leadership in mobilizing support for reducing debt through taxation came from within the nation's financial leadership, both inside and outside of government. Throughout the nineteenth century and into the early twentieth, the national interest group of financial leaders, in whose formation Alexander Hamilton had played a crucial role, knew that the nation had to maintain the trust of European lenders in order to sustain the flow of investment capital and, in that context, vigilantly attempted to maintain the credibility of the American government, at all levels, as a borrower by insuring an adequate flow of tax revenues. The domestic lenders of capital to American governments became increasingly important, particularly during the Civil War, and also exercised formidable political power in consolidation efforts. During the twentieth century, particularly during the two world wars, the social composition of the class of domestic holders of debt became much broader and deeper, enhancing political support for taxation as a means of consolidation. Within government, the leadership of the Federal Reserve (created in 1913) and the Department of Treasury joined to become a major force for fiscal responsibility. The Federal Reserve and virtually all Secretaries of the Treasury sought consistently to ease the pressure on long-term interest rates and avoid crowding out private investment. For example, during the late 1990s, after the most recent successful consolidation, Alan Greenspan, Chairman of the Federal Reserve Board between 1987 and 2006, embraced the surplus budgets of the Clinton administration. Greenspan rejected the proposal by Congressional Republicans that they should be used for tax cuts, arguing that "the surplus should be used to pay down the national debt to the public" (Greenspan 2007: 185). Robert Rubin, Clinton's Secretary of the Treasury, concurred, explaining later that consolidation was a response to the demand by "bondholders" for

> a higher return, based both on the larger-term fiscal outlook and on the risk that the politics of reestablishing fiscal discipline would be too difficult and that, instead, our political system would attempt to shrink the real value of the debt through inflation.

In retrospect, Rubin speculated on the possibility that deficit reduction had an even more important confidence-building effect than the reduction of interest rates. Consolidation attacked what "had become a symbol of the government's inability to manage its own affairs—and of our society's inability to cope with economic challenges more generally, such as our global competitiveness, then much in question" (Rubin and Weisberg 2003: 120, 122).

The calls by financial leaders for fiscal responsibility won increasing support on Main Street as the middle-class grew in relative size and influence in the nineteenth and early twentieth century. Fiscal virtue became increasingly associated in the popular mind with the political and economic strength of the republic. This built on what Hamilton and Gallatin tried to establish as a tradition—or culture—of long-term fiscal discipline that would be associated with national identity. Thus, throughout all of the consolidations, there was a reservoir of elite and popular support for what economist Herbert Stein called "The Old-Time Religion" of balanced-budgets, and this support often extended to support for higher taxes (Stein 1996: 243).

The nation's leadership usually tried to sell the tax increases associated with major consolidations in terms of not only enhancing financial responsibility but also fulfilling a social contract—making payments for earlier social commitments. This message worked better politically if the earlier financial commitments had been made on behalf of broadly popular enterprises—projects whose popularity rested on more than enhancing the workings of capital markets. This was the case, for example, in the consolidation efforts that paid for the nation's three most popular wars—the American Revolution, the Civil War (popular in the victorious North), and World War II—and to pay for the Louisiana Purchase and the New Deal. Perhaps the least popular consolidation was the one the Reagan administration launched in 1982. This was because the public had difficulty understanding the benefits of discretionary social spending. Only shortly before the launch of the consolidation, Reagan, and the neo-liberal movement that had helped elect him, had mounted a politically potent critique of welfare programs, and the public tended to exaggerate their importance as a share of public spending.[21] This perception laid a foundation for the Economic Recovery Tax Act of 1981, and for future resistance to tax increases that generated revenues that seemed to benefit only small segments of American society. Having just promoted the massive tax cut in 1981, Reagan chose not to re-educate the public with regard to the programs funded by higher taxes, or the importance of the increases for financial markets. In fact, he avoided describing the base-broadening measures he supported as tax increases, referring to them instead as "revisions in the tax code to curtail certain tax abuses and enhance tax revenues" (quoted in Brownlee and Steuerle 2003: 162).

When consolidators called for significant tax increases, the public's attitudes toward the fairness of the proposed new taxes shaped the success of the consolidation programs. The consolidations during the eighteenth and nineteenth centuries relied mainly on consumption taxes. They were regressive but the public accepted them partly as a matter of necessity. The Constitution severely restricted wealth or property taxation at the national level, large-scale income taxation was administratively impractical, and the public far preferred consumption taxes to head or poll taxes. In addition, the public often regarded consumption taxes as fair. The taxes could be designed to tax the wealthy (luxury taxes), or to tax behavior thoughtful to be sinful or unhealthy (e.g., consuming alcohol or tobacco products). When a larger public purpose (such as the Louisiana Purchase, paying off Civil War debts, funding Civil War pensions, or building the Panama Canal) seemed reasonable, the public tended to accept even broad-based consumption taxes with relatively little complaint. The taxes could be reduced or avoided entirely by prudent living. And horizontally-equitable consumption taxes seemed fair in that they taxed citizens with the same consumption patterns at the same rates. During the twentieth century, income taxes that could raise substantial revenues became practical and the idea of taxation according to "ability to pay" became broadly popular, heavily influencing tax policy during consolidations from the time of World War I to the present. Consumption taxes continued as important revenue sources, at both the state and even the federal level, but consolidations usually proceeded more successfully when they relied on progressive income taxes. In the most recent consolidation, an important factor in winning crucial margins of support in Congress for the tax increases of George H.W. Bush and Bill Clinton was the progressivity of the taxes adopted to reduce deficits and debt.[22]

Consolidation Collapse, 2001–present

The preceding survey of the political lessons from the seven US consolidations, 1789—2001, might lead one to be highly optimistic about prospects for successful consolidations in the twenty-first century. However, optimism must confront the failure thus far of fiscal consolidation in the wake of the surge of debt that began in 2001 during the administration of George W. Bush and continued during the presidency of Barack Obama. The primary force behind the surge was the program of tax cutting, mainly for the benefit of the wealthiest Americans. The victories of George W. Bush and Congressional Republicans in 2000 put them in control of both the presidency and Congress for most of Bush's time in office—the first time the Republicans had had such control since the 1920s. This control enabled an extended program of tax cutting similar in some ways to the tax cutting led by Secretary of the Treasury Andrew Mellon during the 1920s. Further swelling the deficits were the wars that followed the terrorist attacks of 9/11, and the enactment of an expensive prescription-drug benefit within Medicare, creating deficits that increased the ratio of debt to GDP from 34 percent in 2000 to 40 percent in 2008. The recapture of the Senate and the House in 2006 ended the Bush tax cuts but the onset of the "Great Recession" in late 2007 brought larger deficits. A depressed tax base coupled with the stimulus spending of both the Bush and Obama administrations accelerated the rate at which the debt grew. Between 2008 and 2013 the ratio soared to 70 percent, the highest level reached since 1950. Economic recovery has recently reduced the level of deficits but the recovery has continued to be slow and public debt has continued to accumulate.

Prospects for an Eighth Successful Consolidation: Applying the Lessons from the Seven

In light of the slow recovery from the Great Recession, *immediate* adoption of a vigorous program of fiscal consolidation would be premature, dampening consumption and putting the recovery at risk. Also, the long-run economic costs and risks of postponing consolidation are modest. The debt that has mounted since 2001 is still much lower, relative to GDP, than during World War II. Moreover, high interest costs to the federal government do not yet pose a heavy financial burden. In 2011, interest costs took 6.4 percent of federal outlays vs. 6.9 percent in 1941, before the great financial mobilization for World War II (US Government Accountability Office). For the time being, the United States is able to borrow easily and inexpensively. And most of the national debt (53 percent in 2013) is still owned by Americans rather than foreigners. In any case, the federal government does not need to purchase the currencies of other nations to pay off its foreign debts, which are denominated in dollars. Finally, taking into account need for investments in social infrastructure that produce high rates of social return (along with greater national income and a larger tax base) over many generations, it may well be the case that the current level of debt is too small.

However, planning for the nation's fiscal future will require addressing, at some point, the historically high debt to GDP ratio. Interest rates will not remain permanently at their current, historically rock-bottom levels, and interest costs are likely to increase as a share of the federal budget. Current commitments to future increases in entitlement spending will further drive up public debt, as well. In November 2013 the Congressional Budget Office projected that in 20 years, under current law, demographic changes will increase the ratio of public debt to GDP to about the same level attained during World War II (see Figure 8.1). It is generally anticipated that the greatest funding needs at the federal level will be largely in the realm of healthcare provided under Medicare and Medicaid. When the time for long-term fiscal consolidation does come, what will be the prospects for success? What form will the consolidation take? Should the consolidation achievements prior to 2001 lead to optimism for another success? Or have the fundamental political and economic conditions changed, perhaps moving the nation toward some combination of crippling interest costs, drastic collapse of important federal programs, and excessive inflation?

The extent to which adjustments on the expenditure side of the federal budget will be able to contribute to fiscal consolidation is highly uncertain. The emergence of peace dividends, a common element in successful consolidations in the past, is already contributing to the easing of deficits, but international instability makes impossible counting on defense budgets for fiscal relief. The likelihood of adjustments in domestic obligations providing relief is at least as uncertain. During the recovery from the "Great Recession" support has grown for the shrinking of domestic discretionary spending that took hold during the 1980s and 1990s. But that sector of public spending has already been squeezed and can make only very minimal contributions in the future to serious consolidation. To deal effectively with long-term deficits and the mounting federal debt through reform of the expenditure side of the budget will require retrenchment of entitlements—most importantly, the benefits that flow from the Social Security, Medicare, and the Affordable Care Act.[23] However, public support today for that kind of retrenchment seems minimal, particularly with regard to Social Security and Medicare. Previous episodes in consolidation have never included drastic reductions in entitlement spending, and proposals to do so now encounter broad popular hostility. Recall the "Tea Party" activists brandishing signs warning: "Don't touch my Medicare." We do not seem to be at the beginning of a new era, one in which the American public will be prepared to scale back what it regards as the entitlements of citizenship. Nonetheless, gradual and relative modest adjustments of Social Security, capable of stabilizing that particular set of programs, may prove politically feasible, just as were the 1983 reforms initiated by the Greenspan Commission.[24] With regard to the containment of healthcare expenditures, the most promising avenue seems to be the search for efficiency gains in delivery. The frightening long-term scenarios proposed both in partisan rhetorical exercises and in main-stream economic modeling may well generate public support for greater efficiency, and perhaps the Affordable Care Act will be able to make good on promises of cost-saving reforms in healthcare delivery.

As in the past, the sources of fiscal consolidation are more likely to lie on the revenue rather than the expenditure side of the budget. Most promising is the stimulation of revenue growth through economic expansion, the *sine qua non* of successful consolidations in the past. In fact, recovery from the "Great Recession" has already somewhat reduced federal deficits, and prospects for continued recovery, albeit at a relatively slow rate, seem good. Sustained economic recovery might also have the political effect of allowing the leadership of the Democratic Party to feel more comfortable pushing for tax increases than they did during the "Great Recession" and its aftermath. Economic recovery would almost certainly—eventually—force increases in long-term interest rates and, as was the case between 1982 and 1993, create incentives for financial leaders to support tax increases. It is worth remembering that one of the major reasons that the Bush administration felt unconstrained in cutting taxes was that, in contrast with its predecessors, it did not face significant resistance from capital markets. Both the private and public sectors found that ample low-cost credit was available at home and abroad, particularly in China and Japan.[25] Democratic and Republic leaders, linked by key elements of the financial community, could devise a package of measures that would both raise tax revenues and reform the tax code. With continuing economic expansion, all that might be necessary for at least a first wave of significant consolidation would be a set of moderate increases in top marginal income tax rates, expansion of the scope of taxation of dividends and capital gains (and indirectly of accumulated wealth), increases in estate taxes, and reducing loopholes enjoyed by wealthy individuals and corporations. Also, a credible "soak-the-rich" threat on the part of Democratic leaders, coupled with the prospect of increasing interest rates and cost of capital, might become the opening wedge for winning support from the financial sector for raising new revenues through not only reform of old taxes but adopting a new tax: a value added tax (VAT). Tax reformers might ease middle-class resistance to a VAT as excessively regressive by earmarking—formally or informally—VAT revenues for broad-gauged social programs like healthcare or even Social Security, by using a VAT to replace the even more regressive Social Security payroll taxes and by enacting a VAT with a progressive element.[26]

One could counter this relatively sanguine assessment by arguing that political conditions have changed since the 1990s, making increases in any taxes—especially progressive taxes—essentially impossible. Without doubt the list of political obstacles to new taxes is substantial: the increasing concentration of wealth and power in the United States (Piketty 2014: 294–300); the Supreme Court's rulings in the Citizens United and McCutcheon cases; the Tea Party-driven makeover of the Republican Party that bore fruit in 2010; and the tactical advantages that the Constitution and Congressional rules and customs have given the Tea Party brand of Republicans in blocking tax measures favored by a majority of Americans. However, the increasing concentration of wealth has two edges: one obstructing tax increases and the other making expansion of progressive taxation more likely as public discontent grows over rising levels of income and wealth, and over the emphasis of the Bush tax cuts for the wealthiest Americans. And, the continuing influence of the parasitic Tea Party depends on the health of its host (the Republican Party). In addition, the baggage of other issues, such as those within the realms of social choice and immigration policy, may well produce larger Democratic—and pro-tax—majorities in the not-too-distant future. Meanwhile, popular support for progressive taxation of high incomes seems to be growing, reflected in the recent increases of the top marginal rates on personal income and the taxation of high incomes to help fund the Affordable Care Act.[27] One could point out as well that Obama and the Democrats in Congress have had politically viable opportunities to increase progressive taxes earlier but chose not to exercise them. In his first administration, Obama did so wisely in order to avoid the risk of making the "Great Recession" worse, or to produce a major aftershock (like the Recession of 1937–38). In his second administration, Obama may have been excessively cautious. One could speculate that if in December 2012 Obama had been willing to go off "the fiscal cliff" and force repeal of the Bush tax cuts, Obama would have won popular applause and obtained the bargaining power to increase taxes without jeopardizing economic recovery. Even though President Obama and the Senate Democrats did not fully seize their political advantage in December 2012, the growth in national support for the Democratic Party that began in 2006 may well turn out to provide an effective base for the federal tax increases and reform required for long-run programs of fiscal consolidation. If enough moderate Republicans would join Democrats in forming a coalition on behalf of tax increases and reform, this might well mark a successful return to the pragmatic centrism that characterized the seven major consolidations in the fiscal history of the United States.

Notes

1 This essay profited greatly from the advice of Steven Bank, Edward McCaffery, Daniel Shaviro, Dennis Ventry, and all of the authors of other essays in this collection.

2 I take as the definition of "fiscal consolidation" the Organization for Economic and Co-operative Development's formulation: "policy aimed at reducing government deficits and debt accumulation" (http://stats.oecd.org/glossary/detail.asp?ID=984). However, as I explain later in the chapter, I believe the concept of fiscal consolidation ought to embrace the financing of unfunded entitlement obligations as well as accumulated debt. Also, I focus on the process of reducing deficits and debt over long periods of time rather than on the process of short-run (i.e., annual) budget adjustments. The best study of the latter in the United States is the econometric analysis by

economist Henning Bohn. Controlling for war-time spending and cyclical fluctuations, he concludes that from 1916 to 1995 fiscal policy in the United States was sustainable in the sense of satisfying an inter-temporal budget constraint. (Bohn 1998: 962). In contrast with an econometric analysis, my long-run, historical approach to understanding fiscal and debt policy focuses on an assessment of the role of institutions and their social setting. For other examples of this approach see the essays in Martin et al. 2009.

3 For lack of space I set aside two complicated but important topics. The first is the history of the numerous consolidation efforts by state and local governments in the United States. (See Martin 2008 and Hubbard and Kane 2013 for recent discussions of the significant case study of Proposition 13 and its aftermath in California.) The second is the history of debt management policies (e.g., the determination by the Treasury of loan durations and interest rates). Classic studies of public finance, such as Studenski and Krooss 1952, often paid close attention to this topic.

4 I believe several important Keynesian liquidity-traps have called for significant and sustained levels of deficit spending and increases in national debt. In addition, I take the view that expanding sovereign debt, particularly when, as in the United States, such debt is denominated in its own currency, can enhance domestic financial stability and economic growth by creating a pool of safe assets. And, that debt can represent investments in public goods with high rates of social return.

5 With regard to long-term fiscal consolidation, some classic histories of American public finance are Love 1931, Myers 1970, and Studenski and Krooss 1952. For a thoughtful trans-national history of public finance that contains engaging sections on the United States, see Macdonald 2003. For an efficient survey of deficit spending at the federal level from the Great Depression into the 1990s, see Morgan 1995. For the best survey of the ways in which the issues of balanced budgets have entered American politics, see Savage 1988.

6 There have been only two major episodes of runaway inflation in US history–the first during the American Revolution and second during another revolution, within the Confederate South in the Civil War.

7 Richard Bonney, Patrick K. O'Brien, W. Mark Ormrod, and others have pioneered in developing the concept of the modern fiscal state and moving beyond Joseph Schumpeter's "tax state" model to incorporate debt finance and thus understand the crucial linkages between successful national states and financial markets. See Schumpeter 1954 and the contributions to Bonney 1995 and Bonney 1999. For an extension of the concept of the modern fiscal state to the experience of China and Japan, see He 2013.

8 For a summary of the elements of Hamilton's program, see Brownlee 2003. Among the most important recent contributions to the vast literature on the career and accomplishments of Alexander Hamilton are Chernow 2004, Edling and Kaplanoff 2004, McCraw 2012, Sylla 2011, and Wright 2008.

9 Throughout the essay, the data on the ratio between federal debt and national income is from Congressional Budget Office 2010.

10 The severe difficulties in reconstructing measures of national product during the early republic mean that this measure is highly uncertain for the 1790s. McCraw has usefully pointed out a more reliable measure of reduction of the debt burden: an impressive decline of the ratio of debt to federal receipts from 46 to 1 in 1790 to 8.6 to 1 in 1800. There seems no doubt about the general result of Hamilton's tax increases combined with the economic growth during the decade. McCraw 2012: 100.

11 Gallatin continued to serve as Secretary of the Treasury until 1814. His 13-year period of service in that office was the longest in US history.

12 The Confederacy's tax effort fell far short of this, but the actual level is impossible to measure and meaningless, given the runaway inflation that took hold there and the importance of a wide variety of other compulsory confiscations of property.

13 McAdoo's plan failed but it may have influenced Congress to commission, in 1927, a statue of Gallatin on the opposite side of the Treasury from Hamilton's. Depression and war delayed completion of Gallatin's statue until 1947.

14 The crucial founding document was the Commission on Economy and Efficiency 1912. For Benjamin Strong's proposals see Strong 1916–17. On the tortured enactment of the act, see Stewart 1989: 172–215. The quotation is on 211. On the initial implementation of the act, see Meyer 1989: 47–48.

15 Throughout this essay I use publicly held debt as the appropriate measure of the federal debt. This measure includes all the debt held by investors, both foreign and domestic (including the Federal Reserve), who are outside the federal government. What is called "gross debt" includes the debt held by the public plus the debt held by the federal government itself, most of which is held by trust funds such as Social Security and Medicare. For justification for focusing on publicly held debt, see Congressional Budget Office 2009: 14–15, The CBO comments that this debt "has no direct, immediate impact on the economy. Instead it simply represents credits to the various government accounts that can be redeemed as necessary to authorize payments for benefits or other expenses."

16 Glenn Hubbard and Tim Kane erroneously asserted that "Every major debt spike" before the current one "was driven by war" (Hubbard and Kane 2013: 252–253).

17 I would emphasize, again, that the rubric of a "modern fiscal state" provides a more powerful description of the financial structure of the federal government in the United States since 1789 than does that of a "tax state." I would also note that there seems little reason to follow the conclusions of some analysts of the history of public finance that the globalization of finance during the 1970s marked the decline or end of the "tax state" and its replacement by a "debt state." For suggestions of the rise of a "debt state," see, for example, Streck 2011, Krippner 2011, and Block 2009: 68–73.

18 Eisaku Ide and I have argued that the current fiscal difficulties in Japan and the United States consist not only in fiscal imbalances measured by deficits and debts but also by a structural deficiency in key types of public investment and social service expenditure. See Ide 2012 and Brownlee 2012.

19 The classic statement of this interpretation is Peacock and Wiseman 1961.

20 Political scientist Andrea Campbell has noted the contribution of Eisenhower's restraint to the muting of tax issues and the relative popularity of the tax system during the 1950s. (Campbell 2009: 58–61).

21 For a suggestion of the connections between "the racialization of poverty" and public dissatisfaction with taxes during the 1980s, see Campbell 2009: 62.

22 On the historic significance of the "ability to pay" criterion see Brownlee 2006.

23 For a powerful discussion of the potential future burden of healthcare entitlements see Steuerle 2014: 30, 73–80, 101–103, and 127–129.

24 Even Hubbard and Kane, who are pessimistic about consolidation without Constitutional reform, describe Social Security reform as "the easy nut to crack" (Hubbard and Kane 2013: 255).

25 Two factors accounted for this. The first was the growing demand of China for US debt—a demand driven by China's effort to keep its currency from appreciating and thus undermining its export markets in the United States. The second was that, in contrast with the previous two administrations, the administration of George W. Bush made no serious effort to reduce the flow of investments by fighting the undervaluing of a trading partner's currency.

26 Central to Hubbard and Kane's case for continued gridlock without Constitutional reform is a prisoners' dilemma model in which the Republicans are always better off maintaining high spending and the Democrats are always better off maintaining low taxes regardless of the behavior of the other party. (Hubbard and Kane 2013: 258–261) I believe this model is poorly specified in that they unduly discount the possible advantages for Democrats in supporting progressive tax increases and for Republicans in supporting deficit-reducing tax increases in the face of threats of rising long-term interest rates or inflation.

27 Also of significance may be the 2012 success in California of Proposition 30, a referendum measure that enacted a significant set of tax increases dominated by hikes in upper-bracket income taxes.

References

Adams, Henry Carter. 1884. *Taxation in the United States, 1789–1816*. Baltimore: Johns Hopkins University.

Bank, Steven A., Kirk J. Stark, and Joseph J. Thorndike. 2008. *War and Taxes*. Washington, D.C.: Urban Institute Press.

Block, Fred. 2009. Read Their Lips: Taxation and the Right-Wing Agenda. In *The New Fiscal Sociology: Taxation in Comparative and Historical Perspective*, ed. Isaac William Martin, Ajay K. Mehotra, and Monica Prasad, 68–85. New York: Cambridge University Press.

Bohn, Henning. 1998. The Behavior of U.S. Public Debt and Deficits. *Quarterly Journal of Economics* 113: 949–963.

Bonney, Richard, ed. 1995. *Economic Systems and State Finance*. Oxford: Clarendon Press.

Bonney, Richard, ed. 1999. *The Rise of the Fiscal State in Europe, c.1200–1815*. Oxford: Clarendon Press.

Brown, E. Cary. 1956. Fiscal Policies in the 'Thirties: A Reappraisal. *American Economic Review* 46: 857–879.

Brownlee, W. Elliot. 1979. *Dynamics of Ascent: A History of the American Economy*. New York: Alfred A. Knopf.

Brownlee, W. Elliot. 1993. Social Investigation and Political Learning in the Financing of World War I. In *The State and Social Investigation in Britain and the United States*, ed. Michael J. Lacey and Mary O. Furner, Washington, D.C. and Cambridge, UK: Woodrow Wilson Center Press and Cambridge University Press.

Brownlee, W. Elliot. 2003. Hamilton's Economic Policies. In *Dictionary of American History*, 3rd Edition, Volume 4, ed. Stanley I. Kutler. New York: Charles Scribner's Sons.

Brownlee, W. Elliot. 2004. *Federal Taxation in America: A Short History*, 2nd Edition. Washington, D.C. and New York: Woodrow Wilson Center Press and Cambridge University Press.

Brownlee, W. Elliot. 2006. Social Policy and Tax Regimes in the United States, 1763 to the Present. *Social Philosophy and Policy* 23: 1–27.

Brownlee, W. Elliot. 2008. Wilson's Reform of Economic Structure: Progressive Liberalism and the Corporation. In *Reconsidering Woodrow Wilson: Progressivism, Internationalism, War, and Peace*, ed. John Milton Cooper Jr. Washington, D.C. and Baltimore: Woodrow Wilson Center Press and Johns Hopkins University Press.

Brownlee, W. Elliot. 2012. The Fiscal Crisis in the United States and the History of Tax Consent: Summary. *Keio Economic Studies* 48: 101–103.

Brownlee, W. Elliot and C. Eugene Steuerle. 2003. Taxation. In *The Reagan Presidency: Pragmatic Conservatism and Its Legacies*, ed. W. Elliot Brownlee and Hugh Davis Graham. Lawrence: University Press of Kansas.

Campbell, Andrea. 2009. What Americans Think of Taxes. In *The New Fiscal Sociology: Taxation in Comparative and Historical Perspective*, ed. Isaac William Martin, Ajay K. Mehrotra, and Monica Prasad, 48–67. New York: Cambridge University Press.

Chernow, Ron. 2004. *Alexander Hamilton*. New York: Penguin Press.

Commission on Economy and Efficiency. 1912. *The Need for a National Budget*, 62nd Congress, 2nd Session, House of Representatives, Document #854. Washington: GPO.

Congressional Budget Office. 2009. *The Long-Term Budget Outlook*. Available at: www.cbo.gov/sites/default/files/cbofiles/ftpdocs/102xx/doc10297/06-25-ltbo.pdf.

Congressional Budget Office. 2010. *Historic Data on Federal Debt Held by the Public*. Available at: www.cbo.gov/publication/21728.

Congressional Budget Office. 2013. *The 2013 Long-Term Budget Outlook*. Available at: www.cbo.gov/publication/44521.

Edling, Max M. and Mark D. Kaplanoff. 2004. Alexander Hamilton's Fiscal Reform: Transforming the Structure of Taxation in the Early Republic. *The William and Mary Quarterly* 61: 713–744.

Greenspan, Alan. 2007. *The Age of Turbulence: Adventures in a New World*. New York: Penguin Press.

He, Wekai. 2013. *Paths toward the Modern Fiscal State: England, Japan, and China*. Cambridge: Harvard University Press.

Hubbard, Glenn and Tim Kane. 2013. *Balance: The Economics of Great Powers from Ancient Rome to Modern America*. New York: Simon & Schuster.

Ide, Eisaku. 2012. From the Affluent Society to the Intolerant Society: Fiscal Mechanism of Generating the Poor Tax Consent in Japan. *Keio Economic Studies* 48: 105–108.

Krippner, Greta R. 2011. *Capitalizing on Crisis: The Political Origins of the Rise of Finance*. Cambridge: Harvard University Press.

Love, Robert A. 1931. *Federal Financing: A Study of the Methods Employed by the Treasury in its Borrowing Operations*. New York: Columbia University Press.

Macdonald, James. 2003. *A Free Nation Deep in Debt: The Financial Roots of Democracy*. Princeton: Princeton University Press.

Martin, Isaac William. 2008. *The Permanent Tax Revolt: How the Property Tax Transformed American Politics*. Stanford: Stanford University Press.

Martin, Isaac William, Ajay K. Mehrotra, and Monica Prasad, eds. 2009. *The New Fiscal Sociology: Taxation in Comparative and Historical Perspective*. New York: Cambridge University Press.

McAdoo, William Gibbs. 1917. Memorandum in Explanation of the Proposed War Loan Bill, August 1917; McAdoo to George Cooksey, October 22. William G. McAdoo Papers. Library of Congress.

McClenahan Jr., William M. and William H. Becker. 2011. *Eisenhower and the Cold War Economy*. Baltimore: Johns Hopkins University Press.

McCraw, Thomas K. 2012. *The Founders and Finance: How Hamilton, Gallatin, and Other Immigrants Forged a New Economy*. Cambridge: Harvard University Press.

Meyer, Annette E. 1989. *Evolution of United States Budgeting: Changing Fiscal and Financial Concepts*. Westport, CN: Greenwood Press.

Morgan, Iwan W. 1995. *Deficit Government: Taxing and Spending in Modern America*. Chicago: Ivan R. Dee.

Myers, Margaret G. 1970. *A Financial History of the United States*. New York: Columbia University Press.

Oberholtzer, Ellis Paxson. 1970. *Jay Cooke: Financier of the Civil War*, Volume I, reprinted from 1907 edition. New York: Burt Franklin.

OECD (Organization for Economic Co-operation and Development). *Glossary of Statistical Terms*. Available at: http://stats.oecd.org/glossary/detail.asp?ID=984.

Peacock, Alan T. and Jack Wiseman. 1961. *The Growth of Public Expenditure in the United Kingdom*. Princeton, NJ: Princeton University Press.

Piketty, Thomas. 2014. *Capital in the Twenty-First Century*. Cambridge: Harvard University Press.

Rubin, Robert E. and Jacob Weisberg. 2003. *In an Uncertain World: Tough Choices from Wall Street to Washington*. New York: Random House.

Savage, James D. 1988. *Balanced Budgets and American Politics*. Ithaca: Cornell University Press.

Schumpeter, Joseph. 1954. The Crisis of the Tax State. In *International Economic Papers: Translations Prepared for the International Economic Association*, ed. Alan T. Peacock et al. London: Macmillan.

Stein, Herbert. 1969. *The Fiscal Revolution in America*. Chicago: University of Chicago Press.

Stein, Herbert. 1996. The Fiscal Revolution in America, Part II. In *Funding the Modern American State, 1941–1995: The Rise and Fall of the Era of Easy Finance*, ed. W. Elliot Brownlee. Washington, D.C. and Cambridge, UK: Woodrow Wilson Press and Cambridge University Press.

Steuerle, C. Eugene. 2014. *Dead Men Ruling: How to Restore Fiscal Freedom and Rescue Our Future*. New York. Century Foundation Press.

Stewart, Charles III. 1989. *Budget Reform Politics: The Design of the Appropriations Process in the House of Representatives, 1865–1921*. Cambridge: Cambridge University Press.

Streck, Wolfgang. 2011. The Crises of Democratic Capitalism. *New Left Review* 71: 5–29.

Strong, Benjamin. 1916–17. Letters to William Gibbs McAdoo, Secretary of the Treasury, December 11, 1916, February 13, 1917, and February 19, 1917. Papers of William Gibbs McAdoo, Library of Congress.

Studenski, Paul and Herman E. Krooss. 1963. *Financial History of the United States: Fiscal, Monetary, Banking, and Tariff, including Financial Administration and State and Local Finance*, 2nd edn. New York: McGraw-Hill.

Sylla, Richard. 2011. Financial Foundations: Public Credit, the National Bank, and Securities Markets. In *Founding Choices: American Economic Policy in the 1790s*, ed. Douglas A. Irwin and Richard Sylla. Chicago: University of Chicago Press.

U.S. Government Accountability Office. Budget and Federal Debt. Available at: www.gao.gov/special.pubs/longterm/debt/budgetdebt.html.

Wilkins, Myra. 1989. *The History of Foreign Investment in the United States to 1914*. Cambridge: Harvard University Press.

Wright, Robert E. 2008. *One Nation under Debt: Hamilton, Jefferson, and the History of What We Owe*, New York: McGraw Hill.

9 Politics, Fiscal Performance, and External Sources of Budget Discipline in the United States, 1970–2013

Joseph J. Thorndike

Introduction

Fiscal nostalgia is endemic among US politicians of a certain age. Confronted by the prospect of a large (and largely unaddressed) long-term fiscal gap, aging politicos invoke the lessons of an earlier, ostensibly more disciplined budgetary era. Once upon a time, these elders insist, lawmakers refused to tolerate oceans of red ink. Faced with an unsustainable fiscal future, they made hard decisions in the budgetary present.

This narrative casts today's political leaders in a poor light. "Where have the heroes gone in the fiscal cliff debate?" bemoaned one political veteran during a budget showdown in 2012. (Frenzel 2012) Real heroes make real compromises. Intransigence can pay short-term political dividends (especially in an era of hotly contested primaries and uncompetitive general elections). But ideological purity is the enemy of genuine fiscal prudence.

Once upon a time, things were better. In the decades immediately following World War II, Democrats and Republicans worked together in the service of the nation. "Politicians in Washington during the Midcentury Moment actually did gather at five o'clock to sip bourbon and branch water in Capitol hideaways and then roll out bipartisan compromises on the floor the next day," wrote political commentator Michael Barone. "Genuine friendships and constant communication were established across party lines, despite great enmities—remember that this was also the era of Joe McCarthy." (Barone 2013)

Or so the story goes.

In fact, there are elements of truth to this narrative of fiscal and political declension. By almost any measure, US fiscal performance has deteriorated over time. To pick just one salient measure, the nation's annual budget deficit has risen substantially. Between 1950 and 1968, yearly deficits averaged 0.6 percent of GDP; from 1970 to 2011, the shortfall averaged 2.9 percent of GDP. Even excluding the extraordinary deficits associated with the recession starting in 2008, the deficit averaged 2.4 percent of GDP between 1970 and 2007 (Office of Management and Budget 2012b: 24–25).

These deficits have left the United States with a large and growing debt burden, another indicator of long-term fiscal trends. Publicly held federal debt reached 106 percent of GDP immediately after the end of World War II but declined steadily until it reached a low of 25 percent in 1981. It then climbed back into the 30 to 40 percent range by the mid 1990s and stayed there until the Great Recession of 2008. Since then, slow economic growth has combined with deliberate fiscal stimulus programs to push total debt to more than 70 percent of GDP. Under current projections, it will continue to rise for decades, reaching 100 percent of GDP by 2038 (Nelson 2013; Congressional Budget Office 2013, Figure 1–1). (See Figure 9.1.)

These debt levels are high by US historical standards, but they are also high when compared to debt levels in many other nations. Among countries with advanced economies, the United States currently ranks sixth in levels of net government indebtedness. US debt will reach 85 percent of GDP in 2013, according to estimates from the International Monetary Fund—less than Greece (173 percent), Japan (140 percent), Portugal (118 percent), Italy (110 percent), and Ireland (106 percent), but more than 19 other nations (IMF 2013).

By the numbers, then, budgetary Cassandras seem to have a point: things are bad and getting worse. They also seem to be right about the political aspect of fiscal declension. Partisan and ideological polarization has been increasing for decades. It is easy to romanticize the bipartisan cooperation of the early postwar years, but empirical research confirms that partisan divisions have, indeed, grown more severe in recent decades. Based on voting patterns, Democratic and Republican members of Congress have moved further apart on almost every issue but especially on fiscal policy. Moreover, this increased polarization—which began in the 1970s and has now reached heights unseen for a century or more—followed on the heels of a "fifty-year blurring of partisan divisions," according to one leading study (McCarty et al. 2006; Sinclair 2006; Abramowitz 2010; Mann and Ornstein 2012).

In other words, the rise of political polarization has been correlated with the decline in American fiscal performance. But this unified theory of American

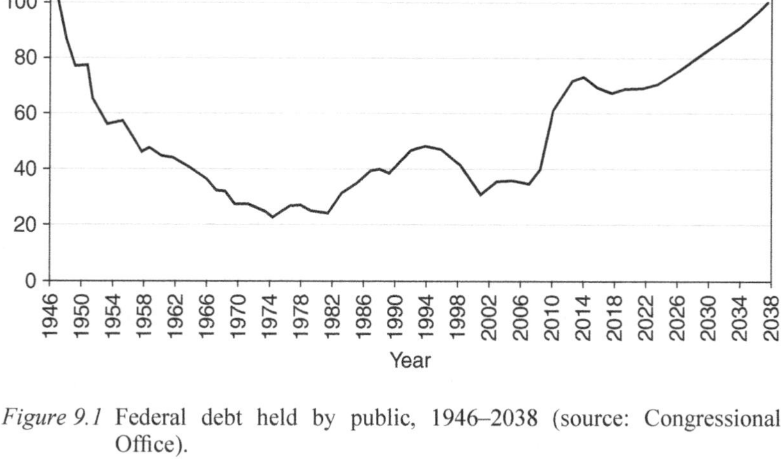

Figure 9.1 Federal debt held by public, 1946–2038 (source: Congressional Budget Office).

fiscal declension is a bit too simple. Shot through with moralistic notions of political virtue, it obscures moments of genuine bipartisan cooperation, or at least bipartisan tolerance, during the fairly recent past. When it comes to fiscal policy, these episodes are obscured by long-term statistics about fiscal performance over the last 40 years. Deficit averages, in particular, tend to hide significant temporal variation, with periods of shrinking shortfalls overwhelmed by periods of growing ones. And in fact, since 1970, the overall growth in US deficit finance has been punctuated by at least two distinct periods of shrinking shortfalls and even budgetary surpluses. The first of these episodes ran from 1985 to 1989, the second from 1993 to 2001 (Office of Management and Budget 2012b). (See Figure 9.2.)

These episodes of fiscal consolidation were the product, at least partially, of intentional policy reform. Both followed on the heels of major changes to the federal budget process: the Gramm–Rudman–Hollings Balanced Budget and Emergency Deficit Control Act of 1985 (GRH) and the Omnibus Budget Reconciliation Act of 1990 (OBRA). Both laws were controversial, their passage fraught with partisan conflict. But both, ultimately, also passed with genuine bipartisan support.

Historically, the willingness to compromise seems to have increased in tandem with budget deficits. Both episodes of fiscal consolidation began when annual deficits exceeded 3 percent of GDP, and they intensified when shortfalls reached 4 percent of GDP. For instance, the fiscal consolidation of the mid to late 1980s developed after a run of deficits averaging just under 5 percent of GDP. Similarly, the fiscal consolidation of the mid to late 1990s developed after a string of annual deficits that averaged 4.4 percent over a three-year period. (Office of Management and Budget 2012b) There is nothing magical about deficits in the 3 percent to 4 percent range, but the political salience of large annual deficits seems to play a role in promoting fiscal consolidation.

If the past can provide clues to the future, then the United States may be heading for another period of fiscal consolidation, or at least a serious effort at

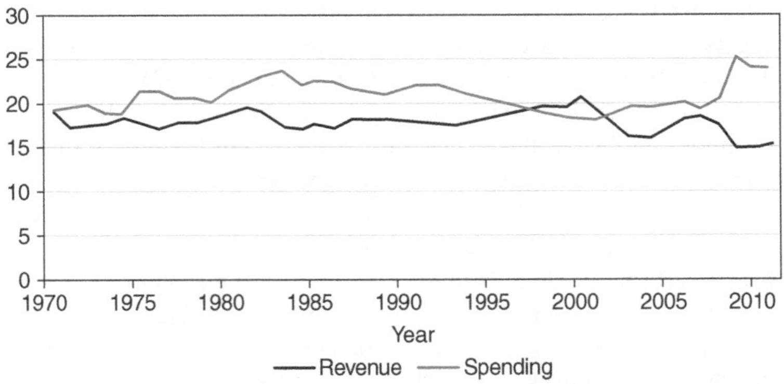

Figure 9.2 Taxes and spending as share of GDP, 1970–2011 (source: Office of Management and Budget).

budget process reform. The 2008 recession pushed annual deficits to extraordinary heights, with help from a deliberate program of expansionary fiscal policy; between 2008 and 2012, deficits averaged 7.8 percent of GDP, topping out in 2009 at 10.9 percent. Over the past couple of years, the numbers have improved somewhat, with the 2013 deficit coming in at 4.1 percent of GDP. Official estimates for fiscal 2014 suggest a further decline to just 2.8 percent of GDP. Shortfalls moreover, are expected to continue shrinking (Congressional Budget Office 2014).

But the good news is not likely to last. CBO expects deficits to start rising over the next decade, reaching about 4.0 percent of GDP by 2024, thanks to the pressures of the aging population, rising healthcare costs, an expansion of federal subsidies for health insurance, and growing interest payments on federal debt. Meanwhile, US federal debt held by the public will reach 78 percent of GDP by FY 2024—far above the 39 percent average sustained during the past 40 years (Congressional Budget Office 2014).

Historically, this sort of gloomy outlook has prompted fiscal consolidation and, indeed, Washington has been gripped for several years by a crisis atmosphere regarding budget policy. But addressing the nation's slow-moving fiscal crisis has been complicated by political stalemate. Since the 1980s, Republicans and Democrats have staked out starkly divergent views on fiscal policy generally and tax policy in particular. While it is important not to exaggerate the bipartisan cooperation of past episodes, it has become increasingly difficult to find common ground between Democrats and Republicans when it comes to spending and tax decisions.

Both parties have changed their views on fiscal policy since the 1970s. Arguably, Democrats have become more open to fiscal consolidation, even at the cost of spending cuts that might threaten cherished social programs. Indeed, some analysts have argued that Democrats, not Republicans, have become the true fiscal conservatives, especially at the presidential level. "When it comes to economic policy, Republican and Democratic administrations have switched places since the 1960s," argued Harvard economist Jeffrey Frankel in 2003 (Frankel 2003, 18).

Indeed, since the 1980s, Republicans have replaced their historical focus on balanced budgets with a sustained drive for tax reduction. This shift was clearly articulated by Vice President George H.W. Bush during his 1988 run for the presidency: "No new taxes," he declared to great applause during the party's national convention. Implicitly, this declaration made overall fiscal performance a secondary concern. Another Republican Vice President, Dick Cheney, made the party's transformation explicit when he reassured a nervous Treasury Secretary that "deficits don't matter" (Suskind 2004, 291).

The persistent partisan divide over tax policy—a crucial element of the fiscal declension narrative—has prompted a search for new ways to break, or at least circumvent, the policy stalemate. Politicians in both parties have again been tinkering with the budget process. In particular, they have been experimenting with "planned disasters"—arbitrary and wholly artificial fiscal crises designed to prompt action and promote compromise. The late 2012 crisis over the so-called "fiscal cliff"—a mass-expiration of various tax cuts enacted during the 2000s—was one example. So, too, was the budget showdown of October 2013, when conflicts over fiscal policy led to a partial suspension of federal government operations. This latter crisis also featured a debate over the extension of federal borrowing authority, which in the United States requires specific congressional authorization separate and apart from spending and tax decisions. Failure to extend the "debt ceiling," which raises the prospect of national default, has long been treated by lawmakers as a possible catalyst for fiscal reform; it is the nation's oldest planned disaster, dating back to the first world war (Kowalcky and LeLoup 1993).

Recent budget showdowns have all featured an artificial crisis designed to force action from recalcitrant politicians. Indeed, these crises have become almost routine, reinforcing the narrative of fiscal declension. But artificial crises are nothing new in US fiscal politics. Both the Gramm–Rudman law of 1985 and the OBRA legislation of 1990 used automatic spending cuts to encourage a search for better alternatives. These prods to action were designed to be both unpleasant and avoidable.

The efficacy of such budget enforcement devices has been the subject of vigorous debate. But they seem to have played an important role in episodes of fiscal consolidation during the 1980s and 1990s. Their principal impact, however, has been more political rather than structural. No Congress can limit the freedom of future Congresses to make—and unmake—policy decisions; statutory constraints on tax and spending policy are inherently fragile and always reversible. And indeed, Congress has repeatedly demonstrated that it will loosen budget constraints when they prove too cumbersome or impractical. Evaluated as binding limits on legislative behavior, the budget process reform of the 1980s and 1990s were a failure.

Politically, however, such reforms enjoyed real success. By focusing legislative and presidential attention on issues of fiscal performance, budget reforms have fostered episodes of meaningful fiscal consolidation. The 1990 reforms were especially successful in this respect, thanks to pay-as-you-go (PAYGO) rules for both spending hikes and tax cuts. By forcing lawmakers to justify any deficit-increasing measure—and compelling them to find a way to pay for such measures—PAYGO helped reshape fiscal politics in the 1990s. Ultimately, budget process reform has proven most effective when designed to keep lawmakers from making the fiscal situation worse, rather than compelling them to make it better.

This chapter explores the history of US fiscal performance since 1970, with a special focus on these attempts to create new sources of fiscal discipline through changes to the budget process. Section 2 briefly outlines the history of fiscal policy in the United States since 1970, exploring several factors that seem to have negatively affected fiscal performance, including reduced rates of economic growth, partisan division over fiscal policy, declining trust in government, and fundamental changes to the federal tax system. Section 3 takes a closer look at the federal budget process, including its creation by the Congressional Budget and Impoundment Control Act in 1974 and its major revision by GRH and

OBRA. Section 4 provides a capsule history of fiscal policy in the years since these landmark budget reforms, including their replacement by more informal forms of external budget discipline. The chapter concludes in section 5 with an assessment of both formal and informal devices of budget discipline, as well as some observations about their future potential.

US Fiscal Policy since 1970

In many respects, US fiscal policy since World War II has been a story of relative continuity. The tax system, in particular, has remained remarkably constant. The law itself, of course, has been in a state of constant flux, as lawmakers have tinkered with it in ways both large and small. But in broad strokes, the federal revenue system retains, today, many of the basic elements first introduced in the 1930s and 1940s, including a broad-based, progressive individual income tax, a modestly graduated corporate income tax, and a flat-rate wage levy designed to fund major social programs (including retirement security and health insurance for the elderly). (Brownlee 2004: 121) The overall burden of these taxes on the economy has remained remarkably steady, with federal taxes accounting for somewhere between 15 and 20 percent of GDP every year, and almost always falling very near the middle of that range (between 1950 and 2011, federal taxes averaged 17.8 percent of GDP). (Office of Management and Budget 2012b: 21–22)

These elements of revenue continuity, however, can obscure important changes in the structure of federal taxation. Rates, in particular, have fallen for both individual and corporate taxpayers. Beginning in the 1960s and continuing for the next 40 years, lawmakers have pushed rates steadily downward. To use an imperfect measure, the top rate declined from a postwar high of 92 percent in 1953 to a low of 28 percent in 1988. (National Taxpayers' Union undated) While the revenue loss of these rate reductions was offset by other factors (including economic growth, inflation, and base-broadening tax reform), the changing rate structure transformed the individual income tax into a less polarizing and better-tolerated revenue tool.

In addition, deliberate policy changes and exogenous economic factors worked to reduce the contribution of corporate income taxes to overall revenue collection. (See Figure 9.3.) Corporate profits grew tremendously over this period, but the increasing globalization of American business has removed a large share of these profits from the taxman's grasp. Moreover, business taxpayers have grown increasingly sophisticated at manipulating the tax laws to minimize tax liabilities. As a result, the contribution of this tax to total federal revenue has fallen from 26.5 percent in 1950 to just 12.0 percent in 2012 (Office of Management and Budget 2012b: 21–22).

Perhaps the most important change in the federal tax system during the postwar decades, however, has been the growing role of Social Security taxes in financing overall federal spending. Lawmakers pushed Social Security tax rates upward for roughly 40 years; levied at a rate of just 3.0 percent in 1950, the tax reached 12.4 percent in 1990 (Tax Policy Center 2013). Except for a brief dip in

2011 and 2012, it has remained at that level ever since. As a result, the contribution of these taxes-to-total revenue has risen dramatically, rising from 11.0 percent of total revenue in 1950 to 34.0 percent in 2012 (Office of Management and Budget 2012b: 32–33).

Despite these changes—or perhaps because of them—the federal tax system has provided ample revenue for much of the postwar period, financing a steady expansion of the federal state and its spending programs. These were years of enviable fiscal performance—years that economist Eugene Steuerle has dubbed the "Easy Financing Era." (Steuerle 1996) During this period, stretching from the end of World War II to roughly the mid-1970s, revenues expanded steadily thanks to a combination of robust economic growth, inflation-driven "bracket creep" (in which rising prices pushed taxpayers into steadily higher tax brackets with higher marginal tax rates), and rising payroll taxes (which were simultaneously better tolerated and less salient to the taxpaying public than other revenue tools) (Steuerle 1996: 416–423).

Changing Fiscal Politics

Buoyant revenues kept deficits to manageable, or at least sustainable, levels. But by the mid-1970s, the system was starting to fail. Conservative economist William Niskanen has described this breakdown—or at least the failure to adequately address it—as a "moral problem" rather than an economic one. By spending too much and taxing too little, adult Americans of the late twentieth century were saddling their children with a heavy burden of outstanding debt. Accustomed to getting more than they paid for when it came to federal government services, they were unwilling to either get less or pay more (Niskanen 1992: 32–33).

Niskanen traced the origins of this moral failure to a change in the nation's written and unwritten fiscal constitution. For the first 140 years of American history, he maintained, federal borrowing was constrained by formal constitutional restrictions on the government's authority to spend, as well as by an informal political agreement that limited borrowing to wars and recessions. Formal restrictions were vitiated by the Supreme Court in the 1930s, however, and informal restrictions fell prey to the Keynesian revolution in economic thought (and the quasi-legitimacy it gave to deficit finance) (Niskanen 1992: 20).

Partisan changes also played a role in the decline of US fiscal performance after 1970. In particular, the Republican Party redefined the meaning of fiscal conservatism, shifting the focus of its electoral appeal from balanced budgets to tax cuts. This transformation was part of a much broader battle for control of the Republican Party—a battle that moderates lost and conservatives won (Kabaservice 2012; Rae 1989). And while some of the victorious conservatives still embraced traditional norms of fiscal responsibility, including balanced budgets, a large and growing number did not consider smaller deficits the *sine qua non* of Republican-style economics. Tax cuts were simply more important.

The new Republican focus on tax cuts founds its roots not in Washington but in states and localities around the nation. Subnational tax revolts, including the famous Proposition 13 adopted by popular vote in California, were both inspiration and proving ground for national anti-tax movements. Republican party leaders capitalized on state-level victories to help build momentum for a national focus on tax cutting (Martin 2008, 2013). Economic trends fueled this ideological and political transformation, as slowing growth, rising inflation, and sluggish employment and wage growth bolstered the resonance of anti-tax appeals. As the historian Molly Michelmore has observed, "The brand of tax politics embraced by Republican leaders in the mid-1970s nationalized earlier popular opposition to taxation and resonated powerfully with members of a silent majority buffeted by the era's relative economic decline" (Michelmore 2012).

The rise of supply-side economics helped facilitate the shift in GOP (Repubican) fiscal policies, lending intellectual support to the political drive for tax cuts. Supply-siders made a case for tax cuts rooted in the effect such cuts would have on the demand side of the economic equation; by increasing incentives to save and invest, cuts would jumpstart a sluggish economy. And given the high marginal rates, especially on upper bracket personal income, the opportunities for improving incentives were substantial (Collins 2000, ch. 6).

One of the chief political champions of the new thinking (which was not, in fact, especially new, having influenced tax policies at least as far back as the 1920s in fairly explicit fashion) was Jack Kemp, a congressman from upstate New York. Kemp tried mightily to move the debate over tax cuts away from distributional issues and on to issues of growth. Tax relief, he insisted, was not an end in itself, but a tool to spur the economy (Collins 2000: 175).

Professional economists were not wholly persuaded by the arguments offered up by Kemp and other supply-side evangelists (a group that included, among others, the economists Arthur Laffer and Norman Ture, as well as *Wall Street Journal* editorial writer Jude Wanniski). As the 1970s drew to a close, the nation was again mired in recession, and many fiscal experts believed that demand-side stimuli were the best prescription for recovery. Even many old-school Republican economists were dubious; one of President Eisenhower's chief advisers, Neil H. Jacoby, acknowledged that the country needed tax cuts but warned that it needed a balanced budget even more. Indeed, revenue losses worried even some economists who supported the Kemp cuts, including Republican fiscal experts like Alan Greenspan, Paul McCracken, and Herb Stein (Collins 2000: 177).

Such concerns notwithstanding, supply-side arguments helped bolster the already potent movement for tax reduction. And supply-siders found a powerful champion in the person of Ronald Reagan, who made the Kemp tax cuts a centerpiece of his successful 1980 presidential campaign. Reagan's "pleasure principle economics," as journalist Sidney Blumenthal later described them, would transform federal taxation—and American fiscal performance (Brownlee and Graham 2003).

The End of Easy Finance

Changing economic conditions paved the way for the political changes described above, including the Republican Party's elevation of tax cuts to the top of its policy agenda. In particular, slowing economic growth had begun to reduce the growth rate for federal revenues, which had proven so dependable for much of the postwar period. Meanwhile, rising inflation had produced rising tax fatigue, as taxpayers' rising prices and wages pushed taxpayers into higher tax brackets with higher marginal rates. Together, slow growth and "bracket creep" combined to give Reagan the opening he needed for his tax cutting campaign. Indeed, the Reagan Revolution—a catchall term for the Republican political ascendancy that began around the end of the 1960s and found its first great victory in the 1980 election of Ronald Reagan to the White House—was a product of these concurrent trends (Niskanen 1992: 13–16; Baker 2007; Bartlett 2009).

Once in office, Reagan brought an end to the era of easy finance, replacing it with a "Fiscal Straightjacket Era" marked by tight budgets and increased political conflict of tax and spending policy. The Economic Recovery Act of 1981 provided for sweeping individual and business tax cuts (Brownlee and Graham 2003). In particular, the law slashed individual rates by 23 percent, curbing the revenue buoyancy of this levy. Perhaps even more important, ERTA indexed individual tax brackets for inflation, thereby eliminating the inflation-driven bracket creep that had been a key mechanism of federal finance for the entire postwar era (Steuerle 1996: 424). By 1990, according to one estimate, indexing alone had reduced federal revenue by $180 billion a year, while rate cuts had cost another $80 billion annually. Thanks to Reagan, observes historian W. Elliot Brownlee, "relatively invisible, politically low-cost means of increasing tax revenues had vanished" (Steuerle 1996: 426; Brownlee 2004: 118).

Fiscal Consolidation and Budget Reform

Paradoxically, the Reagan tax cuts also marked the starting point for a period of fiscal consolidation, at least if such episodes are defined to include the crisis period that precedes actual fiscal improvement. In conjunction with a pair of back-to-back recessions beginning in 1980 and continuing through 1982, ERTA caused a sharp reduction in federal revenues and a corresponding increase in annual deficits. Worried by the rising tide of red ink, key officials in the Reagan administration began looking for ways to raise additional revenue, while also curbing expenditures. A pair of revenue-raising tax bills followed in short order, the first in 1982 and the second two years later. Together, these laws took back roughly a third of the 1981 tax cut. By itself, the 1982 law constituted the biggest tax increase since 1951, and in conjunction with the 1983 legislation, it raised taxes by an average of 1.37 percent of GDP during its first four years (Tempalski 2011). Ultimately, through these and subsequent laws, Reagan rolled back about half his original 1981 tax cut (Bartlett 2011).

In the short term, deficits continued to rise, reaching 4 percent of GDP in 1982 and 6 percent in 1983. These shortfalls increased pressure not simply to raise taxes incrementally, but to make more fundamental changes to the machinery of fiscal policy making. Two pieces of major fiscal legislation resulted from this pressure. In 1986, Congress and the president moved forward on an ambitious program of wholesale tax reform, marked by major expansions of the tax base (chiefly through a reduction in tax expenditures and so-called "loopholes"), as well as a reduction in rates. While the package itself was close to revenue neutral, tax reform renewed the foundation of federal taxation and ensured the continuing vitality of the postwar tax regime; it set the stage for a new era of revenue buoyancy (Brownlee 2004: 165–177; Steuerle 2004, ch. 7; Conlan et al. 1990; Birnbaum and Murray 1987).

While arguably the most important tax legislation of the late twentieth century, however, the Tax Reform Act of 1986 was not the principal expression of fiscal consolidation as a political phenomenon. That distinction belonged to the Gramm–Rudman–Hollings Balanced Budget and Emergency Deficit Control Act of 1985 (GRH). In conjunction with the Budget and Emergency Deficit Control Reaffirmation Act of 1987, GRH recast the budget process by establishing specific deficit targets for Congress and providing for automatic spending cuts if lawmakers failed to make their numbers.

Following the enactment of GRH, the nation's fiscal performance improved somewhat. Between FY 1986 and FY 1987, deficits fell from 5.0 percent to 3.2 percent of GDP. They continued to fall for two more years, reaching 2.8 percent in 1989, as spending fell and revenue rose, both modestly—see Figure 9.3. At the same time—and not coincidentally—the economy was performing reasonably well, with annual GDP growth rates in the range of 3 to 4 percent (despite the slump that immediately followed the stock market crash of 1987).

Many of GRH's champions were quick to claim credit, at least for the deficit numbers. The improving budget picture encouraged a certain complacency on the deficit front, making modest improvements seem good enough to many

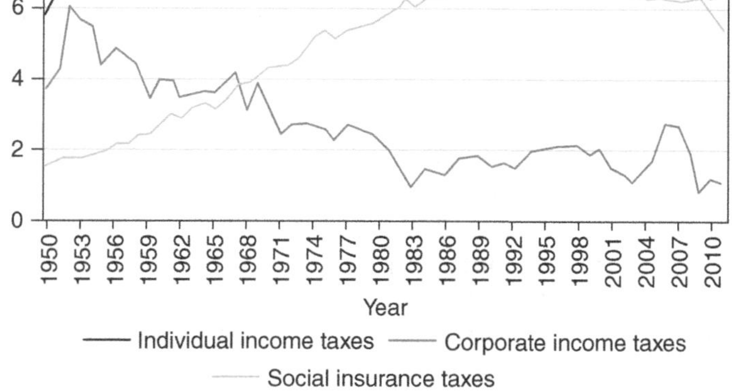

Figure 9.3 Federal receipts by source as a share of GDP, 1950–2011 (source: Office of Management and Budget).

observers. At the same time, the electoral cycle also encouraged lawmakers to soft-pedal deficit worries, since few candidates wanted to run on a program of painful austerity.

By 1990, however, that complacency had run its course. Once again, a recession helped drive down tax receipts, increasing the size of the annual deficit, and boosting pressure for further budget process reform. (Birnbaum and Murray 1987; Conlan et al. 1990) Spending, meanwhile, was starting to edge up; while GRH had managed to impose some degree of budget discipline in the late 1980s, it was proving unequal to the task (Steuerle 2004: 154). In 1990, the deficit jumped to 3.9 percent of GDP, on its way to 4.5 percent and 4.7 percent in the next two fiscal years.

This budgetary failure renewed the drive for structural reform of the federal budget process, and in 1990 President George H.W. Bush negotiated a landmark budget deal with congressional Democrats, providing for roughly $500 billion in deficit reduction over five years. Notably, the bill also included a major overhaul of GRH, replacing its inflexible overall spending caps with a series of separate targets for domestic, international, and defense spending.

Initially, many of Bush's colleagues in the Republican Party balked at the deal, furious that the president had reneged on his "no new taxes" pledge from the 1988 campaign. But Democratic support for the compromise was strong, as party leaders welcomed new revenue that might protect their cherished domestic programs from further spending cuts. Congress ultimately approved a package of tax hikes and moderate spending cuts, as well as some budget process reform. According to Treasury Department estimates, the law increased federal revenues by an average of $31.7 billion in each of its first four years, or 0.50 percent of GDP (Tempalski 2011).

Within two years, the federal budget began a process of steady improvement that would last the rest of the decade, bolstered by another major deficit reduction package passed in 1993 at the urging of President Bill Clinton. The Omnibus Budget Reconciliation Act of 1993 featured rate increases for the individual income tax, especially in the upper brackets, as well as an increase in corporate tax rates. These and other tax provisions raised an average of $47 billion in each of the law's first four years, or 0.63 percent of GDP (Tempalski 2011).

Together, the 1990 and 1993 budget laws represented a second distinct episode of fiscal consolidation. Arguably, they might be viewed as refinements to a process that began in 1985 with GRH, but the changing political dynamics of fiscal policy making—including a shift in the presidency from Republican to Democratic control and a hardening of the GOP opposition to tax hikes as a means of deficit reduction—argue for viewing the two episodes as separate. So, too, does the distinct lull in deficit reduction efforts during the late 1980s.

The 1990 and 1993 budget deals proved more successful than GRH in actually reducing the deficit. Spending as a share of GDP fell steadily through the 1990s, while tax rates rose. The result was a shrinking, and eventually disappearing, deficit. By 1998, the United States was running a surplus, and it would continue to do so through FY 2001. To be sure, robust economic growth was the principle explanation for this robust fiscal performance. But the strict pay-as-you-go spending rules adopted in the 1990 budget deal almost certainly played an important role, too.

After 2001, the federal budget fell back into deficit, thanks again to a recession, as well as to large tax cuts passed in 2001 and 2003 at the behest of President George W. Bush. These laws reduced federal revenues, respectively, by 0.68 and 0.59 percent of GDP, making them the biggest tax cuts since the early Reagan years (Tempalski 2011). The tax cuts had originally been conceived as a response to budget surpluses, but Republicans later defended them as an appropriate response to the nation's sluggish economy in the early 2000s. Between 2002 and 2006, deficits ranged between 1.5 percent and 3.5 percent of GDP, but this subpar fiscal performance did not produce any meaningful drive for fiscal consolidation. Lack of interest in addressing the fiscal shortfall may well have stemmed from the relatively small size of annual deficits, at least after FY 2004. Also, the increasingly hard-line anti-tax stance of the Republican Party made the traditional compromises of previous fiscal consolidation efforts much more problematic, even in the face of growing deficits. With Republicans unwilling to agree to *any* tax increases no matter the circumstance, Democrats had little incentive to compromise on spending cuts, especially for major social welfare programs that were increasingly driving deficits. The resulting stalemate was even more stubborn than the one that had prompted Reagan-era policy makers to enact the GRH reforms.

The deep recession of 2008 brought annual deficits to extraordinary heights not seen since World War II. Advocates of fiscal stimulus welcomed those deficits as a support for aggregate demand and argued for even larger deficit spending. But politically, such large annual shortfalls—reaching 10.1 percent of GDP in 2009 and only slightly less for the next two years—have dramatically increased interest in budget reform.

Budget Process Reform

The two episodes of fiscal consolidation after 1970 both featured structural reform of the legislative fiscal process. In both periods, reform was borne of frustration—of a sense that existing procedures and budgetary institutions were unable to cope with large and growing deficits. Advocates of structural reform insisted that lawmakers needed some source of external discipline if they were ever going to adequately address difficult fiscal problems.

But the two episodes of fiscal consolidation differed in the kinds of structural reform that they embraced. In particular, they differed in the degree of specificity and flexibility allowed within the new framework. The initial, stricter version embodied in GRH enacted in 1985 proved largely unsuccessful, its targets too tight and inflexible to be workable in the real world of US politics. The second latter attempt at structural budget reform in 1990, by contrast, was more flexible and, not coincidentally, more successful.

The Federal Budget Process

Fiscal policy in the United States unfolds within a statutory process described by one official government report as "enormously complex" (Heniff et al. 2012, unpaginated summary.) This process derives principally from the Congressional Budget Act of 1974. Designed to bolster congressional authority within the budget process (relative to the president), the law has been much revised since its original passage. Nonetheless, it continues to provide a basic framework for fiscal policymaking.

Until the third decade of the twentieth century, the US budget process was, in the words of one historian, "decentralized and chaotic from start to finish" (Thurber 2013: 319). Budget requests and funding decisions were made without meaningful coordination by either the executive or legislative branch; the process, such as it was, involved a series of ad hoc decisions by executive branch agencies and congressional tax and spending committees (Heniff et al. 2012: 1).

The early decades of the twentieth century, however, prompted lawmakers to look for a better system. Spending rose steadily between 1900 and 1920, especially—and for obvious reasons—during World War I. Even more important, deficits became increasingly common, with government books in the red for more than half the years in this time frame (Heniff et al. 2012: 1).

In a bid to create more fiscal discipline, Congress passed the Budget and Accounting Act of 1921. The law made relatively few changes to congressional procedures, but it significantly bolstered the president's role in shaping fiscal policy. The act consolidated all executive branch spending requests within a unified presidential budget. Even more important, it created a new Bureau of the Budget within the executive branch, and charged this agency (later renamed the Office of Management and Budget) with coordinating budget requests and providing relevant information to executive branch and congressional officials. This bureaucratic innovation significantly expanded the institutional capacity of the executive branch within the budget process (Thurber 2013).

In other respects, however, the 1921 act left Congress with the upper hand in fiscal policy. The president's unified budget request brought some order to the making of fiscal policy, but it functioned as little more than a recommendation. Lawmakers were free to revise it—and they wielded this freedom with enthusiasm. The law also established the General Accounting Office (GAO) and made it the chief auditing instrument of the federal government (Heniff et al. 2012, 1).

At the same time, however, the budget process remained highly decentralized within Congress. New rules consolidated the authority of the House and Senate appropriations committees to shape spending bills, but budget decisions were still distributed across a wide array of independent-minded subcommittees. As one scholar has summed up the new process:

> For fifty years after passage of the 1921 [legislation], the congressional budgetary process and the constitutional "power of the purse" simply meant adding up the decentralized decisions about appropriations from the House and Senate Appropriations Committees, each with thirteen subcommittees.
>
> (Thurber 2013: 320)

Later decades brought further attempts at budget process reform, but none were especially successful or durable until 1974 (Thurber 2013: 321). That year, after a string of budget battles between the White House and Congress, and in the wake of the Watergate crisis, lawmakers moved decisively to revamp the budget process. The Budget and Impoundment Control Act of 1974 (CBICA) had been precipitated by President Richard Nixon's provocative decision to simply ignore congressional priorities and refuse to spend certain appropriated funds (a process known as impoundment) (Thurber 2013: 321). Outrage at that challenge coalesced with simmering discontent about the structural weakness of congress within the budget process. "During the past half century, the Congress has seen a consistent escalation of executive influence over budget and fiscal policies," explained Senate Budget Committee Chair Edmund Muskie, D-Maine. "The Congressional Budget and Impoundment Control Act of 1974 will give us the means to reverse that erosion" (Thurber 2013: 321–322).

The CBICA made numerous changes to the budget process, beginning with sharp restrictions on presidential impoundment authority. More important, however, it also established new procedures for congressional budgeting, centered on a new concurrent budget resolution. The resolution is not a law, and as such does not require presidential approval. But it does give Congress a vehicle for establishing broad fiscal priorities—and by implication, to challenge the priorities of the executive branch (Thurber 2013: 322). Indeed, the 1974 legislation made budget fights a fixture of late twentieth century US national politics, as a newly empowered Congress squared off against a series of determined presidents. Compromise was necessary and inevitable under the new process. But, as one leading authority has noted, "first, they fight" (Schick 2007: 19).

Among its various institutional reforms, CBICA created independent budget committees in both the House and Senate. Charged with developing the budget resolution, these committees expanded the institutional capacity of Congress to manage fiscal policy making. So, too, did a new Congressional Budget Office (CBO), which serves as a counterpart to the president's OMB. The creation of OMB was especially significant, since it freed Congress from its dependence on executive branch fiscal expertise (Thurber 2013: 322–323; Joyce 2011).

In the wake of CBICA, the new federal budget process unfolded along a clear timeline and with equally clear lines of responsibility. While subsequent legislation has revised this procedure—sometimes in significant fashion—it continues to serve as the basis for federal budgeting.

Step 1: Presidential Budget

In February, the president is required to submit to Congress a detailed budget request for the fiscal year beginning October 1. Developed by OMB, this request establishes priorities both general and specific. It lays out aggregate tax and spending levels, while also establishing very specific spending priorities for all federal programs governed by the annual budget (as opposed to other spending and tax policies governed by permanent law, including many social welfare entitlements and almost the entire federal tax system). This so-called "discretionary" spending includes about half of all federal spending, including most money going to national defense, education, and research.

If the president chooses, the executive budget request can also identify changes to non-discretionary spending and tax policy. And in practice, most presidential budgets *do* include a variety of such recommendations, especially regarding tax policy (Center on Budget and Policy Priorities 2011).

The president's budget is not binding. As with all White House budgets submitted since the 1920s, it serves as a recommendation to Congress (Heniff et al. 2012: 10). As the White House itself explains in some detail:

> The Congress considers the President's budget proposals and approves, modifies, or disapproves them. It can change funding levels, eliminate programs, or add programs not requested by the President. It can add or eliminate taxes and other sources of receipts or make other changes that effect the amount of receipts collected.
>
> (Office of Management and Budget 2012a: 126)

In other words, lawmakers are free to ignore the president's budget request, and they often do. Indeed, it has become almost routine for budgets to be summarily dismissed as "dead on arrival" within moments of their public release—and sometimes even before. Still, the president's request carries symbolic and political weight.

Step 2: Congressional Budget Resolution

After receiving the president's budget, the House and Senate Budget Committees set about developing their own budget resolution. This resolution is wholly independent of the president's request, and it often differs dramatically in both general and specific terms. The resolution reflects congressional tax and spending priorities, which can themselves be internally diverse, especially in years when partisan control of the House and Senate is divided. In theory, the budget resolution must pass both houses by April 15, but, in practice, it is usually late, sometimes failing to pass entirely (Heniff et al. 2012: 12).

The budget resolution is far less specific than the president's budget request, establishing spending priorities for broad categories rather than specific programs. It also sets a revenue target for the next budget, as well as five to 10 following years. After passage, spending targets from the budget resolution are passed along to House and Senate Appropriations Committees, which then divide the total among their various subcommittees. These subcommittees (and the full Appropriations panel) retain broad discretionary authority to allocate spending among various programs and agencies; while the Budget Committees can and do provide guidance on how such allocations should be made, the appropriations committees are usually free to ignore such requests (Heniff et al. 2012: 13).

Step 3: Enforcement

Enforcement of the budget resolution depends on parliamentary rules in each house. Any violation of the resolution—including spending increases or tax cuts inconsistent with the resolution—can be challenged by a "point of order," which often requires a supermajority of lawmakers to approve the violation (Heniff et al. 2012: 15–16).

Another enforcement technique—currently in use but not included in the original budget process of 1974—is sequestration. First developed in 1985 as part of the Gramm–Rudman budget reform (discussed below), sequestration provides for the automatic cancellation of budgetary resources to achieve specified deficit reduction targets. Sequestration has been a feature of the budget process, off and on, for more than a quarter century. It currently serves as an enforcement technique for PAYGO legislation (also discussed below) and for deficit targets under the Budget Control Act of 2011 (Heniff et al. 2012: 16–17).

Step 4: Reconciliation

Congress sometimes uses a process called "reconciliation" to modify budget decisions. Reconciliation legislation packages disparate budget decisions within a single bill, including both tax and spending provisions. Reconciliation bills are immune from routine parliamentary obstructions, including the Senate filibuster. But the content of such bills is also restricted to relevant fiscal provisions; non-fiscal policy changes and other "extraneous" provisions are not permitted. So, too, are tax and spending provisions that lose money long run.

The budget process established in 1974 was hardly a resounding success. Indeed, many critics considered it an abject failure, especially as far as Congress was concerned. "[T]he only kind of budget resolution that can pass today is one that lies," complained one unhappy lawmaker in the 1980s.

> We did it under Carter, we have done it under Reagan, and we are going to do it under every president for as long as we can, because you can not get members under the existing system to face up to what the real numbers do. You always wind up having phony economic assumptions and all kinds of phony numbers on estimating.
>
> (Thurber 2013: 323)

Such complaints were fueled by the persistence of large and growing deficits, especially during the early 1980s; by 1983, the budget shortfall had reached 6 percent of GDP and it neared that level for several years (Office of Management and Budget 2012b). By the middle of the decade, Congress was determined to stem the flow of red ink, and budget process reform seemed like the most logical approach.

Gramm–Rudman–Hollings

In 1985, Congress passed the Balanced Budget and Emergency Deficit Control Act, commonly known as Gramm–Rudman–Hollings after its chief sponsors. This law, which was substantially revised in 1987, was designed to improve the budget process by creating a source of fiscal discipline insulated from political pressures.

GRH was designed to ensure deficit reduction even in the face of political failure. The initial version of the law established a series of declining deficit targets, culminating in FY 1991 with a balanced budget. In 1987, a second round of GRH legislation revised and liberalized this ambitious schedule, pushing the balance target back to 1993. The crucial feature of the GRH law was its enforcement mechanism. Under the legislation, if Congress failed to meet its annual deficit target (measured by projections at the *start* of the fiscal year, not actual deficits at end), then automatic, across-the-board spending cuts, known as sequestration, would do the work that lawmakers could not do for themselves (Schick 2007: 22; Keith 1986). Such cuts would affect most but not all federal outlays. Certain types of spending—including some big-ticket items, like interest on the federal debt, as well as Social Security and Medicare spending—were exempt. As a result, automatic cuts were expected to fall principally on "discretionary" spending (a category that included almost everything the federal government did outside the major entitlement programs) (Heniff et al. 2012: 15–16; Thurber 2013: 8–9).

To some degree, GRH was designed from the start to be an empty threat. "Because implementation of a required sequester was automatic under these procedures," recalled an official history of the Senate Budget Committee, "and perceived to be a drastic action, many regarded it as providing a strong incentive for Congress and the President to reach agreement through the regular process of legislation to meet the established budgetary goals" (Schick 1985: 85–113). In other words, GRH was not designed to be a budgetary procedure as much as a budgetary safeguard. It was created to impart discipline to a notoriously undisciplined fiscal process.

Almost immediately after its passage, however, GRH ran into legal problems. In early 1986, a three-judge federal panel ruled that the act violated the Constitution's separation of powers doctrine. By assigning the authority to trigger automatic cuts (known as sequestration) to the Government Accounting Office (GAO), an arm of Congress, the law vested executive authority in a legislative body, the court found. The Supreme Court, in affirming the lower court's decision, explained the problem succinctly:

> To permit an officer controlled by Congress to execute the laws would be, in essence, to permit a congressional veto. Congress could simply remove, or threaten to remove, an officer for executing the laws in any fashion found to be unsatisfactory to Congress. This kind of congressional control over the execution of the laws ... is constitutionally impermissible.
>
> (Senate Committee on the Budget 2006)

The legislative authors of GRH had anticipated this objection and included an alternative mechanism for sequestration in the law itself. As a result, sequestration actually occurred in 1986 when Congress failed to meet its first deficit target. But the following year, when budget projections suggested that Congress was on pace to miss the next set of GRH targets by a wide margin (about $50 billion over the target of $108 billion), political leaders began to call for revisions to the law itself.

In 1987, another debt ceiling bill provided the legislative vehicle for another round of budget process reforms. The Budget and Emergency Deficit Control Reaffirmation Act of 1987 revised deficit goals to make them more attainable and pushed the target date for budget balance back from 1991 to 1993. The legislation also provided for a more permanent solution to the constitutional problem by reassigning the trigger role for a sequester to the Office of Management and Budget in the executive branch.

Ultimately, however, the 1987 law could not rescue GRH from its own problems. Between FY 1986 and FY 1990, Congress missed deficit targets every year. The overages ranged from $5 billion to $205 billion, getting much worse over time. In fact, the deficit (measured in dollar terms, not as a percentage of GDP) was higher in 1990 than it had been in 1984, before GRH was enacted. Critics argued that even the law's modest improvements were illusory, the product of budget gimmickry and "smoke and mirrors." Real budgetary and fiscal reform, they insisted, was stubbornly elusive (Senate Committee on the Budget 2006; Schick 2007: 22).

Indeed, even one of the law's original sponsors despaired of its efficacy. "I'm filing for divorce on grounds of infidelity and irreconcilable differences," declared Sen. Ernest F. Hollings, D-SC. (Senate Committee on the Budget 2006, 49) A key Republican staffer from the era gave a more specific diagnosis of the ills plaguing the law. "Gramm–Rudman–Hollings was so contrary to the culture and the Constitution and whole flow of legislative history," he said, "the first thing we did was to ignore it" (Senate Committee on the Budget 2006: 51).

Budget Enforcement Act of 1990

As the failures of GRH became more apparent (thanks chiefly to the series of missed deficit targets), lawmakers began to search for new mechanisms for imposing fiscal discipline. The crisis came in the summer of 1990, when projections pegged the FY 1991 deficit at $230 billion—so far above the $64 billion target as to make any sort of sequester unworkable (and almost unthinkable) (Schick 2007: 22). Congress responded by enacting the Budget Enforcement Act (BEA), part of the larger Omnibus Budget Reconciliation Act of 1990 (OBRA 1990) that featured a landmark, bipartisan compromise on deficit reduction measures. Signed by Republican President George H.W. Bush, who had campaigned in 1988 on his "no new taxes" pledge, OBRA 1990 actually included some $158 billion in new revenue over five years, as well as $325 billion in scheduled spending cuts.

Once again, fiscal reform had been triggered by fiscal failure. As the Senate Budget Committee recalled in its official history of the period, "As is often the case with important legislation, the enactment of OBRA 1990 occurred in response to significant budgetary and economic challenges and followed a difficult legislative path" (Calmes 2011, ch. 2). The projected FY 1991 shortfall had prompted Bush to open negotiations with the Democrat-controlled Congress. The president was still clinging to the "no new taxes" pledge of his 1988 campaign, but by early June he had agreed to include new revenue in the eventual compromise package (Calmes 2011).

Republicans in Congress, however, proved a tough sell for their titular leader in the White House. After much hemming and hawing, however, GOP lawmakers eventually agreed to accept new revenues as the price of workable compromise. Negotiators made the final package more palatable to fiscal conservatives by including not just revenue increases, but spending caps and budget process reform as well.

In particular, OBRA replaced the inflexible overall spending caps of the original GRH legislation with new, more flexible spending targets. The change was a recognition of reality, both economic and political. As one budget expert later observed:

> One of the lessons Congress and the president derived from the failure of GRH was that it is futile to set fixed annual deficit limits that cannot be adjusted for changes in economic conditions or for reestimates of program expenditures. Fixed limits can be overtaken and rendered unworkable by unforeseen developments.
>
> (Schick 2007: 23)

Even as it loosened the strictures inherited from GRH, however, OBRA created new budget enforcement rules. The law's new, more flexible deficit targets, which could be adjusted by the president in response to economic exigencies, were paired with other budget rules designed to constrain legislative freedom (albeit more modestly than GRH). For instance, the law established five-year discretionary caps for different categories of discretionary federal spending (as opposed to entitlement spending). Separate caps applied to domestic, international, and defense spending, giving Congress a modest amount of flexibility while still imposing some sort of discipline through structural constraint. More important, the law also included pay-as-you-go requirements (PAYGO) that required lawmakers to "pay" for new tax cuts, as well as any increase in "mandatory" or entitlement spending. PAYGO required that such measures be offset by spending cuts or tax increases elsewhere in the budget. As one scholar later noted, "PAYGO made the budget process a zero-sum game" (Senate Committee on the Budget 2006: 53; Thurber 2013: 12).

OBRA 90 moved the goalposts of fiscal policy, raising deficit targets and thereby making success more likely—or failure less certain, depending on your degree of optimism. The law also provided that these targets could be adjusted to reflect large-scale economic trends and a variety of technical factors. (President

Clinton would soon use this flexibility to avoid sequestration in future years.) Sequestration could still be triggered, in theory at least, if OMB certified violations of the PAYGO rules or the flexible spending caps. But the likelihood of such across-the-board spending cuts was substantially diminished. The size of BEA sequestration cuts, moreover, was likely to be much more manageable than those implied by the inflexible GRH deficit targets (Reischauer 1993: 7).

The Efficacy of Budget Process Reform

Budget experts of the 1980s and 1990s considered GRH and OBRA to be a mixed bag. In general, they took a dim view of the former but found much to like in the latter. Robert Reischauer, who served as director of the CBO from 1989 to 1995, offered a typical assessment. "The approach taken in 1990, when the BEA was passed, has been much more successful than that included in Gramm–Rudman–Hollings," he said in 1993 testimony to the House Committee on Government Operations (Reischauer 1993: 7).

More specifically, Reischauer faulted GRH for pairing unrealistic goals with non-credible enforcement mechanisms. "In an effort to live within the short-term budget constraints, the President and the Congress evaded the targets by relying on overly optimistic economic assumptions and outright budget gimmickry," he said. "This smoke-and-mirrors strategy enabled policymakers to appear to live within the annual constraints, while doing little to reduce the actual deficit" (Reischauer 1993: 2–3). By contrast, BEA's more flexible approach seemed to be working. Key elements of the 1990 legislation were defensive in nature, designed to protect the larger budget compromise embodied in the OBRA legislation. "It was enacted to enforce compliance with the deficit-reducing actions agreed to at the 1990 budget summit, but not to force further reductions or to compensate for unrealized expectations about the economy," Reischauer explained. By their very nature, PAYGO rules were devoted to the status quo (Reischauer 1993: 3; Penner and Steuerle 2004).

Both GRH and BEA coincided with some degree of budgetary improvement, although establishing causal links is difficult. Between 1985 and 1989, the deficit as a share of GDP fell from 5.1 percent to just 2.8 percent. A general speedup in economic growth after the recession of the early 1980s accounts for some of this improvement. Sagging growth at the end of the 1980s brought a return to deficit finance during the G.W. Bush presidency (World Bank undated). But after 1992, deficits began to shrink again, this time dropping precipitously from 4.7 percent of GDP in FY 1992 to 0.3 percent in FY 1997. By 1998, the budget was in surplus, where it remained through FY 2001. Again, economic growth makes it difficult to assign credit for this improvement solely to budget process reform and BEA rules in particular. But as one leading expert pointed out, budget policies were unquestionably a key factor. "Although the surplus would not have emerged without a cooperative economy, it also would not have occurred if budget policy in the 1990s had repeated the mistakes of the 1980s," concluded public policy scholar Allen Schick (Schick 2007: 28). In a period of rapid economic growth, spending constraints and PAYGO tax rules did more than protect the budgetary status quo: they provided the institutional framework for dramatic fiscal consolidation.

Budget Policy after the Reforms

The budgetary good news of the late 1990s did not survive much beyond the end of the decade. Spending caps disappeared in the late 1990s, and by 2002, PAYGO statutes were gone, too. (Keith 2007: 1). Absent structural constraint, federal budgeting took a turn for the worse—or at least the less disciplined. Throughout the early and mid 2000s, spending rose modestly but revenues fell dramatically. As a result, deficits returned, growing from 1.5 percent of GDP in 2002 to 3.5 percent in 2004. After a few years of modest improvement, they skyrocketed with the start of the Great Recession in 2008. Indeed, they reached levels not seen since World War II, hitting 10.1 percent of GDP in 2009 (Office of Management and Budget 2012b: 24–25).

To some degree, the red ink of the late 2000s was deliberate, as lawmakers used spending hikes and tax cuts as a means to stimulate the economy. Deficits also derived from the lower tax revenues that always accompany diminished economic activity. But the deficits of the 2000s were also structural, reflecting the budgetary impact of pre-crisis tax and spending policies, including the sweeping tax cuts of 2001 and 2003.

Whatever their cause, the extraordinary deficits of 2009 and beyond prompted calls for fiscal consolidation. But a lack of structural limitations on deficit finance, combined with partisan disagreement over the wisdom and extent of

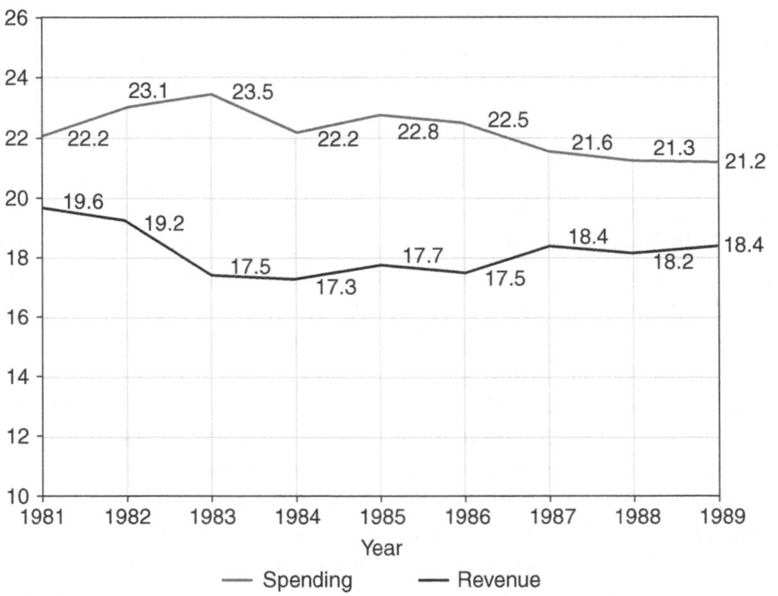

Figure 9.4 Taxes and spending in 1980s (source: Office of Management and Budget).

renewed austerity, led to a series of artificial budget crises. Like the budget process reforms of the 1980s and 1990s, these planned disasters (which took the form of debt limit extensions, government shutdowns, and wholesale expiration of temporary tax cuts) were designed to force compromise on reluctant political belligerents. And to some extent, they achieved this goal, in the sense that lawmakers resolved each crisis in some non-disastrous fashion. But planned disasters failed to achieve any sort of meaningful, long-term fiscal consolidation. Indeed, resolution of the planned disasters reflected an embrace of fiscal self-indulgence, not a commitment to budgetary self-discipline.

The End of Consolidation

The demise of structural budget constraints took place during an era of fiscal optimism. On the eve of President George W. Bush's inauguration, the CBO projected that the late 1990s surpluses would continue for years to come, totaling $5.6 trillion through 2011 (Congressional Budget Office 2012a; Bartlett 2012). But such estimates assumed that current fiscal policies would continue unchanged, and that economic growth would remain relatively robust. In fact, however, neither condition proved true.

Early in his presidency, Bush proposed a sweeping tax cut, justified by surplus predictions. Congress embraced the idea, passing the Economic Growth and Tax Relief Reconciliation Act of 2001, which reduced income tax rates across the board; according to one estimate, marginal rates fell for 62 percent of taxpayers (Steuerle 2004: 201). The law also featured a variety of other tax benefits for both individual and business taxpayers, including a larger child credit, a reduction in the so-called marriage penalty, and full repeal of the federal estate and gift tax. Most of the law's provisions were phased in gradually over the course of a decade—and all were slated to expire in 2011 (although supporters of the bill clearly intended and expected its provisions to be made permanent) (Tax Policy Center undated; Labonte 2010).

The terror attacks of September 11, 2001 brought a significant slowdown to the US economy. In fact, annual GDP growth had been slowing even before 9/11, falling from 4.1 percent in fiscal 2000 to just 0.9 percent in 2001 (World Bank undated). In any case, the downturn of 2001 depressed revenues while also fostering calls for additional tax cuts to stimulate the economy. "The terrorism threat combined with the economic slowdown," recalled tax expert C. Eugene Steuerle, "to give Congress and the president excuses to throw budgetary caution to the wind" (Steuerle 2004: 210).

Spending rose modestly in 2002 and 2003, while tax revenues plummeted. The resulting deficit, however, did nothing to slow the drive for additional tax cuts. In 2002, Congress passed the Job Creation and Worker Assistance Act, which liberalized depreciation allowances and carryback provisions for businesses, while also extending a variety of expiring tax credits (Tax Policy Center undated). In 2003, lawmakers followed up with the Jobs and Growth Tax Relief Reconciliation Act, which accelerated many of the phased-in tax cuts enacted in 2001. It also included a variety of additional tax cuts, including lower rates for capital gains and dividends, as well as even more liberal depreciation provisions (Tax Policy Center undated).

The tax cuts enacted between 2001 and 2003 dramatically reduced federal revenues. And while tax cuts as a form of economic stimulus was hardly a novel idea at the start of the twenty-first century, the size and extent of these tax cuts was dramatic. The 2001 tax cut was the second largest enacted since 1968, according to one Treasury Department estimate (Tempalski 2011). And as a group, the Bush tax cuts pushed federal revenues to their smallest share of GDP since the 1950s, bottoming out at 16.1 percent of GDP in 2004 (Office of Management and Budget 2014: 26–27).

The onset of the Great Recession brought a renewed commitment to fiscal stimulus in the Keynesian tradition—and large tax cuts in particular. The Emergency Economic Stabilization Act of 2008 and the American Recovery and Reinvestment Tax Act of the American Recovery and Reinvestment Act of 2009 both slashed federal revenues, both for individuals and businesses (Tax Policy Center undated). Spending also rose, especially in the 2009 legislation, which carried a net price tag of nearly $1 trillion.

Disaster Budgeting

The sea of post-2008 red ink brought renewed calls for fiscal consolidation. Although shortfalls were largely intentional, fiscal stimulus lost its luster in the face of huge deficits. Republicans had always been reluctant champions of compensatory fiscal policy, and they had opposed the 2009 stimulus legislation unanimously. But in the face of large deficits, even many Democrats committed themselves to a renewed austerity drive, tacitly accepting conservative warnings that the nation was mortgaging its future. In 2010, President Barack Obama even used his state of the union address to endorse a spending freeze for discretionary programs. "Like any cash-strapped family," he said, "we will work within a budget to invest in what we need and sacrifice what we don't. And if I have to enforce this discipline by veto, I will" (Obama 2010).

But major differences continued to divide the parties when it came to fiscal policy. Republicans remained committed to much larger and faster fiscal consolidation than their Democratic counterparts. Deadlock was the all but inevitable result, with the Republican-controlled House of Representatives squaring off against Obama and the Democratic Senate. To cope with this stalemate, policy makers came to rely on a series of arbitrary deadlines and manufactured crises. These planned disasters were designed to force reluctant lawmakers to take some sort of action. And while they achieved this goal, they failed to force much in the way of *productive* action, at least if that goal is defined in terms of meaningful fiscal consolidation.

The first planned disaster came in late 2010, when President Barack Obama began negotiating with Republican leaders over the fate of the Bush tax cuts, most of which were slated to expire at the end of the year. After protracted discussions, the parties agreed to extend the tax cuts for two years, while also creating a new, temporary reduction for the Social Security payroll tax. The Tax

Relief, Unemployment Insurance Reauthorization, and Job Creation Act was projected to cost about $858 billion over 10 years—a steep price tag at any time, but especially in the midst of large and growing deficits (Joint Committee on Taxation 2010).

The compromise provided a breathing spell but a distinctly temporary one; when the two-year extension ran its course, lawmakers would be faced with another mass expiration of previously enacted, ostensibly temporary tax cuts. The creation of this follow-on crisis was not accidental; lawmakers were free to resolve the expiration crisis permanently by making permanent some, all, or none of the expiring provisions. But instead, they opted deliberately for a repeat of the 2010 budget crisis.

First, however, they would have to tackle another, different sort of artificial crisis. In the summer of 2011, the federal government reached the limit if its borrowing authority. Since 1917, Congress had imposed an overall limit on federal debt. In lieu of authorizing every bond issue individually (standard practice before World War I), lawmakers simply required the Treasury Department to stay within an overall borrowing cap. Periodically, this debt limit has had to be increased, as the economy has grown, spending has risen, and lawmakers have continued to approve unbalanced budgets. And in theory, these increases should be uncontroversial, since they are simply a reflection of prior tax and spending decisions. As the Government Accountability Office has explained: "The debt limit does not control or limit the ability of the federal government to run deficits or incur obligations. Rather, it is a limit on the ability to pay obligations already incurred" (Government Accountability Office 2011). Nonetheless, debt limit extensions have historically served as flash points in budgetary politics. Such measures are "must-pass" legislation, in the sense that failure to raise the limit raises the prospect of default. But lawmakers have often leveraged that imperative to pursue other policy goals.

Such was the case in the summer of 2011, when Republican leaders threatened to reject a debt limit increase. The resulting crisis was more severe than past arguments over raising the limit, chiefly because Republicans seemed to be unusually serious about their threat to reject an increase. But the crisis ended in yet another compromise, marked by a short-term extension of the ceiling coupled with a variety of promised spending cuts. The compromise, embodied in the Budget Control Act of 2011, also provided for the creation of a bipartisan congressional joint select committee—widely known as the "supercommittee"—that was charged with crafting a major deficit reduction package. If the supercommittee failed to reach an agreement, the compromise provided for large, automatic, across-the-board spending cuts that would take effect in steps, the first coming in January 2013. "The process presumably is intended to encourage agreement on deficit reduction," observed the Congressional Research Service, chiefly by mandating an alternative budget enforcement process that was even more unappealing than most likely compromises (Heniff Jr. 2011: unnumbered page).

The next budget crisis came in late 2012. Known as "the fiscal cliff," it was a direct outgrowth of the previous planned disasters. At the end of the year, the

Bush tax cuts—extended for two years in 2010—were again due to expire. At the same time, automatic spending cuts mandated by the Budget Control Act were also slated to take effect. Together, such measures would have produced major reductions in the federal deficit, totaling $502 billion between fiscal 2012 and fiscal 2013 (Levit 2013: 1). But according to most observers, including the CBO, the resulting fiscal contraction was likely to tip the US economy into recession (Congressional Budget Office 2012b: 1). In other words, policymakers once again faced a crisis of their own creation. The simultaneity of these automatic policy changes was certainly no surprise—they were evident to anyone and everyone engaged in crafting the original policy proposals.

Like previous planned disasters, the fiscal cliff was resolved with a compromise. In this respect, it was a success. But it was not a compromise consistent with meaningful fiscal consolidation, since it featured a wholesale and permanent extension of most of the Bush tax cuts, combined with a delay in automatic spending cuts required under the Budget Control Act. In its first two years alone, it was projected to reduce federal revenue by more than $280 billion; over ten years, it was expected to cost $1.53 trillion (Levit 2013: 4). In other words, it was an expensive sort of compromise, made possible by the embrace of deficit spending, not a rejection of it.

Taken as a whole, the planned fiscal crises of twenty-first century politics shared several key traits. First, each was triggered by an arbitrary deadline that policy makers had imposed upon themselves, not by some external force or condition; in fact, each represented an effort to *create* an external prod to action—external, at least, relative to the usual budget and political process. Second, each crisis was also resolved in temporary fashion, with lawmakers creating new deadlines to guarantee a near-term recurrence. Planned disasters were inherently ad hoc, existing outside the regular budget process, but their serial reappearance imparted some of the regularity associated with more traditional budget process constraints. Third, each manufactured crisis was carefully designed to create an imperative for compromise, chiefly through the creation of unappealing, automatic fiscal mechanisms that lawmakers would (presumably) work hard to avoid.

In many respects, the manufactured crises of 2012–13 resembled the budget process reforms of the 1980s, especially Gramm–Rudman–Hollings, with its arbitrary deficit targets and automatic mechanism for spending cuts. Like GRH, however, planned disasters produced little in the way of real fiscal consolidation. Politically, they served as an expression of concern, and they may have helped focus public attention on issues of taxation and federal spending. But as a mechanism for actually achieving fiscal consolidation, they were a failure.

Conclusion

Do budget process reforms work? History gives reason for both caution and optimism, but policy makers are clearly interested in the possibility of reviving them. Current Treasury Secretary Jacob Lew, who helped craft fiscal policy in the 1980s and 1990s, has spoken approvingly of GRH and BEA. “I don’t know that we ever would have been able to accomplish the deficit reduction that we did in 1990, 1993, 1997, without an environment that had been shaped by having that collection of enforcement mechanisms in place," he said in 2011 (Calmes 2011). Ultimately, the specific budget mechanisms don't need to work precisely as advertised, Lew explained. "The real truth is nobody ever wants to find out," he said. "The purpose of these mechanisms is to discipline those in the policy process to make decisions" (Calmes 2011).

Lew's argument may overstate the efficacy of sequestration threats, which were the principal enforcement mechanism of GRH. But his emphasis on the political aspect of budget process reform—as opposed to its legislative specifics—is important.

Viewed as a political lever, rather than a specific procedural reform, the budget legislation of the late 1980s and early 1990s seems to have a reasonable claim to success. The hortatory effect of this legislation may have focused attention on key issues of fiscal performance, chiefly by establishing a severe threat of independent remedial action. Even when GRH was failing as policy—as measured by success at reaching specific deficit targets—it was succeeding on the level of fiscal politics. By keeping policy makers focused on fiscal consolidation, it provided the political context, if not the specific mechanism, for budget compromise.

Ultimately, however, the most effective element of budget process reform enacted in the late twentieth century seems to have been the PAYGO rules established in BEA. Indeed, President Obama has cited PAYGO as "a big reason why we had record surpluses in the 1990s" (Obama 2010). Ultimately, this sort of defensive budget rule is more effective than ambitious forward-looking deficit reduction programs like those embedded in GRH. Future targets are all well and good—until the future actually arrives, at which point Congress has demonstrated that it will abandon uncomfortable goals. As one scholar has observed: "the rules cease to operate once they deviate too far from consensus policy" (Auerbach 2009: 43).

Specific deficit targets are especially vulnerable to congressional backsliding because they fail to account for economic factors outside the legislative process. Macroeconomic conditions can often make deficit reduction difficult, rendering specific targets all but impossible to achieve. PAYGO rules, on the other hand, focus legislative attention on things that lawmakers actually *can* control: tax and spending decisions that depart from existing baselines. As one former director of the Congressional Budget Office has observed, 1990s PAYGO rules "imposed restraints on legislated policy changes—something that Congress controlled—rather than trying to design policies targeting a deficit that was more immediately affected by the economy than by congressional actions." PAYGO, in other words, was less ambitious but more feasible (Penner 2002).

The success of PAYGO rules at promoting fiscal consolidation is uncertain. If nothing else, it can be difficult to distinguish between the beneficial effect of PAYGO and the deficit reduction derived from robust economic growth in the mid to late 1990s. But the circumstantial case for the efficacy of PAYGO is hard to ignore: US fiscal performance improved rapidly after PAYGO rules were imposed, and it deteriorated sharply after they disappeared in 2002. If nothing else, PAYGO seems to have prevented Congress from frittering away the fiscal windfall delivered by the surging economy of the late 1990s. And it did so by connecting the long-term effects of fiscal decisions to the short-term dynamics of fiscal politics. As one budget observer has noted:

> The concept of PAYGO represents the simple truism that budgeting is about trade-offs. PAYGO requires that Congress identify the means for offsetting the costs of new tax cuts or mandatory spending programs, thereby allowing Congress the flexibility to implement the policies it chooses along with the responsibility of paying for those policies.
>
> (MacGuineas 2007)

Ultimately, however, PAYGO is a defensive reform, designed to protect past budget improvements. But PAYGO is only valuable if the status quo is worth protecting. PAYGO doesn't solve budget problems, it just prevents them from getting worse. If the United States hopes to resolve its long-term fiscal challenges, policy makers will still have to muster the political wherewithal to reach meaningful deficit reduction. And budget process reforms are unlikely to help much with that task.

References

Abramowitz, Alan. 2010. *The Disappearing Center: Engaged Citizens, Polarization, and American Democracy*. New Haven: Yale University Press.

Auerbach, Alan. 2009. "US Experience with Federal Budget Rules." CESifo DICE Report, Ifo Institute for Economic Research at the University of Munich, 7(1): 41–48.

Avi-Yonah, Reuven S. 2004. "Corporations, Society, and the State: A Defense of the Corporate Tax." *Virginia Law Review* 90: 1193–1255.

Baker, Dean. 2007. *The United States since 1980*. New York: Cambridge University Press.

Bank, Steven A. 2010. *From Sword to Shield: The Transformation of the Corporate Income Tax, 1861 to Present*. Oxford: Oxford University Press.

Barone, Michael. 2013. "Washington Is Partisan—Get Used to It." *Wall Street Journal*. http://online.wsj.com/news/articles/SB10001424052702303680404579140080429918194?mod=WSJ_Opinion_LEADTop, accessed August 10, 2014.

Bartlett, Bruce. 2009. *The New American Economy: The Failure of Reaganomics and a New Way Forward*. 1st edn. New York: Palgrave Macmillan.

Bartlett, Bruce. 2011. "Reagan's Forgotten Tax Record." *Capital Gains and Games*, 22 February. http://capitalgainsandgames.com/blog/bruce-bartlett/2154/reagans-forgotten-tax-record, accessed August 10, 2014.

Bartlett, Bruce. 2012. "The Fiscal Legacy of George W. Bush." *New York Times*, June 12. http://economix.blogs.nytimes.com/2012/06/12/the-fiscal-legacy-of-george-w-bush/?_r=0, accessed December 16, 2014.

Berkowitz, Edward D. 1995. "Social Security and the Financing of the American State." In *Funding the Modern American State, 1941–1995: The Rise and Fall of the Era of Easy Finance*, edited by W. Elliot Brownlee, 149–194. Washington, D.C. and New York: Woodrow Wilson Center Press and Cambridge University Press.

Birnbaum, Jeffrey H. and Alan S. Murray. 1987. *Showdown at Gucci Gulch: Lawmakers, Lobbyists, and the Unlikely Triumph of Tax Reform*. 1st edn. New York: Random House.

Blumenthal, Sidney. 1997. "Seeking Insolvency." *World Policy Journal* 14(2): 19.

Brownlee, W. Elliot. 1996. "Tax Regimes, National Crisis, and State-Building in America." In *Funding the Modern American State, 1941–1995: The Rise and Fall of the Era of Easy Finance*, edited by W. Elliot Brownlee, 37–106. Washington, D.C. and New York: Woodrow Wilson Center Press and Cambridge University Press.

Brownlee, W. Elliot. 2004. *Federal Taxation in America: A Short History*. 2nd edn. Woodrow Wilson Center Series. Washington, D.C., Cambridge, UK, and New York: Woodrow Wilson Center Press and Cambridge University Press.

Brownlee, W. Elliot and Hugh Davis Graham. 2003. *The Reagan Presidency: Pragmatic Conservatism and its Legacies*. Lawrence: University Press of Kansas.

Calmes, Jackie. 2011. "Idea Rebounds: Automatic Cuts to Curb Deficits." *New York Times*, May 15. www.nytimes.com/2011/05/16/us/politics/16fiscal.html?pagewanted=all&_r=0, accessed August 10, 2014.

Center on Budget and Policy Priorities. 2011. *Policy Basics: Introduction to the Federal Budget Process*. Washington, D.C.

Collins, Robert M. 2000. *More: The Politics of Economic Growth in Postwar America*. Oxford and New York: Oxford University Press.

Congressional Budget Office. 2012a. *Changes in CBO's Baseline Projections since January 2001*. Washington, D.C.

Congressional Budget Office. 2012b. *Economic Effects of Policies Contributing to Fiscal Tightening in 2013*. Washington, D.C.

Congressional Budget Office. 2013. *The 2013 Long-Term Budget Outlook, Supplemental Data*. Washington, D.C.

Congressional Budget Office. 2014. *Updated Budget Projections: Fiscal Years 2014 to 2024*. Washington, D.C.

Conlan, Timothy J., Margaret Tucker Wrightson, and David R. Beam. 1990. *Taxing Choices: The Politics of Tax Reform*. Washington, D.C.: CQ Press.

Frankel, Jeffry. 2003. "Trading Places." *Milliken Institute Review*, March: 18–25.

Frenzel, Bill. 2012. "Where have the Heroes Gone in the Fiscal Cliff Debate?" *Real Clear Markets*, December 12. www.realclearmarkets.com/articles/2012/12/12/where_have_the_heroes_gone_in_the_fiscal_cliff_debate_100040.html, accessed August 10, 2014.

Government Accountability Office. 2011. *Debt Limit: Delays Create Debt Management Challenges and Increase Uncertainty in the Treasury Market*. Washington, D.C.

Heniff Jr., Bill, Elizabeth Rybicki, and Shannon M. Mahan. 2011. *The Budget Control Act of 2011*. Washington, D.C.: Congressional Research Service.

Heniff Jr., Bill, Megan Suzanne Lynch, and Jessica Tollestrup. 2012. *Introduction to the Federal Budget Process*. Washington, D.C.: Congressional Research Service.

IMF (International Monetary Fund). 2013. *World Economic Outlook 2013: Transitions and Tensions*. Washington, D.C.

Joint Committee on Taxation. 2010. *Estimated Budget Effects of the "Tax Relief, Unemployment Insurance Reauthorization, and Job Creation Act of 2010."* U.S. Congress, last modified June 7, 2014. www.jct.gov/publications.html?func=startdown&id=3715, accessed August 10, 2014.

Joyce, Philip G. 2011. *The Congressional Budget Office: Honest Numbers, Power, and Policymaking*. American Governance and Public Policy Series. Washington, D.C.: Georgetown University Press.

Kabaservice, Geoffrey M. 2012. *Rule and Ruin: The Downfall of Moderation and the*

Destruction of the Republican Party, from Eisenhower to the Tea Party. Studies in Postwar American Political Development. New York: Oxford University Press.

Keith, Robert. 1986. *Changes in the Congressional Budget Process Made by the 1985 Balanced Budget Act (P.L. 99–177)*. Edited by Congressional Research Service, Washington, D.C..

Keith, Robert. 2007. *Pay-As-You-Go Procedures*. Congressional Research Service, Washington, D.C.

Kowalcky, Linda K. and Lance T. LeLoup. 1993. "Congress and the Politics of Statutory Debt Limitation." *Public Administration Review* 53(1): 14–27.

Labonte, Marc. 2010. *What Effects would Expiration of the 2001 and 2003 Tax Cuts Have on the Economy?* Congressional Research Service, Washington, D.C.

Levit, Mindy R., Margot L. Crandall-Hollick, Jim Hahn, Jim Monke, Janemarie Mulvey, and Julie M. Whittaker. 2013. *The "Fiscal Cliff" and the American Taxpayer Relief Act of 2012*. Washington, D.C.: Congressional Research Service.

MacGuineas, Maya. 2007. *Testimony on Renewing Statutory PAYGO*. Washington, D.C.: New America Foundation.

Mann, Thomas E. and Norman J. Ornstein. 2012. *It's Even Worse than it Looks: How the American Constitutional System Collided with the New Politics of Extremism*. New York: Basic Books.

Martin, Isaac William. 2008. *The Permanent Tax Revolt: How the Property Tax Transformed American Politics*. Stanford, CA: Stanford University Press.

Martin, Isaac William. 2013. *Rich People's Movements: Grassroots Campaigns to Untax the One Percent*. Studies in Postwar American Political Development. New York: Oxford University Press.

McCarty, Nolan M., Keith T. Poole, and Howard Rosenthal. 2006. *Polarized America: The Dance of Ideology and Unequal Riches*. Cambridge, MA: MIT Press.

Michelmore, Molly C. 2012. *Tax and Spend: The Welfare State, Tax Politics, and the Limits of American Liberalism. Politics and culture in modern America*. Philadelphia: University of Pennsylvania Press.

National Taxpayers' Union. undated. *History of Federal Individual Income Bottom and Top Bracket Rates*. www.ntu.org/tax-basics/history-of-federal-individual-1.html, accessed August 10, 2014.

Nelson, Rebecca M. 2013. *Sovereign Debt in Advanced Economies: Overview and Issues for Congress*. Washington, D.C.: Congressional Research Service.

Niskanen, William A. 1992. "The Case for a New Fiscal Constitution." *Journal of Economic Perspectives* 6(2): 13–24. doi:10.2307/2138406.

Obama, Barack. 2010. "Remarks by the President in State of the Union Address." Office of the President. www.whitehouse.gov/the-press-office/remarks-president-state-union-address, accessed June 7, 2014.

Office of Management and Budget. 2012a. *Budget of the United States Government, Fiscal Year 2013: Analytical Tables*. Washington, D.C.: Government Printing Office.

Office of Management and Budget. 2012b. *Budget of the United States Government, Fiscal Year 2013: Historical Tables*. Washington, D.C.: Government Printing Office.

Office of Management and Budget. 2014. *Budget of the United States Government, Fiscal Year 2013: Historical Tables*. Washington, D.C.: Government Printing Office.

Penner, Rudolph G. 2002. *Repairing the Congressional Budget Process*. Washington, D.C.: Urban Institute.

Penner, Rudolph G. and C. Eugene Steuerle. 2004. *Budget Rules*. Washington, D.C.: Urban Institute.

Pollack, Sheldon David. 2003. *Refinancing America: The Republican Antitax Agenda*. Albany: State University of New York Press.

Rae, Nicol C. 1989. *The Decline and Fall of the Liberal Republicans: From 1952 to the Present*. New York: Oxford University Press.

Reischauer, Robert D. 1993. "Statement of Robert D. Reischauer, Director, Congressional Budget Office, before the Subcommittee on Legislation and National Security Committee on Government Operations, U.S. House of Representatives." www.cbo.gov/sites/default/files/1993_05_13reischauertestimony.pdf, accessed June 7, 2014.

Schick, Allen. 1985. *Explanation of the Balanced Budget and Emergency Deficit Control Act of 1985—Public Law 99–177 (The Gramm–Rudman–Hollings Act)*, edited by Congressional Research Service. Washington, D.C.

Schick, Allen. 2007. *The Federal Budget: Politics, Policy, Process*. 3rd edn. Washington, D.C.: Brookings Institution Press.

Senate Committee on the Budget. 2006. *Committee on the Budget, United States Senate, 1974–2006*. 109th Congress, 2nd Session.

Shaviro, Daniel N. 2009. *Decoding the U.S. Corporate Tax*. Washington, D.C.: Urban Institute Press.

Sinclair, Barbara. 2006. *Party Wars: Polarization and the Politics of National Policy Making*. Julian J. Rothbaum Distinguished Lecture Series. Norman, OK: University of Oklahoma Press.

Steuerle, C. Eugene. 1996. "Financing the American State at the Turn of the Century." In *Funding the Modern American State, 1941–1995: The Rise and Fall of the Era of Easy Finance*, edited by W. Elliot Brownlee, 409–444. Washington, D.C. and New York: Woodrow Wilson Center Press and Cambridge University Press.

Steuerle, C. Eugene. 2004. *Contemporary U.S. Tax Policy*. Washington, D.C.: Urban Institute Press.

Sullivan, Martin A. 2011. *Corporate Tax Reform: Taxing Corporate Profits in the 21st Century*. New York: Apress.

Suskind, Ron. 2004. *The Price of Loyalty: George W. Bush, the White House, and the Education of Paul O'Neill*. New York: Simon and Schuster.

Tax Policy Center. 2013. *Historical Social Security Tax Rates [1]*. www.taxpolicycenter.org/taxfacts/content/pdf/ssrate_historical.pdf, accessed June 15, 2014.

Tax Policy Center. undated. *Major Enacted Tax Legislation, 2000–2009*. www.taxpolicycenter.org/legislation/2000.cfm, accessed August 10, 2014.

Tempalski, Jerry. 2011. *Revenue Effects of Major Tax Bills: Updated Tables for All 2010 Bills*. Washington, D.C.: US Department of the Treasury.

Thorndike, Joseph J. 2012. "The Durability of a Dysfunctional Tax: Public Opinion and the Failure of Corporate Tax Reform." *Kansas Journal of Law and Public Policy* 21: 347–450.

Thurber, James A. 2013. "The Dynamics and Dysfunction of the Congressional Budget Process: From Inception to Deadlock." In *Congress Reconsidered*, 319–345. Thousand Oaks, CA: CQ Press.

World Bank. undated. *GDP Growth (annual %)*. http://data.worldbank.org/indicator/NY.GDP.MKTP.KD.ZG?page=4, accessed June 15, 2014.

10 Weaving the Basket

Elusive Fiscal Convergence in the European Union

Edward A. Fogarty

Introduction

Fiscal performance is like much else in Europe: the past hangs heavily in the air, ever poised to repeat itself. In ancient Rome, emperors used a *fiscus* ("basket" or "treasury") to collect and store revenues from the provinces—revenues used to sustain the empire in the face of internal instability and external attacks. Two millennia later another pan-European polity is seeking to build a stronger *fiscus* to banish its post-2009 debt crisis. Will this new fiscal basket hold together, or will the European Union (EU) too fall prey to internal (fiscal) rot and external (speculative) attacks?

The European Union's debt crisis is surely reflective of problematic fiscal performance. Yet the prevailing tale of two Europes—a disciplined "core" of northern European countries and a frail "periphery" of primarily southern Europeans—is at best only partly accurate. This narrative captures real cross-national differences but obscures both the near-past fiscal difficulties of some northern countries and the extent to which southern countries' problems have been magnified by Economic and Monetary Union (EMU), the regime governing the euro. Rather than focusing on the debt crisis itself, this chapter examines the post-1990 fiscal regime in the "eurozone" and its goal to improve fiscal performance in peripheral eurozone countries such as Italy, Spain, and Greece. As it demonstrates, both the regime rules and the convergence toward fiscal orthodoxy they prescribed have been shaped by both the internal contradictions of the regime itself and the inherent difficulties in reconciling the irresistible force of German hegemony and the immovable objects of persistent "varieties of capitalism" in Europe.

Any analysis of fiscal policy coordination in the EU must begin from the understanding that, while the EU is a single polity, it is an *international* polity. Macroeconomic policy making in the eurozone reflects the complexity of this polity: the subset of EU members that adopted the single currency, the euro, delegated monetary policy to the European Central Bank (ECB); fiscal policy, by contrast, remains primarily in national hands—and thus requires international coordination underpinned by rules. In this context, fiscal policy dynamics respond largely to international political and economic conditions; factors addressed elsewhere in this book—such as party alignments and international economic integration—are rather less germane. In a multilevel international polity such as the European Union, fiscal policy is closely associated with national sovereignty, and thus EU-level fiscal coordination, not to mention integration, is *hard*.

This chapter explores how EU member states have struggled since the mid-1990s to promote fiscal rectitude and safeguard the single currency regime. The first section briefly discusses the path *not* chosen: full economic union, in which governments would delegate much greater supranational fiscal authority to the EU—and thus sacrifice more sovereignty to solve the dilemmas of international coordination. The next section addresses the co-evolution of EU fiscal performance and the supranational rules its members adopted to promote convergence toward fiscal orthodoxy. The subsequent section considers both the design flaws in these rules as well as non-institutional explanations for EU fiscal performance, focusing on the uneasy balance between the power of dominant creditor states (notably Germany) and the persistence of diversity in the economic models of different EU countries. The chapter concludes with a consideration of the likely success of reformed fiscal rules adopted during the debt crisis within a continent whose citizens are increasingly skeptical about EU authority.

European Union Fiscal Authority

There are two distinct fiscal arenas in the European Union. The main focus of this chapter is the collective fiscal performance of the member states of the EU. Yet the EU has some fiscal capacity itself—though this capacity is quite low. By identifying the limits on the EU's supranational fiscal authority we can get an initial glimpse into the politics of fiscal coordination in Europe.

The European Union lacks the *sine qua non* of fiscal authority, the power to raise its own revenues through direct taxation. Brussels acquires revenues through voluntary transfers by member state governments, with seven-year budgets agreed through tough intergovernmental bargaining.[1] The EU does have some directly collected revenues drawn primarily from tariff duties levied on goods and services entering the EU's single market, and also draws revenue from a harmonized value-added tax and member state charges based on gross national income. The size of the EU budget is approximately 1 percent of total EU GDP, or €150 billion ($207 billion) for 2014. (As a basis of comparison, the United States, with an economy roughly the same size of the European Union's, had a (proposed) federal budget in 2014 of $3.8 trillion.)

The EU spends its relatively scarce resources quite differently from its member governments. It has a limited role in traditional areas of interest for national governments, such as defense, public health, and education. (Also, because it cannot borrow, the EU spends nothing on debt service.) Rather, the EU has focused its spending on two particular areas: the Common Agricultural Policy (CAP) and "structural funds," or aid to poor regions. Agriculture has long been the single biggest area of EU expenditure, primarily reflecting France's leading role in setting EU priorities in its early days. Agricultural expenditures were 41 percent of the EU budget in 2012, after peaking at 73 percent in 1984—

with funds that once went to production and export subsidies now focused on price supports and "environmental maintenance."[2] Structural funds, for their part, emerged in the 1970s as a means to promote solidarity within a growing community that included new members (e.g., Ireland, Greece) significantly poorer than the original six (West Germany, France, Italy, Netherlands, Belgium, Luxembourg). Structural funds are allocated to regions rather than countries, reflecting internal regional diversity of countries such as Italy—and allowing all member states to claim at least some structural funds for their poorer regions. Yet while both the CAP and (especially) structural funds are tangible forms of intra-EU solidarity, there has been little move toward a transfer union in which funds would be transferred automatically from Brussels to governments or households of member states experiencing the effects of cyclical economic downturns.

Indeed, it is the absence of a transfer union and the power of direct taxation that defines the limits of EU fiscal authority. While it is beyond the scope of this chapter to explain these limits, certain conditions that help explain these limits are also relevant to international fiscal coordination in the EU. First, the European Union is not a state: despite their delegation of major policy areas to Brussels, EU members are sovereign states that remain reluctant to cede authority to the EU in areas of core sovereignty (taxation, defense) or that are politically sensitive (health, education). Second, EU fiscal affairs follow the standard dynamics of distributional politics: budgetary agreements reflect a compromise between net contributors to the EU budget (wealthier countries and/or those with small agricultural sectors), which seek to limit their transfers, and net recipients (poorer countries and/or those with larger agricultural sectors), which seek to maximize their receipts. The combination of all member states' continued defense of central sovereign authorities and wealthier countries' incentives to avoid large, automatic transfers presents large and perhaps insuperable barriers to supranational control over an expanded EU budget, at least for the foreseeable future.

Indeed, distributional politics is central to understanding the rules the EU has adopted to manage fiscal externalities—the external effects of individual countries' taxation and spending choices—in the absence of supranational fiscal authority. In the EU generally but especially in the euro area, fiscal externalities are high: an individual state's fiscal expansion can benefit others through a stimulus of economic activity within the single market, but a state's unsustainable fiscal policy that produces a debt crisis—as with that in Greece in 2009—can threaten financial disaster for all. To understand fiscal performance in the EU—and to put the debt crisis in its proper context—one must appreciate the fact of high fiscal interdependence and the demand for, and difficulties of, rules and institutions to manage these externalities.

EU Rules and Fiscal Convergence

A standard narrative of the EU debt crisis is that the 2008 global financial crisis exposed the unsustainability of peripheral and/or southern European member states' fiscal policies and ultimately necessitated a rescue by the more fiscally responsible northern European creditor countries.[3] While this narrative has some basis in reality, it accurately describes the fiscal malpractice of only one country, Greece, and tends to obscure the strong fiscal performance of crisis-beset countries such as Spain and Ireland and the rather more checkered record of the purported fiscal paragon, Germany.

The EU established its own measures of fiscal performance in the rules it adopted to manage fiscal externalities in the eurozone. Thus we must first consider how these rules sought to socialize members to a specific definition of sustainability—and to promote convergence among all EU states (notably Italy) toward a German/northern Europe model of orthodoxy. Beginning in the early 1990s, EU members adopted a set of fiscal targets as well as procedures to promote compliance with them. Yet these EU rules formed an awkward regime: they created a different set of rules for members participating in EMU and those that did not (see Table 10.1), and for eurozone countries they created unbalanced macroeconomic policy authority between a supranational monetary policy (conducted by an independent ECB) and intergovernmental fiscal rules.

This section first describes the rules adopted by the EU and eurozone to promote convergence toward a model of fiscal orthodoxy, from before the birth of the euro in the late 1990s to the adoption of tighter fiscal rules in 2011–12. Then it briefly examines the actual fiscal performance of the EU, euro area, and a sample of member states during 1995–2013. Variation in member states' fiscal performance not only indicates the limited effect of EU rules but also calls into question the received wisdom about northern European rectitude and southern European profligacy.

Table 10.1 EU and eurozone members

EU member (year joined)	*Year joined eurozone*	*EU member (year joined)*	*Year joined eurozone*
Austria (1995)	1999	Italy (1958)	1999
Belgium (1958)	1999	Latvia (2004)	2014
Bulgaria (2007)	*	Lithuania (2004)	2015
Croatia (2013)	*	Luxembourg (1958)	1999
Cyprus (2004)	2008	Malta (2004)	2008
Czech Republic (2004)	*	Netherlands (1958)	1999
Denmark (1973)	*	Poland (2004)	*
Estonia (2004)	2011	Portugal (1986)	1999
Finland (1995)	1999	Romania (2007)	2007
France (1958)	1999	Slovakia (2004)	2009
Germany (1958)	1999	Slovenia (2004)	2007
Greece (1981)	2001	Spain (1986)	1999
Hungary (2004)	*	Sweden (1995)	*
Ireland (1973)	1999	United Kingdom (1973)	*

Notes

* All member states are required to adopt the euro when they meet the Maastricht criteria except for Denmark and the United Kingdom, which negotiated the right to opt out of the euro in the Maastricht Treaty. Formally, all EU members participate in the EMU, though the common monetary and fiscal rules apply almost exclusively to states using the euro.

EU Fiscal Rules, 1991–2012

The Maastricht Treaty (or Treaty on European Union, TEU), agreed in late 1991, contained both a provisional architecture for the EMU and the first foray into EU fiscal rules. Several articles of the treaty stipulated measures to protect the independence of the new European Central Bank and impose market discipline on countries that would use the euro, including articles forbidding monetary financing of national budget deficits and intergovernmental bailouts. The TEU also articulated precise maximum levels for budget deficits (3 percent) and public debt (60 percent)—two of the "Maastricht criteria" (or "convergence criteria") for countries aiming to adopt the euro—and created an "excessive deficit procedure" (EDP) to monitor and if necessary punish eurozone members that repeatedly exceeded the deficit target. Germany insisted on these articles' inclusion to ensure that countries with poor fiscal reputations, such as Italy, would be forced to converge toward more orthodox practices—and thus could not free ride on northern Europeans' fiscal credibility and pursue economic expansion through borrowing (Dinan 2010).

Over the subsequent two decades, including the first decade of the euro, these rules would be expanded and strengthened before being weakened, partially overturned, and then resuscitated (see Table 10.2). Here the focus is on two interrelated elements of these rules: the extent of the obligation they impose on member states, both to consult with the EU in making their budgets and to face punishment if they are in noncompliance; and the extent to which they delegate authority to both the European Commission (the EU's executive arm) and the European Court of Justice (ECJ) to undertake monitoring and punishment free from member state interference—specifically, via the intergovernmental European Council.

The Stability and Growth Pact (SGP) drew on both the TEU and a 1995 German Finance Ministry proposal for a "stability treaty" to strengthen the EU's fiscal rules. The SGP formalized the 3 percent Maastricht ceiling for budget deficits, which facilitated monitoring and peer review. Through its "corrective arm" the SGP increased budgetary consultation with and monitoring by the Commission, and formalized the excessive deficit procedure to warn and if necessary punish member states (with fines) that breached deficit limits. The SGP's "preventive arm," for its part, was primarily advisory, entreating member governments to aim for balanced budgets over the medium term—thereby including a bit of flexibility regarding deficits with reference to the economic cycle.

Yet, as Heipertz and Verdun (2009) argue, the SGP proved merely "declaratory": the Commission lacked the independent authority to enforce compliance, as demonstrated when Germany and France breached the SGP's deficit targets in 2003 and 2004. In accordance with the wishes of the German and French governments, in March 2005 the Commission and member states agreed to soften the application of the excessive deficit procedure, moving the SGP away from *ex post* punitive measures and promoting more *ex ante* coordination and consultation regarding national budgets. This reform retained the basic goal of promoting fiscal sustainability but left the SGP toothless and weakened the Commission's position as an impartial enforcer of the rules.

Table 10.2 EMU fiscal rules, 1991–2012

Agreement	*Year*	*Pre-budget consultation requirements*	*Enforcement*	*Delegation to EU institutions*
Maastricht Treaty	1991	–	–	Commission monitoring
Stability and Growth Pact (SGP)	1997	Preventive arm: promote balanced budgets over economic cycle	Corrective arm: review and initiate fines for excessive deficits	Enhanced Commission monitoring and enforcement role
SGP revision	2005	Enhanced prior consultation	Weakened enforcement: put EDP "in abeyance"	Enhanced Commission monitoring, weakened enforcement
Two-pack and six-pack	2011	Enhanced prior discussion and approval of national budgets	Enhanced enforcement: earlier imposition of fines, also applicable to debt and current account imbalances	Enhanced Commission monitoring and enforcement
Fiscal Compact and ESM	2012	Increased for all, but especially for states receiving ESM funds	Enhanced enforcement: tougher fines	Enhanced Commission and ECJ monitoring and enforcement

In the context of a weakened SGP, the 2008 global financial crisis triggered a series of fiscal crises in the euro area. Panic began with Greece in 2009 and subsequently engulfed Ireland, Portugal, and Cyprus—and, more dangerously, threatened the solvency of two of the largest eurozone countries, Spain and Italy. The EU's institutional response to the crisis was, in effect, to destroy and rebuild the foundations of the existing regime. It rescinded key provisions of the TEU, overturning the "no bailout clause" by permitting intergovernmental rescues of governments facing imminent default on their public debt. Greece, Ireland, Portugal, and Cyprus have all drawn on the new funds—the temporary European Financial Stability Facility (EFSF) and then the permanent European Stability Mechanism (ESM)—created by EMU members to deter speculative attacks on eurozone government bonds and, if necessary, serve as a lender of last resort.[4]

During the same period, EU and eurozone members pursued both EU legislation and an intergovernmental treaty to intensify fiscal coordination and strengthen EU institutions' oversight of national budgeting (see Buti and Carnot 2012). In late 2011 the entire EU membership adopted the "six pack," a set of six reforms that reinforced surveillance of member states' expenditures and debt levels (as well as more general macroeconomic imbalances), following an earlier measure to intensify *ex ante* coordination in national budgeting. At the same time, members of the eurozone adopted the "two pack," reforms involving a deeper level of fiscal coordination among countries using the single currency, including synchronized adoption of national budgets and enhanced monitoring by and consultation with the Commission. (Members must submit national budgets to the Commission for approval before national parliaments vote on them.) EU members simultaneously negotiated an international treaty, the Fiscal Compact, which required signatories to adopt national legislation and/or constitutional amendments enshrining a "debt brake" akin to the one adopted by Germany in 2009.[5] The compact enhanced the EU's capacity to punish fiscal profligacy by requiring a qualified majority of members to vote *against* punishment rather than for it—a change that would make the sort of deferral of punishment Germany and France had earlier engineered much more difficult.[6]

Overall, the fiscal rules adopted during the debt crisis have essentially doubled down on the original rules in the TEU and SGP. They reasserted the underlying rationale to promote, or now *require*, convergence toward fiscal orthodoxy, especially in the eurozone but also the EU as a whole. The reformed rules reaffirmed the initial fiscal targets (3 and 60 percent) and strengthened the excessive deficit procedure, even as they intensified EU involvement in national budgeting processes—which Schimmelfennig (2014: 325) called "*ex ante* control over national budgets." And even though EU members rescinded the TEU's "no bailout clause," the ESM—essentially, a European IMF—possesses more intrusive mechanisms of EU authority over member states forced to seek financial rescue. Greece, as well as Ireland, Portugal, and Cyprus, essentially lost their fiscal sovereignty within the context of their bailout packages, forced to adopt reforms handed down by the "troika" (the EU, IMF, and ECB) or face the loss of loans to stave off default. So, after the demise of the SGP, members of the EU and eurozone greatly strengthened collective fiscal mechanisms to cope with the debt crisis—and prevent a future crisis—but did not delegate any significant authority to the EU to collect and distribute more of its own resources, and thus the eurozone regime remains unbalanced between supranational monetary *policy* and intergovernmental fiscal *rules*.

EU Fiscal Performance, 1995–2013

The very fact of the debt crisis could be seen as an indicator of poor fiscal performance in the EU—and of the failure of the fiscal regime to attain convergence toward orthodoxy. But if we consider a somewhat longer time horizon the picture is more complex. Prior to the global financial crisis, Italy—the country most clearly targeted by EU rules—was among the EU's most restrained fiscal performers, often running a primary surplus and reducing its debt-to-GDP ratio by roughly 18 percent (see Chapter 4.) Crisis-beset Ireland and Spain were, between 1995 and 2008, better fiscal performers than the "core" stalwarts Netherlands and Germany. In other words, not only was there variation in fiscal performance among EU member states but this variation did not clearly fit the pattern the framers of the EU's fiscal rules might have expected.

Given the differences in the rules between the euro area and the full EU membership, a first question is whether fiscal performance was notably better (or worse) in the eurozone than the overall EU membership. As Figures 10.1 and 10.2 demonstrate, levels of gross public debt and budget deficits in the eurozone and EU27 tracked each other closely, with slightly higher levels of each in the eurozone. Indeed, the eurozone collectively never met the 60 percent debt target, and often failed to meet the 3 percent deficit target. Yet the eurozone's somewhat worse fiscal performance cannot simply be blamed on the weakness of the SGP. First, higher eurozone debt levels reflect the fact that three of its members—Belgium, Italy, and Greece—had the EU's highest levels of public debt (typically

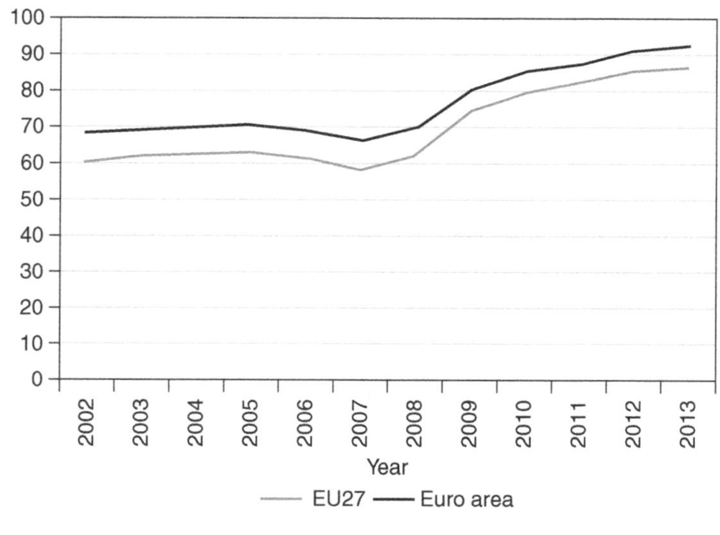

Figure 10.1 Gross public debt in EU and euro area (source: Eurostat).

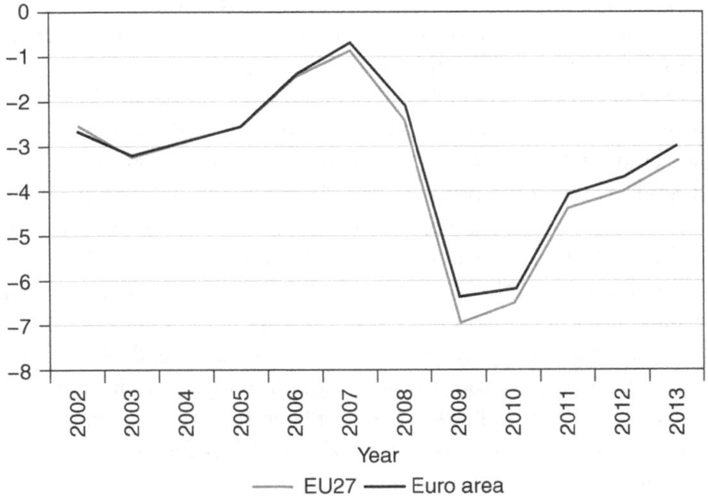

Figure 10.2 Budget deficits in EU27 and euro area (source: Eurostat).

exceeding a 100 percent debt-to-GDP ratio) even before the launch of the euro in 1999, and did not see significant increases in debt levels until after 2008 (along with everyone else). Second, eurozone countries have had (slightly) lower budget deficits than the overall EU membership since 2005—notably, the year that Germany began to restore fiscal rectitude after years of large deficits—and has closed the gap in public debt with the EU27 from roughly 8 percent in 2002–08 to 5 percent since 2009. More generally, both groupings' finances were highly responsive to the economic cycle (see Table 10.3), with debt and deficits

Table 10.3 EU and eurozone growth rates and budget deficits, 2002–13

	EU27		*Euro area*	
	GDP growth	*Budget balance*	*GDP growth*	*Budget balance*
2002	1.3	–2.6	0.9	–2.7
2003	1.5	–3.2	0.7	–3.1
2004	2.6	–2.9	2.2	–2.9
2005	2.2	–2.5	1.7	–2.5
2006	3.4	–1.5	3.2	–1.3
2007	3.2	–0.9	2.9	–0.7
2008	0.4	–2.4	0.4	–2.1
2009	–4.5	–6.9	–4.4	–6.4
2010	2.0	–6.5	2.0	–6.2
2011	1.7	–4.4	1.6	–4.2
2012	1.3	–4.0	–0.7	–3.7
2013	0.1	–3.3	–0.4	–3.0

Sources: European Central Bank, Eurostat, World Bank, OECD.

falling during years of economic expansion (2004–07) and growing during the depth of the global financial crisis (2008–09). Yet deficit reduction since 2010, particularly in the eurozone, has come not as a result of a strong economic rebound but rather of near-universal budgetary austerity.

From the perspective of creditors and debtors in the eurozone debt crisis, we also see trajectories of fiscal performance that do not clearly fit the narrative of "responsible" creditor countries and "irresponsible" debtors. On the debtor side, Greece and Spain reached the brink of default as a result of very different economic and fiscal conditions. Greece, like Italy, was allowed to join the eurozone because its efforts at fiscal rigor in the late 1990s were moving its debt and deficits in the direction of compliance; unlike Italy, Greece did not seek to sustain compliance once it had been admitted—and thus its near-default in 2009 came after years of heavy borrowing. By contrast, Spain reduced its debt-to-GDP ratio by almost half to 36 percent and accrued multiple budget surpluses before the bottom fell out of the housing market that had been fueling Spanish growth. So, while all countries could blame the onset of the global financial crisis for the rapid deterioration of their fiscal positions in 2008–09, only Greece faced default as a result of its own *fiscal* choices in the preceding years.

Meanwhile, the story of Germany's fiscal performance is by now well known. Bearing the burden of integrating the former East Germany, it struggled to meet the standards it had itself demanded of others in the SGP. Indeed, it was Germany's excessive deficits in 2002–04 that led it to demand a reprieve from punishment under the EDP and a reform of the SGP. Yet after 2006 Germany returned to its pre-1990s pattern of fiscal rectitude, putting it in a stronger position to demand such rectitude from its European partners after 2010.

In sum, fiscal performance in the EU does not necessarily accord with the prevailing narratives. The pre-euro narrative, which became the basis of the fiscal regime for the eurozone, was that strong rules were necessary—and likely to be effective—to force spendthrifts like Italy, Spain, and Greece to converge toward Teutonic rectitude. The post-crisis narrative reasserts the morality tale of the virtuous and unvirtuous, despite the fact that Greece was the only case of willful unvirtuousness and, again, Germany itself was for a few years in the camp of the unvirtuous. Nevertheless, we have seen universal austerity and an improvement in fiscal performance since 2009, especially in the euro area—though it is unclear whether austerity, with its growth suppressing effects, has aided or hindered the restoration of fiscal sustainability.

Explaining EU Fiscal Performance

Why did the convergence toward fiscal orthodoxy envisioned in the Maastricht Treaty and the Stability and Growth Pact not emerge? To start from the expectation that an *international* regime with limited enforcement powers could corral countries with distinct political and economic interests and circumstances toward fiscal conformity is to expect too much; fiscal coordination does not come easily. Nevertheless, institutions *do* matter. Explaining EU fiscal performance and cross-national variation therein requires consideration both of the flaws in the design of these rules and institutions and of the magnitude of the challenge any such rules faced in attaining fiscal convergence among a group of countries with quite distinct national economic models.

Rules and Institutions

How much did the EU's fiscal regime affect its members' fiscal performance? It is difficult to say for individual countries. But an effective regime would have produced convergence toward lower debts and deficits in the eurozone, and likely greater stability and orthodoxy within the eurozone than among other EU members—and these were not the outcomes this regime produced. Examining the flaws in the regime can help explain some of the variation, as well as the onset of the debt crisis. It also offers an opportunity for an initial evaluation of the 2011–12 reform of the rules intended to produce the fiscal convergence that the SGP did not.

The main structural flaw in the EMU was, and remains, the imbalance between the supranational monetary regime—in which monetary authority was delegated to the ECB—and the intergovernmental fiscal regime—in which member states coordinated, but ultimately retained national control over, tax and spending decisions.[7] Though the regime was formally called the Economic and Monetary Union, the economic half was decidedly weaker with the previously noted absence of supranational fiscal authority as well as a minimal capacity to promote coordinated economic planning.[8] Krugman (2011), for one, has argued that EU member states' decision not to delegate greater fiscal authority to the EU—specifically, to create a transfer union in which revenues flow automatically from economically successful to struggling states—inevitably led to the financial, and political, crisis in the eurozone after 2009.

Many implications follow from this imbalance between supranational monetary authority and intergovernmental fiscal/economic coordination. One is the extent to which it created a clash of incentives for member states between pursuing national economic interests and complying with EU rules. Because the eurozone is not, by most accounts, an optimal currency area,[9] interest rates that are appropriate for one country might not be for others. During the 2000s, the ECB set rates that were too low for countries experiencing asset inflation (e.g., Spain, Ireland) and too high for those experiencing relative economic stagnation (e.g., Germany, France)—thus causing the former to impose tight fiscal policies to prevent overheating and the latter to pursue deficit spending to stimulate growth. In the absence of supranational taxation/spending authority, eurozone states facing economic stagnation at home and lacking other macroeconomic tools (monetary policy, currency depreciation) to combat it defied—and continue to have incentives to defy—strict limits on debts and deficits.

The design of the euro regime also produced two key credibility problems. The first involved the TEU's "no bailout clause," intended to protect eurozone countries from having to take on others' obligations and thereby to ensure that governments would be constrained by market discipline. But for such market discipline to be operative, bondholders needed to believe members would allow afflicted eurozone governments to default—which they manifestly did not believe during the first decade of the euro. According to Buti and Carnot (2012: 903), interest rate spreads demonstrated that bondholders viewed all eurozone government debt as equivalent and "basically treated all as risk free," assuming "the Union would anyway renege on the no-bailout clause, if needed, to avert a financial crisis." Moreover, the continued reliance on market discipline once the debt crisis erupted in 2009 created self-fulfilling prophecies for European countries (Gros 2012: 41). Markets believed Germany could finance its debt (at essentially any level), and thus it was able to do so because interest rates were low. Alternatively, markets lacked such faith in southern European countries, and as a result they faced higher interest rates—which made servicing their debts more difficult and thus default more likely.[10] Thus a perverse quality of the rules was that they built upon, and ultimately reinforced, the pre-1990s narratives of northern vs. southern European fiscal practice that ultimately effectuated divergence rather convergence between the two.

The second credibility problem involved the EU's own enforcement of the excessive deficit procedure, the EU's mechanism to rein in fiscal free riders (excessive borrowing at reduced interest rates) in case market discipline failed. Part of the difficulty here rested in the nature of the punishment: fining a government for running an excessive deficit may compound rather than solve the problem. More fundamentally, it is politically difficult for EU institutions to punish rulebreakers. The Franco-German success in cajoling the European Council to excuse their fiscal sins in 2003–04 destroyed the authority of the SGP (and the Commission's role therein), not only in exempting them from the rules but in weakening enforcement mechanism applicable to all eurozone countries. But this episode belied an underlying reality: the EU has more leverage to ensure rule compliance when countries want to *join* a given regime—whether it is the Schengen Agreement, the eurozone, or the EU itself—than it does after they've joined. Following Italy's lead, Greece tightened its belt in the late 1990s in a bid to join the eurozone; once it was offered entry, in 2001, it could loosen it with far less fear of repercussions—even more so after the Franco-German actions.[11] So, just as bondholders did not believe they would be punished by a eurozone government default, eurozone governments were given ample reason not to believe they would be fined or otherwise punished by the EU for fiscal profligacy.

The theory underlying the pre-2009 fiscal rules in the eurozone regime was that a supranational fiscal authority to match the ECB's monetary authority was unnecessary (or undesirable), and that a combination of market discipline and enforceable rules would ensure all eurozone governments converge toward fiscal rectitude. Despite the blow this theory suffered with the debt crisis, the main post-2009 reforms to the regime—the six-pack, two-pack, and Fiscal Compact—doubled down on its core logic. To explain this choice, we must consider the power of creditor countries (notably Germany) and the magnitude of their project to achieve fiscal convergence in Europe.

German Hegemony and Varieties of Capitalism

At the end of the Cold War, many asked whether we would come to see a German Europe or a European Germany. The answer, it now seems clear, is both—or at least that is what German leaders have sought to achieve. The Germanization of European fiscal policy (or policies)—i.e., promotion of orthodoxy and market discipline, sometimes called ordoliberalism—has been a project since the Maastricht treaty, with all major rules (no bailout clause, SGP, Fiscal Compact, etc.) reflecting German demands in exchange for its own Europeanization (i.e., surrendering the deutschmark and monetary policy independence). Yet this Germanization of European fiscal policies was very much incomplete by the onset of the debt crisis, reflecting persistent differences in EU members' fundamental economic models—most notably, differences between northern and southern European countries. Thus the capacity of reformed EU rules to induce convergence toward fiscal rectitude will depend in large part on the underlying struggle between the irresistible force of German (and creditor) hegemony and the immovable object of the varieties of capitalism practiced in Europe.

German hegemony, and its orientation vis-à-vis fiscal policy convergence, can best be understood with reference to two longstanding literatures. Hegemonic stability theory describes how an economically dominant state can create regimes that provide collective goods (such as financial stability) and also serve the hegemon's economic self-interest (Kindleberger 1973; Krasner 1976). Liberal intergovernmentalism, for its part, offers an EU-specific theory of how powerful EU members create integrationist treaties or agreements if and only if their national economic interests align (Hoffman 1966; Moravcsik 1998). What these theories highlight is not only the extent to which Germany, as the economically dominant state in Europe, has spearheaded the creation of regimes reflecting its interest in fiscal and financial stability, but also how other EU members' persistent inclination to protect their core sovereignty and national interests limits the extent of Germany's capacity to induce (or compel) fiscal convergence.[12]

The history of the EU and eurozone's rules promoting fiscal convergence, if not the extent of convergence itself, clearly reflects German economic interests (see Dinan 2010; Moravcsik 2012). During the first half of the 1990s, when Germany was negotiating the terms of the euro, it sought EU rules to substitute for the economic rigor it had imposed via the Bundesbank's dominance of monetary policy across Europe during the 1980s. Key eurozone fiscal rules—complete ECB autonomy from political influence (contra French desires), the prohibition of bailouts or monetary financing of national debts, the specific 3 percent and 60 percent targets for fiscal performance, and the formal procedure for punishing states that ran excessive deficits—were adopted on Germany's insistence.[13] Alternatively, when these rules no longer served German interests—notably, the excessive deficit procedure in 2003–04 and the no bailout clause in 2009—it advocated their dismantling. Yet when the debt crisis struck and threatened a perpetual, ruinous cycle of bailouts, it insisted on a Fiscal Compact that mirrored the "debt brake" it had adopted domestically in 2009 and demanded extensive and intensive conditions for fiscal and other economic reforms in Greece, Portugal, and other countries receiving funds from the EFSF and ESM.

Germany promotes European fiscal rectitude (for the most part) for a variety of reasons. Two apply to all EU creditor countries. First, they retain a clear national interest in preventing fiscal free riding—overborrowing by governments benefiting from German and other creditors' financial credibility—and avoiding taking on the financial burdens of other governments. This self-protective interest helps explain not only the rules that have been adopted thus far but also why Germany, Austria, and others have refused to consider new mechanisms to achieve fiscal sustainability throughout Europe that might imply new burdens on their taxpayers, notably Eurobonds.[14] Second, German banks were, by 2008–09, among the most highly exposed to government debt in peripheral countries—with loans totaling $704 billion to Greece, Ireland, Italy, Portugal, and Spain by 2009—and thus defaults would threaten the stability of Germany's banking system.[15]

The third, and least tangible, source of the orthodoxy preference is rooted in Germany's past. Germans' twentieth-century history produced a collective national *angst* regarding the dangers of both debt and inflation, both of which can result from fiscal profligacy (Langenbacher 2010; Newman 2010; Hall 2012). This *angst* was stoked by two existential commitments the Federal Republic made during the 1990s—to sacrifice the deutschmark and to reintegrate the former German Democratic Republic (GDR). Integrating the former GDR involved a real, and large, financial commitment by all Germans, particularly those in the south and west, so national leaders have ardently sought to ensure that adopting the euro would not force Germans to bear the financial burdens of other Europeans. According to Howarth and Rommerskirchen (2013), the Angela Merkel-led governments in Berlin have instead sought to project a German "stability culture" onto the Continent, promoting stability abroad in order to sustain it at home. That the German position has occasionally manifested in sermonizing about fiscal prudence—emphasizing the *moral* in moral hazard—reflects how deeply embedded is the national narrative of economic orthodoxy as perhaps the central pillar of the Federal Republic's postwar revival and rehabilitation.[16]

Hall (2012) offers a framework, based on his work in the varieties of capitalism literature, for understanding why Germany's economic power and preferences may not be sufficient to ensure fiscal convergence. The assumption behind the fiscal rules and broader economic reforms Germany and other creditor countries have promoted is that indebted southern European countries simply need to adopt a specific set of macro- and microeconomic reforms to attain market confidence and economic competitiveness—and thus to replicate their own economic models. As Hall notes, however, northern and southern European countries have categorically distinct economic models—the former oriented toward export-led growth, the latter toward domestic demand—and international constraints on macroeconomic tools are much more onerous on southern European countries. Because northern European countries' economies are largely export-driven, their governments use macroeconomic policy to sustain competitiveness rather than stimulate demand; in southern European countries, domestic demand—and occasional macroeconomic stimulus to support it—are central. The eurozone rules, which limited the scope for fiscal stimulus for governments that had already ceded control over interest rates and currency values, have removed the macroeconomic tools necessary to sustain the southern European model.

Post-2009 reforms to the fiscal rules have thus ratcheted up the pressures on Greece, Italy, Spain, and Portugal to Germanize not just their fiscal policies but their entire economic model. This model does not merely constitute a set of discrete, easily alterable policies to achieve desired economic outcomes; it is deeply embedded in these countries' social and even cultural relationships, and reflects particular constellations of political interests, bargains, and power. While the initial eurozone rules were not strong enough to fundamentally challenge the southern European model or to induce uniform fiscal responses—relative discipline in Italy versus reckless borrowing in Greece—post-2009 fiscal and economic reforms have cut deeper. The reforms have been wrenching for southern European societies, including massive public sector layoffs and youth unemployment exceeding 50 percent in Spain and Greece.[17] Thus they have inevitably sparked political backlash, both against national leaders that have accepted EU diktats and against the EU itself, producing gains for nationalist and extremist parties across southern Europe, including France.[18]

Convergence toward the northern European model and related fiscal rectitude must overcome not only political resistance to a one-sided distribution of the burdens of economic adjustment, but also fundamental questions about whether convergence toward a northern European model is desirable. The status of "export-oriented" or "creditor" country can only be attained if there are "import-oriented" or "debtor" countries elsewhere. Within Europe, Germany and other creditor countries have achieved their status largely because Greece and other debtor countries have been major export markets; in 2012, Germany enjoyed a nearly €55 billion trade surplus with France, Italy, Spain, Greece, Cyprus, and Ireland combined.[19] If debtor countries are reformed to become competitiveness-oriented creditors, current creditors must accept one or both of the following implications: they must either take in more southern European exports themselves to support this transformation, or the EU as a whole must become a mercantilistic trader to support a universal creditor orientation within Europe. The effects of a fully German Europe would be felt globally.

Conclusion

The European Union's single currency regime was conceived, and ultimately still rests, on the premise that it is both necessary and possible to achieve fiscal coordination without real supranational fiscal authority. Yet despite the power and conviction of Germany to promote north-south convergence, the flaws in the prevailing regime and persistent, deep-seated differences between EU member states' economic models enabled the debt crisis and raise doubts about the post-2009 reforms to the regime. The burden of adjustment under the reformed rules has fallen squarely on debtor countries, reflecting to some extent their own fiscal problems and to some extent a failure among creditors to acknowledge how their own economic models (and banks) have contributed to underlying imbalances. Yet the European Commission did formally warn Germany in November 2013 about its excessive imbalances—in its case, an excessive surplus—which may suggest it will attempt to pursue a more balanced enforcement of rules than in the past.

The capacity of the existing regime to solve Europe's fiscal woes ultimately depends on the EU and its member states' responses to several interrelated questions. The first involves the superstructure of the regime and whether enhanced intergovernmental coordination is sufficient to solve the regime's credibility problems or whether greater supranational fiscal authority is necessary. There is little doubt that the reforms—including *ex ante* requirements of nationally embedded "debt brakes" and submission of budgets to the Commission for scrutiny and *ex post* mechanisms for punishing excessive deficits and rescuing governments facing default—strengthen coordination. Yet the imbalance within the EMU regime, with intergovernmental fiscal rules juxtaposed to supranational monetary policy, remains. In the absence of supranational mechanisms such as collectivized debt obligations (i.e., Eurobonds) and automatic transfers between member states (i.e., a transfer union), both political and market actors will have incentives to probe the extent of member states' commitment to these rules and, ultimately, the euro.

A second question, de-emphasized in this chapter but a source of much debate in recent years, involves the definition of appropriate fiscal performance. The definition promoted by Germany and largely codified in the rules is one of Hayekian orthodoxy, involving a strong reliance on market discipline and generalized caution regarding deficits and debt, regardless of the economic cycle. From this approach, strong fiscal performance in the EU is linked almost exclusively with concerns about free riding and negative externalities—i.e., with the concern that fiscal laxity in southern Europe could impose undue burdens on more rigorous northern member states. The buy-in to this Hayekian logic has eclipsed a Keynesian logic, which defines appropriate fiscal performance in terms of the economic cycle: balanced budgets are appropriate during periods of economic expansion, but not during recession and the early stages of recovery. Keynesian critics of the EU's regime, most notably Krugman, have argued that a European economy facing stagnation and possibly deflation—a condition in which the burden of debt increases—should be aiming for larger fiscal stimulus and its attendant deficits, especially in countries like Germany, to offer the *positive* externalities of pro-growth policies. Europe has not been entirely lacking in stimulative fiscal policy—especially immediately after the onset of the global financial crisis—but Hayekian rules such as the Fiscal Compact have further institutionalized constraints on countercyclical fiscal expansion. The adoption of these rules in the face of more pro-Keynesian arguments made by governments in France, Italy, and elsewhere is a strong indicator of the institutionalized power of Germany and its creditor allies.

The imposition of Hayekian rules from above—which French analyst Philippe Legrain has referred to as "fiscal colonialism" in which "European Union institutions have become instruments for creditors to impose their will on debtors"[20]—begs the third question, involving the democratic legitimacy of the

EMU regime. Democratically elected governments must now have their budgets, documents encompassing national priorities for public action, scrutinized and approved by the European Commission before national parliaments may vote on them. If member states suffer a fiscal crisis, they face the fate of Greece and, to a lesser extent other peripheral governments: the almost complete loss of sovereign economic policy authority. As Levi (1988) has argued, legitimate fiscal authority ultimately lies in "quasi-voluntary compliance" with authoritative fiscal institutions. Can such compliance be seen as voluntary in the European Union today?

There is disagreement among scholars regarding the implications of the strengthening of the EMU fiscal regime for the European Union's "democratic deficit." Some have claimed the EU does not suffer from a significant democratic deficit, whether in general (Moravcsik 2004, 2012) or in their procedures for strengthening the post-2009 fiscal regime (Schimmelfennig 2014). Others see more troubling democratic shortcomings, whether as a result of continuing economic integration (Crum 2013) or of a growing elite–mass divide regarding Europe (Fogarty and Wallsten 2013). As noted by Hooghe and Marks (2009) and affirmed by the continuing rise of anti-EU parties, there is no longer a "passive consensus" among European citizens for ever closer union, which means that public skepticism becomes another significant factor standing in the way of national compliance with an intergovernmental fiscal regime. Under such conditions, a fiscal regime that can coerce but not raise or distribute revenue may become increasingly untenable, requiring EU member states to choose between a fully supranational EMU with both automatic fiscal transfers and enhanced mechanisms of democratic accountability or the abandonment of the single currency altogether. As goes the *fiscus*, so goes the empire.

Notes

1 Formally, the European Commission proposes the budget and the European Parliament must give its consent. But because revenues come predominantly from national budgets most of the political wrangling occurs in the intergovernmental European Council.

2 European Commission, "CAP expenditure in the total EU expenditure," available at http://ec.europa.eu/agriculture/cap-post-2013/graphs/graph1_en.pdf (accessed July 6, 2014).

3 See, for example, Josef Joffe, "The euro widens the culture gap," *New York Times*, September 12, 2011.

4 The Spanish government did receive roughly 40 billion from the ESM in 2013 to help capitalize its banks, but managed to avoid an official rescue—and thus avoided required reforms as a condition for the loan.

5 Two EU members, the United Kingdom and the Czech Republic, did not sign the Fiscal Compact.

6 This reform was similar to that adopted in World Trade Organization (WTO) in 1995. Under the WTO's predecessor, the General Agreement on Trade and Tariffs, punishment of a country adopting illegal trade restrictions had to be agreed unanimously—essentially allowing the would-be punished party to block implementation. Under the WTO, punishment is only deferred if there is unanimous agreement among members to defer.

7 For different versions of this claim, see among others Gros 2012; Moravcsik 2012; Delors 2013; Hall 2012; Schimmelfennig 2014; Buti and Carnot 2012; Krugman 2011.

8 Jacques Delors, president of the European Commission from 1985 to 1995, proposed a plan for both increased EU economic coordination and additional tools to spur growth, but

> this was not accepted. Instead, it was deemed sufficient to merely add the word "growth" to the name of the Stability Pact.... In reality, this was purely and simply a budgetary stability pact: no economic coordination; no instruments to stimulate, cooperate, or regulate.
>
> (Delors 2013: 175)

9 According to Michael Cembalest, a leading investment analyst at JPMorgan, all the world's countries beginning with the letter M would make a more appropriate currency union than the eurozone.

10 Gros (2012: 41) notes that countries' fiscal status within the single currency zone may be riskier than outside. Despite the fact that Spain is overall in a better fiscal position than the UK, it faces higher borrowing costs and risks of a debt crisis. According to Gros, "The conclusion seems to be obvious: it is easier to service a high public debt by keeping a national central bank and one's national currency."

11 Between 1995 and 1999 Greece reduced its budget deficit from 9.2 to 3.2 percent of GDP, and its public debt from 97 to 94 percent of GDP. By 2007 its deficit had risen to 6.7 percent and debt to 107 percent—with neither figure coming close to the Maastricht targets in the intervening years.

12 Several northern European countries (notably Austria, Netherlands, and Finland)—which Schimmelfennig (2014) calls the "coalition of solvent countries"—have backed most German positions, particularly during the debt crisis.

13 The German government did not get everything it wanted: in its proposed "stability pact," fines for excessive deficits would have been automatic except if a country experiences an unusually deep recession with a greater than 2 percent contraction of GDP (Heipertz and Verdun 2009: 6).

14 There have been a variety of proposals for Eurobonds, but all would imply the issuance of bonds whose servicing and repayment would formally be a collective EU (or, more likely, euro area) responsibility.

15 Bloomberg View, "Germany's Banks must Assist in Europe's Cleanup," May 24, 2012, available at www.bis.org/publ/qtrpdf/r_qa1203.pdf (accessed July 12, 2014).

16 The Bundesbank has been an influential source of advocacy for orthodoxy. In July 2014 Jens Weidmann, head of the Bundesbank, declared that the ECB's "expansive monetary policy should not last longer than is necessary," and that, "if we pursued our own monetary policy, which we don't, it would look different." Axl Weber, who in 2011 resigned as president of the Bundesbank in protest at ongoing ECB stimulus, declared, "we put too much focus on solidarity, and insufficient focus on [Member States'] own responsibility." Paul Carrel, "ECB Interest Rates Too Low for Germany, Says Bundesbank Chief," *New York Times*, July 12, 2014; David Milliken, "ECB's Weber says EU Too Focused on Solidarity," Reuters, March 9, 2011.

17 Youth unemployment in May 2014 was 57.7 percent in Greece and 54 percent in Spain, as compared to 7.8 percent in Germany and 10.8 percent in the Netherlands. The eurozone average was 23.3 percent. Eurostat news release, "Euro Area Unemployment Rate at 11.6 Percent," July 1, 2014, available at http://epp.eurostat.ec.europa.eu/cache/ITY_PUBLIC/3–01072014-AP/EN/3–01072014-AP-EN.PDF (accessed July 12, 2014).

18 One notable exception to this trend in the 2014 European parliamentary elections was Italy, whose voters strongly backed their current center-left government.

19 Satyajit Das, "Germany's Economy isn't as Strong as Europe Believes," *Wall Street Journal*, December 4, 2013, available at www.marketwatch.com/story/germanys-economy-isnt-as-strong-as-europe-believes-2013–12–04 (accessed July 12, 2014).

20 Philippe Legrain, "Eurozone Fiscal Colonialism," *New York Times*, April 21, 2014.

References

Buti, Marco and Nicolas Carnot. 2012. "The EMU Debt Crisis: Early Lessons and Reforms." *Journal of Common Market Studies* 50(6): 899–911.

Crum, Ben. 2013. "Saving the Euro at the Cost of Democracy?" *Journal of Common Market Studies* 51(4): 614–630.

Dinan, Desmond. 2010. *Ever Closer Union.* Boulder, CO: Lynne Rienner.

Delors, Jacques. 2013. "Economic Governance in the European Union: Past, Present, and Future." *Journal of Common Market Studies* 51(2): 169–178.

Fogarty, Edward A. and Kevin Wallsten. 2013. "The Space between Us: Elite Action, Public Opinion, and the Euro Crisis." Paper presented at the Annual Meeting of the International Studies Association, San Francisco, CA.

Gros, Daniel. 2012. "On the Stability of Public Debt in a Monetary Union." *Journal of Common Market Studies* 50: 36–48.

Hall, Peter. 2012. "The Economics and Politics of the Euro Crisis." *German Politics* 21(4): 355–371.

Heipertz, Martin and Amy Verdun. 2009. *Ruling Europe: The Politics of the Stability and Growth Pact.* Cambridge: Cambridge University Press.

Hoffman, Stanley. 1966. "Obstinate or Obsolete? The Fate of the Nation-State and the Case of Western Europe." *Daedalus* 95(3): 862–915.

Hooghe, Liesbet and Gary Marks. 2009. "A Postfunctional Theory of European Integration: From Permissive Consensus to Constraining Dissensus." *British Journal of Political Science* 39(1): 1–23.

Howarth, David and Chrolotte Rommerskirchen. 2013. "A Panacea for All Times? The German Stability Culture as Strategic Political Resource." *West European Politics* 36(4): 750–770.

Kindleberger, Charles. 1973. *The World in Depression, 1929–1939.* Berkeley: University of California Press.

Krasner, Stephen. 1976. "State Power and the Structure of International Trade." *World Politics* 28(3): 317–347.

Krugman, Paul. 2011. "Eurotrashed." *New York Times Magazine*, January 12.

Langenbacher, Eric. 2010. "Still the Unmasterable Past? The Impact of History and Memory in the Federal Republic of Germany." *German Politics* 19(1): 24–40.

Levi, Margaret. 1988. *Of Rule and Revenue*, Berkeley: University of California Press.

Moravcsik, Andrew. 1998. *The Choice for Europe*. Ithaca: Cornell University Press.

Moravcsik, Andrew. 2004. "Is There a 'Democratic Deficit' in World Politics? A Framework for Analysis." *Government and Opposition* 39(2): 336–363.

Moravcsik, Andrew. 2012. "Europe after the Crisis." *Foreign Affairs* 91(3): 54–68.

Newman, Abraham. 2010. "Flight from Risk: Unified Germany and the Role of Beliefs in the European Response to the Financial Crisis." *German Politics and Society* 28(2): 151–165.

Schimmelfennig, Frank. 2014. "European Integration in the Euro Crisis: The Limits of Postfunctionalism." *Journal of European Integration* 36(3): 321–337.

11 Conclusion

Eisaku Ide and Gene Park

Introduction

The rise of the modern state has reflected the intersection of democratic politics and the market system with governments having taken on major social commitments through the expansion of public spending. One pressing question for the future is whether or not governments will be able to maintain these commitments. In the wake of the global financial crisis, many countries have been left with higher levels of debt and confront sluggish growth. Furthermore, demographic patterns will continue to squeeze public finance systems. Given these trends, the issue of how governments manage their finances is arguably more important than ever. This volume asks what shapes government fiscal performance. What factors influence whether governments pursue fiscal adjustment and the success of these efforts? Much of the existing work approaches this question relying on quantitative analysis. This study proceeds through detailed case studies, employing a broadly historical institutionalist approach. This concluding chapter draws together the themes across the chapters and assesses how this approach can shed new light on these issues.

1 Problem Perception and Fiscal Culture

Research has shown how a variety of factors—fiscal institutions (von Hagen 1992), budget processes (Hallerberg and von Hagen 1997), government fragmentation (Roubini and Sachs 1989), etc.—can exacerbate or mitigate the common pool resource (CPR) problem. As discussed in the Introduction, however, there are legitimate debates about when running deficits and higher debt might be necessary to revive growth. In this volume, it is also clear that there are real differences in the perceptions of the dangers, costs, and benefits of deficits that go beyond the debates of professional economists. The cases here suggest that there are specific, historically conditioned "fiscal cultures" that shape problem perception and the ultimately the management of fiscal policy.

As the chapter on France shows, the legacy of statism continues to shape perceptions of deficits and public debt. Prior to financial deregulation in the 1980s, the government relied on a treasury "circuit" that allowed the government to finance large deficits in order to pursue industrialization. As a consequence of these policies, there is a greater tolerance of rising deficits and growing public debt in French society. According to Tristam and Konishi, some intellectuals in fact view the basic fiscal problem as the reliance on financial markets rather than the level of debt itself, and beyond the centrist parties, the left and right continue to push for fiscal stimulus over consolidation. In South Korea, the statist legacy has shaped fiscal norms, although in the opposite direction of France. The government prior to democratization was firmly committed to fiscal balance as part of its statist economic model. This policy line persisted even after the democratization and was reinforced with the Asian Financial Crisis.

In the US, despite popular images to the contrary, Brownlee finds in his broad survey of fiscal consolidations since the founding of the Republic a resilient culture of "fiscal virtue" and a traditional bipartisan aversion to high debt. Early government leaders, including Alexander Hamilton and Albert Gallatin, an early Treasury Secretary, tried to inculcate these values in the late eighteenth century. Fiscal virtue became associated with the strength of the state and provided elite and mass support for fiscal consolidations. Despite its remarkable longevity, Brownlee notes, however, that since the 1990s the nation's fiscal virtue may be eroding. Thorndike echoes this point, arguing that the Republican party has forsaken fiscal balance for a more ideologically driven anti-tax agenda, which has manifested itself with tax cuts that have eroded fiscal discipline.

2 Role of Market Pressure

While views of the costs of deficits and debt are partly historically conditioned, as discussed above, market signals can create pressure for restoring fiscal balance (Campbell and Allen 1994). Growing deficits and debt may cause interest rates to rise, intensifying what Kemmerling and Truchlewski call "problem pressure." As the costs of fiscal discipline rise, the incentive for a government to pursue fiscal consolidation increases. This dynamic comes across in the cases in this volume, including the chapters on Italy, Sweden, and the US.

The cases in this volume, though, also highlight the partly contingent nature of these pressures. The sensitivity to market pressures depends partly on situation. The US benefits from the dollar's role as the top currency, which has contributed to low interest rates despite rising deficits and debt. By contrast, small and trade-dependent countries, such as Sweden, are more exposed to the international economy. What the cases here, though, illustrate is that government choices and institutions heavily condition the exposure to market signals. Thus, the effect of markets on government fiscal choices is partly reflective of specific government choices and institutions.

As Marzinotto's chapter on Italy shows, financial markets only began to influence policy making after the divorce between the Treasury and Bank of Italy in 1981, which forbids the central bank from financing government deficits. Only afterwards did financial markets begin to influence perceptions about deficits and debt. Similarly in France, the leftist government's dismantlement of its dirigiste financial system expanded the role of financial markets. Perhaps the clearest example of how market signals are mediated by politically created institutions is the eurozone and sovereign debt crisis. Initially monetary union kept interest rates lower for Southern Europe. Then with the global financial crisis, design flaws in the monetary union—the lack of a common fiscal policy to balance the monetary policy of EMU—contributed to the spreading of sovereign debt crisis from Greece to other Southern European countries. As Fogarty's chapter illustrates, these design flaws reflected the difficulty of reconciling Germany's preference for orthodoxy with persistent political-economic diversity within EU.

In the case of Japan, despite financial liberalization, the government has retained greater control over financial resources. The government oversees a large pool of funds from the public pension system and postal savings system, and unlike in Europe, Japan has its own central bank. Both Japan's central bank, the Bank of Japan, and government controlled financial institutions have purchased large amounts of government debt, keeping interest rates low thereby reducing debt-servicing costs. As Shimada and Takahashi show, these interventions have made it possible for the government to run up a remarkable amount of debt.

3 Preferences and Economic Interests

In the classical partisan model (Hibbs 1977), economic preferences influence economic policy choices. Workers prefer looser fiscal policy and favor employment creation; by contrast business tends to be more hawkish toward inflation. Political parties support the policies of their social constituencies. The chapters in this volume suggest that one cannot so easily read preferences off of assumed economic interests.

The chapter on Italy shows that actor and partisan preferences are embedded in the macroeconomic regime. Preferences shifted due to the abolition of central bank financing of debt, currency changes associated with the monetary union in the late 1980s, and the end of wage indexation in 1992. As a consequence of these changes, labor came to support fiscal consolidation as a way to lower interest rates, restore competitiveness, and boost domestic investment. With devaluation closing as an option to restore competitiveness, business backed fiscal consolidation more forcefully. These shifts in the preferences of the key social actors in turn laid the groundwork for political compromise around fiscal consolidation.

Other cases, particularly France and South Korea, illustrate how historical legacies can shape partisan preferences and competition. In neither case has there been a clear split between the left and right over fiscal policy. As a consequence of Gaullism, the right in France historically embraced high taxation and high spending to achieve statist goals. Thus, the cleavage between left and right has been relatively small regarding fiscal issues. In South Korea, the legacy of statism has had the effect of depoliticizing partisan preferences. Under authoritarian rule, the state adhered to a policy of fiscal discipline. Although debt has been ticking up slowly, there is no clear partisan divide over fiscal policy, according to Kang. If the formation of actor and partisan preferences more broadly are as diverse as in our cases, this may explain why the empirical work that has analyzed the effects of partisanship on fiscal policy has been indeterminate.

4 Diffuse Support

The case studies here also suggest that diffuse forms of support play an important factor in fiscal policy, something that work on the new fiscal sociology has begun to highlight (Feldman and Slemrod 2009; Ide and Steinmo 2009; Martin et al. 2009; Thorndike 2009). Specifically, support can be shaped through views of fairness, trust, and social consensus, all of which can potentially lower the political costs of fiscal adjustment.

Brownlee's chapter on the US shows how perceptions of fairness have contributed to fiscal consolidation. As he shows in his chapter, enhancing revenue has been a key to successful fiscal consolidations. Voters have been more likely to accept tax increases when the proposed tax hikes are viewed as fair, which over the course of the twentieth century increasingly came to reflect the principle of "ability to pay." Thus, revenue-side measures, which Brownlee finds have been central to successful fiscal consolidation, have tended to rely on progressive income policy tax changes.

In the case of Sweden, fiscal consolidation and budget reforms also relied on diffuse forms support. The economic crisis of the 1990s led to a widespread sense among the major interest groups and parties that measures to restore fiscal balance were necessary. This facilitated cooperation, but it was not enough to ensure fiscal reforms. The key was to craft a package that voters could accept as balanced. At first, the conservative bourgeois coalition in power until 1994 emphasized heavy expenditure cuts. By contrast the Social Democrats (SAP) proposed expenditure cuts and significant revenue enhancements to spread the burden more evenly. This more balanced approach, which the SAP campaigned on, attracted the support of voters in a general election and allowed the SAP to form a partnership with centrist parties, which proved pivotal to fiscal reform. The SAP-led coalition enacted significant welfare cuts, but the actions, while not necessarily popular, were viewed as fairer and in contrast to the right's proposal not motivated by an attempt to role back the popular welfare state, which SAP had built up for decades. As economic growth returned toward the end of the decade, the social democratic government restored some welfare spending.

Conversely, the lack of trust of government in Japan has hindered fiscal adjustment and contributed to persistent deficits. In lieu of a universal welfare state, the Japanese government has relied on a limited welfare state supplemented by targeted distributive spending. As Shimada and Takahashi argue, this selectivism has undermined trust and the willingness of citizens to accept tax increases. Thus, even though taxes are very low by international standards, the government has been unable to raise adequate revenue to cover its moderate levels of spending.

While it is sometimes assumed that electoral pressure makes it harder for governments to pursue fiscal adjustments, several of the cases here suggest that building social consensus improves the prospects for success. In Sweden, the

Social Democrats (SAP) actually campaigned in 1994 on the basis of its platform to restore fiscal balance in order to win a mandate to carry out tough reforms, as Edlund and Iju note. In Italy, despite a fragile multi-party coalition, during the latter half of the 1990s, the center-left Prodi government built support from the ground up and actually succeeded in passing larger fiscal adjustments than technocratic governments. In both the Italian and Swedish cases, the relatively high degree of organization of interests, particularly labor and business, aided in building consensus. By contrast, in France, where labor, business, and other groups are fragmented, consensus has been more elusive and sectional distributional interests have come into greater play.

5 Rethinking Fiscal Institutions, Budget Process, and Fiscal Rules

While there has been a great deal of research that has found that fiscal institutions, the budget process, and fiscal rules influence fiscal outcomes, this volume suggests that there is a need to examine these claims more carefully. More specifically, the cases here suggest that the underlying conditions that give rise to changes in fiscal institutions and rules are critical in determining the extent to which those reforms actually impact fiscal management.

The two cases where changes to fiscal institutions and the budget process were correlated with the greatest effect on fiscal balance are Italy and Sweden. In Italy, budget reforms during the late 1980s created mid-term planning, limited the ability of the parliament to amend the budget, and imposed limits on spending ministeries. In Sweden, a new fiscal policy framework created a three-year budget, introduced expenditure ceilings for the central government, amended the budget process to enhance top-down decision-making, and imposed a balanced budget requirement on local government. In both countries, however, the reforms were preceded by a shift in priorities toward a deep commitment to fiscal discipline, which proved to be the critical factor in successive drives for fiscal consolidation. In the case of Sweden, this commitment stemmed from the financial crisis of the early 1990s and a sharp rise in interest rates. Thus, the big fiscal adjustments in Sweden preceded and then were concurrent with budget reforms. Edlund and Iju find, though, that the new fiscal policy framework continued to reduce legislative amendments to budget bills thereby enhancing budget discipline.

In the case of Italy, the commitment toward fiscal disciplined stemmed from the shift in the larger macroeconomic regime. As Marzinotto details in Chapter 4, these changes realigned the preferences of the key social partners, paving the way for budget balancing measures, including reform of the fiscal institutions. These preferences have remained relatively stable and continue to shape Italy's fiscal policy. Do such budget changes then exert any independent effect? Marzinotto argues the reforms contributed to fiscal stabilization in the 1990s by ring-fencing the budget during a period of political instability. She also notes, however, that the government only fully implemented the budget reforms after the preferences of social actors had fully shifted toward fiscal consolidation several years after the reforms were passed.

In the absence of deeper societal and political support, the effects of budget reforms are mixed at best. In France, in the context of muted demands for fiscal consolidation, budget reforms have been relatively weak. The French government passed the organic law on public finances (LOLF) in 2001 that gives the executive more discretion to set budget priorites, but the law does not cover local governments, one of the biggest sources of expenditure growth and an area that Tristam and Konishi point out is especially susceptible to the CPR problem. In Japan, the government passed reforms that (1) enhanced the power of the executive and (2) centralized budget-making authority. While the newly created Council on Economic and Fiscal Policy (CEFP) served as a vehicle for Prime Minister Koizumi's fiscal consolidation in the first part of the new century, later prime ministers retreated from consolidation and even abandoned the CEFP.

In the US, the government has used fiscal rules to encourage greater fiscal balance. The Gramm–Rudman–Hollings Balanced Budget and Emergency Deficit Control Act of 1985 set specific deficit targets, which if violated provided for sequestration, the suspension of budget resources. When the targets were violated, the law was revised and then ultimately abandoned. The Budget Enforcement Act (BEA) of 1990 had deeper bi-partisan support and established a "PAYGO" rule whereby spending increases had to offset by cuts elsewhere or tax hikes. Thorndike notes that the BEA proved to be more durable, but ultimately it lapsed. As legislative gridlock increased after the global financial crisis, a bipartisan congressional committee agreed to across-the-board cuts unless the legislature could agree on a deficit reduction plan, but ultimately it resulted in little deficit reduction. One problem with such fiscal rules and mechanisms to force cooperation is that they can be violated, raising the question of whether such rules or processes have an effect at all. Thorndike argues that their main effect is to focus political attention.

Even in Germany, which Kemmerling and Truchlewski point out has a relatively conservative fiscal culture, measures to limit debt growth have not succeeded. West Germany in 1969 introduced a "debt brake" into its constitution to slow down debt growth, but debt continued to increase steadily nonetheless. In response to the ineffectiveness of the debt brake, the government introduced new targets to limit structural deficits for the federal government and the federal states (Länder) in 2006. It is still to early to tell what effect, if any, these changes will have.

In terms of executive–legislative relations, at first glance the South Korean case seems to conform well to theoretical expectations. South Korea is a clear case with a strong executive in the budget process, which should alleviate the CPR problem, and compared to other OECD countries, the government indeed has had low deficits (aside from the Asian Financial Crisis) and low debt. The Korean case, though, illustrates how even given constitutional delineation of authority, there is still room for contestation and institutional innovation. Since democratization in the late 1980s, the legislature has become increasingly assertive, passing measures to enhance oversight of the budget. Also, the executive, rather than using its authority to internalize the costs of its spending, in fact has relied on the expansion of extra-budgetary institutions to circumvent legislative control. Kang argues the executive's use of public corporations has weakened fiscal discipline through extra-budgetary means.

Given the difficulty of imposing deficit and debt targets at the national level, it is not surprising the EU's fiscal restraints have had a weak effect. On the one hand, Italy's move toward fiscal discipline tracked the policy direction of the EU. But as Marzinotto notes, the shift toward fiscal consolidation stemmed from the changing incentives of Italy's key social actors. As the chapters in this volume show, the fiscal rules had weak effects on restraining spending in other countries. Both France and Germany violated the deficit target; and even with the new enhanced fiscal compact created during the sovereign debt crisis, France has continued to miss new targets. As Fogarty points out in Chapter 10 on the eurozone, deficit and debt targets failed due to two credibility problems. First, the no-bail out clause had no credibility from the markets, which undercut market discipline. Second, the procedures for dealing with countries breaking the rules had low credibility. France and Germany were able to violate the deficit targets and used their political weight to convince the European Council not to take action against them, further undermining credibility. Furthermore, the possibility of imposing fines was not credible since this might only exacerbate the fiscal crisis. More fundamentally, Fogarty argues that the fiscal rules may be the wrong prescription in a slow growth environment and in the context of a regional economy with large gaps between current account surplus and deficit countries. The new fiscal compact, while requiring national legislation or constitutional change and strengthened measures for remediation, do not address these basic problems, thus Fogarty remains skeptical of their desirability.

Directions for Future Research

Collectively these finding suggest that there is room to expand the range of causal factors to consider. While the work on fiscal institutions and fiscal rules has advanced our understanding, we should also to be sensitive to the underlying factors that produce budget reforms. This includes looking more carefully at preference formation and how support for budget reform emerges in the first place. Also, the chapters highlight the need to move beyond explanations that assume specific economic preferences to consider fiscal cultures and diffuse forms of support stemming from perceptions of fairness, trust, and social consensus. The volume shows that such factors matter and can shape the otherwise harsh political tradeoffs that leaders must make. The chapters also illustrate that these are not variables that only matter at the margins. Indeed, this volume reveals that many of these factors have strong effects that can be more decisive than those cited in the existing literature. In Italy, realigned social preferences overcame extreme government fragmentation and instability. Despite the conventional wisdom that elections are inauspicious for fiscal consolidation, in Sweden social buy-in allowed the government to campaign on its fiscal adjustment package to win a public mandate.

This volume illustrates that historical institutionalism can help bring such new causal mechanisms to light, but there is still much more work to be done and other methodologies will be required. In particular, there is a need to better understand the factors that shape diffuse forms of support and the evolution of preferences. While only touched upon in this conclusion, there is also a need to unpack "spending" and "taxation." Deficits are often treated as a relatively abstract gap between the two. But as the chapters here show, there is significant variation in the kinds of spending as well as revenue, and each are embedded in very different institutional contexts and social logics that create specific kinds of political constraints. We hope that this volume inspires more research on all of these issues.

References

Campbell, John L. and Michael Patrick Allen. 1994. "The Political Economy of Revenue Extraction in the Modern State: A Time-Series Analysis of U.S. Income Taxes, 1916–1986." *Social Forces* 72(3): 643–669.

Feldman, Naomi and Joel Slemrod. 2009. "War and Taxation: When Does Patriotism Overcome the Free-Rider Impulse?" In *The New Fiscal Sociology: Taxation in Comparative and Historical Perspective*, edited by Isaac William Martin, Ajay K. Mehrotra and Monica Prasad, 138–154. New York: Cambridge University Press.

Hallerberg, Mark and Jürgen von Hagen. 1997. *Sequencing and the Size of the Budget: A Reconsideration.* Centre for Economic Policy Research Discussion Paper No. 1589, London.

Hibbs, Douglas A. 1977. "Political Parties and Macroeconomic Policy." *American Political Science Review* 71(4): 1467–1487.

Ide, Eisaku and Sven Steinmo. 2009. "The End of the Strong State? On the Evolution of Japanese Tax Policy." In *The New Fiscal Sociology: Taxation in Comparative Perspective*, edited by Isaac William Martin, Ajay K. Mehotra and Monica Prasad, 119–137. New York: Cambridge University Press.

Martin, Isaac William, Ajay K. Mehrotra, and Monica Prasad. 2009. *The New Fiscal Sociology: Taxation in Comparative and Historical Perspective*. New York: Cambridge University Press.

Roubini, Nouriel and Jeffrey Sachs. 1989. "Political and Economic Determinants of Budget Deficits in the Industrial Democracies." *European Economic Review* 33(5): 903–933.

Thorndike, Joseph. 2009. " 'The Unfair Advantage of the Few': The New Deal Origins of 'Soak the Rich Taxation'." In *The New Fiscal Sociology: Taxation in Comparative and Historical Perspective*, edited by Isaac William Martin, Ajay K. Mehrotra and Monica Prasad. New York: Cambridge University Press.

von Hagen, Jürgen. 1992. *Budgeting Procedures and Fiscal Performance in the European Communities*. European Commission Economic Paper 96.

Index

Page numbers in *italics* denote tables, those in **bold** denote figures.

For Product Safety Concerns and Information please contact our EU representative GPSR@taylorandfrancis.com Taylor & Francis Verlag GmbH, Kaufingerstraße 24, 80331 München, Germany